GRAINGER COUNTY TENNESSEE INVENTORIES OF ESTATES AND WILLS NOV. 1833–MAY 1852

Abstracted

by

Mary E. Reeves

Please direct all correspondence and orders to:

www.southernhistoricalpress.com
or
SOUTHERN HISTORICAL PRESS, Inc.
PO BOX 1267
375 West Broad Street
Greenville, SC   29601
southernhistoricalpress@gmail.com

ISBN #0-89308-284-8

Printed in the United States of America

This book is dedicated
to my Mother,
Pearl Elizabeth LeGere Beavers,
whose ancestors fill this book.

CONCERNING THE FORMATION OF
TENNESSEE COUNTIES

The Carolinas were settled in the seventeenth century as a proprietary colony with a sea to sea charter. While Tennessee was the western part of what later came to be known as North Carolina, six counties were created. Washington (1777), the first to be created from the western areas of Burke and Wilkes counties (North Carolina), encompassed the entire area and was later to be named Tennessee. Washington enjoyed the distinction of being the only county until 1779 when Sullivan County was created. The remaining counties to be created while Tennessee was yet a part of North Carolina were: Greene (1783), Davidson (1783), Hawkins (1786), and Sumner (1786).

The Territory of the United States of America South of the River Ohio was organized in 1790, and while in this condition, four counties were created: Jefferson (1792), Knox (1792), Sevier (1794), and Blount (1795). A total of ten counties were in existence by the time Tennessee was admitted to the Union in 1796. Between the admission of Tennessee as the sixteenth state and the end of the century, eight more counties were added, making a total of 18 by 1800. Counties added during this early period of statehood were: Carter (1796), Grainger (1796), Montgomery (1796), Robertson (1796), Cocke (1797), Smith (1799), William-son (1799), and Wilson (1799).

By the end of the first decade 20 new counties were created, making a total of 38 by 1810. This number was increased to 47 during the next decade. By 1830 there were 62 counties in Tennessee, which were supple-mented with 10 additional counties by 1839, for a total of 72. Twelve additional counties were added before 1860, for a total of 84. The remaining counties were created in the decade of the 1870's when 12 additional counties were created, making a total of 96 counties, the maximum number. This number remained through 1919, when James County - created in 1871 - was dissolved and absorbed in January 1920 by Hamilton County.

Inventories of Estates and Wills
Nov 1833-May 1852

Grainger County, Tennessee

Abstracted by
Mary E. Reeves

Volume 1 - November 1833 - February 1839

Index pages 1 through 12.

p. 13   Will - John MALICOAT. Wife Ellender, son Dedmond, son William, dau
Dicy NASH, dau Mary WALKER, dau Susannah NASH, son James. Executors John,
Dedmond and William MALICOAT. Signed John x MALICOAT 25 Apr 1831. Wit: James
K. MALLICOAT, William C. MALLICOAT, Nathan x THACKER. Recorded 4 Nov 1833,
P. S. COCKE, clerk.

p. 14   Inventory - Personal Estate of Winston ATKINS, decd. Mentions: two
Negro girls GRASE and ANDRA. Signed Peter ATKINS. Recorded 4 Nov 1833
Pleasant S. COCKE, clerk.

        Will - Edward DANIEL, Sr. Wife Anna; son Isaac; dau Jemima DANIEL;
son William; named to receive equal part of $500.00 in order of age Ester MAYES,
Elizabeth MAYES, Anna HODGE, John DANIEL, Joseph DANIEL, Edward DANIEL, Jr.,
Mary MAYES, Rebecca SUNDERLAND, Sally MAYES and Jemima DANIEL....among all said
and singular of legal heirs in my family of children there being 12 in number
whose names are refered to in the course of this instrument. Signed Edward
DANIEL 6 Feb 1830. Wit: James KENNON, James LACY, James GREENLEE. Recorded
9 Nov 1833 P. S. COCKE, clerk.

p. 16   Account of Sale - Edward DANIEL, Sr., decd. Mentions: Isaac DANIEL,
Wyly McGEE, William DANIEL, Joseph DANIEL, Legand MAYES, Thomas MAYES, William
HODGE, Jesse HODGE, James SUNDERLAND, Dudley MAYES, Jonathan MAYES, William
McDANIEL, Edward DANIEL, Henry BOWEN, John DANIEL, Philip DANIEL, Edward TATE,
John HIXON, John WILLIAMS, Robert MITCHELL, Eliha A. TAYLOR, Samuel POLLARD, John
HILL. Recorded 11 Nov 1833 P. S. COCKE, clerk.

p. 20   Will - William HANKINS, decd. Wife Anna; son-in-law Russile SMALLWOOD;
son-in law John LARGE; Negro man SAM to be set free and given 15 acres of land
in Grainger Co.; son Thomas; mentions McKINEY line to David SHARP's; Estate to
be divided between rest of heirs (not named). John LARGE and Thomas HANKINS,
Executors. Signed 9 Oct 1832 William HANKINS. Wit: William CORAM and Frederick CORAM. Recorded 11 Nov 1833 P. S. COCKE, clerk.

p. 21   Inventory - William HANKINS, decd. Signed Thomas HANKINS and John x
LARGE. Recorded 11 Nov 1833 P. S. COCKE, clerk.

        Account of Sale - William HANKINS, decd. Mentions: Thomas HANKINS,
James HAMILTON, John A. McKINEY, Step. M. SKAGG, David SHARP, Edward HANKINS,
G. B. MITCHELL, Thornton CORUM, Obed. CHASE, Thomas HANKINS, Sr., Thomas MOORE,
Bird PATE, Brite HODGES, Benjamin SMITH, Samuel SHARP, Wilsone HODGES, William

CARATHERS, Seth McKINNEY, James HANKINS, John CHILES, Step. MORE, John CHASE, William LAMON, John LARGE, Pryor GOURING (?), Henry HANKINS, Henry CAVENDER, John CORUM, Alen STONE, Philip MAHONEY, Step. C. RENTFROW, Step. HANKINS, Elias WARD. Recorded 11 Nov 1833 P. S. COCKE, clerk.

p. 23   Account of Sale - Bartlet GODSEY, decd. Mentions: Widow, John MORRIS, R. RIGGS, Jno NOE, D. SHIELDS, N. RIGGS, Isaac MARSHFIELD. Recorded 1 Jul 1834 P. S. COCKE, clerk.

p. 24   Guardian Report - Green B. MITCHELL, Guardian of Hanna C. HANKINS, 18 Feb 1833. Recorded 2 Jul 1834 P. S. COCKE, clerk.

        Guardian Report - Green B. MITCHELL, Guardian for the three minor heirs of James FORGISON, decd. 18 Feb 1833. Recorded 2 Jul 1834 P. S. COCKE, clerk.

        Settlement - John W. LIDE, Adm. of the Estate of Spotswood LIPSCOMB, decd. Mentions: Shff S. BUNCH, Thomas WHITESIDE, John SHIELDS, P. WESTERN, James BLAIR, E. S. LIPSCOMB, Chas CAMPBELL, Peter GODWIN, S. JOHNSON, Thomas POINDEXTER, Robert J. McKINNEY, R. HYNDS, Esq., A. McCONNEL, James PELTER, Joseph COBB, H. HOUSTON, P. B. COBB, Carter B. PINN, T. TURLEY, Thomas WATSON, A. SPOON, DEDDEP & MILES, William McCOLLUM, Willis I. BRADLEY, John KIRKHAM, Zera McGEE, Levy GODWIN, Willis BRADY, Baxter IVY, John GOWEN, Thomas GOWEN, Pryor BIBA, Wilson C. DUNAVANT, James GOWEN, Jesse COUNTS, James McGOULDRICK, James LINDSEY, McKEE & ASHBROOK, P. B. BELL, P. DARBY, I. RIDDLEBERGER, H. T. GORHAM, James SMITH, I. McVEY. Signed 22 Feb 1832 C. McANALLY, Jas COBB, Joseph RICH, Commissioners. Recorded 3 Jul 1834 P. S. COCKE, clerk.

p. 27   Will - Peter HARRIS, decd. 17 day of Mar 1823, wife not named, sons Thomas HARRIS and Isaac HARRIS, John HARRIS and Jesse HARRIS. Executors John and Jesse HARRIS. Signed Peter HARRIS. Wit: John LONG and Robert LONG. Recorded 5 Jul 1834 P. S. COCKE, clerk.

p. 28   Inventory - Peter HARRIS, decd. Mentions: Three Negroes JACOB, SALLY and child MATILDA, Jesse HARRIS, Samuel HARRIS. Signed 20 May 1834 John HARRIS, Executor. Recorded 5 Jul 1834 P. S. COCKE, clerk.

        Account of Sale - Peter HARRIS, decd. 25 Jun 1833. Mentions: Will B. McGEE, Zera McGEE, Morning HARRIS, Jesse HARRIS, John SMITH, Nehemiah HARRIS, Thomas TURLEY, Hughs O. TAYLOR, Raleigh STUBBLEFIELD, John COCKE, William P. LONG, Negro man JACOB, Robert LONG, Negro woman SALLY, one Negro girl, G. S. LONG, Nehemiah HARRIS, Sr., Charles RICE, Thomas HARRIS, John GODWIN, William LONG. Signed John HARRIS, Executor. Recorded 8 Jul 1834 P. S. COCKE, clerk.

p. 30   Inventory - John MALICOAT, decd, given by Dedman MALICOAT, Executor. Mentions: Robert KING, Thomas NASH, Claiborn NASH. Signed 10 Jun 1833 William MALICOAT and Dedman MALICOAT, Executors. Recorded 8 Jul 1834 P. S. COCKE, clerk.

        Sale - John MALICOAT, decd. 14 Jun 1833.

p. 31   Settlement - Delphia GRADY, Admx for Estate of Kinney GRADY, decd, dated 19 Nov 1832. Mentions: the children. Signed Thomas ACUFF, Samuel x DOTSON, Sr. Benjamin LEWIS. Recorded 8 Jul 1834 P. S. COCKE, clerk.

Inventory - Estate of Bartlet B. GODSEY, decd. Mentions: regimental coat. Signed Elizabeth x GODSEY, Admx., 20 Aug 1832. Recorded 8 Jul 1834 P. S. COCKE, clerk.

p. 32   Settlement - Elizabeth JACK, Admx of John F. JACK, decd. Mentions: William D. JENNINGS, two Negroes RENA and LOUISA, E. WILLIAMS, William F. TATE Adm of the Estate of John BROWN, decd., John CUMMINS, Isaac LEBOW, John A. McKINNEY, Mary EDWARDS, John W. LIDE, Hugh G. MOORE, John SHIELDS & CO., James L. ETTER, Thos GILL, Isaiah PAIN, George A. BOWEN, F. S. HEISKELL, Wm A. ANDERSON, taxes for 1832, Henry HIPSHER, B. CRAIGHEAD, C. McANALLY, Lemuel MOORE, N. A. SENTER. Signed 6 Aug 1833 C. McANALLY, Samuel B. TATE, Thomas GILL, Commissioners. Recorded 9 Jul 1834 P. S. COCKE, clerk.

p. 33   Inventory - Estate of John GRAY, decd. Recorded 9 Jul 1834 P. S. COCKE, clerk.

p. 34   Account of Sale - Estate of John GRAY, decd. Mentions: John BOX, James MALLICOAT, Thomas PERRY, John GREENLEA, Samuel McNEICE, John EATON, John GRAY, Robert CARDWELL, Samuel POLLARD, Major POLLARD, John MAYES, Jane GRAY, John WILLIAMS, William GRAY, James JAMES. Signed Sarah GRAY, Admx. Recorded 9 Jul 1834 P. S. COCKE, clerk.

p. 35   Account of Sale - Winston ATKINS, decd, sold 15 Aug 1833. Mentions: Mary ATKINS, Meredith ATKINS, Peter THACKER, Jesse THACKER, John KENNON, George H. EVINS, John MALLICOAT, James CRAIG, Daniel CLONCH, Winright ATKINS, John RUCKER, W. J. BOWMAN, Manuel ATKINS, Nathaniel THACKER. Signed Peter ATKINS, Adm. Recorded 9 Jul 1834 P. S. COCKE, clerk.

p. 37   Account of Sale - John DENNIS, decd, sold 14 and 15 Jun 1832. Sold by William DENNIS, Adm. Recorded 9 Jul 1834 P. S. COCKE, clerk.

p. 39   Additional Account of Sale - John DENNIS, decd, held Sep 1832 and Nov 1832 by William DENNIS. Recorded 10 Jul 1834 P. S. COCKE, clerk.

p. 40   Settlement - Executors of the Estate of William HAMILTON, decd. Mentions: this being the 2nd, John STONE, Jacob GRIFFEN, Cardwell LEAMON, Owen DYER, Esq., Nathaniel ROBINSON. Signed 20 Aug 1833 G. B. MITCHELL, Robert BLAIR, Robert GAINES, Executors. Recorded 10 Jul 1834 P. S. COCKE, clerk.

p. 41   Guardian Report - M. E. C. WATKINS in account with James JOHNSON, Guardian. Mentions: 1828 taxes on your land, 1829, 1831 taxes, 1832 settlement made with Adm of John K. WATKINS, decd; 26 days traveling by horse to and from Paris; 1833 disposition from W. McAFREY and Jas WATSON of Knoxville; H. BROWN, Esq., of Knoxville; George BARKER land agent; 1829 Robert KING, John McNAIR; 1833 R. McADORY and George BARKER; suit pending in Henry Co. Court against Julian TREASURE the Adm of John K. WATKINS, decd. Signed James JOHNSON. Recorded 10 Jul 1834 P. S. COCKE, clerk.

p. 42   Settlement - T. D. KNIGHT and D. SHIELDS, Executors of the Estate of John SHIELDS, decd. Mentions: SHIELDS, JOHNSON & RICE, John SHIELDS CO.; hire of two NEGRO men for 1830; rent of mills and part of plantation 1830; William and John SHIELDS; the firm of SHIELDS, WOODS and SHIELDS; hire of Negro man KELLERY

from 1 Jan 1831 to 1 Mar 1833; hire of Negro man NELSON for 1831 and 1832; sale
of papers from R. KING to CROZIER; David SHIELDS; William BRIGGS; Jacob NOE;
Elizabeth KIRKHAM; Major Hugh HOUSTON; William L. WILLS; H. O. TAYLOR; John
WOODS; cash paid from 19 Dec 1830 to 15 Feb 1832 to KNIGHT & SHIELDS; T. WHITE-
SIDE; John CRUSE; NEGROES of the Estate of John BROWN, decd. Signed 6 Aug 1833
C. McANALLY, Joseph RICH, Thomas GILL. Then mentions: minor heirs; Jno SHIELDS.
Recorded 10 Jul 1834 P. S. COCKE, clerk.

p. 46   Account of hire of Negroes BERRY and RHODA and child belonging to the
Estate of John BROWN, decd. Mentions: Ethelred WILLIAMS, Joseph Mc_____.
Signed William T. TATE, Adm. Recorded 11 Jul 1834 P. S. COCKE, clerk.

p. 47   Settlement - William F. TATE, Adm of John BROWN, decd. 17 May 1833.
Mentions: hire of NEGROES; Ethelred WILLIAMS; CRAIDHEAD & MASSENGILE; Benjamin
CRAIGHEAD; John LAFFERTY; Samuel BUNCH, Sheriff; HEISKELL & BROWN; William DANIEL;
James LACY; Peter MAY; Nathaniel HURD; William E. COCKE; Hugh HOUSTON; Samuel
WEST; Charles McANALLY; Richard GRANTHIM; George MOODY, Samuel B. TATE; Robert
BLANE; Stephen SMITH, Abram McCONNEL; Dr. John W. LIDE; John COLLINSWORTH; William
COOSE; Thomas DENNIS; William WILLIAMSON; William F. WILLIAMS; John M. BRABSON;
Thomas S. WILLIAMS, Bolser SHIRLEY; Hugh HOUSTON; Abner HUGES; William S. DIER;
James COCKE; John BOWEN; James CHECK; John HIXON; Daniel ROBINSON; Pleasant S.
COCKE; Edward TATE; James R. COCKE; Wilson DIER; John EASLEY; John CUMMINGS;
John DUGLASS; Robert H. HYNDS; R. C. CROZIER; D. WOOLDRIDGE; R. LOID; John
DANIEL; Charles CAMPBELL; Reese BOWIN; Elizabeth JACK; Jackson SMITH, Jr. Signed
18 May 1833 C. McANALLY, Thomas GILL, Warham EASLEY. Recorded 11 Jul 1834 P. S.
COCKE, clerk.

p. 50   Inventory - Estate of Adam STARNES, decd. 15 Feb 1834. Mentions:
Benjamin NEELY, James STARNES, Eli RECTOR. Recorded 11 Jul 1834 P. S. COCKE,
clerk.

p. 51   Account of Sale - Adam STARNES, decd. Mentions: William and Martin
DONEHEW, John HILL, William CLARK, Isaac DYER, Wrinant (?) COFFMAN, Joel
FIELDS, James VITTETOE, Nath. POPEJOY, Thomas McMILLIN, William HICKLE, Mark
MUNROE, Eli RECTOR, I. D. POPEJOY, Joseph HILL, William SHARP, Lewis ELLIS,
Stephen ATKINS, W. WILLIS, D. GOANS, John HICKLE, Samuel DOTSON, J. DENNIS, James
STARNES, Isaac SEAMORE, William DYER, John ROBERTSON, H. JENNINGS, A. MULLINS,
B. SHIRLEY, William WYRICK, Hugh DUFF, John STARNES, R. JENNINGS, S. DENNIS, E.
WILLIS, John CHANDLER, J. BEELER, William C. MALLICOAT, William HOLLINGSWORTH,
John CLARK, George ROBERTSON, Hugh PETERS, A. EVANS, Robert DUFF, __hereley
STARNES, J. KINDER, Cla. ACUFF, William DYER, W. C. SMITH, Willson C. JOHNSON,
Martin CLEVELAND, Jno HICKMAN, William MARTIN, George JENNINGS, William NORRIS,
E. MERRETT, William CUTTS, James NORRIS, William HILL, Moses BROCK, James
DYER, William VITTETOE, William BURNETT, A. McMAHAN, E. CLARK, Thomas WAGGONER,
N. BRANSON, Joseph CLARK. Recorded 11 Jul 1834 P. S. COCKE, Clerk.

p. 52   Inventory - James RAGSDALE, decd. Signed 22 Aug 1833 A. P. GREEN, Adm.
Recorded 12 Jul 1834 P. S. COCKE, clerk.

         Account of Sale - James RAGSDALE, decd. Sold 14 Sep 1833. Mentions:
Robert MITCHELL, Hugh JONES, Hugh HOUSTON, Pleasant S. COCKE, Benjamin CRAIGHEAD,
William PHILLIPS. Signed A. P. GREEN, Adm. Recorded 12 Jul 1834 P. S. COCKE.

p. 53   Settlement - A. P. GREEN, Adm of James RAGSDALE, decd. Mentions: Archibald P. GREEN, Adm., Pleasant S. COCKE, William E. COCKE, Isaac P. SIMPSON, David BARTON, John WILLIAMS. Signed Pleasant S. COCKE, Hugh JONES, William K. LATHIM, Commissioners. Recorded 12 Jul 1834 P. S. COCKE, clerk.

p. 54   Inventory - Estate of Thomas TURLEY, decd. Signed Joseph RICH, Adm. Recorded 12 Jul 1834 P. S. COCKE, clerk.

         Account of Sale - Thomas TURLEY, decd. Mentions: Joseph BEETS, Nelson A. SENTER, John COCKE, Widow TURLEY, Thomas WHITESIDE, Reubin GROVER, William F. WILLIAMS, Zera McGEE, Henry BOWEN, Jacob KIRKHAM, David McANALLY, A. G. LIVINGS- TON, John NOE, Jr., Richard MOORE, James MAYES, Richard STUBBLEFIELD, J. LIVINGS- TON, Hardy JOHNSON, Willie B. McGEE, Daniel TURLEY, Thomas WATSON, Jr., Franklin RAYL, Reese BOWEN, Wilson OLIVER, Jacob GODWIN, Caleb CROSBY, Jesse LIVINGSTON, H. O. TAYLOR, Warham EASLEY, Thomas McANALLY, John G. TURLEY, David COUNCE, Levi SATTERFIELD, Thomas GILL, Esq. Signed Joseph RICH, Adm. Recorded 12 Jul 1834 P. S. COCKE, clerk.

p. 58   Settlement - Elizabeth ESTES, Admx of George W. ESTES, decd. Mentions: Betsey ESTES, Admx.; HAYES & GIBBONS; Thomas MANN; S. J. & RICE; 10 Aug 1832 F. BOYD taxes; H. JOHNSON 1829 taxes; BENLY & HUNTER & CO.; T. D. KNIGHT; George BURCH; Joseph SHANNON; SHIELDS, JOHNSON & RICE; John COCKE; Russil RIGGS, William ROBINSON; G. S. LONG; C_____ AUSTIN; Archibald AUSTIN; Jas CARMICHAEL; Celia MANN; HAYNES & GIBSON; A. SHIPLEY; Joseph WILLIAMS; Dr. William MURRY. Signed 10 Aug 1832 John HARRIS, Joseph SHANNON, David SHIELDS, Commissioners. Recorded 12 Jul 1834 P. S. COCKE, clerk.

p. 59   Will - James HILL, decd. Wife Rachel, dau Catharine, son Abel, son John, dau Rachael Minerva, son Kanedy Corlson, 2 young children Rachel Manerva and Kanda Corlson when they come of age. Executor son John HILL. Signed 28 Jun 1832 James HILL. Wit: John HILL, Stephen FROST, Lorenzo D. FROST. Recorded 14 Jul 1834 P. S. COCKE, clerk.

p. 60   Inventory - James HILL, decd. 3 Nov 1832. Signed John HILL, Rachel HILL, Executors. Sale held 3 Nov 1832. Recorded 14 Jul 1834 P. S. COCKE, clerk.

p. 62   Will - Rice MOORE, decd. Wife Elizabeth, son John, son William, that William BARHAM alias William MOORE have 1 yr schooling to be paid by wife, 3 daus Nancy BRYAN, Elizabeth McANALLY and Mary McANALLY. Charles McANALLY and John BRYAN, Executors. Signed 1 Apr 1833 Rice MOORE. Wit: William T. TATE, John S. MILLS, Mackness MOORE. Recorded 14 Jul 1834 P. S. COCKE, clerk.

p. 63   Account of Sale - Peter HAMILTON, decd. Sale held 15 Aug 1833. James HAMILTON, Adm. Recorded 16 Jul 1834.

p. 65   Account of Debts - Due the Estate of John DENNIS, decd. Mentions: BLAIR & FRANKLIN, Mark MUNROE, Jesse JENNINGS, son John DENNIS, James STRANGE and William LEMMONS. Signed 21 May 1834 William DENNIS, Adm. Recorded 11 Jul 1834 P. S. COCKE, clerk.

         Inventory and Account of Sale - Elijah HIPSHERE, decd. Mentions: William McCOY, Jacob HIPSHERE, John HIPSHERE, William EVANS, Enoch DAULTON,

Matilda DAULTON, A. G. HELTON, A. JOHNSON, Thomas HAYES, Colbert HIPSHERE. Sold 1 Apr 1834, signed Henry HIPSHERE, Adm. Recorded 17 Jul 1834 P. S. COCKE, clerk.

p.66   Settlement - Ninean and Andrew CHAMBERLAIN for the Estate of Jeremiah CHAMBERLAIN, decd. Mentions: G. HENDERSON; Jacob KINDER; Thomas MAYES and James LACEY; Samuel BETTIS and Ralph CROW; Richd WATKINS and Isaac WATKINS; Daniel C. CHAMBERLAIN; David TATE, Jr.; 21 Sep 1829 taking inventory; E. TATE; Blackwell Meeting House; Jno STIFFY; Samuel BUNCH; Thomas S. WILLIAMS; Robert LOYD; William E. COCKE; Ephraim RIGGS. Signed 18 Nov 1831 E. TATE, Thomas WEST, Sr., James LACY. Recorded 18 Jul 1834 P. S. COCKE, clerk.

p. 68   Settlement - Agnes CERSAY, Admx of John CERSAY, decd. Mentions: Agness KERSEY, Admx of Estate of John KERSEY, decd; E. TATE; 7 heirs (not named); Agness KERSEY's widows part; William FIELDING who intermarried with Litty KERSEY an heir Agness KERSEY, Junr one of the heirs; John KERSEY, Junr an heir. Signed Reuben DICKSON, Henry ALLSUP, Edward TATE, Commissioners. Recorded 18 Jul 1834 P. S. COCKE, clerk.

p. 69   Settlement - Alexr HAMILTON and Mathew CAMPBELL, Executors of William HAMILTON, decd. Mentions: William LAY; Richard MALONE; Nathaniel ROBERSON; John STONE and Jacob GRIFFIN; Cardwell CUMONS; A. E. McHAFFER; taxes paid 1827 and 1829; John COLVIN; Samuel McBEE, Alexander HAMILTON's share of the Estate; William HAMILTON's share of the Estate; Robert BLAIR; William W. BLAIR. Signed 18 May 1830 Robert GAINS, William LANE, G. B. MITCHEL, Commissioners. Recorded 18 Jul 1834 P. S. COCKE, clerk.

p. 70   Settlement - Henry WISENER, Adm of Nathan BATES, decd. Green B. MITCHEL Robert BLAIR and Robert GAINES appointed Commissioners Feb 1831. Mentions: Stephen FRENCH, Warham EASLEY, J. MOORE, Thomas CHAMPLAIN, J. W. LIDE. Signed 14 May 1831. Recorded 18 Jul 1834 P. S. COCKE, clerk.

p. 72   Settlement - Mathew CAMPBELL, Guardian of the minor heirs of William HIXON, decd. Mentions: John BULLARD. Signed 20 Aug 1833 Robert BLAIR, Greenberry MITCHEL, Robert GAINES appointed Feb 1833 Commissioners. Recorded 18 Jul 1834 P. S. COCKE, clerk.

          Guardian Report - James R. COCKE, Guardian of William A. BROWN. Signed James R. COCKE, Guardian 19 Feb 1833. Recorded 18 Jul 1834 P. S. COCKE, clerk.

p. 73   Guardian Report - D. SHIELDS, Guardian of the minor heirs of Jno SHIELDS decd. Dated 20 May 1833. Mentions: James SHIELDS and Joseph COBB; JOHNSTON & RICE; SHIELDS, WHITEMAN & CO.; 1/3 to widow. Signed D. SHIELDS, Guardian. Recorded 18 Jul 1834 P. S. COCKE, clerk.

          Guardian Report - Guardian for heirs of John BARNARD, decd. Mentions: rent of small plantation for 1830; maintenance of heirs paid to their Grandmother Bedi BARNARD. Signed George BARNARD 22 Feb 1831. Recorded 19 Jul 1834 P. S. COCKE, clerk.

p. 74   Guardian Report - George BARNARD, Guardian of minor heirs of John BARNARD, decd. Signed George BARNARD, Guardian. Recorded 19 Jul 1834 P. S. COCKE, clerk.

Guardian Report - George BARNARD, Guardian of minor heirs of John BARNARD, decd. Signed 18 Nov 1833 George BARNARD, Guardian. Recorded 19 Jul 1834 P. S. COCKE, clerk.

Account of Sale - Estate of John VINYARD, decd. Mentions: William BRADLEY, Nicholas VINYARD, Andrew VINYARD, Mitchell M. NEMORE, Daniel VINYARD, Hiram NEMORE, Jeremiah R. GOANS, Stephen GREAR, Jacob VINEYARD, G. B. MITCHELL, Preston MITCHELL, John MITCHELL, John NANCE, Jacob GRUBB, Mary VINYARD, Martin VINYARD, Silas MYNETT, Edward CHURCHMAN, Thomas SMITH, Hiram M. NEMORE, Cuff CHURCHMAN, James R. FORREST, James R. HAGGARD, Richard CORAM, Joel COFFY, Jacob GRABEL, Mathas VINYARD, Pearce W. BRADSHAW, William BEARD, James S. TOLBERT, Samuel VINYARD, Nathaniel GREAR, Lavina BRADSHAW, John NEMORE, James FARLEY, Rowland CHILDS, Paul CHILDS, Nathaniel GREEN, Garder MAZE. Signed G. B. MITCHEL, Daniel VINYARD, Adms. Recorded 21 Jul 1834 P. S. COCKE, clerk.

p. 78   Will - Joel HAMMERS, Sr., decd. Wife Hannah; given already to several children. Signed 8 Aug 1832 Joel x HAMMAR. Wit: James KENNON and Enos HAMMAR. Recorded 21 Jul 1834 P. S. COCKE, clerk.

p. 79   Inventory - Joel HAMMAR, decd. Mentions: Nicholas COUNER, Jr. Signed Thomas DYER, Executor. Recorded 21 Jul 1834 P. S. COCKE, clerk.

p. 80   Will - Jonathan MUMPOWER, decd. Wife Jane, son Anderson, daus Elizabeth, Sally, Susan, Dulcenia, Mary WILLS, Nancy MILLS and Ann HARRY (?). Signed 10 Jan 1831 Jonathan x MUMPOWER. Wit: Rice MOORE, John BRYAN and William R. BEGGS. Recorded 22 Jul 1834 P. S. COCKE, clerk.

p. 81   Inventory - Stephen TEAGUE, decd. Signed Easter x TEAGUE. Recorded 22 Jul 1834 P. S. COCKE, clerk.

Guardian Report - David ELKINS, Executor and Adm of heirs of Joseph ELKINS, decd. Signed 15 Feb 1834 David ELKINS, Sr. Recorded 23 Jul 1834.

p. 82   Guardian Report - William H. MOFFITT, Guardian of John S. MOFFITT. Mentions: report given 21 Feb 1832. Signed 18 Feb 1834 William H. MOFFIT, Guardian. Recorded 22 Jul 1834 P. S. COCKE, clerk.

Additional Account of Sale - Jeremiah CHAMBERLAIN, decd. Mentions: Thomas CHAMBERLAIN, James KENNON, John CARDWELL, Abraham WATKINS, James POLLARD, William DANIEL, John GRAY, Hugh McHANEY, Samuel M. POLLARD, George SPARKMAN, Robert CARDWELL, David COCKRAM, John IVY, Isaac J. WATKINS. Recorded 23 Jul 1834 P. S. COCKE, clerk.

p. 83   Will - Adam STARNES, decd. Wife Pheroba; Nathan to have 1 year school; sons Conrad and James H. Signed Adam STARNES, Sr. 28 Dec 1833. Executors sons Conrad and James H. Wit: Edward CLARK and ____enard BURNETT. Recorded 23 Jul 1834.

p. 84   Guardian Report - G. B. MITCHELL, Guardian of the minor heirs of William HANKINS, decd. Signed 17 Feb 1834 G. B. MITCHELL.

Guardian Report - G. B. MITCHELL, Guardian for the minor heirs of James

FORGENSON, decd. Signed 17 Feb 1834 G. B. MITCHELL.

Recorded 23 Jul 1834 P. S. COCKE, clerk.

Inventory - John FORGISON, decd. J. KENNON, Adm. Mentions: one NEGRO boy. Recorded 24 Jul 1834 P. S. COCKE, clerk.

p. 85   List of the Debts Owed Estate of Jno FORGISON, decd. Mentions: Philimo≡ HODGES, John MAYES, Henry COUNTS, William HODGES, Richard FORGISON, William CARTE≡ John KIDWELL, Thomas GILMORE, Josiah BUNCH, James WILLSON, William and Isaac DANIEL, Dixon SMITH and James GALLION, Thomas McBROOM and Robert STUBBLEFIELD, James KINNON, Jacob KLINE, Warham EASLEY, Chesley MORGAN, Samuel WEST, Legand MAYES, Joseph McCAIN. Signed James KENNON, Adm. Recorded 24 Jul 1834 P. S. COCK≡

p. 86   Account of Sales - John FORGISON, decd. Mentions: James WILSON, Allen D. MORGAN, John GILMROE, Lea DYER, Isaac DYER, John COLLISON, Stephen BUTLER, Samuel COLLISON, Charles ACUFF, Hugh HOUSTON, Thomas SMITH, James SIMMONS, James MASSENGILL, John DAVIS, Daniel ROGAN, Bloser SHIRLEY, Thomas WEST, John MORGAN, Jr., Thomas RAY, Samuel POLLARD, John W. EATON, Noah WILLIS, Chesley MORGAN, Edward WEST, George DUTTON, Lewis KINNEY, William GILMORE, John GILMORE, Wilson DYER, John CRAIN, William DYER, Thomas DYER, Joshua D. CURL. Recorded 4 Aug 1834 P. S. COCKE, clerk.

p. 89   Additional Account of Sales - Peter HARRIS, decd. Mentions: Land sold to John COCKE on 7 Dec 1833. Signed John HARRIS, Executor. Recorded 4 Aug 1834 P. S. COCKE, clerk.

p. 90   Will - Elizabeth SATTERFIELD, decd. Dated 26 Mar 1834. The Last Will and Verbal Request of Elizabeth SATTERFIELD a few minutes before she departed this life. We, William CARTER and George ROBERSON, being present was called on by her to take notice that she wished Mary SMITH to take her little girl, Mary, and raise her, and my wearing clothes to go with her. Rest of the children to stay on land and support selves. Wit: William CARTER, George ROBINSON. Recorded 4 Aug 1834 P. S. COCKE, clerk.

p. 90   Inventory - Andrew CHAMBERLAIN, decd. Recorded 4 Aug 1834 P. S. COCKE, clerk.

p. 91   Account of Sale - Andrew CHAMBERLAIN, decd. Mentions: Thompson CHAMBERLAIN, 1 Negro man JOE, David TATE, 1 Negro woman HANNAH, Pleasant WILLIAMS 1 Negro boy JIM, Lea DYER, 1 Negro girl POLLY, Simeon WILLIFORD, Robert CARDWELL, Robert FRANKLIN, James WILLIAMS, Samuel WEST, Ninian CHAMBERLAIN, Isaac DANIEL, Robert MITCHELL, Thomas WEST, James MALICOAT, Thomas COCKE, Hugh McELHANEY, Jonathan WILLIAMS, Enos HAMMER, Jr., John CARDWELL, John HOWERTON, Lawrence BRADLEY, John KINDER, John VOSS, Robert WATSON, I. I. WATKINS, Cornelius GOFORTH, John McDANIEL, James GARRETT, James MALLICOAT, John GREENLEE, James WATSON, Lawrence BRAND, James CHURCHMAN, John GREENLEA, Sr., Eli SPOON, John GRAY, Pleasant CHURCHMAN, William SMITH, Samuel McNEAR, William MAYES, James LACY, Jame≡ HODGES, Massa COCKRAM, John COCKE, John IVY, David KIDWELL, John RAMSEY, John HIXON, Robert MITCHELL, William HODGE, Isaac HULL, Reubin CHURCHMAN, James MALLICOAT, Isaac I. WATKINS, Neal GOFORTH, James JAMES, Isaac PHILLIPS, David KITTS, John BOX, John HIXON, John GREENLEE, Joel PHILLIPS. Recorded 5 Aug 1834

P. S. COCKE, clerk.

p. 94   Account of Notes and Accounts - Andrew CHAMBERLAIN, decd. Mentions: Thomas WEST, I. I. WATKINS, James CHAMBERLAIN, John MEEK, James EATON, John CARDWELL, James LACY, John DAVIS, John COPELAND, Arthur CARNEY. Signed James KENNON, Adm. Recorded 5 Aug 1834 P. S. COCKE, clerk.

p. 95   Will - George NORRIS, decd. Wife Priscilla; son Thomas; son William; son George; Lucinda NORRIS (no relation given) during her widowhood and Calvin and Mahala NORRIS heirs of Brown NORRIS, decd. Signed 30 Nov 1833 George NORRIS. Executor son Thomas. Wit: William BAKER, Jarret x NORRIS. Recorded 6 Aug 1834 P. S. COCKE, clerk.

p. 96   Guardian Report - Heirs of Carter DOLTON, decd. Mentions: years 1831, 1832 rents. Signed C. McANALLY, Guardian, 19 Feb 1834. Recorded 6 Aug 1834 P. S. COCKE, clerk.

          Inventory - Miller W. EASLEY, decd. Mentions: 7 Negroes JANE, PRIMUS, ABRAHAM, ISAAC, WILSON, AGNESS and PETER; John EASLEY. Signed 19 Aug 1834 Warham EASLEY and Mary x EASLEY, Executors. Recorded 12 Sep 1834 Thomas COCKE, clerk.

p. 97   Will - Michael MASSINGELL, decd. Grandson Solomon MASSINGILL; granddau Mary M. M. MASSENGILL; grandson William M. COCKE; granddaus Mary I. WHITESIDE (?) and Narcissa F. BRIDGEMAN; Negro boy RUSSEL; Negro girl SALLY ANN; Negro boy WASHINGTON; Negro woman MARGARET; Negro woman PAT; Negroes ABRAHAM, BOB, JOHN, CHARLOTTE, BILL and CALVIN. Son Robert Executor. Signed 1 Jan 1834 Michael x MASSENGILL. Wit: Henry ALSUP and Thomas WEST. Recorded 3 Nov 1834 T. S. COCKE.

p. 98   Will - Samuel WEST, Sr., decd. Wife Elizabeth; daus Mary CAMBERLAND, Rachel DOUGLAS, Elizabeth LOVE, Fanny Harcesea WEST, Jane (?) A. WEST and Eliza C. WEST; oldest sons Thomas and James; son Edward; son Samuel; son Alexander; son Robert R., not of lawful age. Executors James WEST, friend James KENNON. Signed 26 Jul 1834 Samuel x WEST. Wit: Thomas WEST and John BOILS (?). Recorded 3 Nov 1834 Thomas S. COCKE, clerk.

p. 99   Will - Joseph HILL, Sr., decd. 20 Apr 1833; wife not named; 4 sons William, John, Jesse and Robert; 2 daus Sarah DUNAHEW and Elizabeth HILL. Executors 2 oldest sons William and John. Signed Joseph HILL. Wit: Willis L. PRATT and Jesse x HILL. Recorded 4 Nov 1834 Thos S. COCKE, clerk.

p. 100   Will - Andrew ELDER, decd. Wife Elizabeth. Executors Elizabeth ELDER. Signed 28 Aug 1824 Andrew x ELDER. Wit: Henry x HIPSHIRE, William HAYES, Jr. and Js BOWEN. Recorded 4 Nov 1834 Thos S. COCKE.

          Will - Abraham JAMES, decd. Wife Nancy. Executor Nancy JAMES. Rest of heirs have received their portion. Signed 23 Apr 1834 Abraham JAMES. Wit: James L. WEST and Thomas GILMORE. Recorded 4 Nov 1834 Thos S. COCKE.

p. 101   Will - Meridith DOLTON, decd. 29 Apr 1834; sons Coalby and Reuben; wife and children (not named); mentions land next to Ann McGINNIS; OGAN debt; SHIELDS debt; LAFFERTY debt; OGLE debt. Executor Coalby DOLTON. Signed Meridith DOLTON. Wit: William HAYES, Moses PAYNE, John HIPSHEAR. Recorded 4 Nov 1834 T. S. COCKE.

Will - Benjamin HOWELL, decd. Wife Agnes alias Agnes GRISSOM; Permilia WALKER (no relation given); Executor Calib HOWELL. Signed Benjamin HOWELL 5 Feb 1833. Wit: Goodwin PRICE and Joseph DANIEL Recorded 5 Nov 1834 Thos S. COCKE.

p. 102   Will - Shurrad MAYS, decd. Wife Elizabeth; 5 sons Thomas, William, Goodwin, Dudley and Jonathan MAYS; daus each provided for by their grandfather Thomas SMITH of VA; Levi SATTERFIELD and Joseph DANIEL Executors. Signed 11 Apr 1829 Shurrad x MAYS. Wit: Elijah SIMS, Joshua KIDWILL. Recorded 5 Nov 1834 Thos S. COCKE.

p. 103   Account of Sales - Stephen W. SENTER, decd. 25 Mar 1830. Mentions: Samuel B. TATE, Hughs O. TAYLOR, Abram McCONNELL, John W. LYDE, Thomas BRYANT, Mrs. SENTER (Widow), Wiley B. KYLE, Mastin HENDERSON, Richard STUBBLEFIELD, David SHROPSHIRE, William LINN, John CUMMINGS, H. B. KILE, Joel EMBRY, T. D. KNIGHT, Thomas WHITESIDE, George MARLOCK, Warham EASLEY, David McANALLY, Thomas JOHNSON, T. B. EVANS, David COUNTS, Wm MAYS, Alexander HELTON, Joseph PROFFITT, Pleasant JENNINGS, Charles McANALLY, Fountain HARRIS· Signed Nelson A. SENTER, Adm. Recorded 17 Dec 1834.

p. 110   Inventory - Elizabeth SATTERFIELD, decd. Mentions: notes on Thomas BROWN, William DENNIS, John SATTERFIELD. Signed William DENNIS, Adm. Recorded no date.

Account of Sales - James STOKES, decd. Court at Aug 1834 term. Mentions John HOLT, Ephraun PURVIN, Rowland McGILL, Goodwin PRICE, Walter SHROPSHIRE, John DENSON (?), Nicholas NOE son of John NOE, Sr. Signed William McGILL, Adm. Recorded no date.

p. 111   Account of Sales - Isazah MIDKIFF, decd. Sold 6 Apr 1834 by John IVY, Adm. Mentions: Godwin PRICE, Walter SHROPSHEAR, Paskil TURNER, John SPOON, BLACKHEAD note, Moses SMITH, Phillimon IVEY, John RAMSEY, Cutbert IVEY, Thomas K. HOWELL, David COUNTZ, James MAIZE, Prior BIBA, Ephraim PA___IN, M. N. JEFFERIES, Walter D. COWEN. Signed John IVY, Adm. Recorded 6 Jul 1836 E. TATE, clerk.

p. 112   Will - Ruth STIFFY, decd. Bros and sis David HENDERSON, Joseph HENDERSO Abraham HENDERSON, John HENDERSON, Robert HENDERSON, Mary CONLEY, Sally GREEN, Betsy McDANIEL and Margaret HALEY; Jane GRAY, Betsy MALLICOAT, Sarah GRAY, John S. GRAY, Louisa GRAY, Mary GRAY, William M. GRAY and Amanda GRAY the children and heirs of my nephew John GRAY, decd. Edward TATE Executor. Signed 8 Apr 1834 Ruth x STIFFY. Attest: Wm MAYES, John CLARK, John CARDWELL. Recorded 6 Jul 1836 E. TATE, clerk.

Inventory - Rachel COUNTZ, decd. Signed 17 Feb 1835 Thomas McBROOM, Executor. Recorded 6 Jul 1836 E. TATE, clerk.

p. 113   Will - David ELKINS, decd. Dear wife (not named); son David; dau Patsy; dau Mary. Executors Wife, my trusty friends and son David. Signed David x ELKINS (no date). Attest: John HILL, David ELKINS, Jr., John D. POPEJAY, Nathaniel x POPEJAY. Recorded 10 May 1836 E. TATE, clerk.

Inventory - David ELKINS, decd. Signed David ELKINS, Jr. Executor. Recorded 10 May 1836 E. TATE, clerk.

p. 114   Will - Robert McGINNIS, decd. Wife Lettice; 2 sons Christopher and Andrew; son Joseph; mentions land owned by heirs of Meredith DOLTON and Henry HIPSHIRE; 5 following children Nobel, Archabald, William, Mary who is inter-married with Clabourn W. LATHAM, and my youngest dau Nancy; all SLAVES to wife. Executor son Andrew. Signed 5 Feb 1836 Robert McGINNIS. Wit: C. M. McANALLY, Dan'l DONALDSON, John LATHAM, Jr. Recorded 10 May 1836 Edward TATE, clerk.

p. 115   Sales of Edward CHURCHMAN, decd. Mentions: Negro man DICK sold to Sarah CHURCHMAN for $248.25. Signed Massey COCKRAN and Alen x D. MORGAN. Recorded 10 May 1836 E. TATE, clerk.

         Settlement - G. B. MITCHELL and Daniel VINEYARD, Adms of John VINEYARD, decd. Mentions: Elizabeth MITCHELL, Matthias VINEYARD, Andrew VINEYARD, Nich-olas VINEYARD, John VINEYARD, Mary VINEYARD, Gordim MAYES, Martin VINEYARD, William VINEYARD, James MAYES, Stephen GREER, James (?) CAMPBELL, Harmon G. LEA. Recorded 10 May 1836 E. TATE, clerk.

p. 116   Account of Sales - Isaac DYER, decd. Signed Nancy DYER, Adm. Recorded 7 Jun 1836 E. TATE, clerk.

         Account of Sales - Ruth STIFFY, decd. Mentions: Elizabeth MALLICOAT; Jane WILLIAMS; Negro man ISAM hired 1 yr to William HIGHTOWER; Negro woman FANNY 1 yr hire to Pleasant WILLIAMS; Negro woman NANCY 1 yr hire to Sarah GRAY; 346 acre plantation to Pleasant WILLIAMS. Signed E. TATE Executor. Recorded 7 Jun 1836 E. TATE, clerk.

p. 119   Inventory - Robert McGINNIS, decd. Mentions: 8 NEGROES; debts owing; notes on Aaron McGINNIS; 1 note on Thomas HAYES; account on William McGINNIS; account on Andrew McGINNIS; John OGAN's Estate. Signed 6 Jun 1836 Andrew McGINNIS. Recorded 8 Jun 1836 E. TATE, clerk.

p. 120   Will - Obadiah WALTERS, decd. Wife (not named); 2 sons Israel and Isaac; dau Mary; granddau Leete Jane WALTERS, son Lemuel; the rest of all my children $1.00 to each with what I have partioned to them; trusty friends James COLVIN and Lemuel WALTERS to be my Executives. Signed Obadiah x WALTERS. Wit: George W. VITTITO, William P. McBEE, Israel x WALTERS. Recorded 8 Jun 1836 E. TATE, clerk.

p. 121   Inventory - Aquilla MITCHELL, decd. Mentions: notes on William HODGES and Phillamon HODGES, Augustin BOWERS and Robert MASSENGILL. Signed 6 Jun 1836 G. B. MITCHELL, Executor. Recorded 9 Jun 1836 E. TATE, clerk.

p. 122   Inventory - Samuel BROWN, decd. Signed 2 May 1836 William BROWN, Adm. Recorded 9 Jun 1836 E. TATE, clerk.

p. 123   Account of Sales - Robert GOINS, decd. Signed 6 Jun 1836 Bailes E. GOINS and Robert C. GOINS, Executors. Recorded 9 Jun 1836 E. TATE, clerk.

         Guardian Report - John CHILES, Guardian of minor heirs of John AMES, decd, to whit: William, Elizabeth, James and Edward. Signed 18 May 1835 John CHILES, Guardian. Recorded 6 Jul 1836 E. TATE, clerk.

p. 127   Will - Abraham JAMES, decd. Apr 23, 1834 all to wife Nancy as for rest
of heirs they have received their respective portions. Signed Abraham JAMES.
Attest: James T. WEST and Thomas GILMORE. Recorded 6 Jun 1836 E. TATE, clerk.

       Will - Rachel COUNTS. Son Jesse COUNTS; son-in-law Prior P. BUNCH and
his 4 children, sons of my dau Susan; son James M.; daus Patsey and Nancy;
Executor Thomas McBROOM. Signed Rachel x (his mark) COUNTS 28 Jul 1834. Wit:
William M. MOODY and Robert CRAIGHEAD. Recorded 6 Jul 1836 E. TATE, clerk.

p. 128   Will - Robert MORROW, decd. Wife Rosanna; dau Nancy; son Robert;
mentions land bought from Robert NASH; wife and dau to live with son Robert; 5
children yet alive George, Elizabeth ATKINS, John, Barbara KITTS, Mark; to heirs
of dau Peggy WYRICK, decd; dau Polly ATKINS, decd; Executor Robert MORROW. Signe
Robert x MORROW 11 Jan 1834. Wit: James SALLING, William HAMILTON and William
LAY. Recorded 6 Jul 1836 E. TATE, clerk.

       Guardian Report - John BARNARD, decd. Dec 1833. Report for 1832, 1833
and 1834. Signed George BARNARD, Guardian 18 Nov 1834. Recorded 6 Jul 1836
E. TATE, clerk.

p. 130   Will - Daniel TAYLOR, decd. 30 Nov 1834; wife Jane; son George; son
Morgan; dau Keziah; son Greefield (?); dau Destimony; dau Elizabeth; dau Mourning
son Daniel; son Hugh O.; son James; dau Nancy; dau Jane; Executors Hughs O.
TAYLOR, Jr., James TAYLOR and Hughs W. TAYLOR. Signed 30 Nov 1834 Daniel TAYLOR.
Wit: H. O. TAYLOR, John W. T. McANALLY, John HARRIS. Recorded 6 Jul 1836 E.
TATE, clerk.

p. 131   Inventory - Edward CHURCHMAN. Taken 16 Oct 1835. Signed Massy COCKRUM
and Allen D. x MORGAN. Recorded 7 Jul 1836 E. TATE, clerk.

p. 132   Settlement - Estate of Peter HAMILTON, decd. 15 Aug 1835. Mentions:
James HAMILTON; Nancy REDMAN; 10 legatees Katherine HAMILTON, Polly CASEY, Peter
HAMILTON, Nancy COBB formerly Nancy REDMAN, James HAMILTON, Joseph P. HAMILTON,
Sarah DURRET, Hiram HAMILTON, Vander HAMILTON, and Lorenzo D. HAMILTON. Signed
Robert BLAIR, Harmon G. LEA, William READER. Recorded 7 Jul 1836 E. TATE, clerk.

p. 134   Settlement - Estate of Jeremiah CHAMBERLAIN, decd. Neman CHAMBERLAIN
Executor, 4 Dec 1833. Signed and dated 29 May 1835 Robert GOINS, Harmon LEA,
G. B. MITCHELL. Recorded 7 Jul 1836 E. TATE, clerk.

p. 135   Inventory Sale - Edward CHURCHMAN, decd. Signed Massy COCKRUM and Allen
D. x MORGAN, Adms. Recorded 7 Jul 1836 E. TATE, clerk.

p. 140   Settlement - John STIFFY, decd. Edward TATE, Executor. Mentions:
payment of notes by Robert LOYD on JENNINGS note; William JENNINGS; Doct Wm E.
COCKE; Reuben STIFFY; John CAMPBELL; William MAYES; Hugh HOUSTON (rental, 6 mos,
on sawmill); William MAYES (rent on sawmill). Signed 15 Jan 1835 E. TATE,
Executor.

p. 142   Sale of Personal Property - Ruth STIFFY, decd.

       Above two Recorded 7 Jul 1836 Edward TATE, clerk.

p. 144   Guardian Report - Thomas DENNIS, Guardian of the heirs of John DENNIS, decd. Mentions: 4 yrds of Cambrick for Aleneth DENNIS $3.00; 1 yd Callico for Cyntha DENNIS $.37; William DENNIS going to school $1.75. Signed Thomas DENNIS 16 Feb 1835. Recorded 16 Feb 1836 E. TATE, clerk.

p. 145   Settlement - John LARGE and Thomas HANKINS, Executors of the Estate of Wm HANKINS, decd. Signed Harmon G. LEA, William COWAN, James S. TALBOT 10 May 1835. Recorded 8 Jul 1836 E. TATE, clerk.

p. 146   Settlement - James HANKINS, Adm of the Estate of John AMES, decd. Signed Harmon G. LEA, William COWAN, James S. TALBOT 16 May 1835. Recorded 8 Jul 1836.

p. 127   Inventory - Joseph HILL, decd. Signed Margaret HILL, Admx. Recorded 9 Jul 1836 E. TATE, clerk.

   Account of Hire - Negroes BERRY and RHODA and child belonging to the Estate of John BROWN, decd, returned to court 16 Feb 1836. Hired Negro BERRY to John COCKE for 12 mos for $60.00. Hired Negro RHODA and child to Joseph WORLEY for 12 mos for $9.00. Signed Wm G. TATE, Adm. 16 Feb 1836. Recorded 9 Jul 1836 E. TATE, clerk.

p. 148   Will - Robert GAINS, decd. Youngest son Pryor Anderson GAINS; all my children namely Elizabeth DAVIS, Anna COWIN, Baylis E. GAINS, Robert C. GAINS, James P. GAINS, Preston H. GAINS, Mahayley GAINS, Prior A. GAINS, Mildreth GAINS; two oldest sons Bailis E. GAINS and Robert C. GAINS Executors. Signed 28 Jun 1833 Robert GAINS. Wit: Thos SMITH, Joseph SMITH, Robert H. SMITH. Recorded 9 Jul 1836 E. TATE, clerk.

p. 149   Inventory - Robert MONROW, decd. 7 Jan 1835. Signed Robert MONROW. Recorded 9 Jul 1836 E. TATE, clerk.

p. 150   Inventory - William ROBERTSON, decd. Signed Thomas x ROBERTSON 18 Feb 1835. Recorded 9 Jul 1836 E. TATE, clerk.

   Settlement - James WILLSON and Jacob KINDER, Executors for the Estate of Eve FUESTONE, decd. Henry JOHNS, sole devisee. Signed James T. WEST, David N. TATE, I. B. BOYD. Recorded 9 Jul 1836 E. TATE, clerk.

p. 151   Inventory - Joseph BRYANT, decd. Signed Elizabeth BRYAN. Recorded 9 Jul 1836 E. TATE, clerk.

   Account of Sales - Joseph RICH, Adm. of the Estate of Thomas TURLEY, decd. Land purchased 3 Mon of Aug 1835 by Robert LONG and John HARRIS. Signed Joseph RICH 18 Aug 1835. Recorded 9 Jul 1836.

p. 152   Will - Shurad MAYES, decd. Beloved wife Elizabeth MAYES; 5 sons Thomas, William, Godwin, Dudley and Jonathan MAYES; my daus each to be provided for by their grandfather Thos SMITH of VA as specified in his last will and testament which see; Levi SATTERFIELD and Joseph DANIEL Executors. Signed Shurad x MAYES 11 Apr 1829. Wit: Elijah SIMS and Joshua KIDWELL. Recorded 9 Jul 1836 E. TATE, clerk. (see p. 10; p. 102 of microfilm)

Account of Sales (2nd) - Adam STARNES, decd. Held 15 Sep 1834. Signed James H. STARNES 16 Feb 1835. Recorded 9 Jul 1836 E. TATE, clerk.

p. 153   Account of Sales - Henry IVEY, decd, by Benjamin IVEY, Adm. 13 Sep 1834. Recorded 9 Jul 1836 E. TATE, clerk.

p. 154   Account of Sales - William HANKINS, decd. Held 14 Nov 1833. Recorded 9 Jul 1836 E. TATE, clerk.

p. 156   Account of Sales - Thomas SHIPLEY, decd. 9 Apr 1835. Mentions: Thomas SHIPLEY, Nathaniel SHIPLEY, Adam SHIPLEY. Signed Adam SHIPLEY and William SHIPLEY, Executors, signed in open court 18 May 1835. Recorded 9 Jul 1836 E. TATE, clerk.

p. 158   Settlement - William MALLICOAT, Executor of the Estate of John MALLICOAT decd. Signed Aug 1835 by Rail x JENNINGS, John LATHAM, John DODSON, Joel DODSON. Recorded 9 Jul 1836 E. TATE, clerk.

p. 159   Inventory - Jenny DYER, widow of Isaac DYER, decd. Signed 13 Feb 1836 Janny DYER. Recorded 11 Jul 1836 E. TATE, clerk.

p. 160   Account of Sales - Estate of James HILL, decd and Rachel HILL, former Exectrix of James HILL, decd. 19 Dec 1835. Signed John HILL, Executor. Recorded 11 Jul 1836 E. TATE, clerk.

p. 164   Inventory - Estate of Robert WATSON, decd. 17 Nov 1835. Signed E. TATE Adm. Recorded 11 Jul 1836 E. TATE, clerk.

Account of Sale - Robert WATSON, decd. Recorded 11 Jul 1836 E. TATE.

p. 165   Inventory - 12 Nov 1835 James HILL, decd, as Rachel HILL, the widow of said James HILL, has deceased on date mentioned above. Signed John HILL, Executor. Recorded 11 Jul 1836 E. TATE, clerk.

p. 166   Settlement - Warham EASLEY and Mary EASLEY, Executors of Millar W. EASLEY, decd. Signed 17 Aug 1835 John COCKE and Hugh JONES. Recorded 11 Jul 1836 E. TATE, clerk.

Additional Account of Sales - Ruth STIFFY, decd. Recorded 11 Jul 1836 E. TATE, clerk.

p. 167   Inventory - Felps REED, decd. Signed Mar 1835 George G. REED, Adm. Recorded 12 Jul 1836 E. TATE, clerk.

p. 169   Account of Sales - Felps REED, decd. Recorded 12 Jul 1836 E. TATE.

p. 172   Petition - Aug Session 1835, Felps REED, decd. Slaves belonging to said Estate: TENEE, age 46, JOHN, ELIAS, STUCKY, JUDY and POLLY and another female (name not recollected), age 3. Said REED left 5 children, 5 grandch the heirs of his deceased son, Thomas. Petition to sell slaves; ELIAS, a free man of color, husband of TENEE and father of JUDA, POLLY and younger one. Signed George G. REED, Adm. Recorded 12 Jul 1835 E. TATE, clerk.

p. 173   Account of Sales - Felps REED, decd. Sold 12 Sep 1835. Recorded 12 Jul 1836 E. TATE, clerk.

p. 175   Account of Sales - Robert MONROW, decd. Recorded 12 Jul 1836 E. TATE.

Guardian Report - David SHIELDS, Guardian of the heirs of John SHIELDS, decd, including the widows account in Aug 1833. Signed D. SHIELDS. Recorded 12 Jul 1836 E. TATE, clerk.

p. 178   Settlement - Thomas NORRIS, Executor for George NORRIS, decd, who was the Adm of Brown NORRIS, decd. Signed 15 Nov 1834 James LALLING, Alexander HAMILTON and John CHESNEY. Recorded 12 Jul 1836 E. TATE, clerk.

p. 179   Will - Zera MAGEE. Wife Mary monies on hand and Negro girl LOUISA; oldest son Nehemiah; oldest dau Louisa wife of Ambrose EVANS; son Willie; son James; my dau Sarah wife of John MAYES; Nehemiah H. MAGEE and Willie B. MAGEE Executor. Signed 15 Aug 1835 Zeree MAGEE. Wit: James CARMICHAEL, Sr. and D. C. CARMICHAEL. Recorded 12 Jul 1836 E. TATE, clerk.

p. 181   Will - Benjamin RAY, decd. Wife Saly; sons Sterling RAY, Caswell RAY, Chester RAY and Robert RAY; note on hand on Levi MILLAR; Lewcinda my dau; dau Lidy; son Jesse RAY; daus Annie RAY, Mary RAY, Lewcinda RAY; Jincy SPARKMAN my dau; friend Henery ALSUP, Executor. Signed Benjamin x RAY 8 Feb 1832. Wit: Thomas RAY, Adonijah KEY, Jacob ARNET. Recorded 12 Jul 1836 E. TATE, clerk.

p. 182   Settlement - Robert EATON, Adm of the Estate of Elizabeth ALBERT, decd. Signed John T. CURL, Hugh JONES, Chesley JARNAGIN. Recorded 13 Jul 1836 E. TATE, clerk.

p. 184   Will - Evan HARRIS, decd. Wife Rachel; son Isaac; son Israel; 3 daus Elizabeth, Mary and Nancy; dau Martha and children; other 5 children Robert, Jane, John, Stewart and Temple; son Isaac HARRIS sole Executor. Signed 14 Oct 1834 Evan HARRIS. Wit: James WHITLOCK, Samuel x RAY. Recorded 13 Jul 1836 E. TATE, clerk.

p. 185   Petition - Feb term 1836, Massy COCKRUM and Allen D. MORGAN, Adms of the Estate of Edward CHURCHMAN, decd. All heirs, 12 in number, are of age. Petition to sell Negro DICK and money to be distributed among heirs. Signed 15 Feb 1836 Massy COCKRUM and Allen D. x MORGAN. Recorded 13 Jul 1836 E. TATE, clerk.

p. 186   Account of Sales - Estate of Samuel WEST, Sr., decd, as sold 10 Sep 1834. Returned to Court 18 Nov 1834 James T. WEST, Executor. Recorded 13 Jul 1836 E. TATE, clerk.

p. 187   Inventory - 16 Aug 1834 John OGAN, Sr., decd. Signed Peter OGAN. Recorded 13 Jul 1836 E. TATE, clerk.

Additional Account of Sales - Jahu SIMMONS, decd. Signed Robert SIMMONS, Green x SIMMONS, Adms. Recorded 13 Jul 1836 E. TATE, clerk.

p. 188   Will - David McANALLY, Sr., decd. Wife Nancy; 3 children; my dau Sarah BAINES; dau Polly CARROLE; son Thomas. Signed 18 Sep 1834 David McANALLY. Wit:

John LATHAM, Thomas P. McANALLY, E. McANALLY, H. WILLIAMS. Recorded 13 Jul 1836
E. TATE, clerk.

        Account of Sales - Estate of John BROWN, decd. Hire of Negroes BERRY
and RHODA and child for $46.00 to Ethelred WILLIAMS for 12 mos; RHODA to Joseph
WORLEY for 12 mos at $16.00. Dated 17 Feb 1835. Recorded 13 Jul 1836 E. TATE.

p. 189   Account Inventory - Sale of the property of Elizabeth SATTERFIELD, decd.
Signed William DENNIS, Adm. Recorded 13 Jul 1836 E. TATE, clerk.

p. 190   Will - Aquilla MITCHELL, decd. Wife (not named); oldest son William
MITCHELL; land joining James DAVIS; second son Benjamin MITCHELL; third son
Aquilla MITCHEL; three daus Celia MAYSE, Rhoda GALLIAN and Nancy ARMSTRONG;
Green B. MITCHELL Executor. Signed 11 May 1822 Aquilla x MITCHELL. Wit: Peter
GILMORE, Thomas GILMORE. Recorded 13 Jul 1836 E. TATE, clerk.

p. 191   Commissioners Report - Nov session 1835: Commissioners appointed at Aug
session 1835 for Jane BROWN, widow of John BROWN, decd, to lay off support for a
period of 1 year; to decide if William A. BROWN was one of the family and cash
value of the Estate. Commissioners: Nicholas COUNTS, Jacob KLINE. Recorded
14 Jul 1836 E. TATE, clerk.

p. 192   Additional Sales - John VINEYARD, decd. Signed G. B. MITCHELL, Daniel
VINEYARD, Adms. Recorded 14 Jul 1836 E. TATE, clerk.

p. 193   Account of Sales - Jahu SIMMONS, decd. Mentions: Charles CRANE, Sr.,
Drury ROCH, Hardin CAMRON, Thomas RAY, David COATS, James EYATS, James JARNAGIN,
Pleasant CRANE, Martha SIMMONS, David BROCKUS, Thompson CHAMBERLAIN, John SIMMONS,
Henry ALSUP, Samuel BOX (?), John CRAIN, Abram FULKERSON, John COLLISON, John
COTHRUM, Isaac MITCHELL, Houston CHESHER (?), Martin RIGHT, Edward WEST, Jacob
ARNETT, Elijah BECKUM, Green SIMMONS, Thomas RAY, Samuel SMITH, James WEST,
William BROWN, Robert RAY, John HENSLEY, Alexander HIGGS. Recorded 14 Jul 1836
E. TATE, clerk.

p. 195   Guardian Report - Helen M. LIPSCOMB, minor, in account with her Guardian
J. W. LIDE for her use 1832 from GLOVER & ROSS; J. H. FYFFE, Esqr, goods 1833;
CLEAGS & CRUTCHFIELD 1832, 33, 34; S. BOGART & CO. 1832, 33, 34; W. W. ANDERSON
1834; shoes made by Henry HEWINGER 1834 ($1.25); tuition Athens Female Academy
1832, 33, 34, Rev. J. H. NORMENT, principal; J. W. LIDE, Guardian for minor heirs
of Spotswood LIPSCOMB, decd, from 22 Aug 1827 to 7 Apr 1829 to be charged for use
and occupency of Intestate plantation mill. Signed C. McANALLY, Joseph COBB and
Joseph RICH. Recorded 14 Jul 1835 E. TATE, clerk.

p. 196   Guardian Report - Margaret T. LIPSCOMB, minor, J. W. LIDE, Guardian.
Accounts with J. H. FYFFE 1833, 34; Athens Female Academy 1834; Rev. John G.
LARKIN tuition 1833, 34; Henry HINEGAR for shoes. Signed G. W. LIDE, Guardian
17 Aug 1834. Recorded 14 Jul 1836 E. TATE, clerk.

        Guardian REPORT - Caroline S. LIBSCOMB, now Caroline S. SMITH, J. W.
LIDE, Guardian. Pay Rufus STANLEY for stage hire to and from Knoxville going to
school; goods from CLEAGS & CRUTCHFIELD 1832; goods from J. H. FYFFES 1832.
Signed J. W. LIDE, Guardian. Recorded 14 Jul 1836 E. TATE, clerk.

p. 197   Settlement - Commissioners appointed to settle three settlements with John W. LIDE, Adm of the Estate of Spotswood LIPSCOMB, decd. Mentions: Joseph RICH, Jacob NOE, Lewis DAVIS, Thomas JONSTON assignee of William BALL. Signed 18 Aug 1835 C. McANALLY, Joseph RICH, Joseph COBB, Comm. Recorded 14 Jul 1836.

        Guardian Report - G. B. MITCHELL & John A. McKENNY, Guardians of the minor heirs of John PERRIN, decd. Signed 14 Feb 1835. Recorded 14 Jul 1836.

p. 198   Account of Sales - Hughs KENNON, decd. Mentions: Peter HOLSTEIN, John MOODY, John HANEY, Robt LOYD, Godwin MAYES, John CRAIN, John KENNON, Sr., Edmond PEMBLETON, James JOICE, Joseph BEETS, Winny KIRK, Alex. JOYCE, Eli GREENLEA, Philip HODGES, Ezekiel BOATMAN, John JOICE, Sr., Maddison STRATTON, Andrew COFFMAN. Signed 15 Feb 1836 Charles CRAIN, Jr., Recorded 15 Jul 1836 E. TATE, clerk.

p. 199   Guardian Report - G. B. MITCHELL, Guardian for Hannah C. HANKINS; Guardian for the minor heirs of James FURGASON, decd; for William & Lanty SMALLWOOD. Signed Green B. MITCHELL 15 Feb 1836. Recorded 15 Jul 1836 E. TATE, clerk.

        Commissioners Report - James LACY, George G. SATTERFIELD & Godwin MAYES. 1 yr support for Coley KENMORE, widow of Hughs KENNON, & family consisting of dau & son. Signed 3 Dec 1835. Recorded 15 Jul 1836 E. TATE, clerk.

p. 200   Commissioners Report - E. TATE & Jacob KINDAR. 1 yr support to family of Edward CHURCHMAN, decd. Signed E. TATE, Jacob x KINDAR 8 Dec 1835. Recorded 15 Jul 1836 E. TATE, clerk.

        Commissioners Report - James F. WEST, Elijah MITCHEL & Joseph DYER. 1 yr support of widow & family of Jahu SIMMONS, decd. Recorded 15 Jul 1836 E. TATE. Signed: James F. WEST, Elijah x MITCHEL & Joseph DYER 17 Nov 1835.

p. 201   Commissioners Report - Isaac BARTON, Obadiah BOOZ, John EASTERLY, James SHIELDS & John ROBERTSON, Estate of John MOFFET, decd. Mentions: Joseph COBLE, Esq., surveyor; Elinor SHANNON formerly Elinar MOFFET widow of John MOFFET, decd; dower lands on Cedar Creek on DONALDSON's line; William H. MOFFET an heir; John S. MOFFET an heir. Signed 16 Jun 1835. Recorded 15 Jul 1835 E. TATE, clerk.

p. 203   Settlement - Estate of Henry IVY, decd, Benjamin IVEY, Adm. 17 Jun 1836. Signed M. N. JEFFERYS, Joseph DANIEL & James LACY 1 Jul 1836. Recorded 15 Jul 1836 E. TATE, clerk.

p. 204   Account of Sale - Samuel BROWN, decd. Sold 1 Jul 1836. Mentions: Harrison BROWN, Chester JARNIGAN, Demsy PARRISH, Thos JETT, Willson, DYER, notes on James HUSTON & Elijah S. HAND or HARRELL, Judgement on Joshua HIGHTOWER. Signed William BROWN, Adm. Recorded 15 Jul 1836 E. TATE, clerk.

p. 205   Guardian Report - (no name given, this is an account of a sale). Mentions: James MASSENGILL, John L. DAVIS, Willie TALLY, Aquilla MITCHEL, Benjamin MITCHEL, Edward WEST, Berry MITCHEL, Jesse PASLEY, Godwin MAYES, Daniel VINEYARD, Jubal MITCHEL, fifty cents to the Cryer. Signed Godwin MAYES, Guardian. Recorded 15 Jul 1836 E. TATE, clerk.

p. 206   Settlement - 20 Jun 1836 on Andrew PHILLIPS, Adm of the Estate of
Samuel PHILLIPS, decd. Signed George MOULDER, Jacob YEADON, John BULLARD.
Recorded 15 Jul 1836 E. TATE, clerk.

          Settlement - Peter ADKINS, Adm of the Estate of Winston ADKINS, decd.
Mentions: E. WILLIAM, John MALLICOAT, Mary ADKINS, Emanul ADKINS, Winright
ADKINS, John KENNON, Jacob SHIELDS, Meredith ADKINS, Peter ADKINS, Jane ADKINS,
Harrison ADKINS. Signed 30 Jul 1836 John LATHAM, Jr., John LATHAM, Sr., Jeremiah
BOWMAN, Commissioners. Recorded 3 Aug 1836 E. TATE, clerk.

p. 207   Account of Sale - Elizabeth ARMSTRONG, minor heir of Nancy ARMSTRONG,
decd, by Aquilla MITCHELL, Guardian. Mentions: Edward WEST, Aquilla MITCHELL,
J. S. TALBOT, Benjamin MITCHELL, Jubal MITCHELL, Chesley RAY, Elijah MITCHELL,
John L. DAVIS, John BOILES, Joseph DYER, Hardin CAMPBELL, Richardson RAY. Signed
Aquilla x MITCHELL. Recorded 2 Aug 1836 E. TATE, clerk.

p. 208   Settlement - John FURGASON, decd, James KENNON, Adm. Mentions: Henry
COUNTZ, John MAYES, Richard FURGASON, Phillamon HODGES, William HODGES, William
CARTER, John KIDWELL, Thomas GILLMORE, Josiah C. BUNCH, James WILLSON, Isaac and
William DANIEL, Hughs KENNON, Dixon SMITH, Wm ROCH, Thomas GILLMORE, Robert
STUBBLEFIELD, James KENNON, Jacob KLINE, Warham EASLEY, Chesley MORGAN, Samuel
WEST, Sr., Legan MAYES, J. M. McCLAIN, Sheriff LOYD, Jessee COUNTZ. Signed James
T. WEST, B. CRAIGHEAD, R. LOYD, Commissioners. Recorded 3 Aug 1836 E. TATE, cler

p. 210   Settlement - A. (Andrew) CHAMBERLAIN, decd, James KENNON, Adm. Mentions
Noah JARNAGIN on account of legacy; Elizabeth CARNEY from Estate of Mary EDWARDS,
decd, was transfered from John CARNEY and wife to A. CHAMBERLAIN; Constable LOYD
collected money for Andrew CHAMBERLAIN; John L. DAVIS, John CALDWELL, James LACY,
Arthur CARNEY, J. J. WATKINS, John COPELAND, James CHAMBERLAIN, John TALBOT, P.
S. COCKE, Hugh HOUSTON, E. LEFEW, Thomas WEST, Jr., Thompson CHAMBERLAIN, John
SWAIN, Compton HARRIS, J. A. McKENNY, Hugh GRAHAM, M. MENDINGHALL, Ruth GREENLEA,
George HENDERSON, William M. MOODY (jailor), William GRAHAM, J. B. REECE, David
TATE, J. B. SNIDER, William C. COCKE, A. COLLINGSWORTH, James EATON, Samuel
McNEICE, James LACY, Richard HAYWORTH, Daniel EATON, John W. EATON, James JAMES,
Dr. COCKE, Larence BRADLEY, O. R. WATKINS, John WILLIAMS, David BARTON, Isaac
PHILLIPS. Signed Wm E. COCKE, Jno T. CURLE, John COCKE. James KENNON rendered
services as Adm in years 1833, 34, 35, 36. Dated Aug 1836.

p. 214   Will - Richard ACUFF, decd, Planter. Wife Martha; 2 daus Anna ACUFF and
Joice ACUFF; all my children, namely: Clabourn ACUFF, Anderson ACUFF, Alford
ACUFF, Sally McPHETERS, Frances CLARK, Rachel HAMMER, Anna ACUFF, Joice ACUFF and
Martha HARMON; my son-in-law John CLARK. Signed Richard ACUFF 6 Apr 1835. Wit:
Joseph CLARK, Joseph WILLIAMS. Recorded 7 Sep 1836 E. TATE, clerk.

p. 215   Inventory - Estate of John DANIEL, decd. 6 Sep 1836. Signed John PRATT
Adm. Mentions: James CLARK of Cocke Co., TN. Recorded 7 Sep 1836 E. TATE.

p. 216   Account of Sale - John DAVIS, decd. Sold by John PRATT, Adm. 1 Sep 1836
Mentions: Hamilton IVY, Walter D. COWEN, James B. BOYD, Thomas K. HOWELL, Paskil
TURNER, Prior BIBER, Samuel RAYEL, Ryal JENNINGS, John SMITH, Godwin PRICE,
Jacob PERKYPILE, Walter D. COWEN, Edward MAYES, Godwin PRICE, John PROTT, Joseph
BEETS, Cut Bird IVY, Philip ROBERTS, Thomas WATSON, Francis YOUNG, John IVY,

Thomas HILL, Henry J. HODGES, Philip IVEY, William ALEXANDER. Signed John PRATT, Adm. Recorded 12 Oct 1836 E. TATE, clerk.

p. 217   Settlement - 3 Oct 1836 James T. WEST, Executor for Estate of Samuel WEST, decd. Mentions: William DICKSON; Henry ALSUP; James KENNON, Adm of the Estate of Jno FURGASON, decd; Thomas DYER; William JAMES; Benjamin PECK; Daniel SPENCER; Henry ALSUP; John COLLINGSWORTH; Michael MASSENGILL; Estate of A. CHAMBERLAIN, decd; Samuel SMITH; David BARTON; Robert CALDWELL; Presley S. CHISHIR; Thomas LOYD; Wm E. COCKE; Hugh HOUSTON; William BRECZETTON; Dixon SMITH; John ANDERSON; Daniel MURPHY; P. S. COCKE; John BOILS; Mathison GRIFFIN; Samuel BUNCH; John DUGLAS; Lea DYER; George BURKET; Peter GILMORE; Samuel LOUS. Signed John T. CURLE, John BOYLES and G. B. MITCHELL. Recorded 12 Oct 1836 E. TATE.

p. 219   Settlement - Robert and Green SIMMONS, Adms for Jahu SIMMONS, decd. Mentions: Unity WHITEHEAD; Elijah MITCHELL; Isaac HARRIS; James T. WEST; Joseph DYER; Wm E. COCKE; John BOILES; Thomas SMITH; the receipts of all the heirs of Jahu SIMMONS, decd, to wit: John SIMMONS, Elizabeth CRAIN, Martha SIMMONS, James SIMMONS. Signed Sep 1836 John BOILS, Thos SMITH, James T. WEST. Recorded 17 Oct 1836 E. TATE, clerk.

p. 220   Settlement - James WHITLOCK, Adm of the Estate of Thomas SMITH, decd. Mentions: John SMITH, William SMITH, Isaac HARRIS and his wife Rebeka HARRIS, Samuel SMITH, Lewis EVANS and Bethany EVANS. Signed 5 Nov 1836 Harmon LEA, G. B. MITCHELL, William CARMETT (?). Recorded 12 Nov 1836 E. TATE, clerk.

p. 221   Settlement - Estate of Hughs O. KENNON, decd, Charles CRAIN, Adm. Mentions: Abraham McCONNEL, Charles CRAIN, Jr., Reece BOWMAN, Hugh HOUSTON, Jacob KLINE. Signed 28 Oct Jacob KLINE, Wm M. MOODY, E. TATE. Recorded 12 Nov 1836.

p. 222   Guardian Report - George BARNARD, Guardian of the heirs of John BARNARD, decd, for the year 1836. Paid Julius HACKER for 3 timber trees. Signed 1 Dec 1836 George BARNARD, Guardian. Recorded 9 Dec 1836 E. TATE, clerk.

     Guardian Report - Thomas DENNIS, Dec 1836, bills paid for the heir of John DENNIS, decd. Recorded 9 Dec 1836 E. TATE, clerk.

     Inventory - George BULL, decd. Recorded 9 Dec 1836 E. TATE, clerk.

p. 223   Will - George BULL, Planter. To be buried beside my wife in Grainger Co; my son Clabourn BULL; my dau Martha alias Patty and my dau Hannah BLACKMAN's three children called George, Paulinda and Elizabeth; other two daus Elizabeth IAMS and Margaret BARNARD; land where on John EPPERSON now lives; grandson George BULL; Clabourn BULL, Executor. Signed 8 Nov 1836 George BULL. Wit: Peter OGAN, Robt x BARNARD, John EPPERSON. Recorded 9 Dec 1836 E. TATE, clerk.

p. 225   Account of Sale - Richard ACUFF, decd. Mentions: Benjamin BRANSON, Anderson ACUFF, Thomas ACUFF, William HAMMERS, the Widow ACUFF, John ROBERTSON, Clabourn ACUFF, James ACUFF, Pleasant WATSON, Peter WOLFINBARGER, Reuben WOLFIN-BARGER, William CLARK, William HERROLD, Joseph WILLIAMS, Joseph CLARK, John D. ACUFF, Joel DOTSON, Henry WILLIAMS, Samuel DOTSON, William ACUFF, Sr., Anderson FRY, Robert WATSON, Mark MONROW, Robert FRY, Benjamin ACUFF, Benjamin FRY, James STARNES, Pleasant JENNINGS, Claburn NASH, William LEFEW, George DYER, David

DOLTON, James SELLERS. Sale held 10 Oct 1836 Signed John CLARK, Executor.
Recorded 9 Dec 1836 E. TATE, clerk.

p. 228   Inventory - Joseph HILL, Adm of the Estate of Isaac DYER, decd.
Mentions: William DENNIS; William DONEHOO; Robert DYER; Pleasant PARKER; Joel
FIELDS; Jefferson WYRICK; Joseph HILL; Isaac DAMEWOOD; George DYER; Thomas
DENNIS; Sampson SHARP; George DYER, Jr.; Isaac DYER; Edward MERRET; William
SHARP; John HICKLE; Thomas MYNATT; Perrin CARDWELL; James DALE; John McKINNEY;
Thomas ROOCHARD; John WYRICK, decd; William DYER; an account on the Widow, Fanny
DYER. Signed 30 Dec 1836 Joseph HILL, Adm. Recorded 3 Jan 1837 E. TATE, clerk.

p. 229   Inventory - William CLARK, decd. 17 Dec 1836. Mentions: Henry HIPSHEA
Robert FRY. Signed John CLARK, John P. JENNINGS. Recorded 3 Jan 1837 E. TATE.

p. 230   Inventory - David BEELAR, decd. Signed George DYER. Recorded 3 Jan
1837 E. TATE, clerk.

        Guardian Report - Green B. MITCHELL, Guardian for minor heirs of James
FORGASON, decd. Signed 16 Feb 1835. Recorded 3 Feb 1837 E. TATE, clerk.

        Guardian Report - Green B. MITCHELL, Guardian for the minor heirs of
William HANKINS, decd. Signed 16 Feb 1835. Recorded 3 Feb 1837 E. TATE, clerk.

p. 231   Guardian Return - Heirs of John BARNARD, decd, for the year 1835. By
clothing for Starling and clothing and boarding Sally, two of the heirs. Signed
George BARNARD, Guardian, 13 Nov 1835. Recorded 13 Feb 1837 E. TATE, clerk.

        Inventory - John HILL, Jr., decd, taken 30 Jan 1837. Signed Willis L.
PRATT. Recorded 13 Feb 1837 E. TATE, clerk.

p. 232   Inventory - George JENNINGS, decd. Signed Elizabeth x JENNINGS.
Recorded 13 Feb 1837 E. TATE, clerk.

        Guardian Report - G. B. MITCHEL, Guardian of the heirs of Russel C.
SMALLWOOD, decd. Recorded 13 Feb 1837 E. TATE, clerk.

        Guardian Report - G. B. MITCHEL, Guardian of the minor heirs of James
FURGASON, decd. Recorded 13 Feb 1837 E. TATE, clerk.

p. 233   Guardian Report - Minor heirs of John PERRIN, decd. Signed G. B.
MITCHEL and John A. McKENNY. Recorded 13 Feb 1837 E. TATE, clerk.

        Guardian Report - G. B. MITCHEL, Guardian of the minor heirs of William
HANKINS, decd. Recorded 13 Feb 1837 E. TATE, clerk.

        Commissioners Report - 28 Jan 1837. Lay off provisions for 1 yr for
Widow of David BEELER, decd. Signed John CLARK, Anderson ACUFF, John ROBERTSON.
Recorded 13 Feb 1837.

p. 234   Account of Sale - Richard ACUFF, decd. 14 Jan 1837. Mentions: Martha
ACUFF, Pleasant D. WATSON, Joseph LEFFEW, Benjamin BRANSON, Thomas MOYERS, Willia
LEFFEW, John ACUFF, Sr., Clabourn ACUFF, Thomas ACUFF, William ACUFF, Alford

ACUFF, John ROBERTSON, Anderson ACUFF, William McPHETRIDGE, Samuel DOTSON, Simeon
ACUFF. Signed John CLARK, Executor. Recorded 13 Feb 1837 E. TATE, clerk.

p. 235   Account of Sale - David BEELAR, decd.   28 Jan 1837. Mentions: Polly
BEELAR, John BEELAR. Signed George DYER. Recorded 14 Feb 1837 E. TATE, clerk.

        Account of Sale - George BULL, decd. Mentions: Benjamin BRAY, Peter
WOLF, William CARPENTER, George ALLEN, Mathew RUSSELL, John PRASHER, Henry MASON,
William IAMS, John McDANIEL, James McDANIEL, William JOHNSTON, Robert BARNARD,
Manil NASH, John McDANIEL, Sterling HAYES, Green BRENDEN, William HIPSHEAR, Henley
HUSH, John ALLEN, Thomas McANALLY, James McANALLY, Jeremiah HUTCHESON, Nelson
PERTTS (?), Jesse CARPENTER, Henry MASON, Edwin MASON, Clabourn BULL. Signed
6 Feb 1837 Clabourn BULL, Executor. Recorded 14 Feb 1837 E. TATE, clerk.

p. 237   Inventory - William D. JENNINGS, decd. Mentions: Royal JENNINGS;
Estate of William CLARK, decd; William PASLEY; John COCKE; John ROBERTSON; a
PENDLETON; John PRINCE. Signed Ryal JENNINGS, Sr. Recorded 14 Feb 1837 E. TATE.

p. 238   Settlement - James H. STARNES, Adm of Adam STARNES, decd. Mentions:
Martin CLEVELAND, William SHARP, Gray GARRET, Wrenard BURNET, P. S. COCKE, Robert
FIELDS, Jacob B. SNIDER, Edward CLARK, Clabourn JONSTON, John CHANDLER, John
STARNES, Jonas NIELY, Joshua WASHMAN, Charles McANALLY, Coonrod STARNES, CRAIG-
HEAD & MASSINGILL, Alexander McMAHAN, Benjamin FORD, Hugh JONES, Eli RECTOR,
John MULLINS, Robert MULLINS, William and Phereba SHARP, Phereba STARNES, Robert
CUTTS, Robert MULLINS, Eli RECTOR and Lydia RECTOR, Levi HUBBLE. Signed 28 Jan
1837 Joseph CLARK, John ROBERTSON, Wrenard BURNET. Recorded 14 Feb 1837.

p. 239   Settlement - Adams STARNES, decd, Estate to James H. STARNES. Mentions:
Benjamin NEALEY. Recorded 14 Feb 1837 E. TATE, clerk.

        Guardian Report - Benjamin BRAY, Guardian of Polly M. OGAN for the
Estate of Peter OGAN, decd. Mentions: William BLACKMAN; D. BARTON, Esq. 19 May
1835; Anderson HETTON and Henry MASON Jan 1837. Signed Benjamin BRAY, Guardian
3 Feb 1837. Recorded 14 Feb 1837 E. TATE, clerk.

p. 241   Settlement - James DYER, Sr., William DENNIS and Joel FIELDS, Commissioners. David ELKINS, Executor of David ELKINS, decd, Guardian of Drury ELKINS and
Sarah ELKINS minor heirs of Joseph ELKINS, decd. Signed 13 Jan 1837. Recorded
8 Mar 1837 E. TATE, clerk.

        Inventory - Evan HARRIS, decd. Mentions: Shadauk INMAN, Samuel SMITH,
James and Jesse HODGES. Signed Isaac HARRIS 6 Mar 1837. Recorded 8 Mar 1837
E. TATE, clerk.

p. 242   Settlement - William SHARP and Eli DENNIS, Feb 1837, commissioners to
settle with William DENNIS, Adm of the Estate of John DENNIS, decd. Mentions:
John SHARP, Nathan SHELLY, Robert CUTT, Eli CLARK, James DYER, Sr., Samuel
PETTYBONE, Gilbert VANDERGRIFF, Doctor COCKE, taxes for 1832, John CRAZIR, George
SEAMORE, Adam STARNES, William DYER, Benjamin CRAIGHEAD, Martin BAKER, Gray
GARUT, Robert CARDWELL, John HILL, Sr., Joseph DENNIS, Charles McANALY, James
DYER, Robert FIELDS, John SELLERS, Robert MULLENS, William T. CARDIN, William
SHARP, Eli DENNIS. Signed 18 Feb 1837 Eli DENNIS, William SHARP. Recorded

8 Mar 1837 E. TATE, clerk.

p. 243   Inventory - Abel DALE, decd.   14 Feb 1837.   Signed Abner DAIL, Adm.
Recorded 8 May 1837 E. TATE, clerk.

p. 244   Account - Hireing of Negro BERRY and RHODA and child belonging to the
Estate of John BROWN, decd.   6 Mar 1837.   Mentions: John COCKE, Thomas W. HUMES,
Ethelred WILLIAMS.   Signed Wm T. TATE, Adm.   Recorded 8 Mar 1837 E. TATE, clerk.

        Account of Sale - William CLARK, decd.   16 Jan 1837.   Mentions: Pleasant
JENNINGS, Joseph WILLIAMS, John LATHAM, Martin CLEVELAND, Rial JENNINGS, Thomas
WHITESIDE, William HIPSHEAR, William RUCKER, William HAYES, Harmon HAYES, William
PAIN, Benjamin COFFY, Thomas McANALLY, Andrew COLLINS, George COFFY, Deadman
MALLICOAT, George GENNINGS, Martin BAKER, Clabourn W. LATHAM, William GRAHAM,
William HARREL, Wainright ATKINS, Colby DALTON, Enoch DOLTON, Alexander HETTON,
Ausbury COFFY, Robert BURNET, Jacob KLINE, Charles McANALLY, Joseph CLARK, David
NOE, John SHEARER, James L. ACUFF, Robert GRESSUM, Joel DODSON, Isaac BULLEN,
Roadman HARRELL, John ALLEN, Elizabeth CLARK, Joseph WILLIAMS.   Signed John P.
JENNINGS, John CLARK.   Recorded 8 Mar 1837 E. TATE, clerk.

p. 247   Commissioners Report - Estate of William CLARK, decd.   Lay-off 1 yr to
support widow and family.   Signed 11 Jan 1837 John LATHAM, Jr., William HAYES,
John LATHAM, Sr.   Recorded 11 Apr 1837 E. TATE, clerk.

        Account of Sale - John HILL, Jr., decd.   17 Feb 1837.   Signed Willis L.
PRATT, Adm.   Recorded 11 Apr 1837 E. TATE, clerk.

p. 249   Will - Hughs O. TAYLOR, decd.   Wife Elizabeth; dau Louisa; son Hughs W.;
dau Amelia; son Elikee A.; dau Rachel; son George G.; dau Amanda A.; son Thomas
D.; son Jabin (?) L.; my son Elbert E and my dau Edna E. when they become of age;
Black boys MICGER and GEORGE; Black boy SAMUEL; where Thomas BRIAN now lives;
Abraham BURCHIL lives; Hughs W. and Elika A. TAYLOR, Executors.   Signed Hughs O.
TAYLOR 26 Jul 1836.   Wit: Robert LONG, Caleb CROSBY, James MAYES.   Recorded
11 Apr 1837 E. TATE, clerk.

p. 250   Account of Sale - Estate of Abel DIAL, decd, closed on 17 Mar 1837.
Signed Abner DIAL, Adm. 1 Apr 1837.   Recorded 11 Apr 1837 E. TATE, clerk.

p. 252   Inventory - Estate of Niman RIGGS, decd.   Mentions: William HARRIS,
James HODGES, Russel CROW, James SHIELDS, Eli KEEN, Peter HUNT.   Signed Henry
BOATMAN, Joseph RIGGS, Adms.   Recorded 11 Apr 1837 E. TATE, clerk.

p. 254   Account of Sale - Estate of Niman RIGGS, decd.   24 Mar 1837.   Mentions:
Ezekiel BOATMAN, John BARREN, Pleasant WISTER, Russel CROWE, Elizabeth RIGGS,
David NOE, William HETTON, James KNIGHT, Samuel RIGGS, Eli HODGES, F. H. IVEY,
Jesse LIVINGSTON, John IVEY, James JONES, Thomas DOGGET, Joseph RICH, Joseph
RICH, Jr., David N. RICH, G. P. MOODY, Willie B. McGEE, E. MILLIKAN, John COCKE,
J. B. ELLEDGE, Henry BOWEN, Andrew REECE, James McGEE, Thomas REECE, David
COUNTZ, Jesse WILLIAMS, Walter D. COWEN, William HARRIS, John EASTERLY, George
BOATMAN, William SPOON, Isaih REECE, John BARROW, William JONSTON, Eli HODGES,
Thomas RUSSEL, Elijah BARTON, Azariah RIGGS, Isaac NEWMAN, William SNIDER,
Simmeon WILLIFORD, David COUNTZ.   Recorded 11 Apr 1837 E. TATE, clerk.

p. 257   Commissioners Report - Lay-off 12 mos provisions for Sarah HILL, widow of John HILL, decd. Signed 16 Feb 1837 Joel FIELD, William DENNIS, David ELKINS. Recorded 2 May 1837 E. TATE, clerk.

Commissioners Report - Robert MONROW, Adm of the Will of Robert MONROW, decd. Mentions: Gray GARRET, G. CARDIN, Calliway HODGES, John MONROW, William HAMILTON. Signed 29 Apr 1837 James SALLING, William COLVIN, William DENNIS. Recorded 2 May 1837 E. TATE, clerk.

Commissioners Report - 15 Apr 1837. Court order dated 7 Mar 1837. Mentions: John EASTERLY, Joseph SHANNON, Isaac BARTON, Commissioners; G. G. REED Adm of the Estate of Felps REED, decd; George G. REED; sale 10 Mar 1835; Jesse RIGGS; 5 heirs; sale Sep 1835; total aggregate for 6 heirs; Willie REED; William A. REED; James THOMPSON; Ellis RIGGS; balance of money to be divided between 6 heirs: Willie REED, William A. REED, James THOMPSON, Ellis RIGGS and said Adm. George G. REED, except John F. NOE who has received his share. Recorded 2 May 1837 E. TATE, clerk.

p. 260   Settlement - Felps REED, Esqr, in account with George G. REED beginning Jan 1834 to Feb 1836. Mentions: Nelson REECE as clerk; William DONALDSON as clerk at Crying Sale; Atto BARTON for counsel; Job GARRITSON for coffin. 15 Apr 1837. Settlement with George REED, Adm of the Estate of Felps REED, decd. Signed John EASTERLY, Joseph SHANNON, Isaac BARTON, Commissioners. Recorded 2 May 1837 E. TATE, clerk.

p. 262   Will - Josiah SMITH, Planter. To be intered at Rutledge; the land where I now live and tract where Calvin HUDDLESTONE and Coleman CEMORE now live; the field Negroes GRACE, SAM and CHARLES, these I have moved with the other two ESTER and FRANK is yet in the Alabama State of my Father, decd; "to be used by her in her widowhood"; sons John, Josiah, James; land purchased from Jacob VANDAGRIFF; daus Polly HUDDLESTON, Lucy CEMORE, Dorcus HUDDLESTON and Nancy SMITH my youngest; beloved wife Nancy SMITH, Extrix. Signed 19 Apr 1837 Josiah x SMITH. Wit: J. B. BUTCHER, Allen HURST, Thomas BLACKBOURN. Recorded 6 Jun 1837 E. TATE, clerk.

p. 263   Account of Sale - John BROWN, decd. 3 Jul 1837. William T. TATE, Adm. Recorded 17 Jul 1837 E. TATE, clerk.

Account of Sale - William D. JENNINGS, decd. Mentions: Agustus JENNINGS, John RUCKER, Pleasant JENNINGS, Elisha WALKER, Emanuel ATKINS, John LATHAM, Lewis M. ELLIS, John P. JENNINGS, G. W. JENNINGS, William HARRIL, John BUNCH, Timothy DOLTON, Elizabeth CLARK. Signed Royal JINNINGS, Jr., and Ryal x JINNINGS, Sr. Recorded 18 Jul 1837 E. TATE, clerk.

p. 266   Settlement - William T. TATE, Adm for the Estate of John BROWN, decd. Mentions cash rec'd since last settlement; hire 2 NEGROES, 20 Feb 1834; Robert BLAIN, 20 May 1833; David COUNTZ, 24 May 1833; Godwin MAYES, 7 Aug 1833; Henry B_____ (written over, can not read), 7 Sep 1833 and 18 Feb 1834; Henry COUNTZ, 6 Mar 1834; William MAYES, 15 Apr 1834; Henry BROWNLOW, 15 Apr 1834; Thos L. COCKE, 8 Jan 1834, 15 Apr 1835; hire NEGROES 18 Feb 1835; Robert FRY, 8 Jan 1835; Thomas SOLOMAN, 15 Apr 1835; Zacheriah CAMPBELL, 15 Apr 1835; Henry BROWN, 17 Aug 1836; Elias DAVIS, 15 Jan 1837; Benjamin LEWIS, 30 Apr 1837; James BYON,

12 May 1837; Jonathan WILLIAMS, 27 Jul 1837; David NOE, 27 Jul 1837; Samuel H.
COPELAND, John MORGAN, Joseph SMITH, John COFFEE, 6 Aug 1834; Thomas L. WILLIAMS,
3 Jan 1833; R. LOYD, 1 May 1834; Isaac DANIELS, Ethelred WILLIAMS, Robert J.
McHENRY, Esqr, 25 Feb 1837; Warham EARLY, Thomas GILL, C. McANALLY, Thos COCKE,
16 Feb 1837. Signed 2 Aug 1837 C. McANALLY, Thomas GILL, Commissioners. Recorde
16 Aug 1837 E. TATE, clerk.

p. 269   Inventory - Josiah SMITH, decd, Planter. Mentions: Brewis COX, James
C. MORE, MOSS, Owen DYER, Elisha HAMPTON, William DAUGHTRY, Jeremiah SAVAGE, Jame
HUNDLY, Isaac AUKEY, Isaac B. BUTCHER, Moses WILLIS. Signed 7 Aug 1837 Nancy x
SMITH. Recorded 16 Aug 1837 E. TATE, clerk.

p. 270   Guardian Report - John LATHAM, Guardian, heirs of Meredith ATKINS, decd.
Mentions: Maria ATKINS and her children; Jane ATKINS, she having become of age
on 14 Mar 1837. Signed 4 Sep 1837 John LATHIM, Guardian. Recorded 11 Oct 1837
E. TATE, clerk.

p. 271   Settlement - John HILL, Jr., Executor of James HILL, decd. 29 Aug 1837.
Mentions: Robert BLAIR, Robert BLEVINS, Julian FRAZIER, Samuel SHIELDS, Henry
WIENER, James DYER, Jr., James DYER, Sr., Abel HILL, Katherine SHARP, John HILL,
minor heirs Manerva and Canada HILL. Signed William LEWIS, John LEWIS, William
DINNES, Commissioners. Recorded 11 Oct 1837 E. TATE, clerk.

p. 272   Settlement - Estate of Sherad MAYES, decd, Levi SATTERFIELD and Joseph
DANIEL, Executors. Mentions: Robert CARDWELL and Joshua KIDWELL. Signed M. N.
JEFFRYS, James LACY, Commissioners. Recorded 12 Oct 1837 E. TATE, clerk.

p. 273   Inventory - Samuel McNEICE, decd. Signed 2 Oct 1837 Jane x McNEICE,
Admx. Recorded 15 Oct 1837 E. TATE, clerk.

p. 274   Settlement - Edward TATE, Adm., Estate of Robert WATSON, decd. Oct 1837
Mentions: Doctor Wm C. COCKE, James JONES, Sarah WATSON, Hardin WATSON, Ruth
GREENLEA, Jehu SIMMONS, James WATSON, William KIDWELL, William FREEMAN, Samuel
WATSON, Margaret ROACH, Benjamin McFARLAND, John EASLEY, Signed 6 Nov 1837 Wm E.
COCKE, B. F. McFARLAND, Jno EASLEY, Commissioners. Recorded 7 Nov 1837 E. TATE.

p. 275   Guardian Report - Thomas DYER, Guardian of the minor heirs of Marvel
WICKLIFF. Mentions: Isaac WICKLIFF, Adm. Signed 6 Nov 1837 Thomas DYER.
Recorded 7 Nov 1837 E. TATE, clerk.

p. 276   Guardian Report - Edward TATE, Guardian of William M. GRAY, the Estate
of Ruth STIFFY, decd. Mentions: John S. GRAY; James and William WILLIAMS;
Robert LOYD, Sheriff; James MALLICOAT; William E. COCKE, Justis of the Peace.
Signed Edward TATE, Guardian. Recorded 7 Nov 1837 E. TATE, clerk.

p. 277   Guardian Report - Edward TATE, Guardian of Ruth STIFFY up to her death.
Mentions: Sale 11 Mar 1836; James GALLIAN, year ending 11 Mar 1836; Estate of
John STIFFY, decd; Feb 1837 business for Ruth STIFFY; Pleasant WILLIAMS keeping
Ruth STIFFY until her Death; Thos S. COCKE; W. M. MOODY; James MALLICOAT; Robert
LOYD; John MAYES; Thomas WILLIAMS; Gray GARRET, lawyer; Charlie CATES. Signed
E. TATE, Guardian. Recorded 8 Nov 1837 E. TATE, clerk.

p. 278   Commissioners Report - William MAYES acting Justice of the Peace appt'd
Commissioner to lay-off a yr supply for widow and family of Samuel McNeice, decd.
Signed F. B. S. COCKE, _____ AUSTIN, John GRAY, Commissioners. Recorded 8 Nov
1837 E. TATE, clerk.

p. 279   Will - George G. REED, decd. Sister, Adeline RIGGS; daus Caroline M.
REED, Mary Addaline, Sidney Jane, Eliza Adalade; sons Thomas, Noah; servant man
JOHN; my friends Ellis RIGGS and James THOMPSON, Executors. Signed 24 Sep 1837
George G. REED. Wit: William S. MANNON, David NOE, Felps RIGGS, Ellis RIGGS,
James THOMPSON. Recorded 10 Nov 1837 E. TATE, clerk.

p. 281   Account of Sale - Robert GOINS, decd. Signed 6 Nov 1837 B. E. and R. C.
GOINS, Executors. Recorded 10 Nov 1837 E. TATE, clerk.

p. 282   Settlement - Thomas HANKINS and John LARGE, Executors of William
HANKINS, decd. Mentions: Thomas MOORE, David SHARP, James GALLANT, G. B.
MITCHELL, R. C. SMALLWOOD, Stephen MOORE, William CARUTHERS, Edward HANKINS.
Signed 5 Oct 1837 William DINNES, Harmon G. LEA, Commissioners. Recorded 10 Nov
1837 E. TATE, clerk.

p. 283   Guardian Report - Thomas DENNIS, Guardian of the minor heirs of John
DENNIS, decd, year ending 1 Dec 1837. Signed 4 Dec 1837 Thomas DENNIS, Guardian.
Recorded 8 Dec 1837 E. TATE, clerk.

p. 284   Settlement - Massy COCKRUM and Allen D. MORGAN, Adms for Edward CHURCH-
MAN, decd. Mentions: Negro DICK; Laurence BRADLEY; Cornelius GOWFORTH; R. HAY-
WORTH; R. LOYD, Sheriff; E. TATE; Legatees William CRAFORD, Michael DYKE, Philip
SNIDER, Mary CHURCHMAN, William FREEMAN, Sarah CHURCHMAN, Elizabeth CHURCHMAN
and Elias DAVIS; John COCKE; John M.BRATSTON. Signed 1 Jan 1838 Isaac DANIEL,
William MAYES, David N. TATE, Commissioners. Recorded 5 Jan 1838.

p. 285   Account of Sale - Jane McNEICE, Admx for Samuel McNEICE, decd. Signed
1 Jan 1838 Jane x McNEICE. Recorded 5 Jan 1838 E. TATE, clerk.

p. 286   Guardian Report - James MALLICOAT, Guardian of Amanda GRAY. Signed 1
Jan 1838 James x MALLICOAT, Guardian. Recorded 5 Jan 1838 E. TATE, clerk.

p. 287   Guardian Report - James LACY, Guardian for Mary GRAY now Mary TATE.
Mentions: Edward TATE, Executor of the wills of John and Ruth STIFFY, decd;
support of Mary GRAY Sep 1837; 13 Nov 1837 cash to Mary TATE; Clabourn and David
BURNET; Dixon SMITH and Isaac DANIEL. Recorded 6 Feb 1838 E. TATE, clerk.

p. 288   Settlement - Edward TATE, Executor of Ruth STIFFY, decd. Mentions:
James MALLICOAT; Dr. COCKE; Joth WILLIAMS; Sarah GRAY; John L. GRAY; Robert
LOYD; Pleasant WILLIAMS who intermarried with Jane GRAY an heir; Sarah GRAY an
heir and John L. GRAY an heir; James MALLICOAT who intermarried with Elizabeth
GRAY an heir; James MALLICOAT, Guardian of Louisa GRAY and James MAYES who
intermarried with said Louisa an heir; James MALLICOAT, Guardian of Amanda GRAY
an heir; James LACY, Guardian of Mary Ann GRAY and Edward L. TATE who intermarried with said Mary Ann an heir; Edward TATE, Guardian of William M. GRAY an
heir; P. WILLIAMS. Signed 2 Feb 1838 Wm E. COCKE, B. F. McFARLAND, Commissioners.
Recorded 12 Feb 1838 E. TATE, clerk.

p. 290   Settlement - George DYER, Adm for David BEELAR, decd. Mentions: John
BARNET, Daniel McFETRIDGE, A. NOEL, Jacob KLINE, Daniel BEELER, Robert FRY,
Martin CLEVELAND, Smith STRANGE, E. TATE, J. CLARK, John SHARP, the Widow.
Signed 27 Jan 1838 John ROBINSON, William SHARP, Joseph CLARK, Commissioners.
Recorded 12 Feb 1838 E. TATE, clerk.

p. 291   Guardian Report - Benjamin BRAY, Guardian of Polly M. OGAN, Estate of
Peter OGAN, decd. Mentions: James McDANIEL, Robert BARNARD, William HAYS, Henry
HIPSHEAR. Signed B. BRAY 5 Mar 1838. Recorded 10 Mar 1838, E. TATE, clerk.

p. 292   Guardian Report - Carter DOLTEN, decd. Mentions: years 1833, 34, 35,
36 and 37. Signed C. M. McANALLY, Guardian 3 Mar 1838. Recorded 10 Mar 1838.

          Account of Sale - 29 Mar 1838. William MOORE, decd. Signed John P.
McANALLY, Adm. Recorded 25 Apr 1838 E. TATE, clerk.

p. 293   Guardian Report - Godwin MAYES, Guardian of Nancy MAYES alias Nancy
JOICE, Susanna MAYES alias Susanna BURNET, Elizabeth MAYES, Martha MAYES and
Rachel MAYES. Mentions: G. B. MITCHELL, Nancy and James JOICE, Vendiman BURNET
and wife. Signed 5 Feb 1838 Godwin MAYES, Guardian. Recorded 13 Feb 1838 E. TAT

p. 294   Guardian Report - G. B. MITCHELL, Guardian for Hannah C. HANKINS.
Signed 5 Feb 1838 G. B. MITCHELL.

          Guardian Report - G. B. MITCHEL, Guardian for William and Lanty SMALL-
WOOD. Signed 5 Feb 1838 G. B. MITCHELL.

          Guardian Report - G. B. MITCHEL, Guardian of the minor heirs of James
FURGASON. Signed 5 Feb 1838 G. B. MITCHEL.

          Guardian Report - We the Guardians of the minor heirs of John PERRIN.
Signed 5 Feb 1838 G. B. MITCHEL.

          Recorded 13 Feb 1838 E. TATE, clerk.

p. 295   Inventory - Eli HODGES, decd. Signed Henry HOLSTEIN and John M.
HODGES, Adms. Recorded 7 May 1838 E. TATE, clerk.

p. 296   Account of Sale - Eli HODGES, decd. 18 Apr 1838. Mentions: Elizabeth
HODGES, Elis HODGES, William HODGES, Walter D. COWEN, John WALKER, Daniel B.
CLEEK, John WARD, John M. HODGES, John McCANN, John COX, Andrew J. ADEN, Joshua
HAZELWOOD, J. HUNT, F. J. MORRIS. Signed Henry HOLSTON, John M. HODGES, Adms.
Recorded 10 May 1838 E. TATE, clerk.

p. 298   Commissioners Report - James CARMICHAEL and Andrew COFFMAN and Isaac
BARTON, Commissioners, Apr 1838, Estate of Eli HODGES, decd. Lay-off 1 yr
supply for Widow and family. Signed 16 Mar 1838 James CARMICHAEL, Andrew
COFFMAN. Recorded 26 May 1838 E. TATE, clerk.

p. 299   Will - Jane CAMPBELL, decd. Husband, Matthew CAMPBELL; Margret CAMPBELL
no relation given; John CAMPBELL, no relation given; Alexander CAMPBELL, no
relation given, not of age; Jane CHASE, no relation given; Nancy CHASE, no

relation given; to the heirs of Sarah STONE, no relation given; James CAMPBELL bro of Margaret CAMPBELL; claims on Bird PATE, John CHASE, Jacob P. CHAISE and Richard THORNBURG; my husband and children. William LAWYERS and Margaret CAMPBELL, Executors. Signed Jane x CAMPBELL. Wit: 17 Apr 1838 Julian FRAZIER and George W. ARNOLD. Recorded 22 May 1838 E. TATE, clerk.

p. 300   Settlement - G. B. MITCHEL, Executor of the Estate of Aquilla MITCHEL, decd. 3 Apr 1838. Mentions: John GALLIAN and Rhoda, his wife; Godwin MAYES, Guardian of the heirs of Celia MAYES an heir; Aquilla MITCHEL, Guardian of Elizabeth ARMSTRONG an heir; John BOILES; E. TATE; Thos S. COCKE; Evan SMITH; Elijah MITCHEL; Nancy MITCHEL. Recorded 22 May 1838 E. TATE. clerk.

p. 301   Settlement - Apr 1838, James KENNON, Adm for the Estate of Andrew CHAMBERLAIN, decd. Mentions: James CHAMBERLAIN; James BOX, R. J. McKENNY; James MALLICOAT; Isaac DANIEL consent on a Judgement D. TATE vs James KENNON, Adm of A. CHAMBERLAIN and Nenian CHAMBERLAIN, Executor of Jeremiah CHAMBERLAIN, decd; James E. WILLIAMS; William BRAZETTON; R. LOYD; John COPPOCK; T. D. KNIGHT; John T. CURL, Adm; John COLLISON. Signed John T. CURL and John COLLISON, Commissioners. No recording date.

p. 302   Guardian Report - Elizabeth RIGGS, Guardian of Mahala RIGGS, Malinda RIGGS, Levenia RIGGS, Joshua RIGGS, Elizabeth RIGGS and Keziah RIGGS, minor heirs of Nenian RIGGS, decd. Signed 22 May 1838 Elizabeth x RIGGS, Guardian. Recorded 6 Jun 1838 E. TATE, clerk.

p. 303   Inventory - 2 Apr 1838, Jesse HODGES, decd. Signed William B. HODGES and Edward HODGES, Adms. Recorded 6 Jun 1838 E. TATE, clerk.

p. 304   Account of Sale - Jesse HODGES, decd. Mentions: William HODGES, Ann HODGES, James MAGER, Edward HODGES, Joshua KIDWELL, Robert JOICE, James HODGES, John IVY, William MAYES, Isaac DANIEL, John GREENLEA, William HAMMERS, Craven CREWS, John CAMRON, Dixon SMITH, Jemima HODGES, Alpeus (?) OWENS. Signed 4 Jun 1838 William B. HODGES, Edward HODGES, Adms. Recorded 6 Jun 1838 E. TATE, clerk.

p. 305   Commissioners Report - Jesse HODGES, decd. Mentions: widow and family. Signed F. B. S. COCKE, Chiba AUSTIN, Enos HAMMERS. Recorded 6 Jun 1838 E. TATE.

p. 306   Inventory - 15 Mar 1838 Samuel RAIL, decd. Mentions: an account on Walter D. COWEN. Signed Isaac HAMMER, Adm. Recorded 6 Jun 1838 E. TATE.

p. 307   Account of Sale - Samuel RAIL, decd. Sold by Isaac HAMMER, Adm, 15 Mar 1838. Mentions: James DENNISTON, J. M. HODGES, Mary RAIL, E. SPOON, Jesse RAIL, James CHURCHMAN, Nat HAUN, Walter COWEN, Jo. M. NOLLY, Samuel BETTIS, John IVY, Francis YOUNG, Wm DAY, Richard THORNHILL, William A. HARRIS, Stephen JONSTON, ____ NOE, O. R. WATKINS, Robert POTTER, William POENDEXTER, William KELLY, Thos C. HASKINS, John PRATT, P. WILLIAMS. Signed Isaac HAMMER, Adm. Recorded 6 Jun 1838 E. TATE, clerk.

p. 309   Commissioners Report - Widow Mary RAIL, 1 yr support. Signed 15 Mar 1838 John IVY, Francis YOUNG, Caleb HOWELL, Commissioners. Recorded 6 Jun 1838.

p. 310   Inventory - John DENNIS, decd. Mentions: Levi DENNIS, William DENNIS.

Signed Levi DENNIS, Adm. Recorded 7 Jun 1838 E. TATE, clerk.

p. 311   Account of Sale - John DENNIS, decd. Mentions: Sarah DENNIS, William
DENNIS, Jr., Lewis M. ELLIS, Thomas McMILLEN, John STARNES, Abel DAIL, William
HILL, John VITTITO, Daniel HOLT, Eli DENNIS, John DENNIS, Solomon WYRICK, Plea-
sant STARNES, Jackson DYER, George DYER, Moses BROCK, William SHARP, Green B.
DUTHREG. Signed Eli DENNIS, Adm. Recorded 7 Jun 1838 E. TATE, clerk.

p. 314   Will - Hannah HAMMER, decd. Two daughters Sarah DYER and Magdalin
THOMPSON; Dr. Wm E. COCKE; the daughters of my former husband Joel HAMMER viz
Elizabeth HAMMER now Elizabeth KENT and Ruth HAMMER now Ruth COUNTZ, Martha
HAMMER now Martha COUNTZ; my son Ezra HAMMER; Thomas DYER, Executor. Signed 10
Apr 1836 Hannah x HAMMER. Att: Reuben GROVE & John KENNON. Recorded 12 Jul
1838 E. TATE, clerk.

p. 315   Inventory - Deadman MALLICOAT, decd, Nathaniel MALLICOAT, Adm.
Mentions: Colbert HAYES, Richard HOPSON. Signed Nathaniel MALLICOAT, Adm.
Recorded 12 Jul 1838 E. TATE, clerk.

p. 316   Commissioners Report - 20 Jun 1838, Estate of Deadman MALLICOAT, decd.
Mentions: 1 yr support of widow & family; John DOTSON, John RUCKER, John NASH,
John OLIVER, Nathaniel MALLICOAT. Signed John LATHAM, Henry WILLIAMS, John
DOTSON, Commissioners. Recorded 12 Jul 1838 E. TATE, clerk.

        Commissioners Report - 9 Jun 1838. Estate of John DENNIS. Lay-off 1 yr
support for widow & family. Signed 9 Jun 1838 Mark MONROW, William x MARTIN,
Henry x NEEDHAM. Recorded 12 Jul 1838 E. TATE, clerk.

p. 317   Will - William WILLIAMS, Sr., decd. Nancy YEADEN, James & William
WILLIAMS, Anna McBEE, John WILLIAMS, Elizabeth SPYRES, Polly HAYNES, Rebecka
BUTCHER, Patsey WALTERS, Matilda BUTCHER, David WILLIAMS, Daniel WILLIAMS,
Elijah WILLIAMS & Campbell WILLIAMS all my children; my wife Mary WILLIAMS;
youngest son Campbell WILLIAMS. Signed 29 Jun 1838 William x WILLIAMS, Sr.
Wit: Samuel x CLOUD, Ezra BUCKNER, William x WAGGONER. Recorded 15 Aug 1838
E. TATE, clerk.

p. 318   Account of Sale - Deadman MALLICOAT, decd. Mentions: Gilbert HAYES,
Clabourn DOTSON, Edmond MALLICOAT, Benjamin OLIVER, Colbert HAYES, Cleveland
COFFEE, William MALLICOAT, Rhodeman HARREL, Winwright ADKINS, T. P. McANALLY,
Colbert HIPSHEAR, Henry HIPSHEAR, Martin HAYNES, Louvina MALLICOAT, Joel MALLI-
COAT, Henry WILLIAMS, John LATHIM, James MALLICOAT, Sterling HAYES, James NASH,
John RUCKER, Martin MAYER, Nathaniel THACKER, William McCOLLINS. Signed Joel
MALLICOAT, Adm 6 Aug 1838. Recorded 15 Aug 1838 E. TATE, clerk.

p. 320   Inventory - Gilbert PATTERSON, decd. Signed 6 Aug 1838 Thomas DYER &
Thornton CHESHIRE, Adms. Recorded 15 Aug 1838 E. TATE, clerk.

p. 321   Commissioners Report - Gilbert PATTERSON, decd. Set apart to widow &
family. Signed 6 Aug 1838 James T. WEST, Charles CATES & Drury ROACH, Commissioners. Recorded 15 Aug 1838 E. TATE, clerk.

        Will - Thomas HENDERSON, decd. Wife Mary HENDERSON; two Negroes LUCY &

THOMAS; my children Mariah L. HENDERSON, William Y. HENDERSON, Rutha A. HENDERSON, Dianah J. HENDERSON & Mary L. HENDERSON; Negroes HANABAL, RHODA & GEORGE; James MOORE, Executor. Signed Thomas HENDERSON 9 Jun 1838. Att: 11 Jun 1838 N. A. SENTER, Larkin JONSTON, Samuel B. TATE. Recorded 14 Sep 1838 E. TATE, clerk.

p. 323   Will - David TATE, Sr., decd. Legal heirs Edward TATE, Margaret NOE, David TATE, John K. TATE, Samuel B. TATE, William T. TATE & Milton TATE; Negro slave TABBY; wife Comfort; Edward & William TATE, Executors. Signed 30 Jul 1834 David TATE. Wit: John x DAVIS, Benjamin H. OWENS, David N. TATE. Recorded 18 Sep 1838 E. TATE, clerk.

p. 324   Inventory - Meredith COFFEE, decd. Rice COFFEE, Adm. Mentions: Joel WATKINS, James COFFEE & Rice COFFEE. Signed Rice COFFEE, Adm, 3 Sep 1838. Recorded 18 Sep 1838 E. TATE, clerk.

p. 325   Commissioners Report - To Esther COFFEE, Consort & family of Meredith, decd. Signed Henry ALSUP, Jubal MITCHEL, William MITCHEL, Commissioners. Recorded 18 Sep 1838 E. TATE, clerk.

p. 325   Inventory - Thomas HENDERSON, decd. 13 Jul 1838. Mentions: William I. (?) JONES, Pleasant WHITLOW, Charles JONES. Signed James MOORE, Executor. Recorded 18 Sep 1838 E. TATE, clerk.

p. 326   Inventory - John LATHIM, decd. Signed 4 Sep 1838 C. W. LATHIM, Adm. Recorded 18 Sep 1838 E. TATE, clerk.

p. 327   Will - Joseph BRYAN, decd. Children: John BRYAN, Thomas BRYAN, Joseph BRYAN, Rachel PROFFIT wife of John B. PROFFIT, Betsy STERLING wife of Thomas STERLING & Patsey GRADY wife of Duglas GRADY, James Morgan BRYAN; slaves CINDY & WILLIAM; wife Betsy BRYAN; minor son James & his four sisters Jeney Ann, Letitia, Peggy & Amanda BRYAN, all minors. Betsey BRYAN, wife, Executrix. Signed 19 Feb 1831 Joseph BRYAN. Wit: John POINDEXTER, Sterling COCKE. Recorded 19 Sep 1838.

p. 329   Will - Fanny DYER, decd. Names children: Cynthia DYER, Elizabeth DYER, Anna DYER & Nancy DYER; my dau Catherine DYER; Hamton DYER; Pleasant DYER heir of Isaac DYER, decd; Robert DYER, Isaac DYER & George DYER (not relation given); my friend James DYER, Jr., Executor. Signed 12 Sep 1838 Fanny x DYER. Wit: William DENNIS, Joseph HILL, Pleasant DYER. Recorded 8 Oct 1838 E. TATE, clerk.

p. 331   Will - Samuel RAY, decd. Wife Angy; my dau Elizabeth; all my children (not named); Isaac HARRIS & Preston MITCHELL, Executors. Signed 4 Aug 1838 Samuel x RAY. Wit: James TALLY & Aquilla MITCHEL, Jr. Recorded 8 Oct 1838.

p. 332   Account of Sale - John LATHIM, decd. Mentions: Andrew McGINNIS, James LATHIM, Thomas WHITESIDE, John P. JENNINGS, George H. EVANS, William HARREL, Henry WILLIAMS, Jacob GODWIN, Henry JENNINGS, Colby DOLTON, John RUCKER, Welbern TAYLOR, Abraham McCONNEL, James MALLICOAT, Thomas P. McANALLY, Edward McGINNIS, Dowell COLLINS, James HAYES, William P. McGINNIS, Elisha WALKER, Reuben DALTON, Hamilton EVANS, Enoch McKEY, Ransom DAY, Maichail WEB, William C. MALLICOAT, Nat MALLICOAT, Tanay DALTON, Colbert HAYES, Gilber HAYES, Roadman HARREL, Jno OLIVER, Thomas McGOLDRUK, Welbert TAYLOR, Chesley THOMAS, Edmund MALLICOAT, A. P. GREEN, Cleveland COFFEE, Joseph McGINNIS, Thomas YOUNG, David COLLINS, William

HIPSHEAR, Harrison ATKINS, Benjamin BRANSON, M. B. DALTON, Michael FARMER, Dennis ROBERTS, John LONG, Fraqua McNELY, Charles McANALLY, Jesse L. COFFEE, Hamilton EVANS, Nero COLLINS, Pleasant JENNINGS, George COFFEE, O. H. P. McGINNIS. Signed C. W. LATHIM, Adm.   Recorded 7 Nov 1838 E. TATE, Clerk.

p. 338   Account of Sale - Additional Sale of the Estate of John DENNIS, decd. Mentions: Joseph HILL, William DENNIS, Jr., Sarah DENNIS, Eleanor EASLEY, David ELKINS, William PETERS, Eli DENNIS.   Signed 27 Sep 1838 Levi DENNIS, Adm. Recorded 7 Nov 1838 E. TATE, clerk.

          Inventory - Samuel RAY, decd.   2 Oct 1838.   Mentions: Robert RAY, Isaac B. DYER, Jacob ARNET.   Signed Isaac HARRIS, Preston MITCHEL, Executors.   Recorded 7 Nov 1838 E. TATE, clerk.

p. 339   Account of Sale - Samuel RAY, decd.   17 Oct 1838.   Mentions: Hardin CAMRON, Jacob ARNETT, Balis G. GAINES, Thomas DAVIS, Hardin SPARKMAN, Henry CARBACK.   Signed Isaac HARRIS, Preston MITCHEL, Executors.   Recorded 8 Nov 1838.

          Inventory - Fanny DYER, decd.   Signed 15 Sep 1838 Joseph HILL, Executor. Recorded 8 Nov 1838 E. TATE, clerk.

p. 340   Account of Sale - Estate of Fanny DYER, decd.   Mentions: John D. POPE-JOY, Nathaniel POPEJOY, William DENNIS, William SHARP, Goldman B. CARDIN, Daniel ELKINS, James VITTITO, Clabourn ACUFF, Josiah WYRICK, John COX, William DENNIS, Jr., Robert ATKINS, George DYER, Jr., Andrew SHARP, Anderson DYER.   Signed Joseph HILL, Adm.   Recorded 8 Nov 1838 E. TATE, clerk.

p. 341   Settlement - Aquila MITCHEL, Guardian of Elizabeth ARMSTRONG to 6 Oct 1838.   Mentions: G. B. MITCHEL, COOK & MASSENGILL & Co., T. & S. SMITH, Urijah KEYS.   Signed 6 Oct 1838.   Recorded 8 Nov 1838 E. TATE, clerk.

p. 342   Settlement - Mary FURGASON, Guardian of Nancy, Mary Ann, James, Martha, John, Rabecka, William, Witt & Joseph FURGUSON, minor heirs of John FURGASON, decd.   Mentions: James KENNON, Adm of the Estate of John FURGASON, decd;   26 Jul 1836 money received for rents 1835 through 1837; Elizabeth FURGASON who inter-married with Isaac LOWE (?); Nancy FURGASON when she came of age 20 Jun 1838. Signed 5 Nov 1838.   Recorded 12 Nov 1838 E. TATE, clerk.

p. 343   Settlement - Joseph HILL, Executor of Isaac DYER, decd.   9 Oct 1838. Mentions: Fanny DYER, decd; Isaac DYER, Eli DENNIS, Thomas S. COCKE, Wm SHARP, Eli HART (?), S. & M. SHIELDS, Samuel WYRICK, BLAIN & FRANKLIN, Claborn JONSTON, John LAIN, E. TATE, John SMITH, George DYER, Martin CLEVELAND, PICKET & BALLARD, James DAVIS, James SALLING, Abel DAIL, Abner DAIL, John McKINNY, Thomas ROOKARD, William DYER.   Signed E. TATE.   Recorded 12 Nov 1838.

p. 345   Settlement - David WATSON, Executor for the Estate of Philip FREE, decd. 26 Oct 1838.   Mentions: cash received on account of the sales of the personal property of said decd, sold on 14 Mar 1826; B. CRAIGHEAD; Lewis M. ELLIS an heir; Rial JENNINGS Guardian of Lewis M. ELLIS; Sheriff BUNCHE for taxes 1827; Wm E. COCKE, clerk; Sheriff LOYD for taxes 1829; William E. TATE Adm of the Estate of John BROWN, decd; Negro man named ABRAHAM.   Signed Lewis M. ELLIS 25 Sep 1838. Recorded 12 Nov 1838 E. TATE, clerk.

p. 346   Account of Sale - William WILLIAMS, decd, by Robert HUDDLESTONE, Guard-
ian of Campbell WILLIAMS. Mentions: John CYRUS, Carlisle HAYNES, Jacob BUTCHER,
David YADON, Daniel WILLIAMS, Elisha SAVAGE, William COOK, Christian OUSLEY,
George LONG, Benjamin SMITH, John SWAFORD, John F. HUDDLESTONE, James DAVIS,
William WAGGONER, Martin COOK, Christopher HITCH, Thomas WAGGONER, Ezra BUCKNER,
James COOK, Allen HURST. Signed Allen HURST, John CYRUS 5 Sep 1838. No record-
ing date.

p. 350   Account of Sale - Thomas HENDERSON, decd. 18 Oct 1838. Mentions:
William MURRY, George W. MATLOCK, William HENDERSON, Nancy HENDERSON, Mary
HENDERSON, James GRANTHAM, Edmund COLLINS, Peter LAMPSIL, Abls. SULLENBURGER,
Hardy LONG. Signed James MOORE Executor. Recorded 10 Dec 1838 E. TATE, clerk.

p. 351   Inventory - William MILLIKAN, decd. Mentions: John MORRIS, John NEWTON,
Walter COWIN, William DAY, William MILLIKAN, Jr., Reuben BURRIS, Cs. HARRIS,
Gideon MORRIS, Alexander MILLIKAN, David MILLIKAN, John IVY, Samuel MILLIKAN,
Charles HODGES, Eliha MILLIKAN, Jesse HOWELL, Calab HOWELL. Signed Eliha
MILLIKAN, Jesse HOWELL, Adms. 7 Jan 1839. Recorded 11 Jan 1839 E. TATE, clerk.

p. 352   Inventory - Leroy PULLIN, decd. Signed 18 Dec 1838 William DONALDSON,
Adm. Recorded 11 Jan 1839 E. TATE, clerk.

        Commissioners Report - Set apart to Hannah PULLIN, widow of Leroy
PULLIN, decd, she having no family. Signed 20 Dec 1838 William x CHANY, Ellis
RIGGS. Recorded 11 Jan 1839 E. TATE, clerk.

p. 353   Account of Sale - Leroy PULLIN, decd. Mentions: John WHITE, Wm CHANY,
Henry COUNTZ, John MORRIS, Wm BAKER, Wm JONSTON, A. C. EATON, Thomas REECE,
Henry COUNTS, Jno WHITE, James WOOD, Hannah PULLIN, James KNIGHT, Saml HUFF-
MASTER, Peter HUNT, Thomas RUSSEL, Esqr., Wm CARTWRIGHT, Military W. BLACK,
Russel CROW, David SHIELDS, Esqr., John BARN, Hezekiah ROBINSON, Sterling NOE,
Isaiah REECE. Signed 20 Dec 1838 William DONALDSON, Adm. Recorded 11 Jan 1839.

p. 354   Commissioners Report - Charles BIDDLE, decd. Mentions Widow & orphans
(not named). Signed 8 Dec 1838 William MAYES, Reuben GROVE, James LINDERKIN.
Recorded 11 Jan 1839 E. TATE, clerk.

        Inventory - John GREENLEE, Sr., Adm of the Estate of Charles BIDDLE,
decd. Signed John x GREENLEA, Sr., Adm 7 Jan 1839. Recorded 11 Jan 1839 E. TATE.

p. 355   Account of Sale - 19 Jul 1838 Sale of the personal property of Hannah
HAMMER, decd. Mentions: Nicholas COUNTZ, William L. DYER, Elisha THOMASON,
William D. MORGAN, Winny WICKLIFF, Dinah DYER, Enos HAMMER, Thomas DYER, Thomas
WEST. Signed Thomas DYER, Executor. Recorded 11 Jan 1839 E. TATE, clerk.

p. 356   Settlement - Thomas DENNIS, Guardian of the minor heirs of John DENNIS,
decd. 24 Dec 1838. Mentions: cash received of William DENNIS, Adm 19 Oct 1836;
R. M. SCRUGGS. Signed E. TATE, clerk. Recorded 11 Jan 1839 E. TATE, clerk.

p. 357   Settlement - Robert CALDWELL, Sr., Guardian of Jeremiah & Elizabeth
Jane CHAMBERLAIN minor heirs of Andrew CHAMBERLAIN, decd. 7 Dec 1838. Mentions:
James KENNON, Adm; cash received for rent of wards lands 1836, 37, 38 & 39;

James MALLICOAT; William MALLICOAT; P. S. COCKE; Lea DYER, Dpt Shff for taxes 1838; R. LOYD, Shff taxes 1835, 36 & 37; Gray GARRETT, Atto; Wards plantation; R. CALDWELL, Jr.; Joseph COMBS for schooling. Signed E. TATE, clerk. Recorded 11 Jan 1839.

p. 358   Inventory - Joseph HIGHTOWER, decd. Signed 7 Jan 1839 John T. CURL, Adm. Recorded 11 Jan 1838 E. TATE, clerk.

        Will - William DYER, Planter, decd. Wife Nancy; 6 sons Owen DYER, Anderson DYER, Booker DYER, Calliway DYER, Jackson DYER & Wilson DYER; 4 daus Sarah McBEE, Elizabeth McAFEE (?), Mahaly BROCK & Cynthia DONAHOO; sons Owen & Booker DYER, Executors. Signed 7 Feb 1837 Wm DYER. Wit: Martin CLEVELAND, John A. CLEVELAND. 24 Jul 1838 Will ammended. Signed Wm DYER. Wit: Joseph DYER, Thomas DENNIS. Recorded 11 Jan 1839 E. TATE, clerk.

p. 360   Account of Sale - Gilbert PATTERSON, decd. 20 Jul 1838. Mentions: Mary PATTERSON, Elizabeth WEST, Samuel WEST, Martin MILLER, James HANDCOCKE, Thomas WEST, George EZELL. Signed Thornton CH___D, Thomas DYER, Adms. Recorded 7 Feb 1839 E. TATE, clerk.

p. 361   Account of Sale - Deadman MALLICOAT, decd. 25 Jan 1839. Mentions: Cleveland COFFEE, James ASBURY, Clabourn NASH, Anthony HUGHS, notes on Collen HAYES & Ric'd HOPSON. Signed Nathaniel MALLICOAT, Adm. Recorded 7 Feb 1839.

p. 362   Inventory - William CREWS, decd. Taken 7 Jan 1839 by John B. CREWS, Adm. Signed John x CREWS, Adm. Recorded 7 Feb 1839 E. TATE, clerk.

        Account of Sale - William CREWS, decd. Sold 23 Jan 1839. Mentions: Wm COOSE, Robt MARTIN, Cravin CREWS, John PRATT, A. McCONNEL, Wm HAMMER, Daniel FLORA, Robert JOICE, John CAMPBELL, Nimrod CREWS, Thomas CREWS, Adm. Recorded 7 Feb 1839 E. TATE, clerk.

p. 363   Inventory - Alexander BLAIR, decd. Signed Josiah BLAIR, Adm.   29 Dec 1838. Recorded 8 Feb 1839 E. TATE, clerk.

p. 364   Account of Sale - Alexander BLAIR, decd. Sold 29 Dec 1838. Mentions: Mary HENDERSON, Hughs TAYLOR, Richard MOORE, Russel WYATT, Robert D. GRAY, Wm HENDERSON, R. D. GRAY, A. G. SULLENBARGER, John ROYAL, Wm MOFFITT, John POIN-DEXTER, David McANALLY, Nancy BLAIR. Signed Josiah BLAIR, Adm. Recorded 8 Feb 1839 E. TATE, clerk.

p. 367   Will - John IMES, decd. To be buried on my own land; wife Polly IMES; daus Elizabeth HARVEY (?), Rachel PAYNE; grdau Mary IMES; son William IMES; Indian Creek land; gr son John IMES; gr dau POLLY IMES; William IMES, my son, Executor. Signed 5 Jul 1838 John x IMES. Wit: Clabourn BULL, Thomas LACOCK. Recorded 8 Feb 1839 E. TATE, clerk.

p. 368   Account of Sale - John OGAN, decd. Mentions: Henry R. CRAWLEY, Thos McANALLY, Lewis MITCHEL, Charles McANALLY, Henry WILLIAMS, Wilbourn TAYLER, John EPPERSON, David McCOY, John HAYES, Hannah OGAN, Nelson PIRTLE, George BARNARD, William IMES, John PRENCE, Benjamin BRAY, William EVANS, John RUCKER, John HAYES, James McDANIEL, Joel McCOY, Stephen ALLEN, DANIEL Widow, Robert GRISSOM, Joseph

FURGASON, Abjah BRAY, Marshel WELLS, Henry MILLS, George BULL, William HIPSHEAR, Green B. CLOUD, Matthew RUSSEL, John McCOY, A. WOLF, Enoch DOLTON, James HAYES, Peter BUNDEN, J. C. BUNCH, Meredith DOLTON, John PRATHER. Signed Peter OGAN, Adm. Recorded 9 Jan 1841 E. TATE, clerk.

Volume 2 - March 1839 - May 1847

p. 1   Will - Royal JENNINGS, Sr., decd. Low state of health; 3 youngest sons George W., Royal & Augustus F.; two sons John P. JENNINGS & Pleasant JENNINGS; land in Claiborne Co.; land in Broken Valley & Copper Ridge; land adjoining Larkin COLLINS; slave BRITANIA & her 2 children RACHEL & FANNY; dau Nancy; 2 gr ch Caroline & Katherine the 2 oldest daus of my dau Martha; my daus Sarah ELLIS & Polly ROSE & their hus Lewis ELLIS & George ROSE; gr son John PRIOR for the use of his father Pleasant JENNINGS; Negro man LANDY; dau Elizabeth CLARK; Royal JENNINGS, Jr., my son, the Adm of William D. JENNINGS, decd; my sons John P. JENNINGS & Royal JENNINGS, Executors. Signed 25 Nov 1838 Royal his *R* mark JENNINGS. Wit: C. McANALLY, H. WILLIAMS. Recorded 27 Mar 1839 E. TATE, clerk.

p. 2   Inventory - Royal JENNINGS, decd. 6 Feb 1839. Signed John P. JENNINGS, Royal JENNINGS, Executors. Recorded 27 Mar 1839 E. TATE, clerk.

p. 3   Inventory - Samuel VANCE, decd. Signed 2 Mar 1839 John ROBERTSON, Adm. Recorded 27 Mar 1839 E. TATE, clerk.

          Account of Sale - Samuel VANCE, decd. Mentions: John CLARK, Rinehart COFFMAN, John STARNES, Alfoid ACUFF, Sarah VANCE, Mary VANCE, Peter BULEN, Hannah VANCE, Peter BULAR, Peter BEELAR (?), John VANCE, Jacob BEELAR, Joseph VANCE, John GAMBLE, Polly VANCE, Martin CLEVELAND, Wm ARWINE. Signed John ROBERTSON, Adm. Recorded 27 Mar 1839 E. TATE, clerk.

p. 4   Account of Sale - Meredith COFFEE, decd. Mentions: James S. TALBOT, Joel COFFEE, Samuel SMITH, James COFFEE, Henry ALSUP, Thomas TOWSLEY, Ester COFFEE, Aquilla MITCHEL, Edward CHURCHMAN, Joseph TOWNSELY, Richard HANKINS, Mitchel NEMORE, Thomas GREEN, Edmond CHESHIRE, Jacob ARNETT, Mary COFFEE, Robert RAY, Lewas COFFEE, Samuel CRAIN, William NORTHERN, John LEWIS, Richard HARRISON, Clabourn WATKINS, Thomas CHESHIRE. Signed Rice x COFFEE, Adm. Recorded 27 Mar 1839 E. TATE, clerk.

p. 5   Additional Account of Sale - Robert GAINS, decd. Signed 4 Mar 1838 B. E. & R. C. GAINS, Executors. Recorded 27 Mar 1839 E. TATE, clerk.

          Account of Sale - A bill on list of the remainder of William WILLIAMS property, decd, 29 Oct 1838. Mentions: John CYRUS, John WILLIS, Wm WAGGONER, Carlisle HAYNES, Allen HURST to stack flax at Robert HUDDLESTONE, Guardian. Recorded 27 Mar 1839 E. TATE, clerk.

p. 6   Settlement - John P. JENNINGS & John CLARK, Adms for the Estate of Wm CLARK, decd. Mentions: David WETOONS; Wm E. COCKE; McEWEN, Superintendent of Common Schools; Wm DENNIS; Henry ALSUP; William DOTSON; RAMSEY & CRAIGHEAD; Solomon S. SHIPLEY; James FULKERSON; Pleasant JENNINGS; Jacob SHOUTTS; Peter ATKINS; Joshua SHIFFLET; RICE & McFARLAND; R. LOYD, Shff; Joseph CLARK; E. TATE; William McCANN; Thomas P. McANALLY; Royal JENNINGS; Isaac RUTH & Constable

MALLICOAT; Martin CLEVELAND; John LATHAM; William M. MOODY; I. HUTCHISON & R. COFFEE; Stephan RUTH; Dr. Wm E. COCKE; Thomas WHITESIDES; High HOUSTON; Royal JENNINGS, Jr.; Thomas WALKER; G. W. JENNINGS; C. W. LATHIM; John DIXON; Thomas LYMAN; J. A. HOWELL; Edward CLARK; Daniel WIDDER; LAFFERTY & WHITESIDE. Signed 25 Feb 1839 E. TATE, clerk. Recorded 28 Mar 1839 E. TATE, clerk.

p. 7   Settlement - James LACY, Guardian of Mary GRAY who intermarried with Edward L. TATE from the time of the last report. Mentions: Dinon SMITH, Isaac DANIEL. Signed 20 Feb 1839 E. TATE. Recorded 28 Mar 1839 E. TATE, clerk.

p. 8   Settlement - Abner DIAL, Adm for the Estate of Abel DIAL, decd. Mentions: James DIAL; S & M SHIELDS; BLAIN & FRANKLIN; James & Wm WILLIAMS; R. M. SCRUGGS; William C. SMITH; Shff SALLING taxes for 1837; Constable HILL; James DYER; James DYER, Sr.; William DENNIS, Sr.; John DENNIS; cash paid for widow's yr allowance. Signed E. TATE, clerk. Recorded 28 Mar 1839 E. TATE.

        Additional Inventory - William MILLIKAN, decd. Mentions: John HODGES note due 1 Jan 1840. Signed 1 Apr 1839 Elhu MILLIKAN, Jesse HOWEL, Adms. Recorded 15 Apr 1839 E. TATE, clerk.

p. 9   Account of Sale - William DYER, decd. Sold 25 Jan 1839. Mentions: Callaway DYER, Jackson DYER, Nathaniel POPEJOY, Wm DENNIS, Jr., Widow DYER, Alford ACUFF, Silas McBEE, Moses BROCK, Robert FIELDS, James VITTITO, Joseph HILL. Signed Booker DYER, Executor 25 Jan 1839. Supplement: Reubin SELLERS, decd, Samuel WAGNER. Signed Booker DYER, Executor 25 Jan 1839. Recorded 15 Apr 1839 E. TATE.

p. 11   Account of Sale - Royal JENNINGS, decd. 8 Mar 1839. Mentions: James LATHIM, Pleasant JENNINGS, George W. JENNINGS, Elizabeth CLARK, Agustus JENNINGS, William MALLICOAT, Ambrose DAY, Abraham McCONNEL, John WALLER, Levin WALLER, Henry JENNINGS, Harman HAYES, Ezekiel HERALD, Rhodeman HERRALD, Mira JENNINGS, Lewis ELLIS, Thomas WHITESIDE, Charles McANALLY, William HARIL, Marinda DUVAULT, John PHILLIPS, Marlin BOWLS, Green BUNDEN, Henry WILLIAMS, Ransom DAY, Wm HIPSHEAR, Pleasant WATSON. Signed John P. JENNINGS, Royal JENNINGS, Executors. Recorded 15 Apr 1839 E. TATE, clerk.

p. 13   Settlement - Returns of Joshua HAMILTON & JOSEPH RICH, Overseers of the Bean Station to Cumberland Gap Turnpike for year 1838. Mentions: services & supplies from the following: Hezekiah BROCK, Elijah JONES, Wm JONSTONS, Wm PRICE, B. SEWELL, John HODGE, Mrs. BREEDEN, T. HUNT, Stephen HARDY, Joseph HAMILTON, Jacob SHOULTZ, Carban CHEEK, Hugh JONES, Peter BUNDIN, Hugh GRAHAM, Mrs. CHEEK, Wm CLARK, Hubard ADAMS, Mary CHEEK, Jesse DOLTON, Jessee HOLTON, Isam HAYES, Elias BURCHFIELD, Mrs. HOPSON, John CAMPBELL, Fanny BREEDEN, John BURCH, Wm GIBSON, James F. STONE, John McNEIL, Elisha NUNN, Mrs. MILLAR, John QUALES, Western WELL, Rich'd HOPSON, Wm LEFOON, Pleasant MONDY, Jas JONSTON, William HAMILTON, Joseph NOE, John B. ELDUIDGER, Abraham CODLE, Nelson McWILLIAMS, Jacob PIKE, Jesse INDECOT, Joel NANTZ, Eliza COLLINSWORTH, Benj. SEWELL, Charles COLLIER, Andrew CHANNY, Robert BAILES, George W. FAIRCHILDS, John ROWLETS, Elijah JONES, Daniel MARCHIM, Wesley WEBB, John COX, Robert NUCKLES, Jacob ZICK, Robert ZICK, Matilda COX, Henry WILBURN, Pascal NUN, John PROVANCE, Jno HAWKINS, Valentine McCOLLINS, Wm SOLOMON, George HURLEY, John CALLS, Thos POLLARD, Elisah DULS, Anderson HUNT, David LAMBERT, George McCRANE, Wm CONNER, Isacc PIERCEFIELD

(14½ da labor, $10.00), John BROCK, John JONSTON, Samuel HAMILTON, Hugh CAIN,
John CONNER, Jason CADLE, Matthew HAMILTON, Matthew RUSSEL, Jno BROCK, Jr.,
Joshua HAMILTON, Wm GRAHAM, James HUNTER, Wm WELSH, Wm HOUSTON, Joshua CORE,
Martin JONSTON, Wm BEATY, James HARRIS, Wm PRICE, James ASBERY, James BARTLET,
Bluford WOODALL, Nancy TONY, Pryor MONDAY, Jno CONNER, Valentine McCOLM, Henry
CHILDERS, Abraham KELLER, Beal LEA, Hiram JONSTON, Geo BROCK, James HELTON, John
HELTTON, Peter HOPPER, Elijah HOPPER, George HOPPER, Thomas BRIAN, Thomas DOLTON,
P. H. & N. A. SENTER, Thomas WHITESIDE, LAFFERTY & WHITESIDE, F. TAYLOR & Co.,
John P. JENNINGS, Wm HIPSHEAR, Thos McGOLDRICK, McGINNIS & LATHIM, Pleasant
JENNINGS, Ryal JENNINGS, George EVANS, And. McGINNIS, Abram SPOON, Wm HOUSTON,
Reuben DOLTON, Andrew COLLINS, Andrew DOLTON, Griffin COLLINS, Royal COLLINS,
Demsey DOLTON, Griffin COLLINS, Demsey LYNN, Wm COFFEE, Thos HAYES, Colbert
HIPSHEAR, Nathan PERRY, Elijah COFFEE, C. W. LATHIM, Wilburn TAYLOR, Harvey MILLS,
Pleasant WEBSTER. Signed Wm GRAHAM, Comm. 21 Mar 1839, Wm M. MOODY, A. P. GREEN,
Thos McBROOM. Recorded 13 to 17 Apr 1839 E. TATE, clerk.

p. 26   Settlement – B. E. & R. C. GAINS, Executors for Robert GAINS, decd.
Mentions: sale returns for 6 Jun 1836, 10 Nov 1837, 4 Mar 1839; Sheriff TALBOT
tax 1835, 1836; P. MITCHEL, Dpt Sheriff tax 1838; Balis E. GAINS; minor heirs
schooling & board; Robert C. GAINS. Signed 4 May 1838 E. TATE, clerk. Recorded
7 May 1838 E. TATE, clerk.

p. 27   Will – David SHIELDS, decd, of Holstein Paper Mill. Being in moderate
health but lately & frequently attacted with painful diseases which indicate
Death; bros John & James SHIELDS; business of John SHIELDS & Co. at Bean Station,
TN, Cumberland River, KY; business of SHIELDS-WOODS & Co., Spurgevinesville, TN;
nephew David N. RANKIN; sis Sarah or Joanah SHIELDS; bro Milton SHIELDS; bros
John SHIELDS & Milton SHIELDS, Executors. Signed Sunday, 10 Sep 1826 David
SHIELDS. My handwriting being so well known that a Subscribing witness thought
unnesessary. Land in Russelville, TN to bro James SHIELDS. Recorded 7 May 1839.

p. 28   Settlement – Henry BOATMAN, Adm of the Estate of Nenian RIGGS, decd.
31 May 1839. Mentions: William HARRIS, James HODGES, Russel CROW, James SHIELDS,
Peter HUNT, W. D. COWAN, LAFFERTY & WHITESIDE, DEDRICK & ANDERSON, John M. COFFIN,
Joth NOE, Wm SNIDER, Thomas WILLIFORD, Joseph LEBOW, Jon GARRITSON, COFFIN &
McKINNY, Geor. W. RICH, Sheriff THOMASON, Elizabeth RIGGS (Guardian 1 Apr 1839,
25 Aug 1838), Sheriff LOYD. Signed E. TATE. Recorded 10 Jun 1839 E. TATE, clerk.

p. 29   Settlement – Samuel BUNCH & Edward TATE, Trustees of Madison Accademy.
Mentions: monies received 1 Oct 1829 & 9 Dec 1831; 9 Dec 1831 Wm C. COCKE,
Treasurer up to date 2 Apr 1839; Wm E. MOODY, JP. Signed Saml BUNCH, E. TATE,
2 Apr 1839. Signed Wm M. MOODY, JP, 2 Apr 1839. Recorded 13 Jul 1839 E. TATE.

         Commissioners Report – 5 Aug 1839. Provisions for Anah CATE, widow of
Moses CATE, decd. and family for 1 yr from death of her husband. Signed John
DUGLAS, William x MITCHEL, William GILMORE. Recorded 6 Aug 1839 E. TATE, clerk.

p. 30   Guardian Report – 4 Aug 1839. Signed Robert HUDDLESTONE, Guardian of
Campbell WILLIAMS. Recorded 3 Sep 1839 E. TATE, clerk.

         Inventory – Moses CATES, decd. Taken 20 Jul 1839 by Levi SATTERFIELD,
Adm. Recorded 9 Sep 1839 E. TATE, clerk.

          Account of Sale - Moses CATES, decd. Mentions: Ana CATES, Jacob
ARNETT, J. T. WEST, Robert RAY, Wm AUSTIN, Chesley RAY, Wm MAPLES. Signed Levi
SATTERFIELD, Adm 20 Jul 1839. Recorded 9 Sep 1839 E. TATE, clerk.

p. 31   Commissioners Report - Estate of Vincent G. BULL, decd. 5 Jul 1839.
Estate of less than $30.00 given to widow. Signed 14 Sep 1839 Joseph WILLIAMS,
William ESTES, Comm. Recorded 19 Oct 1839 E. TATE. clerk.

          Settlement - William DENNIS, Esq, Adm of the Estate of Elizabeth SATTER-
FIELD, decd. Mentions: David BARTON, John SATTERFIELD, Green SATTERFIELD, James
DYER, Sr., P. L. COCKE, Wm HICKLE & James DYER, Jr., E. TATE. Signed E. TATE
15 Aug 1839. Recorded 19 Oct 1839 E. TATE, clerk.

p. 32   Settlement - Robert HUDDLESTONE, Guardian of Campbell WILLIAMS heir of
William WILLIAMS, decd. 3 Sep 1839. Mentions: Additional estate sales 29 Oct
1838 and 4 Aug 1840; John CYRUS; Marcus COOK; Valentine WEYMIRE; William
WILLIAMS; Owen DYER, B. C. McCRAY & ROSE; Joseph HILL, Dpt Shff; John COX; Wm
WAGONER; Samuel CLOUD; Ezra BUCKNER; Daniel WILLIAMS. Signed E. TATE. Recorded
19 Oct 1839 E. TATE, clerk.

p. 33   Settlement - Andrew McGINNIS, Executor of the Estate of Robert McGINNIS,
decd. Mentions: Thomas HAYES; Peter OGAN, Adm of the Estate of John OGAN, decd;
RICE & McFARLAND; John A. McKENNY; Sheriff LOYD; Peter SUMING (?); H. HOUSTON;
Ethelrod WILLIAMS; LAFFERTY & WHITESIDE; Pryor LEA; Samuel BUNCH; Gray GARETT,
S. S. SHIPLEY, Dowell COLLINS, Deadman MALLICOAT; William RUCKER; William B.
EVANS; Robert CALDWELL; Peter PARSON. Recorded 24 Oct 1839. Signed E. TATE
9 Aug 1839.

p. 34   Settlement - Andrew McGINNIS, Executor of the Estate of Robert McGINNIS,
decd, who was the Adm of the Estate of Lawrence STONE, decd. Mentions: Estate
of Lawrence STONE, decd, against John COCKE & E. JACK, Adms of the Estate of
John F. JACK, decd, and Sterling COCKE, the Security in the Supreme Court at
Knoxville; John A. McKINNEY; Robert KING; James CAMPBELL & CO.; J. W. LIDE;
Pryer LEA; Peter PARSON; Jacob PECK; Tillman A. HOWARD; RICE & HOWARD; nursing
care for Lawrence STONE, decd, during last sickness in the summer and fall of
1818 (7 weeks); Joseph COBB, Josiah BUNCH and Benj. CLOUD, Esqrs; Joseph COLLINS;
Rhoda EVANS: Adm. wife. Signed Wm M. MOODY, JP, Andrew McGINNIS 9 Aug 1839.
Signed E. TATE 28 Aug 1839. Recorded 24 Oct 1839 E. TATE, clerk.

p. 35   Settlement - John CLARK, Executor for the Estate of Richard ACUFF, decd.
Mentions: Benj. LEWIS, Thos ACUFF, James & William WILLIAMS, Martin CLEVELAND,
RICE & McFARLAND, Lewis CAMPBELL, R. ACUFF & C. McANNALLY, Joseph CLARK, Alfred
ACUFF, John ROBINSON, Wm E. COCKE, Benjamin BRANSON, Hezekiah ROOK, Joice
ACUFF. Signed E. TATE 20 Sep 1839. Recorded 24 Oct 1839 E. TATE, clerk.

p. 36   Settlement - Allen HUNT, Executor of the Estate of William WILLIAMS,
decd. Mentions: Campbell WILLIAMS minor son of decd. Signed 4 Sep 1838
Robert HUDDLESTONE, Guardian, and 29 Aug 1839. Signed E. TATE, Samuel CLOUD.
Recorded 24 Oct 1839 E. TATE, clerk.

p. 37   Settlement - Thomas DYER, Executive of the Estate of Hannah HAMMER,
decd, made 16 Oct 1839. Mentions: Wm E. COCKE, COCKE & ARMSTRONG, William

KIDWELL, Elisha THOMASON, Aaron COUNTZ, Nicholas and Martha COUNTZ the legatees, Thomas DYER being the husband of Sarah HAMMER a legatee. Signed E. TATE. Recorded 16 Nov 1839 E. TATE, clerk.

p. 38   Settlement - Nancy SMITH, Executrix of the Estate of Josiah SMITH, decd. Mentions: vs MOSS; Owen DYER; Wm DOUGHTRY; SAVAGE note; James SALLING, Dpt Shff; James & William WILLIAMS; Jeremiah SAVAGE; Peter SHARP; John COX. Signed E. TATE, 20 Sep 1839. Recorded 16 Nov 1839 E. TATE, clerk.

Guardian Report - James LATHIM, Guardian of Martha and E. LATHIM, minor heirs of John LATHIM, decd, appointed 1 Oct 1838. Mentions: hiring of SLAVES to S. S. SHIPLEY, James LATHIM, Jr., & George EVANS; schooling by Miss Eliza HENDERSON. Signed E. TATE 2 Nov 1839. Recorded 16 Nov 1839 E. TATE, clerk.

p. 39   Guardian Report - 2 Nov 1839 James MALLICOAT, Guardian of Amanda GRAY. Mentions: last report 1 Jan 1838; E. TATE, agent for heirs of John & Ruth STIFFY, decd; hiring of SLAVES; RICE & McFARLAND; KLINE & Sons; James & William WILLIAMS; Wm T. TATE; Robert CARDWELL; George MOODY; Benjamin OWENS. Signed 2 Nov 1839 E. TATE. Recorded 16 Nov 1839 E. TATE, clerk.

p. 40   Guardian Report - Mary FURGASON, Guardian of the minor heirs of John FURGASON, decd. Mentions: last report 2 Nov 1838; interest from 26 Jul 1836; Nancy FURGASON who is now of full age; Elizabeth FURGASON, having intermarried with Isaac LOW (?); James FURGASON one of the wards in the past. Signed E. TATE 2 Dec 1839. Recorded 7 Dec 1839 E. TATE, clerk.

Account of Sale - Robert HUDDLESTONE, Guardian of Campbell WILLIAMS. Signed 2 Dec 1839. Recorded 7 Dec 1839 E. TATE, clerk.

p. 41   Account of Sale - Hughs O. TAYLOR, decd. Sold 3 May 1837. Mentions: Warham EASLEY, Hughs O. TAYLOR, Thomas POINDEXTER, Thomas WHITESIDE, J. B. ELLEDGE, Wm M. MITCHEL, John HUNT, Isaac HAINES, John F. NOE, George G. TAYLOR, Eliker TAYLOR, Coleman WITT, Thomas K. HOWELL, Richard MOORE, John R. CHAMBERS, George W. MATTOCK, Willis GRANTHAM, Negro boy MICAGE, Andrew C. ESTON, Negro boy GEORGE. Signed H. W. & E. A. TAYLOR, Executors. Recorded 21 Jan 1840.

p. 42   Settlement - Willis L. PRATT, Adm of the Estate of John HILL, Jr., decd. 21 Jan 1840. Mentions: Samuel SHIELDS, S. & M. SHIELDS, FRAZIER & McKINNY, HUFFMAN & WESTERFIELD, R. M. SCRUGGS, Jesse HILL, Thomas McMILLIN, John HILL, Jr., John HILL, Sr., HILL & JOHNSTON, Martin BAKER, George DYER, Jr., Harman G. LEA surveyor, Sarah HILL widow, Isaac DAMEWOOD, Wm DENNIS, John DENNIS, Jr., David ELKINS, Nancy RANDOLPH, James DYER, Jr., Jarrad NORRIS, tax receipts 1837-38. Signed 21 Jan 1840. Recorded 11 Feb 1840 E. TATE, clerk.

p. 43   Guardian Report - Mary BEELAR, Guardian of the minor heirs of David BEELAR, decd, taken 3 Feb 1840. Mentions: rents & taxes 1838-39. Recorded 11 Feb 1840 E. TATE, clerk.

Additional Account of Sale - Heirs of Robert GAINS, decd. Signed B. E. and R. C. GAINS, Executors. Recorded 11 Feb 1840 E. TATE, clerk.

p. 44   Will - Absalom ROACH, decd. Wife Mary ROACH, daus Anna, Hannah and

Elenor, sons Absalom, James, William, John and Alfred, my friend Robert LOYD
Executor. Signed 5 Jun 1839 Absalom A. x ROACH. Wit: James M. ROACH, Willi
H. ROACH, George x EZELL. Recorded 11 Feb 1840 E. TATE, clerk.

p. 45   Guardian Report - Elizabeth RIGGS, Guardian of the minor heirs of
Nemian RIGGS, decd. Mentions: last report 22 May 1838; Henry BOATMAN, Adm;
Mahaley RIGGS; Levina RIGGS a ward; Joshua RIGGS a ward, Elizabeth RIGGS a
ward; Keziah RIGGS a ward; schooling & taxes 1838. Recorded 8 Feb 1840 E. TATE.

p. 46   Inventory - Joseph LEFFEW, decd. Signed Reas WILLIAMS, Adm. Recorded
10 Mar 1840 E. TATE, clerk.

        Commissioners Report - Allowance for Sary LEFFEW, widow of Joseph
LEFFEW, decd. Signed 18 Jan 1840 David WATSON, Joel DOTSON. Recorded 10 Mar
1840 E. TATE, clerk.

        Account of 3rd Sale - John DENNIS, decd. Mentions: Sarah DENNIS,
William DENNIS, John DENNIS. Signed Levi DENNIS, Adm 26 Feb 1840. Recorded
10 Mar 1840 E. TATE, clerk.

p. 47   Account of Sale - Joseph LEFFEW, decd. 12 Dec 1839. Sale held 18 Jan
1840. Mentions: L. NEAL, H. JINNINGS, W. LEFFEW, T. MAJORS, S. DOTSON, L.
LEFFEW, J. WALLER, A. BUNCH, S. RUCKER, S. LEFFEW, A. HARREL, J. HOWEL, R. SHELTON
P. BRAY, E. JOHNS, J. NASH, B. FARMER, N. WILLIAMS, M. CLEVELAND. Signed Reas
WILLIAMS, Adm. Recorded 10 Mar 1840 E. TATE, clerk.

p. 48   Account of Sale - Thomas HENDERSON, decd. 9 Nov 1839. Mentions:
hiring 2 NEGROES, girl by Louisa HENDERSON and boy by William HENDERSON; Reuben
LONG and Marlin HARRIS. Signed James MOORE, Executor. Recorded 10 Mar 1840.

        Inventory - Dec term 1839. Milton SHIELDS & Benjamin D. BARBSTON,
Adms for David SHIELDS, decd. Mentions: Negro girl MALINDA. Signed Milton
SHIELDS, B. D. BARBSTON, Adms. Recorded 10 Mar 1840 E. TATE, clerk.

p. 50   Account of Sale - David SHIELDS, decd. 23 Nov 1839. David SHIELDS &
B. D. BARBSON, Adms. Recorded 10 Mar 1840 E. TATE, clerk.

p. 51   Guardian REPORT - Additional amount against David SHIELDS, decd, former
Guardian of the minor heirs of John SHIELDS, decd, in favor of the Estate of John
SHIELDS, decd. Mentions: rent ending Feb 1835; Thomas TURLEY Estate; NELSON's
hire due at his death in Jul 1835; T. D. KNIGHT for KELE's hire 1835 & 36; F. B.
EVANS note due 4 Jul 1832; Widow, Mary, of John SHIELDS, decd and minor heirs.
Signed Milton SHIELDS, Benj. D. BRANSON, Adms of David SHIELDS, decd, 2 Mar 1840.
Recorded 10 Mar 1840 E. TATE, clerk.

p. 52   Will - George DYER, decd. My dau Mariah McCUBANS and her children; my
dau Polly BEELAR and her children; Negro girl CLAUSER; my son Willie B. DYER;
Negro HENRY; my son William DYER; Negroes ANDREW and BETSY; my son Charton DYER;
2 Negro boys JOHN and WILLIAM; my son George Washington DYER until he becomes of
age; Negro woman EVELINE and her youngest child, CATHERINE; son William DYER and
son-in-law Jesse BEELAR, Executors. Signed 25 Jan 1840 George DYER. Wit:
Martin CLEVELAND, Charlton DYER. Recorded 11 Mar 1840 E. TATE, clerk.

p. 53   Commissioners Report - Polly ESTES, Widow of John ESTES, decd. In the absence of Joseph W. PATTERSON who is now in Indiana, we set a part 1 yrs provisions for widow and family. Signed 21 Mar 1840 John ROBINSON, John EASTES. Recorded 22 Apr 1840 E. TATE, clerk.

p. 54   Will - John LEBOW, decd. My son Joseph LEBOW, son-in-law William GRAY, my son Isaac LEBOW, my daus Sena, Lucretia and Lucenda, my son John LEBOW, my wife Catherine LEBOW, my son-in-law Sanford JOHNSON, my son Jacob LEBOW and my son-in-law Wm GRAY, Executors. Signed John his *a* mark LEBOW 28 Dec 1825. Wit: C. MOORE, George WILLIAMS. Recorded 22 Apr 1840 E. TATE, clerk.

p. 55   Settlement - Massy COCKRUM & Allen D. MORGAN, Adms for Edward CHURCHMAN, decd. Mentions: last settlement 1 Jan 1838; Robert LOYD, Sheriff; E. CHURCHMAN a legatee; Sarah CHURCHMAN a legatee; Philip SNIDER a legatee; Michael DYER a legatee; Wm FREEMAN a legatee; William CRAWFORD a legatee; E. TATE, Guardian of minor heirs of Thos CHURCHMAN a legatee; Elisha THOMASON, Sheriff, taxes for 1838; A. E. McHAFFEE agent for Moses CRAWFORD and Malinda CRAWFORD one of the legatees. Signed 18 Mar 1840. Recorded 22 Apr 1840 E. TATE, clerk.

        Commissioners Report - Ann ATKINS, Widow of Nathan ATKINS, decd. 1 yr support for her & family. Signed 4 Mar 1840 William SHARP, Joseph HILL, George W. VITTETO. Recorded 8 May 1840 E. TATE, clerk.

p. 56   Inventory - Nathan ATKINS, decd. Mentions: James NEEDHAM, Washington VITTITO, Carter T. DOLTON. Signed 4 May 1840 Mark MONROW, Adm. Recorded 8 May 1840 E. TATE, clerk.

        Account of Sale - Nathan ATKINS, decd. Mentions: Ann ATKINS, James VITTITO, Alfred NOE, Lewis ATKINS, James NEEDHAM, Wm DENNIS, John BURNETT, Stokely VITTITO, Calvin MONROW, Solomon WYRICK, James COLVIN, Joseph WILLIAMS, John NEEDHAM, Alfred NOEL, Isaac GOWFORTH, John CARDIN, G. W. VITTITO, Archibald MULLINS, James H. STARNES, Stephen ATKINS, Joseph WOLFINBARGER, Robert ATKINS, Presley BURNETT, Martin CLEVELAND, Daniel CAPPS, Thomas WILLSON, Elijah ATKINS. Signed 17 Mar 1840 Mark MONROW, Adm. Recorded 8 May 1840 E. TATE, clerk.

p. 58   Inventory - Absalom ROACH, decd. 24 Feb 1840. Mentions: Alfred ROACH, Absalom ROACH, Jr., John ROACH, Wm E. COCKE. Signed Robert LOYD, Executor. Recorded 8 May 1840 E. TATE, clerk.

p. 59   Account of Sale - Absalom ROACH, decd. 24 Feb 1840. Mentions: Joseph NOE, Daniel WOLDRIDGE, Green ROACH, Eli McDANIEL, Samuel JONES, Benjamin FRY, Hamilton ROACH, Absalom ROACH, Clemment MALLICOAT, Alfred ROACH, Thomas WEST, John CALLISON, James McDANIEL, Lacy WITCHER, Green ARNETT, Drury ROACH, John YOUNG, M. E. JEFFERES, John BRABSON, John DUGLASS, John ROACH, Reuben GROVE, Thomas DYER, John T. ROBERTS, Dennis ROBERTS, Vince BARBSTON, James R. HAGGARD, Bird JONES, Henry MAYES, Thomas DAVIS, Henderson DAVIS, James JAMES. Signed Robert LOYD, Executor. Recorded 9 May 1840 E. TATE, clerk.

p. 60   Account of Sale - Joseph HIGHTOWER, decd. Mon., 27 Apr 1840. Mentions: Balser SHIRLEY, Stephen J. GODSEY, BLACK BOY of Henry ALSUP, A. & W. E. KYLE. Signed T. CURL, Adm. Recorded 9 May 1840 E. TATE, clerk.

p. 61   Will - Edward CHURCHMAN, decd. Wife Eda CHURCHMAN; Negro woman NICE;
my daus & their heirs Mary BLEDSOE, Naomy MILLS, Margaret MITCHELL, Nancy MILLS,
Rabeca PERRIN, Jane NANCE, Hannah BRADLEY, Rachel MITCHEL, Matilda CHURCHMAN &
Cynthia COLLET; grson John P. PERRIN son of my dau Sarah; Vaiden PERRIN (no
relation given), Preston MITCHEL & J. BLEDSOE, Executors. Signed 10 Mar 1840
Edward CHURCHMAN. Wit: Thomas LAMAR, Thomas BRADSHAW. Recorded 9 May 1840.

p. 62   Settlement - Henry HOLSTEIN & John HODGES, Adms for Eli HODGES, decd.
Mentions: F. J. MORRIS, Job GARRISTON, Preston LOYD, Lewis RIGGS, Abijah
FOWLER, Joseph TREMAN, Thomas GARLAND, Elizabeth HODGES, widow. Signed 29 Apr
1840. Recorded 9 May 1840 E. TATE, clerk.

p. 63   Settlement - Levi DENNIS, Adm for John DENNIS, decd. 17 Apr 1840.
Mentions: 3 sales 7 Jun 1838, 7 Nov 1838, 10 Mar 1840; Sarah DENNIS, widow;
Wm SHARP & Joseph HILL; E. TATE; John COCKE; Wm DENNIS; Eli DENNIS; John DENNIS;
Wm SHARP, Abner DIAL, Moses BROCK, Mark MONROW, Wm MARTIN, Henry NEEDHAM.
Recorded 9 May 1840 E. TATE, clerk.

p. 64   Inventory - John LEBOW, Sr., decd. 9 Apr 1840. Mentions: 2 tracts of
land in Hawkins Co. called Hotlets Place; David QUEEN; Sally CRAWFORD; BESETER
tract; BENTER tract; Negro woman JUDY; Negro man SAM; Negro girls MATILDA, JANE,
MARTHA, SARAH; J. M. COFFIN & Co.; C. H. COFFIN & Chas J. McKINNEY; Peter BARR;
Hugh A. BASSET; George MATLOCK; A. T. NALL & Robt NALL; Gabriel McCRANE; Wm B.
BASSET; Nathan GRAY; Spencer BASSET; John MAYES; Jesse RIGS; Cyntha FORT; David
McANALLY; John B. PROFFIT; James SHIELDS; P. J. NOE & George WILLIAMS; James
MOOR; Raleigh DOTSON; Isaac LEBOW; John BOYD; David COUNTZ, Henry COUNTZ & Thos
WHITESIDE; Thomas TAYLOR; James BRADLEY; Benjamin HAYWOOD; Thomas GAMWELL; Peter
ELROD; Aquilla JONES; Wm SHROPSHEAR; John R. EASTES; Julias CONNER; James CONN.
Signed William GRAY, Executor. Recorded 5 Jun 1840 E. TATE, clerk.

p. 66   Settlement - Elihu MILLIKAN & Jesse HOWELL, Adms for William MILLIKAN,
decd. 17 May 1840. Mentions: sale recorded 11 Jan 1839 & 1 Apr 1839; Jahu
MAINS; John DENNISON; Crampton G. HARRIS; John NEWTON; Alexander MILLIKAN; E.
TATE; Solomon MILLIKAN a legatee; Eli MILLIKAN, Wm MILLIKAN, Saml S. MILLIKAN,
Alexander MILLIKAN legatees and William CONDRA ficio of the legatees; George
MILLIKAN a legatee; David MILLIKAN a legatee; Elihu MILLIKAN being a legatee;
Jesse HOWELL being a legatee. Recorded 5 Jun 1840 E. TATE, clerk.

p. 67   Settlement - Isaac HORNER, Adm for Samuel RAIL, decd. 1 Jun 1840.
Mentions: Walter D. COWEN, John T. MOFFETT & co., Cramton L. HARRIS, Joel
DENNISTON, John DENNISTON, Eli SPOON. Recorded 5 Jun 1840 E. TATE, clerk.

         Inventory - Wm BEELAR, decd. 4 Jan 1840. Mentions: Daniel CUR,
Andrew BOWERS, Rinehart COFFMAN. Signed Peter WOLFINBARGER, Adm. Recorded
5 Jun 1840 E. TATE, clerk.

p. 68   Account of Sale - William BEELAR, decd. Mentions: Milly BEELAR,
Joseph WILLIAMS, Joseph WOLFINBARGER, Robert FRY, William WOLFINGARGER, James
DOLTON, Willie DYER, Miller BEELAR. Signed 25 May 1840 Peter WOLFINBARGER,
Adm. Recorded 5 Jun 1840 E. TATE, clerk.

         Commissioners Report - 25 May 1840. Estate of William BEELAR, decd.

1 yr support for widow & family. Signed John CLARK, Joseph CLARK, Joseph
WILLIAMS, Comms. Recorded 6 Jun 1840 E. TATE, clerk.

p. 69   Commissioners Report - Set apart for Elizabeth NEEDHAM, widow, and
family of James NEEDHAM, decd. Mentions a note on Presly BURNET. Signed 9 May
1840 Joseph HILL, George VITTITO, Wm SHARP, Comms. Recorded 6 Jun 1840 E. TATE.

          Account of Sale - June term 1840. James EASTES, decd, sale on 28 Mar
1840. Signed Jesse RIGGS, Adm, 1 Jun 1840. Recorded 6 Jun 1840 E. TATE, clerk.

p. 70   Settlement - Abner DIAL, Adm of Abel DIAL, decd. 2 Jun 1840. Mentions:
settlement 1 Mar 1839; John MULLINS a legatee; Wm M. COCKE, clerk, & Bolser
SHIRLEY & E. TATE receipts for Jonathan DIAL a legatee; James DIAL a legatee;
Richard SIMMONS a legatee; Abner DIAL a legatee; widow of Abel DIAL. Recorded
13 Jul 1840 E. TATE, clerk.

          Account of Sale - James NEEDHAM, decd. Mentions: Elizabeth NEEDHAM.
Signed 20 Jun 1840 Lewis ADKINS, Adm. Recorded 13 Jul 1840 E. TATE, clerk.

p. 71   Settlement - John POINDEXTER, Executor for James BLAIR, decd. 3 Jun
1840. Mentions: Hughs O. TAYLOR purchase of NEGRO boy: Samuel MORRISON; rents
during 1832 through 1837; Thos STERLING; balance in hands of Executor after 2
yrs from probate of will; Susanna POINDEXTER; James SPRADLING an heir; E.
WILLIAMS; Russel WYATT an heir; Thomas GAMEWELL; Sterling COCKE; Wm MURRY; John
CUMMINGS; Jesse RIGGS; G. McCRANE; Joseph COBB; James EVANS; James L. ETTER;
James R. COCKE, Dpt Clerk; W. B. WILLIAMS; F. BOYD, Shff taxes 1831-1834; David
McANALLY, Dpt Shff taxes 1835-1837; Wilson WYATT an heir; John LEBOW; labor for
1832 to 24 Sep 1838. Recorded 13 Jul 1840 E. TATE, clerk.

p. 72   Guardian Report - For minor heirs of John SHIELDS, decd. Milton SHIELDS
& B. D. BRABSON, Adms for David SHIELDS, decd, who was the Guardian of the minor
heirs of John SHIELDS, decd. 30 Jun 1840. Mentions: Mary SHIELDS, widow of
John SHIELDS, decd; money in hands of David SHIELDS, Guardian, on 20 May 1833
to 14 Aug 1834 and up to time of death of David SHIELDS; SHIELDS, JOHNSON & RICE;
E. WILLIAMS; John SHIELDS & Co.; James SHIELDS vs Estate of John SHIELDS; KNIGHT
& GILL medical bills; RAMSEY & CRAIGHEAD, printers; Dr. McINTOSH medical services
to NELSON; Orvil RICE; Joseph RICH; James T. SHIELDS an heir; Elizabeth SHIELDS
a minor heir; Abram CULLINS, Atto. Signed 30 Jun 1840. No recording date.

p. 74   Inventory - Edward CHURCHMAN, decd. Mentions: Joel PERRIN, Lewis
COLLET, James HARGIS, James MILLS, Elizabeth CHURCHMAN, John A. & Seth McKINNY,
Daniel MEEK, John BRADLEY, Reed COX, William PERRIN, Seth HAMMER & George
STEPHENS, A. BLACKBURN & Daniel MEEK, M. THORNBURG & John MILLS, C. M. GODLIN,
Lamer BRADSHAW, Obadiah & Jacob P. CHASE, David & Daniel CAMPBELL, Nathan
STANLEY, Alexander REEDER, Reuben NANCE, Banister WILES, Jesse DELAZER, John
MITCHEL, S & M SHIELDS, Robert BLAIN. Signed Preston MITCHEL, Executor, 20 May
1840. Recorded 14 Jul 1840 E. TATE, clerk.

p. 76   Account of Sale - Edward CHURCHMAN, decd. Mentions: James MILLS, G. C.
McBEE, Joel PERRIN, Lewis COLLET, Thomas HANKINS, John MITCHEL, Jefferson NANCE,
Calliway HODGES, William BRADLEY, Samuel EVANS, E. CHURCHMAN, Andrew VINEYARD,
Matilda CHURCHMAN, Martin VINEYARD, Owen DOFFRIN, Edward HANKINS, James LAMAR,

Giles J. BLEDSOE, Benjamin SMITH, Hawkins CAMPBELL. Signed 22 May 1840 Preston
MITCHEL, Executor. Also Negro man HENRY. Signed 17 Jun 1840 Preston MITCHEL,
Executor. Recorded 14 Jul 1840 E. TATE, clerk.

p. 78   Commissioners REPORT - Aug term 1840. John ESTES, decd. 1 yr support
for Mrs. Polly ESTES, widow, & family. Mentions: Joseph W. PATTERSON in IN;
report of 21 Mar last has been lost. Signed John EASTERLY, John RICE 31 Jul
1840. Recorded 13 Aug 1840 E. TATE, clerk.

        Settlement - Nancy SMITH, Exectrix for Josiah SMITH, decd. 25 Aug 1840.
Mentions: last settlement 20 Sep 1839; Owen DYER; Booker DYER; John LAMDON; E.
TATE; Joseph HILL, Dpt Shff taxes 1840. Recorded 15 Sep 1840 E. TATE, clerk.

p. 79   Settlement - Ryal JENNINGS, Adm for William JENNINGS, decd. 25 Aug 1840
Mentions: sales 5 Apr 1838; Lewis A. GARRET, Clerk & Master 21 Oct 1839;
LAFFERTY & WHITESIDE; P. L. COCKE; Hugh JONES; John COCKE, Atto; Andrew McGINNIS:
James & Wm WILLIAMS; E. WILLIAMS; Jesse EVANS; Jacob SHOULTZ; Hugh HOUSTON; John
P. JENNINGS; N. A. SENTER; H. GRAHAM, James FULKERSON; Elizabeth JENNINGS; Shff
THOMASON tax 1839; C. McANALLY; Thomas WHITESIDE, R. CARDWELL; C. BULL;
Archibald McCOY; Thos S. COCKE; G. W. CHURCHWELL, Atto; D. WATSON; Robt MITCHEL;
Ab McCONNEL; COCKE & MASSINGILL; Saml DUNBAR; Wm QUEEN; R. LOYD tax 1837; E.
THOMASON tax 1838; Wm RUCKER; Pleasant JINNINGS; Law Suit at Kingston; Martin
CLEVELAND; Orvil RICE; RICE & McFARLAND to Thos WHITESIDE; Thos LATHIM, Constable
Ethelred WILLIAMS; George W. JINNINGS. Recorded 15 Sep 1840 E. TATE, clerk.

p. 80   Settlement - James MOORE, Executor for Thomas HENDERSON, decd. 27 Aug
1840. Mentions: sale & hiring of NEGROES recorded 10 Dec 1838; Reuben LONG &
Malin HARRIS; Elisha THOMASON, Shff, taxes 1839; E. WILLIAMS; Richard BRAGG;
taxes 1840; E. TATE; David McANALLY; Nathan GRAY; Wesley MILLAR; Wm Y. HENDERSON
a legatee; Louisa HENDERSON a legatee; Wm G. JONES; Pleasant WHITLOW; Charles
JONES. Recorded 15 Sep 1840 E. TATE, clerk.

p. 81   Guradian Report - Robert HUDDLESTONE, Guardian of Campbell WILLIAMS.
From last report 3 Sep 1839 to Aug 1840. Mentions: Dpt Shff HILL taxes 1840;
S & M SHIELDS & Co.; Allen HURST, Adm for William WILLIAMS, decd; Jacob BUTCHER.
Recorded 15 Sep 1840 E. TATE, clerk.

p. 82   Will - Rufus M. SCRUGGS, decd. Wife Mary SCRUGGS, lawful children
(not named), father-in-law Jeremiah JARNAGIN and bro John SCRUGGS, Executors.
Not signed or dated. Wit: Mahala WILLIAMSON, William WILLIAMSON. Recorded
17 Sep 1840 E. TATE, clerk.

        Inventory - 10 Sep 1840. Jarrett NORRIS, decd. Signed William NORRIS,
Adm. Recorded 27 Oct 1840 E. TATE, clerk.

p. 83   Inventory - Rufus M. SCRUGGS, decd. Mentions: Negroes HAMILTON (age
c17), CHARLES (age c23), POLLY (age c23), ANDREW (age c6), WESLEY (age c4); Levi
SATTERFIELD; B. F. McFARLAND; Chesley JARNAGIN; Wm G. EATON; Shady Grove; George
W. MYERS; Jacob SMITH; Robert R. DUFF; George ATKINS; Chesley RAY; John INGLE;
John EDINGTON; John PALMER; George EZELL; Edward SHIPLEY, left the country; Wm
P. JONES. Signed 2 Oct 1840 Jeremiah JARNAGIN, John SCRUGGS, Executors.
Recorded 27 Oct 1840 E. TATE, clerk.

p. 84   Inventory - William ACUFF, decd.   29 Aug 1840.   Signed John D. ACUFF, Adm. Recorded 27 Oct 1840 E. TATE, clerk.

        Account of Sale - 31 Aug 1840.   William ACUFF, decd.   Mentions: Lucinda ACUFF, James L. ACUFF, Thomas ACUFF, Asa ROUTH, Asa EVANS, Ezekill HARREL, Alford BUNCH, Simeon ACUFF, John CAMPBELL, Benjamin BRANSON, Armested BUNCH, John CLARK, Reuben WOLFINBARGER, Pleasant D. WATSON, James L. ACUFF, David KITTS, Frances WHALEN, Ezekill P. HARRELL, Isaac PHILLIPS, Jacob VANDA-GRIFF, Martin CLEVELAND, James DOLTON, Rhodman HARRELL, John CAMPBELL, Anderson ACUFF, James KERBO, William MALLICOAT, Alfred BUNCH, John BRANSON, Samuel RUCKER, Isaac TEAGUE, William WATSON, James JAMES, James PHIPPS, Charles ACUFF, Natheniel BRANSON, John BIRD. Signed John D. ACUFF, Adm. Recorded 27 Oct 1840.

p. 86   Inventory - James WHITLOCK, decd. Mentions: Lewis COATS, Thomas GREEN, John STALSWORTH. Signed G. B. MITCHEL, Adm. Recorded 27 Oct 1840.

p. 87   Account of Sale - James WHITLOCK, decd. Mentions: Isaac HARRIS, Thornton CORUM, Balis E. GAINS, Thomas SMITH, Elisha OWENS, James R. JARNAGIN, James COFFEE, Joel COFFEE, Katherine WHITLOCK, George W. MYERS, James BARTON, Jackson ROAN, Henry ALSUP, Aquilla MITCHEL, Jr., James P. GAINS, Rice COFFEE, Joseph PARROTT, Aquilla MITCHEL, William AUSTIN, Samuel CRAIN, Eliza DAVIS, G. B. MITCHEL, Elisha OWENS, Jubal MITCHEL, John STALSWORTH, Martin MILLAR, Isaac DANIEL, Harvey MALONE, William TILLET, James HINES, Preston WHITLOCK, William WILLIAMS, Solomon TROGDON. Signed 20 Aug 1840 G. B. MITCHEL, Adm. Recorded 27 Oct 1840 E. TATE, clerk.

p. 89   Additional Account of Sale - Robert GAINS, decd. Signed 5 Oct 1840 B. E. & R. C. GAINS, Executors. Recorded 27 Oct 1840 E. TATE, clerk.

p. 90   Guardian Report - James LATHIM, Guardian for Martha & E. LATHIM minor heirs of John LATHIM, decd.   8 Oct 1840. Mentions: last report 2 Nov 1839; tuition of Adaline, Mr. KIDWELL, teacher; board at Mr. GILL's. Recorded 27 Oct 1840 E. TATE, clerk.

        Will - George MOODY, decd.   Wife Rachel; my man LEWIS; all my children now living (not named); my three little grchildren of Jane JONES; my sons John & William M. MOODY, Executors. Signed May 1840 George MOODY. Wit: M. N. JEFFRES, Elizabeth x MAYES. Recorded 27 Oct 1840 E. TATE, clerk.

p. 91   Commissioners Report - James WHITLOCK, decd. 1 yr support for Widow WITLOCK & family. Signed 19 Aug 1840 Aquilla MITCHEL, Henry ALSUP, Solomon TROGDON, Comms. Recorded 10 Nov 1840 E. TATE, clerk.

p. 92   Inventory - George MOODY, decd. Mentions: Moses MILLAR, M. N. JEFFERES, Henry SOLOMON, John IVY, David HORNER, Joel PHILIPS, Moses HODGES, William ROACH, Gabriel ROGERS, Wm M. MOODY. Signed 24 Oct 1840 John MOODY, Wm M. MOODY, Executors. Recorded 10 Nov 1840 E. TATE, clerk.

        Account of Sale - George MOODY, decd. Mentions: William DANIEL, Henry MAYES, George M. LACY, Thomas K. HOWEL, George P. MOODY, Wm E. COCKE, Isaac DANIEL, Jeroam JEFFERES, Edward TATE, Jr., Washington McNEICE, Isaac PHELIPS, Pharoah PRICE, John COCKE, Jr., John B. ELLEDGE, Joshua KIDWELL,

John COCKE, Samuel THORNBURG, Henry M. MOODY, Godwin MAYES, James LACY, Robert
CARDWELL, Jr., George LACY, Hugh McNEICE. Signed 24 Oct 1840 John MOODY, Wm M.
MOODY, Executors. Recorded 11 Nov 1840 E. TATE, clerk.

p. 93   Noncupative Will - George BURKET, decd, on 18 Jul 1840. His mother
Mary BURKET entire estate. Signed and witnessed 10 Jul 1840 Absalom CAMRON,
John CLARK, Price CODY. Recorded 11 Nov 1840 E. TATE, clerk.

p. 94   Will - Samuel COX, decd. My son Jeremiah COX; my son Samuel COX; my
son Edmond COX; my dau Martha GLOSSUP wife of William GLOSSUP; my dau Margaret
WHITE wife of James WHITE; my son Harmon COX; my grdau Priscilla COX dau of my
son Harmon COX; Menritary Washington BLACK son of Peggy BLACK (no relation
given); heirs of my son John COX; my son Levi COX; my son Solomon COX and his
heirs; land purchased from William SMITH; son Solomon COX, Executor. Signed 17
Feb 1838 Samuel x COX. Wit: Elisha BULL, John x WALKER, Thomas REECE, Geo F.
GILLASPIE. Recorded 11 Nov 1840 E. TATE, clerk.

p. 95   Commissioners Report - Oct term 1840. Wm F. WILLIAMS, decd. 1 yr
support for widow & family. Signed 23 Oct 1840 N. A. SENTER, Thos McBROOM, Geo
W. MATLOCK, Comms. Recorded 11 Nov 1840 E. TATE, clerk.

          Guardian Report - G. B. MITCHEL, Guardian of Russel SMALLWOOD from 1st
Mon of Feb 1837 to 28 Nov 1840. Recorded 16 Dec 1840 E. TATE, clerk.

p. 96   Guardian Report & Settlement - G. B. MITCHEL, Guardian of the minor
heirs of John PERRIN, decd. 28 Nov 1840. Mentions: last report 1st Mon of Feb
1837; Katherine PERRIN only surviving heir; coffin for Jesse PERRIN an heir;
taxes 1837 through 1840. Recorded 16 Dec 1840 E. TATE, clerk.

          Guardian Report - 28 Nov 1840. Aquilla MITCHEL, Guardian of Elizabeth
ARMSTRONG. Mentions: last report 6 Oct 1838. Recorded 16 Dec 1840 E. TATE.

p. 97   Account of Sale - Jarrett NORRIS, decd. Mentions: George NORRIS, Blain
NORRIS, John SATTERFIELDS. Signed 5 Dec 1840 William NORRIS, Sr., Adm.
Recorded 28 Dec 1840 E. TATE, clerk.

          Inventory - 7 Dec 1840. Isaac ROUTH, decd. Mentions: John ROUTH,
Rhodeman HERRELL, Patten HOWEL, Hester TEAGUE, Stephen ROUTH, Hezekiah ROUTH,
Hugh ROUTH. Signed Stephen ROUTH, Adm. Recorded 6 Jan 1841 E. TATE, clerk.

p. 99   Account of Sale - Isaac ROUTH, decd. Mentions: Asa ROUTH, Simeon
ACUFF, Hester TEAGUE, Isaac TEAGUE, James ACUFF, Thomas ACUFF, David KITTS,
Armsted BUNCH, Wm LEFFEW, Michael FARMER, James FIPPS, Alfred BUNCH, James
PHIPPS, Washington HARRIS, Isaac PHILLIPS. Signed 7 Dec 1840 Stephen ROUTH,
Adm. Recorded 6 Jan 1841 E. TATE, clerk.

p. 100   Inventory - Wm F. WILLIAMS, decd. Signed 7 Dec 1840 Samuel GILL, Wm
WILLIAMS, Adms. Recorded 6 Jan 1841 E. TATE, clerk. List of notes belonging
to Estate: Thos BRUCHILL, Winston PARTON, Lawson A. R. LONG, James IVY, Frank
RAY (?), Matthew WILLIAMS, Robt R. CORBIN, Moses DUNSMORE, James LYNN, Lewis
BELL, Coonrod STALY, Levi CAMPBELL, Jesse IRVINS, Joseph SLAGLE. Signed and
recorded same as above.

p. 101   Account of Sale - William F. WILLIAMS, decd. Sold on 12 mos time to hiest bidder 12 Nov 1840. Mentions: E. WILLIAMS, G. W. MATLOCK, Marcus DANIEL, Robt MITCHEL, John MAYES, Warham EASLEY, Levi LONG, Thomas BURCHIL, Edward TATE, Thomas COCKE, John LONG, R. M. YANCY, Jerre HANY, Thos GILL, Wm E. COCKE, Ann K. WILLIAMS, F. B. COBB, Jacob NOE, Josiah HOLDER, Richard PEMBERTON, Jacob GODWIN, J. L. KLINE, hire of NEGROES named LEWIS, TOM, SILAS, DICK, GEORGE, ALFRED, PHILLIS plus 2 boys, 2 girls and 2 children. Signed William WILLIAMS, Samuel GILL, Adm., 7 Dec 1840. Recorded 6 Jan 1841 E. TATE, clerk.

p. 103   Will - William DYER, decd. George Washington DYER, my bro; Negroes ANDREW & BETSY; my bro Willie B. DYER; my bro-in-law Jesse BEELAR; my sis Polly BEELAR; Mariah McCUBAN or her legal heirs; my father George DYER's will; my bro Willie DYER, Executor. Signed 12 Dec 1840 William DYER. Wit: Martin CLEVELAND, Elizabeth CLARK, Anderson ACUFF. Recorded 7 Jan 1841 E. TATE, clerk.

p. 104   Settlement - Peter OGAN, Adm for John OGAN, decd. 21 Dec 1840. Mentions: Jacob SHOUTZ; Hannah OGAN, widow; John EPPERSON who intermarried with Phany OGAN a legatee; Wm E. COCKE; Hugh GRAHAM; Jane CLOUD; Wm M. MOODY; Hiram REED; William CLOUD, Dpt Shff; C. McANALLY; George BULL. Recorded 7 Jan 1841.

Additional Account of Sale - George MOODY, decd. Mentions: M. N. JEFFRES, James BOWERS, James LACY. Signed 8 Dec 1840 Wm M. MOODY, Executor. Recorded 7 Jan 1841 E. TATE, clerk.

p. 105   Settlement - Joseph HILL, Executor for Fanny DYER, decd. 1 Jan 1841. Mentions: S & M SHIELDS; G. H. & G. A. CHEEK; George DYER, Aaron HAMILTON, Benjamin NEELY, Eli DENNIS, Wm SHARP. Recorded 7 Jan 1841 E. TATE, clerk.

Commissioners Report - David WATSON, Joseph CLARK, Albartis ARNWINE, Comms. 1 yr for support of Nancy DOTSON, widow of Samuel DOTSON, decd. Signed David WATSON, Joseph CLARK, Comms. 29 Oct 1840. Recorded 7 Jan 1841 E. TATE.

p. 106   Inventory - Samuel DOTSON, decd. Signed 4 Jan 1841. Joel DOTSON, Adm. Recorded 7 Jan 1841 E. TATE, clerk.

Account of Sale - Samuel DOTSON, decd. Mentions: Samuel DOTSON, Nancy DOTSON, Benj. BRANSON, Wm DOTSON, Pleasant KIRBY, Alfred BUNCH, Levin WALLER, Samuel RUCKER, Pleasant KERBO, James NASH, John DOTSON, James A. HOWETH, John WALLER, Ryal JENNINGS, Rhodeman HARREL, Ralph SHELTON, David BRANSON, Edward McGINNIS, Harred HOPSON, Isaac BULLEN. Signed Joel DOTSON, Adm. Recorded 7 Jan 1841.

p. 107   Guardian Report - Thomas DENNIS, Guardian of minor heirs of John DENNIS, decd. 20 Dec 1840. Mentions: last report 24 Dec 1838; Wm P. JONES; D. M. McCOLLUM; Cazwell DENNIS saddle for Cynthia Ann DENNIS a ward on 16 Dec 1840. Recorded 7 Jan 1841 E. TATE, clerk.

p. 108   Guardian Report - Benjamin BRAY, Guardian for Polly OGAN. 19 Dec 1840. Mentions: last report 5 Mar 1838; Robt LOYD, Shff, taxes 1837; H. G. LEA, surveyor; OGAN & PRATHER; McGINNIS & LATHIM; E. THOMASON, Shff, taxes 1389; business of wards for 1835. Recorded 8 Jan 1841 E. TATE, clerk.

p. 109   Account of Sale - 22 Aug 1840. George BURKET, decd. Mentions: James
& Thomas WILLIAMS, Andrew COFFMAN, P. J. JEFFERS, Daniel EATON, Isaac DANIEL,
Absalom CAMRON, Wm E. COCKE, Cornelius GOWFORTH, William ROACH, Isaac PRATT,
John GRAY, Elisha LEFFEW, Joseph DANIEL, Wm SMITH, Pleasant WILLIAMS, E. D.
SUNDERLAND, Jacob KLINE, James SUNDERLAND, George W. McNIECE, John GREENLEA, M.
N. JEFFERS, Isaac PHILLIPS, John BIRD, William HAMMER. Signed 22 Dec 1840 James
SUNDERLAND, Executor. Recorded 8 Jan 1841 E. TATE, clerk.

p. 110   Second Account of Sale - Edward CHURCHMAN, decd. Mentions: Lewis
COLLET, John MITCHEL, Jefferson NANCE, Benjamin SMITH, Hawkins CAMPBELL, Joab
PERRIN, G. B. MITCHEL. Signed 2 Nov 1840 Preston MITCHEL, Executor. Recorded
8 Jan 1841 E. TATE, clerk.

        Settlement - Edward TATE, Executor of Ruth STIFFY, decd. 28 Jan 1841.
Mentions: last settlement 2 Feb 1838; E. THOMASON taxes on NEGROES for 1838;
Isaac DANIEL, Sarah SMITH, Charles CAMPBELL vs E. TATE; COCKE & McFARLAND; James
MALLICOAT who intermarried with Elizabeth GRAY a legatee; James MAYES who intermarried with Louisa GRAY a legatee; John S. GRAY a legatee; Pleasant WILLIAMS who
intermarried with Jane GRAY a legatee; James MALLICOAT, Guardian of Amanda GRAY
a legatee; Sarah GRAY a legatee; E. L. TATE who intermarried with Mary Ann GRAY
a legatee; E. TATE, Guardian of William M. GRAY a legatee. Signed Stephen J.
GODSEY, John T. CURL, Comms. Recorded 1 Feb 1841 E. TATE, clerk.

p. 112   Guardian Report - Examination of the Guardian Report of Edward TATE,
Guardian of William M. GRAY from 1 Nov 1837 time of last report. E. TATE being
Clerk of County Court. Mentions: Estate of Ruth STIFFY, decd; cash, rents,
hiring of NEGROES 1837 to 1841; RICE & McFARLAND; James & Wm WILLIAMS; Wm M.
MOODY; Wm BURGESS; Pleasant WILLIAMS; James MILLICOAT; Jacob KLINE; A. P. & D.
GREEN; John DUNAVANT for making Jane's coat; Isaac DANIEL; taxes 1836 to 1839;
E. L. TATE; Archabald AUSTIN; E. THOMASON, Shff, taxes 1840. Signed 28 Jan 1841
Stephen J. GODSEY, John T. CURL, Comms. Recorded 2 Feb 1841 E. TATE, clerk.

p. 113   Guardian Report - Examination of the Guradian Report of Edward TATE,
Guardian of the minor heirs of Thomas CHURCHMAN, decd. E. TATE being Clerk of
County Court. Mentions: cash received of Massy COCKRUM, Adm of Edward CHURCH-
MAN, decd, 1 Jan 1838; William FREEMAN; Richard GREEN. Signed 28 Jan 1841
Stephen J. GODSEY, John T. CURL, Comms. Recorded 2 Feb 1841 E. TATE, clerk.

p. 114   Will - John HILL, decd. 5 Feb 1840. Wife Nancy; my children Abel,
Pheba & Nancy all that I allowed them at their marriage heretofore; land on
DYER's line; my son William Ramsey comes to age; my dau Penina Pallestine;
Negroes PHILIP & STEPHEN; friends Stephen FROST & John HUBBS, Executors.
Signed John HILL. Wit: William HUBBS, Oliver FIELDS, William HILL, Abel HILL.
Recorded 23 Mar 1841 E. TATE, clerk.

p. 115   Inventory - William WILLSON, decd. Signed 3 Apr 1840 John A. McKINNY,
Julian FRAZIER, Adms. No recording date.

        Account of Sale - 23 & 24 Oct 1840. Wm H. WILLSON, decd. John A.
McANALLY, Julian FRAZIER, Adms. Mentions: Mary A. WILLSON, Joseph JACKSON, Wm
F. MILLS, James L. TALBOT, Benjamin SMITH, S. C. RENTFROW, Jas WILLSON, Martin
MILLAR, Wm MYNATT, Henry BROWN, Edward HANKINS, Thos HUMES, Wm TURNER, Wm

MERCHANT, Archy McKINNY, Jos MYNATT, And. GRAHAM, Steph. M. SKAGGS, James S. TALBOT, C. H. WILLSON, H. B. LEA, M. HANKINS. Recorded 24 Mar 1841 E. TATE.

p. 117   Account of Sale - Property of George Washington DYER minor heir of George DYER, decd. Sold 27 & 28 Jan 1841. Mentions: Lewis M. ELLIS, Robert FRY, Willie DYER, John COFFMAN, Anderson ACUFF, James HOUCETH, James DAULTON, Joseph WOLFINBARGER, Jesse F. BEELAR, John CHANDLER, Jr., Benjamin FRY, Pleasant WATSON, Jacob BEELAR, John CLEVELAND, Pleasant STARNES, David BRANSON, James GRAY, Alfred NOE, Asa ROUTH, Nicholas NICELY, Jackson DYER, William WILLIAMS, Elijah JONES, John NANCE, Washington HARRIS. Signed Martin CLEVELAND, Guardian. Recorded 24 Mar 1841 E. TATE, clerk.

p. 118   Settlement - John B. CREUES, Adm for William CREUES, decd. 6 Feb 1841. Mentions: B. F. McFARLAND, A. P. & D. GREEN, Jacob KLINE; Wm PHILIPS; Abraham McCONNEL, Constable; John JOICE, Caleb GIPSON; taxes 1838-40. Recorded 24 Mar 1841 E. TATE, clerk.

          Guardian Report - Jesse F. BEELAR, Guardian for minor heirs of David BEELAR, decd. Mentions: last report 3 Feb 1840; Jacob BEELAR; 4 wards. Recorded 24 Mar 1841 E. TATE, clerk.

p. 119   Account of Sale - John LEBOW, decd. 1st sale 20 Jun 1840. Mentions: William GRAY, Jr., Albert SULLENBARGER, George W. MATLOCK, Peter BEAR, Isaac LEBOW, John SHELTON, A. R. SULLENBARGER, John HARVILLE. 2nd sale 21 & 22 Oct 1840. Mentions: Katherine LEBOW, Larkin JOHNSON, Jacob FOREST, Jacob FOUST, Peter LAMPSEL, George WILLIAMS, William MOORE, Henry LONG, Enoch DAULTON, Ausburn COFFEE, Clem MOORE, Joseph HICKS, John MAYES, Thomas JONES, Cenah LEBOW, Cynthia FORT, John RUCKER, William DAVIS, P. M. SENTER, Reuben LONG, Jackson McANALLY, Jacob LEBOW, William GRAY, Richard STUBBLEFIELD, Burrel BASSETT, John SHELTON, John HOWELL, Jr., David McANALLY, David COLLINS, Lucretia LEBOW, Lucinda LEBOW, Frederick COBB, William GRAY, Jr., Joseph HICKS, Thos WHITESIDE, James WILLIAMS, David HARRIS, Octovis YOE (?), Negro woman JUDA, Negro man SAM, Negro girls SARAH, MARTHA, JANE & MATILDA. Signed William GRAY, Executor. Recorded 13 Apr 1841 E. TATE, clerk.

p. 125   Inventory - 21 Dec 1840. B. C. McCRARY, decd. Mentions book accompts on: Amos SHARP, Wm HAMILTON, John COX, Sr., Wm CARTER, Lewis HARRELL, Jno F. HUDDLESTON, Carlisle HAYNES, Richard WADE, Wm McFETRIDGE, Christopher WYRICK, Vincent BAYLY, John LANMON, Jeremiah SAVAGE, Thos WILLSON, Wm WAGGONER, Sr., David PERKEY, Abel DIAL, Wm COLVIN, Wm ROGERS, Nancy ELY, Joseph WYRICK, Robert CARDIN, John HILL, John HICKLE, Coleman LEMORE, Ephriam W. McBEE, John TURNER, Abner SMITH, James CEAK (?), Isaac HAMPTON, Andrew J. CARTER, Stephen WILLIS, Jessee BUTCHER, Hiram WYRICK, Thomas HARDIN, John MONROW, George FIELDS, Elias WARRICK, James SELVAGE, Jeremiah SELVAGE, Sterling HAYNES, John MATTHEWS, Elisha SAVAGE, Gold CARDIN, Pheba McCUBBINS, James LAY, John MOORE, Wm LAY, Henry PRICHARD, John WILLIS, Dye TUCKER, Frederick COFFMAN, Ira NEEDHAM, George McCRARY, Thomas MORTON, Benjamin SMITH, A. HURST, Wm SHARP, Daniel CAPPS, Valentine WEYMIRES, John COLVIN, Joel SHARP, George TURNER, Joseph HILL, Nancy CARTER, John CONN, Charles BERRY, John McBEE, Robert HUDDLESTON, Wm GREEN, Daniel McPHETRIDGE, Isaac BUTCHER, Martin COOK, Wm SNODGRASS, John JOHNSON, Isaac SMITH, Mary WILLIS, Loyd HITCH, Joshua GRIST, Andrew GRIST, Robert McBEE, Wm CARTER, Narcissa COX, Ezekiel DOUGHTRY, Levisa WILLIS, Granvill COX, Valentine MOULDER,

Pryor Lee McBEE, John A. BLACKBURN, Jacob CAPPS, Wm WAGGONER, Wm DAVIS, Joab
CAPPS, Benj. PIKE, Robert SMITH, Israel McBEE. List of notes: Isaac L. WILLSON,
Robert CARDIN, A. HURST, John SUTTERFIELD, G. H. McBEE, A HOPKINS, Lewis HERREL,
Samuel WILLSON, John SWAFFORD, James SEMORE, Roddy SAVAGE, Andrew GRIST, John
McCARTER, John RICE, Hiram WYRICK, George FIELDS, Abner SMITH, David PARKER,
Joel SMITH, Edward MERRIT, Robert McBEE, Jonathan POWEL, Andrew A. ELLIS, Thomas
SMITH, James LAY, Thomas BLACKBURN, William MERRIT, Elijah COLVIN, James SMALL,
Asce TOLLIVER, Wm McPHETRIDGE, Zachariah McHONE, George ROSE, Wm GEAR, Thomas
SUMACH, George McCRARY, David & Wm DEVENPORT, Wm HURST, Wm McWILLIAMS, Levi
MARTIN, R. HANSFORD. Signed Calvin HUDDLESTON, Adm, 21 Feb 1841. Recorded 14
Apr 1841.

p. 129   Account of Sale - 22 Dec 1840. C. B. McCRARY, decd. Mentions: Wm P.
YADON, D. F. HUDDLESTONE, Sml WILLSON, Jno F. HUDDLESTON, Ezra BUCKNER, Robert
McBEE, Elisha SAVAGE, John SMITH, Wm P. BUCKNER, Wm COCKE, Sr., Owen DYER, Pheba
McCUBBINS, Alnd. HAMILTON, Jr., Lecta McCRARY, Hastin BUTCHER, A. HURST, Wm
WAGONER, Robert HUDDLESTONE, John McCRARY, Wm DAVIS, Jr., George McCRARY, James
SELVEDGE, Wm HAMILTON, Wm COLVIN, Wm LAY, Sr., George W. C. MORE, James SMITH,
John BEELAR, J. B. BUTCHER, G. B. CARDIN, David EVANS, Coalman C. MORE, Jas COOK,
Jno TURNER, David PARKEY, Levina SENTOR, John WILLIS, Henderson WALLIS, Isaac
HAYNER, Thomas BLACKBURN, Robt McBEE, Leety McCRAY, Joseph HILL, Willie COOK,
John WILLIS, Joseph YADON, Edward BRADEN, Overton W. SENTOR, Isaac CONDRY,
Calvin HUDDLESTONE, John WALTERS, John COX, James SAVAGE, Jno COX, Carlisle
HAYNES, Wm SNODGRASS, Martin COOK, Nancy SHELTON, Eli SHELTON, Jno CYRUS, Aaron
HAMILTON, Peter SHARP, John BAKER, Wesly BUTCHER, Joth. JACKSON, Jesse WAGGONER,
David EVANS, Jno WESTERFIELD, Levi DENNIS, Hugh PETRES, Vincent RALY, Lewis (?)
MONROW, Arch HALE, Robt G. McCUBBINS, Isaac SMITH, Thos HARDIN, Hiram WYRICK,
Calvin HICKLE, Wyley BUTCHER, Joel SMITH, Ezra BUCKNER, Pleasant COOK, Lewis
WHITENER, P. S. CHESHIRE, Noble HOUSLEY, James JOHNSON, Richd WADE, Asa TOLLIVER,
John BLACKBURN, Jefferson WYRICK, Jordan HUNLEY, J. E. WARWICK. Signed Calvin
HUDDLESTONE, Adm. Recorded 19 Apr 1841 E. TATE, clerk.

p. 136   Inventory - William DYER, decd. Signed Willie DYER, Executor. Recorded 20 Apr 1841 E. TATE, clerk.

        Account of Sale - William DYER, decd. Mentions: Benj. GRIFFIN,
Pleasant JINNINGS, James DYER, Isaac BEELAR, James DOULTON, Nicholas NICELY,
Robert FRY, John BOWER, Joseph CLARK, Jos WOLFINBARGER, James GRAY, Pleasant
STARNS, Jesse BEELAR, Jacob BEELAR, Martin CLEVELAND, Charlton DYER, John CLARK,
David DOULTON, Andrew BOWER, Pleasant WATSON, John NANCE, Edward CLARK, Tandy
WOLFINBARGER, Thomas MAJORS, John COFFMAN, Elijah LEFFEW, Isaac PHILIPS, James
MALLICOAT, Asa ROUTH, James STARNES, Benj. FRY, Alfred NOEL, James KERBO,
Anderson ACUFF, James BROCK, Elizabeth KERBY. Signed Willie DYER, Executor.
Recorded 20 Apr 1841 E. TATE, clerk.

p. 137   Inventory - Saml COX, decd. Signed Solomon COX, Executor. Recorded
20 Apr 1841 E. TATE, clerk.

p. 138   Account of Sale - Sold 6 Mar 1841. Samuel COX, decd. Mentions: Henry
BOATMAN, John WALKER, Willie REECE, Jeremiah COX. Signed Solomon COX, Executor.
Recorded 20 Apr 1841 E. TATE, clerk.

p. 139   Settlement - Isaac HARRIS & Preston MITCHELL, Executors for Samuel RAY, decd. 6 Mar 1841. Mentions: Hardin CAMRON, James JAMES, RICE & McFARLAND, Robt RAY, William KIDWELL, Levi SATTERFIELD, Wm McDANIEL, Thos & Sml SMITH, A. BLACK-BURN, Aquilla MITCHEL, Dr. William E. COCKE, J. H. DYER, Henry CARBACK who inter-married with Ann RAY a legatee, Wm M. MITCHEL who intermarried with Eliza RAY a legatee. Recorded 20 Apr 1841 E. TATE, clerk.

p. 140   Second Settlement - Balis E. & R. C. GAINS, Executors of Robert GAINS, decd. 9 Mar 1841. Mentions: settlement 4 May 1839; additional sales 3 Feb 1840 & 5 Oct 1840; S & M SHIELDS; P. MITCHEL, Dpt Shff taxes 1839; FRAZIER & McKINNY goods for minor heirs; Hugh A. DUFF; James P. GAINS, Mitchel NEMO. Recorded 20 Apr 1841 E. TATE, clerk.

p. 141   Guardian Report - Robert CARDWELL, Sr., Guardian of minor heirs of Andrew CHAMBERLAIN, decd. 3 Apr 1840. Mentions: last report 7 Dec 1838; rents 1838-39; taxes 1839-40; Wm T. TATE & Co.; Charles GOWFORTH, Philip COMBS for schooling; John C. TATE for schooling. Signed Robert CARDWELL, Guardian. Recorded 22 Apr 1841 E. TATE, clerk.

p. 142   Guardian Settlement - Thomas DENNIS, former Guardian for minor heirs of John DENNIS, decd. 26 Mar 1841. Mentions: last report 21 Dec 1840; William SHARP late Guardian; Thos McBROOM present Guardian. Recorded 22 Apr 1841.

          Guardian Report - Wm SHARP, Guardian of minor heirs of John DENNIS, decd. 19 Mar 1841. Mentions: former Guardian Thomas DENNIS; heirs chose Thos McBROOM their Guardian. Signed Wm SHARP. Recorded 22 Apr 1841 E. TATE, clerk.

p. 143   Guardian Report - William SHARP, Guardian for minor heirs of William CHEEK, decd. 19 Mar 1841. Mentions: rents 1838 to 1841. Signed Wm SHARP, Guardian. Recorded 22 Apr 1841 E. TATE, clerk.

          Commissioners Report - Stephen FROST, John FROST & Jedidah FIELDS, Comms. 1 yr provisions for Widow DYER & children of George DYER, decd. Recorded 22 Apr 1841 E. TATE, clerk.

p. 144   Second Settlement - William DENNIS, Adm for Elizabeth SATTERFIELD, decd. Mentions: last settlement 15 Aug 1839; James SALLING, Constable; burying expenses for Calvin SATTERFIELD an heir. Signed 12 Mar 1841. Recorded 22 Apr 1841 E. TATE, clerk.

          Commissioners Report - Nancy HILL widow of John HILL, decd. 1 yr supplies. Signed 3 Mar 1841 Wm SHARP, Mark MONROW, Wm MARTIN, Comms. Recorded 22 Apr 1841 E. TATE, clerk.

p. 145   Will - Matilda CHURCHMAN, decd. My dear mother Eda CHURCHMAN; father's estate; my sister Hannah BRADLEY; note on John BRADLEY; my sister Rabeca PERRIN; note on Joab PERRIN; my niece Matilda PERRIN; my niece Cynthia MITCHEL; my niece Jane MITCHEL; Thomas LAMAR, Executor. Signed 6 Mar 1841 Matilda x CHURCHMAN. Wit: Thos NUGIN, James FURGASON. Recorded 22 Apr 1841 E. TATE, clerk.

          Settlement - Commissioners of Bean Station Turnpike Road. Mentions: C. W. LATHIM, gatekeeper; Jno P. JENNINGS, gatekeeper; Joseph RICH, overseer;

Joshua HAMILTON, Claborne Co., overseer; Wm HA_____TON; Benj. S_____; John
LAFFERTY; C. McANALLY. Signed W. T. TATE, John EASLEY, Jacob GODWIN, Comms.
Apr 1841. Recorded 6 May 1841, E. TATE, clerk.

p. 147   Inventory - John HILL, decd. Signed Stephen FROST, John HUBBS, Executors. Recorded 8 May 1841 E. TATE, clerk.

        Inventory - Nancy HILL wife of John HILL, decd. 31 Mar 1841. Signed
Stephen FROST, John HUBBS, Executors. Recorded 8 May 1841 E. TATE, clerk.
($52.12 on hand of which $6.00 is counterfect.)

p. 148   Inventory - John HILL, decd. Mentions notes on: GOLDMAN, Joseph HILL,
Henry FROST, Joel FIELDS, Samuel WAGNER, Robert MARTIN, Pleasant HAMMOCK, Matthia
NORRIS, George ROBINSON, William FLETCHER, Thomas SMITH, Jonathan DIAL, William
DANIEL, Alburtis GRAHAM, Samuel WYRICK, Abel HILL, Jesse HILL, William HILL,
Joseph SMITH, Philip WYRICK, Hugh VANCE, Joseph DENNIS, John HAMMOCK, Jr.,
Edward SHIPLEY, David ELKINS, Wm HILL & James VITTITO. Accompts on: James
PHIPS, Cardwell LEAMORE, David SELLERS, Solomon SKEAGS, Julius HACKER, Joshua
WASHAM, Thomas SMITH, John DENNIS, Sr., Thomas NORRIS, Jr., Michael HILL,
Isaac DAMEWOOD, John PHIPPS, John HAMMOCK, Washington LEAMORE, Mat HUNTER,
Mitchel NICELY, Renard BURNET, Amos EVANS, Benjamin SMITH, Dickson BREWER,
George ATKINS, William SHARP, James VITTITO, James McCUBBINS, John SMITH, Benj.
EDGE, George LEAMORE, Joseph HILL, Sr., Pryor DYER, John HICKLE, Thomas McMULLIN,
Michael GOLDMAN, William HILL, Abner DIAL, James DYER, Sr., William WILLIS,
Greenberry DEDERIDGE, Richard CARDWELL. Signed Stephen FROST, John HUBBS,
Executors. Recorded 8 May 1841 E. TATE, clerk.

p. 149   Account of Sale - John HILL, decd. Mentions: Wm T. CARDIN, Carter
DOLTEN, G. B. CARDIN, Clabourn JOHNSEN, James DYER, Pleasant JENNINGS, Robert
FRY, Joseph KITTS, Levi MONROW, Saml SHIELDS, Sterling CHESNEY, A. T. DYER,
James VITTITO, Fred COFFMAN, Calvin HICKLE, Joseph WILLIAMS, Jackson DYER, Robert
HUDDLESTON, John McCRARY, Abel HILL, J. F. HUDDLESTONE, Owen DYER, Robt HILL,
Pleasant STARNES, Martin CLEVELAND, Joel FIELDS, David COOK, Wm DENNIS, James
HUBBS, Wm HICKLE, Nathaniel POPEJOY, Wm HUBBS, Isaac PHILLIPS, John FROST, David
PARKEY, Lewis ELLIS, Wm HILL, Nancy HILL, Pryor H. DYER, Wm SHARP, John SAWYERS,
G. W. VITTITO, Levi DENNIS. Signed Stephen FROST, John HUBBS, Executors.
Recorded 8 May 1841 E. TATE, clerk.

p. 152   Guardian Report - Elizabeth RIGGS, Guardian of minor heirs of Nenian
RIGGS, decd. 7 Apr 1841. Mentions: last report 20 May 1839; Henry BOATMAN,
Adm of Nenian RIGGS, decd; Elizabeth RIGGS & Keziah RIGGS youngest wards.
Signed Elizabeth x RIGGS, Guardian. Recorded 8 May 1841 E. TATE, clerk.

p. 153   Settlement - Hughs W. TAYLOR & E. A. TAYLOR, Executors for Hughs O.
TAYLOR, decd. Mentions: Elizabeth TAYLOR, widow; Willis GRANTHAM; COCKE,
ARMSTRONG & CO.; Wm DONALDSON; George W. TAYLOR a legatee; Coleman H. WITT who
intermarried with Rachel TAYLOR a legatee; George WITT who intermarried with
Amelie TAYLOR a legatee; Elka A. TAYLOR a legatee; minor heirs; Levina BOAT-
WRIGHT a legatee; Amanda TAYLOR a legatee; George G. TAYLOR a legatee; George
W. TAYLOR a legatee. Signed 27 Apr 1841. Recorded 8 May 1841 E. TATE, clerk.

p. 154   Guardian Report - Elizabeth HODGES, Guardian of the minor heirs of Eli

HODGES, decd. Mentions: John M. HODGES & Henry HOLSTEIN, Adms; John WARD; Eli HODGES a ward; Jacob E. HODGES a ward; schooling from John WARD; schooling from Levina WELLS. Signed Elizabeth x HODGES, Guardian. Recorded 9 Jun 1841 E. TATE.

p. 155   Settlement - Clabourn W. LATHIM, Adm of John LATHIM, decd.   28 May 1841. Mentions: sale 19 Jan 1839; McGINNIS & McCOY; William O. WINSTON; Andrew McGINNIS; Wm HARREL; Hamilton EVANS; Wm HIPSHEAR; Joseph McGINNIS; Dicy NASH; C. M. McANALLY; Peter BUNDEN; James LATHIM, Sr.; Wm D. NELSON; Wm BARNARD; John OLLIVER, Sr., John OLIVER, Jr.; A. P. & D. GREEN; Jacob SHOULTZ: Samuel BUNCH. Recorded 9 Jun 1841 E. TATE, clerk.

p. 156   Settlement - John P. JINNINGS & Ryal JINNINGS, Executors for Ryal JINNINGS, decd.   17 May 1841. Mentions: McGINNIS & LATHIM; Willis AKIN; Clabourn DOTSON; Pleasant STARNES; J. HUTCHESON; John LEBOW; C. McANALLY; Thos LATHIM, Constable; James & William WILLIAMS; David WATSON; RICE & McFARLAND; John COCKE; Thos WHITESIDE; Levin WALLER; John E. WALLER; Lewis M. ELLIS; COCKE MASSENGILL & Co.; Elisha THOMASON, Shff, taxes 1838-39; Wm MURRY; Thomas McGOLDRICK; A. P. & D. GREEN; John EASLEY; Hugh GRAHAM; Cynthia HAWN; Henry JENNINGS; Jacob HARRIL; Jacob SHOULTZ. Recorded 12 Jun 1841 E. TATE, clerk.

p. 157   Second Settlement - Henry HOLSTEIN & John M. HODGES, Adms of Eli HODGES, decd.   28 May 1841. Mentions: last settlement 29 Apr 1840; Wm E. COCKE, Court Clerk, State vs Richard TAYLOR; Wm HOLTON; Joseph SHANNON; Elizabeth HODGES, Guardian of minor heirs; Lucinda HODGES a legatee; Preston LOYD who intermarried with Mary HODGES a legatee; John M. HODGES a legatee; Adms of Eli HODGES, decd, vs Joseph NOE & C. B. IVY; Thos K. HOWELL; John SPOON; James MALICOAT; Jesse HOWELL; Lewis RIGGS. Recorded 12 Jun 1841 E. TATE, clerk.

p. 158   Inventory - George DYER, decd. Signed 23 Mar 1841 Wm DYER, Adm. Recorded 12 Jun 1841 E. TATE, clerk.

        Account of Sale - George DYER, decd. Mentions: John HUBBS, Pryer H. DYER, Dotia DYER, Wm WYRICK, James DAMEWOOD, Robert HILL, James DYER, Jr., Wm P. McBEE, William WILLSON, Wm HOWERTON, Joel FIELD, George DYER, Jedidah FIELDS, Cox RENTFROW. Signed William DYER, Adm. Recorded 12 Jun 1841 E. TATE, clerk.

p. 159   Additional Account of Sale - John LATHIM, decd. 19 Jan 1839. Mentions: Thomas GAINS, Henry WILLIAMS, Andrew McGINNIS, John, Sr. & James LATHIM, Jr. Signed C. W. LATHIM, Adm. Recorded 12 Jul 1841 E. TATE, clerk.

        Inventory - Matilda CHURCHMAN, decd. Mentions: John BRADLEY, Joab PERRIN, James HANKINS, Wm DICK, John MITCHEL, father's estate. Signed 22 May 1841 John BRADLEY, Executor. Recorded 12 Jun 1841 E. TATE, clerk.

        Guardian Report - James MILLICOAT, Guardian of Amanda GRAY. 15 Jun 1841. Mentions: from 1 Jan 1838 to date; Estate of Ruth STIFFY, decd; hire of SLAVES belonging to John STIFFY, decd. Signed James x MALLICOAT. Recorded 9 Jun 1841 E. TATE, clerk.

p. 160   Settlement - John PIOTT, Adm of John DANIEL, decd. 5 Jun 1841. Mentions: Doctor COCKE; John C. WILLIAMS; D. McANALLY, Dpt Shff, tax 1836; Walter D. COWEN receipt for Crying Sale; John CANNON. Recorded 9 Jul 1841.

p. 161   Commissioners Report - To Amy ROBINSON, widow of George ROBINSON, decd.
1 yr support for her & family from death of husband. Signed 15 May 1841 Wm
SHARP, Wm HICKLE, John LAIN. Recorded 9 Jul 1841 E. TATE, clerk.

Commissioners Report - 1st Mon of May last. Estate of William H. WILL-
SON, decd. 1 yr support for widow who had no family, only a small BLACK BOY.
Signed 7 Jun 1841 Benjamin PECK, Warham EASLEY, B. F. McFARLAND, N. A. SENTER, JP.
Recorded 18 Aug 1841 E. TATE, clerk.

p. 162   Guardian Settlement - James LATHIM, former Guardian of Martha & E.
LATHIM, minor heirs of John LATHIM, decd. 30 Aug 1841. Mentions: last report
8 Oct 1840; 4 NEGROES; A. McGINNIS. Recorded 15 Sep 1841 E. TATE, clerk.

Commissioners Report - A division of Salves belonging to Estate of David
TATE, decd. Last will says: John K. TATE to have AMANDA, David TATE to have
LOUISA, Milton TATE to have THOMAS, Edward TATE to have ALSA, Margaret NOE to
have ROSA, Wm T. TATE to have GEORGE, Saml B. TATE to have ELVIRA. Signed Saml
BUNCH, Wm E. COCKE, Thos McBROOM, Comms. Recorded 15 Sep 1841 E. TATE, clerk.

p. 163   Settlement - William HODGES & Edward HODGES, Adms of Jesse HODGES,
decd. 9 Aug 1841. Mentions: William DANIEL, Executor of Edward DANIEL, decd,
part of a Legacy bequeathed to Anna HODGES; Ethelred WILLIAMS; Jacob KLINE;
Matthew SATTERFIELD; Jesse HODGES; RICE & McFARLAND; Henry GROVE; Thomas LOYD;
taxes 1836-39; James & Jesse HODGES note. Recorded 3 Sep 1841 E. TATE, clerk.

p. 164   Second Settlement - Henry BOATMAN, Adm of Nenian RIGGS, decd. 19 Aug
1841. Mentions: last settlement 31 May 1839; William HARRIS; John EASTERLY;
Eli KEAN; David REECE; Elizabeth RIGGS, Guardian of minor heirs. Recorded 3 Oct
1841 E. TATE, clerk.

Guardian Settlement - Robert HUDDLESTONE, Guardian of Campbell WILLIAMS.
24 Aug 1841. Received of Robert HUDDLESTONE, my Guardian, in full my claims of
the Estate of my father William WILLIAMS. Signed 1 May 1841 Campbell WILLIAMS.
Wit: John McCRARY. Recorded 3 Oct 1841 E. TATE, clerk.

p. 165   Second Settlement - James MOORE, Executor of Thomas HENDERSON, decd.
26 Aug 1841. Mentions: last settlement 27 Aug 1840; E. THOMASON tax 1841; Wm
GODWIN; J & J LAFFERTY; Ruth Ann HENDERSON & Dianah HENDERSON two legatees;
John BIGGS; Wm MURRY. No recording date.

p. 166   Settlement - William DONALDSON, Adm of Leroy PULLIN, decd. 25 Aug
1841. Mentions: Saml L. HUFFMASTER, Jesse WILLIAMS, Jehu MORRIS, James M.
DEDRICK, John L. WHITE, Ludville PULLIN, Nenian RIGGS, C. S. HARRIS, D & M
SHIELDS, John COCKE, Atto. Signed E. TATE, clerk. No recording date.

p. 167   Inventory - List of the Book of Moses CATE, decd, 1839. Lists: Robt
RAY, Green ARNETT, Thomas CHESHIRE, James R. RAY, Charles CATE, Jacob ARNETT,
Elijah KEY, Calvin COTNER, Hiram SPENCER, Thos RAY (GREEN), Wm SMITH, Willie
TALLY, Wm GILLMORE, James BOWERS, James DOUGLASS, John ATES, Joshua PASCAL,
David HORNER, Wm FIELDING, Elza DAVIS, Joseph DYER, Hiram ATES, Nedin COX
(moved away), Levi SATTERFIELD, James BROWN, Henderson DAVIS, John BOILES,
Comfort TATE, Sam PARSLEY, Sterling COTNER, Anderson TALLY, Wm YORK, James

DAVIS, David TATE, Sr., George CLEVENGER, John LAWRENCE, Hugh CRAFFORD, Joel FREEMAN, Joseph B. CHURCH, Isaac BRADLEY, Jacob COPPEL, James HODGES, John HAMMONDS, Joseph COMBS, John WILKERSON, Solomon NOE, Benj. CLEVENGER (moved away), Philip COMBS, Saml WATSON, Jackson CHURCHMAN, Wm FREEMAN, Joseph ORR, Alsey MENDINHALL, Eppy LEA, Wm CRAFFORD, Richard HAYWORTH, Margaret GARRETT, Perry TALBOTT, Massy COCKRUM, Jos WILKERSON, Saml LAMDIN, Joseph B. REECE, Wm TROGDEN, Hardin CAMRON (moved away), James TALLY, Meredy ATES, Reubin ATES, Elizabeth WEST, Saml WEST, Jackson COTNER, Thornton CHESHIRE, John DOUGLASS, Calvin COTNER, Thos DAVIS, Quller MITCHELL. Signed Levi SATTERFIELD, Adm. Recorded 3 Oct 1841 E. TATE, clerk.

p. 168   Commissioners Report - Elizabeth BUTCHER, widow of Isaac BUTCHER, decd. 1 yr support for her & family. Signed Alexander HAMILTON, Joseph HILL, Robt HUDDLESTONE, Comms. Recorded 2 Nov 1841 E. TATE, clerk.

        Account of Sale - Fanny DYER, decd. Mentions: James HUBBS, William SHARP, William DYER, Philip WYRICK, Silas MYNATT, Wm WYRICK, Wm DENNIS, Pryor DYER, Wm DONAHOO, Pleasant DYER, William HILL, Sr., Elizabeth DENNIS, Dotio DYER, Thomas MATTHEWS. Second time 1 Nov 1841 Joseph HILL, Adm. Recorded 2 Nov 1841 E. TATE, clerk.

p. 169   Will - Mary PECK, decd. Wife of Benjamin PECK; bur in family burying ground; Frederick Myers WILLIAMSON son of Wm WILLIAMSON when he reaches 21; my hus to give to his son John PECK & the same to Benjamin & Nancy; hus Benjamin PECK, Executor; little yellow servant boy KINDERICK to Wm B. CUNNINGHAM's son Kendrick; my step-dau Nancy Jan PECK. Signed 11 Oct 1841 Mary x PECK. Wit: Jacob PECK, Eliza J. McEFEE. Recorded 5 Nov 1841 E. TATE, clerk.

p. 170   Account of Sale - Moses CATE, decd. Mentions: corn sold to James T. WEST & Lide INGLEBARGER. Signed Levi SATTERFIELD, Adm. Recorded 14 Dec 1841.

        Third Inventory - Joseph HIGHTOWER, decd. John CURL, Adm. Signed 6 Dec 1841. Recorded 14 Dec 1841 E. TATE, clerk.

        Account of Sale - Joseph HIGHTOWER, decd. Sold Sat., 4 Dec 1841. Mentions: Joshua CURL, William ROACH, Jr., Wm P. JONES. Signed John T. CURL, Adm 6 Dec 1841. Recorded 14 Dec 1841 E. TATE, clerk.

        Account of Sale - Joseph HIGHTOWER, decd. Sold 30 May 1840. Mentions: William HIGHTOWER. Signed John T. CURL, Adm. Recorded 14 Dec 1841 E. TATE.

p. 171   Inventory - Isaac BUTCHER, decd. Signed 25 Nov 1841 Allen HURST, Adm. No recording date.

p. 172   Account of Sale - Isaac B. BUTCHER, decd. 11 & 12 Oct 1841. Mentions: Joseph HILL, Elizabeth BUTCHER, Calvin HUDDLESTONE, Thomas BLACKBURN, John COX, John McCRARY, Richard WADE, Hastin BUTCHER, John A. BLACKBORN, Jesse BUTCHER, John SHARP, Jacob SHARP, John TURNER, Squire C. HURST, Julian FRAZIER, George VITTITO, William CALLISON, Abner DIAL, William HARBESON, John SWAFFORD, Lewallen W. BUTCHER, George TURNER, James COOK, Peter SHARP, Hiram WYRICK. Signed 3 Jan 1842 Allen HURST, Adm. Recorded 23 Jan 1842 E. TATE, clerk.

p. 173   Account of Sale - Jan 1840. William H. WILLSON, decd.   John A. Mc-
KINNY & Julian FRAZIER, Adms. Mentions: Calloway HODGES, James HANKINS, James
S. TALBOT, Joseph JACKSON, John RENTFRO, H. T. HANKINS, G. I. JACKSON. Signed
3 Jan 1842. Recorded 23 Jan 1842 E. TATE, clerk.

p. 174   Settlement - Moses CATES, decd. Mentions: Estate being insolvent;
Levi SATTERFIELD, Adm; widow's 1 yr allowance. Signed 8 Dec 1841 Wm T. TATE,
John EASLEY, Thos McBROOM, Comms. Recorded 23 Jan 1842 E. TATE, clerk.

        Third Settlement - Nancy SMITH, Exectrix for Josiah SMITH, decd.   3
Jan 1842. Mentions: Joseph HILL, Dpt Shff, taxes 1841. Recorded 23 Jan 1842
E. TATE, clerk.

p. 175   Will - Robert HUDDLESTONE, decd. Wife Bethena HUDDLESTON; son Daniel
F. HUDDLESTONE; my four daus; Negros JACK & ALEY; my 7 children; son John F.
HUDDLESTON; Negro PLEASANT; son Calvin HUDDLESTONE; Negro boy GREEN; land to
corner of Ezra BUCKNER's; Negro boy JESSE; dau Letty McCRARY; Negro girl MARIAH;
dau Leah Emaline HUDDLESTONE; Negro girl EMALINE; dau Sarah Ann HUDDLESTONE;
Negro boy JIM; dau Jemima Orlena HUDDLESTON; Negro girl RACHEL; $600 from John
CONLEY, my wifes father, as part of her estate; Pheba McCUBBINS & Elizabeth
BUCKNER my 2 step-daus; John F. HUDDLESTONE & Ezra BUCKNER, Executors. Signed
Robert x HUDDLESTONE. Wit: Wm BAKER, James B. SMITH, Daniel x HUDDLESTONE.
Recorded 23 Jan 1842 E. TATE, clerk.

p. 176   Settlement - James COLVIN & Lemuel WALTERS, Executors of Obadiah
WALTERS, decd.   24 Dec 1841. Mentions: William DONAHOO, John HILL & Clabourn
JOHNSON & Co., John SMITH. Recorded 23 Jan 1842 E. TATE, clerk.

        Inventory - 31 Jul 1841. Isaac WALTERS, decd. Mentions: Daniel
McPHETRIDGE, John CARDIN, John F. HUDDLESTONE, Wm LAY, G. W. VITTITOE, Williston
WILLIS, Joseph HILL, Solomon WYRICK, Thomas McMILLIN, James COLVIN, Lemuel
WALTERS, John WALTERS, Negro woman FELLIS c30 yrs, Israel WALTERS, Joseph OAKS.
Signed 31 Jul 1841 Lemuel x WALTERS, Adm. Recorded 11 Feb 1842 E. TATE, clerk.

p. 177   Guardian Settlement - James MALLICOAT, Guardian of Amanda GRAY.   17
Jan 1842. Mentions: RICE & McFARLAND, Wm COX who intermarried with Amanda
GRAY. Recorded 11 Feb 1842 E. TATE, clerk.

p. 178   Settlement - Robert LOYD, Executor of Absalom ROACH, decd.   23 Feb
1842. Mentions: Alfred ROACH, John ROACH, Dr. Wm E. COCKE, RICE & McFARLAND,
Henry GROVE for coffin, Wm CROOSE, Reece BOWEN. Recorded 14 Apr 1842 E. TATE.

        Settlement - Levi SATTERFIELD, Adm for Moses CATES, decd.   12 Feb 1842.
Mentions: Achsee CATES widow of Moses CATES, decd, Wm P. JONES. Recorded
14 Apr 1842 E. TATE, clerk.

p. 179   Inventory - John HILL, Executor for James HILL, decd. Signed 12 Mar
1842. Recorded 14 Apr 1842 E. TATE, clerk.

        Inventory - Ann BEELAR, decd. Signed 2 Apr 1842 William BEELAR, Adm.
Recorded 14 Apr 1842 E. TATE, clerk.

p. 180   Inventory - 7 Jan 1842. Robert HUDDLESTONE, decd. Mentions: Wm
DETHERGE, Lige HURST, Lewis ELLIS, John and George _____, Elisha SAVAGE, B. C.
McCRARY, John McCRARY, John BALLARD, R. H. SAVAGE, Ezra BUCKNER, John F.
HUDDLESTONE, John A. BLACKBOURN, Wm GREEN, Calvin HUDDLESTONE, Daniel F.
HUDDLESTONE, Letty McCRARY, State vs George H. McBEE, Samuel CLOUD vs Carlisle
HAYNES & wife. Signed 4 Apr 1842 John F. HUDDLESTONE, Executor. Recorded 15
Apr 1842 E. TATE, clerk.

p. 181   Guardian Report - Martin CLEVELAND, Guardian of Charlton DYER, minor.
19 Mar 1842. Mentions: John COCKE, Atto; Allen H. MATHIS for tuition. Signed
Martin CLEVELAND. Recorded 15 Apr 1842 E. TATE, clerk.

        Guardian Report - Martin CLEVELAND, Guardian of George M. DYER, minor.
1 Mar 1842. Mentions: Jesse F. BEELER, care of SLAVES, a woman & child for
1841; John COCKE; Wm P. JONES & Co.; Allen MATHIS tuition at Newmarket; Diannah
ANDERSON for midwife fee ($1.50). Signed Martin CLEVELAND. Recorded 15 Apr 1842.

p. 182   Will - 4 Jan 1842. Joseph DANIEL on his death bed wished wife, Polly
DANIEL, & his children (not named). Signed John PIOTT, M. N. JEFFERES. Recorded 15 Apr 1842 E. TATE, clerk.

        Will - Robert FIELDS, decd. Wife Abigal FIELD; all my Black people to
be set free, namely JOSEPH, CRISA, LEWIS, PATTY, PHILLIP, LEA, JANE, GREEN,
PATTON, JOHN & PRYOR; $100 to promote the Gospel; wife Abigail FIELD & William
SHARP, Executors. Signed 9 Nov 1841 Robert FIELD. Wit: 5 Dec 1841 Moses
BROCK, Clabourn JOHNSON. Recorded 15 Apr 1842 E. TATE, clerk.

p. 183   Settlement - Reece WILLIAMS, Adm of Joseph LEFEW. 22 Apr 1842.
Mentions: James & Wm WILLIAMS, Benjamin BRANSON, Constable, Wm M. COCKE & Co.,
James KIRBY, Lewis M. ELLIS, Constable, Thos MAJORS, Hugh JONES, E. THOMASON,
Jacob KLINE & Sons, David WATSON, A. P. & D. GREEN, Wm C. MALLICOAT, John
NANCE, Benj. ACUFF. Recorded 11 May 1842 E. TATE, clerk.

p. 184   Settlement - Wm GRAY, Executor for John LEBOW, decd. 15 Apr 1842.
Mentions: first & second sales; sale of real estate 15 Dec 1840; COFFIN & Co.;
Peter BEAR; Hugh BASSETT, George W. MATLOCK; Robert NALL; Gabriel McCRANE;
William BASSETT; John MAYES; Cynthia FORT; James SHIELDS; James MOORE; Raleigh
DODSON; Isaac LEBOW; John BOYD; David COUNTZ; James CONN; Wm C. JACKSON; Albert
SULLENBARGER; John SHELTON; E. WILLIAMS; Cleon MOORE; Joseph McDANIEL; Thos
JONES; James MOOR; Jesse RIGGS; E. G. EASTMAN; R. DODSON, Dpt Shff taxes 1840;
E. THOMASON, Dpt Shff taxes 1840; Sanford JOHNSON who intermarried with Louisa
LEBOW a legatee; Senah LEBOW a legatee; Catherine LEBOW, widow, a legatee;
Albert SULLENBARGER who intermarried with Lucretia LEBOW a legatee; Lucinda
a legatee; Isaac LEBOW a legatee; Jacob LEBOW agent for Joseph LEBOW a legatee;
William GRAY, Executor, who intermarried with Mary LEBOW a legatee. Recorded
11 May 1842 E. TATE, clerk.

p. 185   Account of Sale - James NEEDHAM, decd. Sold 14 Mar 1842. Signed Lewis
ATKINS, Adm. Recorded 11 May 1842 E. TATE, clerk.

p. 186   Third Settlement - Henry HOLSTEIN & John M. HODGES, Adms for Eli HODGES,
decd. 27 Apr 1842. Mentions: last report 28 May 1841; Joseph NOE, Jr. &

C. B. IVY; Jesse HOWELL; John SPOON; James MALLICOAT. Signed 27 Apr 1842.
Recorded 11 May 1842 E. TATE, clerk.

Commissioners Report - April term 1842. Nicholas NICELY, decd. 1 yr
support for widow & family. Mentions: two hides at Jacob KLINE's. Signed
Martin CLEVELAND, James BROCK, Joseph CLARK 11 Apr 1842. Recorded 11 May 1842.

p. 187   Inventory - Nicholas NICELY, decd. Mentions: Benjamin BRAY, Jeremiah
BOWMAN, Charlton DYER, Jr. Signed Smith STRANGE, Adm, 13 Apr 1842. No recording date.

Will - William CLAY, decd. Wife Rebecka CLAY land in Richland Valley;
my slaves ISAAC, JUDE, LITTLETON, JACK, BRADDOCK, MELLA, JUDY, a girl & dau of
CHANEY & her children, MARY, MARIA, EPHRAIM a lame man, EPHRAIM a boy & a Negro
girl named POLLY; land North Side of Clinch Mts adjoining Richard ACUFF; my grsons Clemment Clabourn CLAY & Hugh Lawson White CLAY, the 1st & 3rd sons of my
son Clement C. CLAY; my 4 daus Cynthia GREEN, Margaret M. BUNCH, Nancy HIGHTOWER
& Maacah KINDRECK; Negro boy HENRY; my son William CLAY now decd without issue;
Negro boy JACOB; Negro woman NAN & her son TOM; Negro woman CHANY & her 2 children, BETTY & LUCINDA; Negro woman ESTHER; Negro woman RACHEL & her two children
SALLY & SAMPSON; wife Rebecka CLAY, son Clement C. CLAY & my son-in-law John
BURCH & Aliston H. GREEN, Executors. Signed 27 Nov 1830 William CLAY. Wit: Luke
LEA, Jr., S. H. BUNCH, James DYER, Sr., Samuel SHIELDS, Noah JARNAGIN. 4 Jan 183.
reacknowledge by Pryor LEA. 21 Aug 1834 reacknowledged by S. S. 26 Mar 1838
reacknowledged by James DYER, Sr.
            Codicil to above Will - Dau Margaret M. BUNCH, wife of John BUNCH.
Signed 4 Jan 1833 William CLAY. Wit: Pryor LEA, Samuel SHIELDS 21 Aug 1834.
26 Mar 1838 reacknowledged by James DYER, Sr.
            Additional Codicil - Son-in-law William P. KINDRICK; Negro girl POLLY;
my dau Maacah KINDRICK; 2 Negro children HARRIETT ELIZABETH & EMILY GREEN born
since my will was made. Signed 12 Jun 1833 William CLAY. Wit: Pryor LEA,
Saml SHIELDS, Luke LEA 28 Jul 1835. 26 Mar 1838 reacknowledged James DYER, Sr.
21 Aug 1834 reacknowledged by S. S.
            Third Codicil - My dau Margaret M. BUNCH, now a widow & relict of John
BUNCH, decd. Signed William CLAY 19 Sep 1838. Wit: Samuel SHIELDS, Harman G.
LEA.
            Fourth Codicil - William P. KINDRICK, husband of my dau Maaca. Signed
9 Dec 1839 William CLAY. Wit: Noah JARNAGIN, Chesley JARNIGAN. Recorded 12
May 1852 E. TATE, clerk.

p. 191   Settlement - Beanstation Turnpike Comms. for 1841. Mentions: Henry
BROWN, William MURPHEY, Johua HAMILTON, James C. MOSES, J. P. JENNINGS, Jonathan
VAUGHN, John LAFFERTY, C. McANALLY. Signed Wm T. TATE, J. GODWIN, John EASLEY,
Comms. Recorded 17 May 1842 E. TATE, clerk.

p. 192   Account of Sale - Nicholas NICELY, decd. Mentions: Elizabeth NICELY,
Reubin WOLFENBARGER, Benjamin BRANSON, John BROCK, Robert FRY, John CLARK,
William WILLIAMS, G. W. VITTITO, Alfred NOE, James BROCK, John CHANDLER, David
BRANSON, Charlton DYER, Jr., Nicholas SATTERFIELD, Edward BRADEN, John C. JERREL.
Signed 3 May 1842 Smith STRANGE, Adm. Recorded 8 Jun 1842 E. TATE, clerk.

p. 193   Inventory - E. HIGHTOWER,decd. Signed Wm P. JONES, Adm. Recorded

8 Jun 1842 E. TATE, clerk.

Guardian Report - G. B. MITCHEL, Guardian of minor heirs of William HANKINS, decd. Mentions: last report 1st Mon Feb 1837. Signed 28 Nov 1840. Recorded 8 Jun 1842 E. TATE, clerk.

p. 194   Settlement - Rice COFFEE, Adm of Meredith COFFEE, decd.   25 May 1841. Mentions: James COFFEE; Wm KIDWELL; Preston MITCHEL; S. & T. SMITH; James G. WALKER; Samuel CRAIN who intermarried with Mahala COFFEE a legatee; James COFFEE a legatee; Joel COFFEE a legatee; Jubel MITCHEL who intermarried with Dorcas COFFEE a legatee; Jacob ARNETT who intermarried with Anna COFFEE a legatee; Henderson DYER who intermarried with Mary COFFEE a legatee; Henry ALSUP agent for Henderson SPARKMAN who intermarried with Eliza COFFEE a legatee; Rice COFFEE, Adm, being a legatee; Rice COFFEE, Atto, for Hardimon SPARKMAN who intermarried with Mira COFFEE a legatee.   Recorded 8 Jun 1842 E. TATE.

p. 195   Settlement - Booker DYER, Executor of William DYER, decd.   14 May 1842. Mentions: James SALLING; Granvill CHEEK; Martin CLEVELAND; Callaway DYER; James DYER, Sr.; William POPEJOY; Thomas DENNIS; Clabourn JOHNSON; Moses BROCK who intermarried with Mahaly DYER a legatee; Silas McBEE who intermarried with Sarah DYER a legatee.   Recorded 8 Jun 1842 E. TATE, clerk.

Settlement - Lewis ADKINS, Adm of James NEEDHAM, decd.   7 May 1842. Mentions: 2 sales, William SHARP, Joseph HILL.   Recorded 9 Jun 1842 E. TATE.

p. 196   Second Settlement - Isaac HARRIS & Preston MITCHEL, Executors for Samuel RAY, decd.   28 May 1842. Mentions: last settlement 6 Mar 1842; COCKE, MASSENGILL & Co.; James WALKER; Benj. WALKER; Jacob ARNETT; Aquilla MITCHEL, Jr.; Henry CARBACK who intermarried with Anna RAY a legatee; Wm M. MITCHEL who intermarried with Eliza RAY a legatee; Isaac HARRIS, Guardian of Mary RAY, Tabitha RAY, Samuel RAY & Abner RAY minor heirs of Saml RAY, decd.   Recorded 9 Jun 1842.

p. 197   Settlement - Mark MONROW, Adm of Nathan ATKINS, decd.   3 Jun 1842. Mentions: sales due 17 Mar 1841; Dr. Alfred NOEL; R. M. SCRUGGS & Co.; Dr. John STARNES; Martin CLEVELAND; Eli DENNIS; Joseph HILL; G. W. VITTETO; Stephen ATKINS; William SHARP; Wm SANDERS; John NEEDHAM; John NANCE; Benj. NEELY; Ann ATKINS, widow.   Recorded 9 Jun 1842 E. TATE, clerk.

p. 198   Guardian Report - Aquilla MITCHEL, Guardian of Elizabeth ARMSTRONG, minor.   28 May 1842. Mentions: last report 28 Nov 1842.   Recorded 10 Jun 1842.

Guardian REPORT - Isaac HARRIS, Guardian of Mary, Tabetha, Samuel & Abner RAY minor heirs of Samuel RAY, decd.   28 May 1842. Mentions: Preston MITCHEL, Executor for Samuel RAY, decd.   Recorded 10 Jun 1842 E. TATE, clerk.

p. 199   Guardian Report - G. B. MITCHEL, Guardian of Russel SMALLWOOD's heirs. 28 May 1842. Mentions: last report 28 Nov 1840.   Recorded 10 Jun 1842 E. TATE.

Guardian Report - G. B. MITCHEL, Guardian of the minor heirs of Wm HANKINS, decd.   28 May 1842. Mentions: last report 28 Nov 1840.   Recorded 10 Jun 1842 E. TATE, clerk.

p. 200   Guardian Report - James MILLS, Guardian of John P. PERRIN. Mentions: cash received from Preston MITCHEL, Executor of Edward CHURCHMAN, decd. Recorded 10 Jun 1842 E. TATE, clerk.

Inventory - Martha COUNTZ, decd, by Thomas McBROOM, Adm. Recorded 10 Jun 1842 E. TATE, clerk.

p. 201   Settlement - John HILL, Executor of James HILL, decd. 6 Jun 1842. Mentions: last settlement 29 Aug 1837; Rachel M. HILL a legatee; minor heirs; James SALLING, Dpt Shff taxes 1836 to 1838; Joseph HILL, Dpt Shff taxes 1839 to 1841; Wm HUBBS present Guardian. Recorded 6 Jul 1842 E. TATE, clerk.

p. 202   Inventory - Joseph DANIEL, decd. 21 Mar 1842. William P. LONG, Adm. Recorded 6 Jul 1842 E. TATE, clerk.

Account of Sale - Joseph DANIEL, decd. Mentions: G. B. MAYES, Mary DANIEL, James CROW, Farbak PRICE, John COCKE, John IVY, M. N. JEFFERES, P. J. JEFFERES, Pharoah PRICE, W. H. DANIEL, Mary DANIEL for John, Robert, Sarah Jane & Issabella, John HOLT. Signed William P. LONG, Adm. Recorded 6 Jul 1842.

p. 204   Guardian Report - Edward TATE, Guardian of William M. GRAY. 1 Aug 1842. Mentions: last report 28 Jan 1841; hiring of SLAVES belonging to heirs of John STIFFY, decd; James MAYES, A. P. & D. GREEN; Jacob KLINE & Sons; Wm M. MOODY; George HANKINS for board at Newmarket; A. H. MATHIS; RICE & McFARLAND. Recorded 5 Aug 1842 E. TATE, clerk.

Guardian Report - Edward TATE, Guardian of the minor heirs of Thos CHURCHMAN, decd. 27 Jul 1842. Mentions: last report 28 Jan 1841; 3 letters from wards in the State of Indiana. Recorded 5 Aug 1842 E. TATE, clerk.

p. 205   Guardian Report - Elizabeth RIGGS, Guardian of the minor heirs of Nenian RIGGS, decd. 2 Aug 1842. Mentions: taxes 1840 & 1841; boarding Elizabeth & Keziah RIGGS, two of her wards. Signed Elizabeth x RIGGS 2 Aug 1842. Recorded 5 Aug 1842 E. TATE, clerk.

p. 206   Guardian Report - Heirs of John HILL, decd, namely Ramsey & Penina Palestine HILL. Mentions: notes on Abel HILL & Stephen FROST; renting DAIL place to Wm DENNIS; running lines between wards & Pheba FIELDS. Signed Martin CLEVELAND, Guardian 1 Aug 1842. Recorded 5 Aug 1842 E. TATE, clerk.

Guardian Report - Martin CLEVELAND for ward G. W. DYER. Mentions: renting farm to Willie B. DYER; notes put in the hands of Lewis M. ELLIS on Deadman NASH & John CHANDLER, Jackson & Booker DYER, Willie B. DYER & Joseph WILLIAMS, Nicholas NICELY, Robert FRY, Jacob & Jessee F. BEELAR, Robt FRY & Anderson ACUFF, Pleasant STARNES & James STARNES, Willie B. DYER & Peter WOLF-INBARGER, Joseph WOLFINBARGER & Charlton DYER, Elijah LEFFEW & Pleasant WATSON, A. NOEL & John NANCE, Anderson ACUFF & Wm WATSON, Asa ROUTH & Stephen ROUTH, Washington RAY & Robert FRY, Nathaniel BRANSON & James DAULTON, Anderson ACUFF & Robert FRY, John COFFMAN & Rinehart COFFMAN, James GRAY & Tandy WOLFINBARGER. Signed Martin CLEVELAND Aug 1842. Recorded 5 Aug 1842, E. TATE clerk.

p. 207   Commissioners Report - Joseph BRYAN, decd. Mentions: Elizabeth BRYAN, widow, one Slave VINE age c42; Eli DENNIS who intermarried with Lettice BRYAN; to James MONROW & his wife Margaret BRYAN, one Slave ELIZABETH c9 yrs; to Jension BRYAN one Slave MALINDA; Amanda BRYAN one Slave William GREEN c14 mos old; heirs to wit: Elizabeth BRYAN, widow, Eli DENNIS & his wife LETICE, James MONROW & his wife Margaret, Jenison & Amanda to pay James M. BRYAN, the son of Joseph BRYAN, decd, $20 ea; one Slave SALLY. Signed 5 Aug 1842 N. A. SENTER, David McANALLY, James MOORE. Recorded 5 Aug 1842 E. TATE, clerk.

p. 208   Guardian Report - Elizabeth CLARK, Guardian of the minor heirs of Wm CLARK, decd, taken 27 Jul 1842. Mentions: John P. JENNINGS & John CLARK, Adms of the estate of Wm CLARK, decd; E. TATE; plantation containing 125 acres. Recorded 5 Aug 1842 E. TATE, clerk.

p. 209   Guardian Report - Wm G. TATE & Wm M. COCKE, Guardians of Martha & Evaline LATHIM, minor heirs of John LATHIM, decd. Mentions: James LATHIM former Guardian; hiring Slaves to wit: Wm E. COCKE LITTLE ALFRED & MATILDA, Robert LOYD BIG ALFRED, A. P. GREEN ABBE; renting plantation to K. McANALLY; E. THOMASON, Sheriff; James LATHIM, Sr; John MAYES boarding Evaline; James L. EASLEY for schooling; Wm T. TATE & Co. Signed 29 Jul 1842. Recorded 5 Aug 1842 E. TATE.

p. 210   Guardian Report - Wm HUBBS, Guardian of Kenada HILL. Mentions: notes on Wm HICKLE, H. & L. FROST, Wm T. CARDIN, Wm HUBBS, John CHESNEY, Wm BOLES & Joseph KITTS, Stephen FROST & Abel HILL. Recorded 6 Aug 1842 E. TATE, clerk.

        Account of Sale - Additional sale, Estate of Alexander BLAIR, decd. Mentions: sale of Slaves ROSE, MALINDA & RACHEL on 21 Mar 1840. Signed Josiah BLAIR, Adm. Recorded 6 Aug 1842 E. TATE, clerk.

p. 211   Guardian Report - Thomas McBROOM, Guardian of the minor heirs of John DENNIS, decd. 26 Jul 1842. Mentions: notes on Martin CLEVELAND, George SEAMORE, George BROCK, James BROCK, Thos McMILLIN, David McMILLIN, Levi DENNIS, Joel FIELDS, Jedidah FIELDS, Wm SHARP, Wm DONAHOO, Booker DYER; Dr. C. M. GOOLIN; coffin for one of wards; SCRUGGS & Co. Recorded 6 Aug 1842 E. TATE, clerk.

p. 212   Guardian Report - Hiram VITTITO, Guardian for Luretter, Ira & Talbot ATKINS. 22 Jul 1842. Mentions: notes by James VITTITO, Geo. W. VITTITO, Elijah ATKINS, Lewis ATKINS, Joseph HILL, Robt ATKINS, Archd MULLINS, Moses ATKINS, Wm SHARP, Solomon WYRICK, Wm WYRICK, Thos WAGGONER, Joseph HILL; Mark MUNROW, Adm of Nathan ATKINS, decd, & Guardian of his minor heirs. Recorded 6 Aug 1842 E. TATE, clerk.

        Guardian Report - Thomas DYER, Guardian of the minor heirs of Marvel WICKLIFF, decd. Mentions: last report 6 Nov 1837 to date 29 Jul 1842. Recorded 6 Aug 1842 E. TATE, clerk.

p. 213   Guardian Report - Mary FURGASON, Guardian of the minor heirs of John FURGASON, decd. Mentions: last report 2 Nov 1838 to date 29 Jul 1842; Martha FURGASON a ward now of age; Rabecka FURGASON a ward; John FURGASON a ward; Dr. NAFF for schooling; James FURGASON a ward now of full age; Sheriff THOMASON taxes for 1839, 40 & 41. Signed Mary x FURGASON. Recorded 6 Aug 1842 E. TATE.

        Will - Robert L. WRIGHT, decd. My dau Lucinda HARRISON; my son Isaac

WRIGHT; my son John WRIGHT; wife Rosanna WRIGHT, my friend Joseph W. PATTERSON, Executors. Signed Robert L. x WRIGHT 27 May 1842. Wit: A. H. TAR, Peter O'BRYAN, John EASTERLY. Recorded 6 Aug 1842 E. TATE, clerk.

p. 214   Will - John DEVAULT, decd. Polly DEVAULT, wife; four NEGROES; all the children when they come of age; the four boys; land in Hawkins Co. containing 319 acres to John B. FINDLEY who holds a bond on land; my father's estate; to John ZACKERY the place I bought of Wm HOWERTON; ZACKERY & wife Executors. Signed John DEVAULT 8 Dec 1835. Wit: John SHARP, William x HOWERTON. Recorded 6 Aug 1842.

p. 215   Account of Sale - The minor heirs of Robert GAINS, decd. Mentions: Daniel VINEYARD, H. G. LEA, Wm BLAIR, R. C. GAINS, Thos GREEN, J. P. GAINS. Signed 5 Sep 1842 B. E. & R. C. GAINS, Executors. Recorded 12 Sep 1842 E. TATE.

p. 216   Settlement - Josiah BLAIR, Adm of Alexander BLAIR, decd. 28 Jul 1842. Mentions: E. WILLIAM, A. C. McCONNEL, David McANALLY, E. TATE, George WILLIAMS, William THOMPSON, John BIGGS, E. THOMASON, note to Hannah BLAIR, note to Josiah BLAIR. Recorded 12 Sep 1842 E. TATE, clerk.

p. 217   Settlement - Willie DYER, Executor of George DYER, decd. 4 Aug 1842. Mentions: Rhodeman HARREL; Charlton DYER; B. L. CAVENDAR, Constable; John WEST-ERFIELD; William DYER note to M. L. ELLIS; David BRANSEN; Joseph WILLIAMS: Charlten DYER, Jr.; William ODEL; James DYER; Martin CLEVELAND; Joseph CLARK; E. THOMASON; E. TATE; Charlton DYER a legatee; 1 clock to Willie DYER which was willed to him by William DYER, decd; Elijah LEFFEW. Recorded 12 Aug 1842. (Note: in the first line it reads William DYER, decd, this was marked out and George DYER, decd was written above.)

p. 218   Settlement - John VANCE & Peter BEELAR, Securities of John ROBINSON, Adm for the estate of Saml VANCE, decd. 8 Aug 1842. Mentions: E. TATE; David RICHARDSON; Saml A. VANCE a legatee; Anna BEELAR a legatee; Mary VANCE a legatee; Mary VANCE, widow, a legatee; Joseph VANCE a legatee; Hannah VANCE a legatee; Sary VANCE a legatee; John VANCE a legatee. Recorded 13 Sep 1842 E. TATE, clerk.

Guardian Report - William SHARP, Guardian for minor heirs of Wm CHEEK. Mentions: wards having arrived at age 21; last report 19 Mar 1841; Clabourn JOHNSON agent of wards. Recorded 13 Sep 1842 E. TATE, clerk.

p. 219   Settlement - Wm DYER, Adm for estate of George DYER, decd. 23 Aug 1842. Mentions: Docy DYER, widow & relict; Joseph HILL, Dpt Shff taxes 1841; E. TATE; Joel FIELDS; Wm DENNIS; John FROST; Stephen FROST; James DYER. Recorded 13 Sep 1842 E. TATE, clerk.

Inventory - Jacob GODWIN, Adm for John SMITH, decd. Mentions: 4 NEGROE in hands of Jacob PECK, Esqr & bill in Chancery Court in Tazwell against PECK former Guardian of John SMITH. Signed Jacob GODWIN, Adm 5 Sep 1842. Recorded 13 Sep 1842 E. TATE, clerk.

p. 220   Inventory - 3 Sep 1842. Estate of Robert HARRIS, decd. Mentions: 300 to 400 acre tract of land; 9 SLAVES, one in Alabamy; John & Seth McKINNEY notes; S. C. RENTFRO & John A. McKINNEY note; Charles HAMES note; Edward HANKINS, John A. McKINNEY & Julian FRAZIER note; S. C. RENTFRO & John A. McKINNEY note;

John MYNATT note; John P. SLADE note; WILLSON & HANKINS note; Aaron HARRISON
note; Thomas PATTERSON note. Signed Isaac HARRIS, Reuben HARRIS, Adms. Recorded
13 Sep 1842 E. TATE, clerk.

Commissioners Report - James M. McANNALLY, decd. Lay off 1 yr provisions
for widow. Signed Hamilton EVANS, John P. JENNINGS, Clabourn BULL, Comms 24 Sep
1842. Recorded 10 Oct 1842 E. TATE, clerk.

p. 221   Inventory - Robert L. WRIGHT, decd. Mentions: note on Wm BARTLEY; a
Judgement against Isaiah REECE; note on Lawsen A. R. LONG; Chessley ROGERS; Isaac
ROGERS, Jesse RIGGS; Jas RANKIN; Joseph RIGGS, Alexander McCAWER. Signed I. W.
PATTERSON, Executive. Recorded 11 Oct 1842 E. TATE, clerk.

p. 222   Inventory - John D. HICKMAN, decd. Mentions: Acpts on Wm SHARP, Francis
HICKMAN, L. M. ELLIS. Signed Stephen ATKINS, Adm 3 Oct 1842. Recorded 11 Oct
1842 E. TATE, clerk.

Account of Sale - Estate of John D. HICKMAN, decd. Mentions: Wm MARTIN,
James HUNTER, Joseph HILL, Lydia HICKMAN, Mary Ann HICKMAN, John B. GRIGSBY.
Signed Stephen ATKINS, Adm 17 Sep 1842. Recorded 11 Oct 1842 E. TATE, clerk.

p. 223   Inventory - John DEVAULT, decd. Mentions: Black girl JULIA c23; Black
boys JONAS & JERRY 13 yrs the 16th of last Jun; Black girl AMANDA 3 yrs the 10th
of last Jun; Black girl HANNAH 11 mos old; notes on John SHARP, Wm HOWERTON, Wm
MYNATT, John BAKER, Ira HOUSESTON, George GRAVES, Michael MILLAR, John HICKLE.
Signed John ZACHERY Oct 1842. Recorded 11 Oct 1842 E. TATE, clerk.

p. 224   Account of Sale - Robert HARRIS, decd. Mentions: Evan HARRIS, Jacob
NUTTY, Samuel JOHNS, the Widow, Jonathan JACKSON, boy slave JAMES, Clabourn
HALEY, Andrew FURGASON, Silas MYNATT, Pryor MYNATT, Calvin MITCHEL, Wm MYNATT,
Balis GAINS, Wm COVIN, James COFFEE, Martin L. MYNATT, Andrew GLOWERS or CLOWERS,
Moses GRAY, James MILLS, Charles HAMES, Thos HAMES, Joel COFFEE, John A.
McKINNEY, James L. TABOT, Anderson DOLIN, Vincent M. JACKSON. Signed Isaac
HARRIS, Reuben HARRIS, Adms. Recorded 12 Oct 1842 E. TATE, clerk.

p. 226   Additional Account of Sale - George BURKET, decd. Mentions: B. H.
OWENS, Wm MILLAR, Absalom CANNON, M. N. JEFFERS, David N. TATE, Samuel POLLARD,
John CLARK. Signed James SUNDULAND, Adm. Recorded 12 Oct 1842 E. TATE, clerk.

p. 227   Settlement - Jeremiah JARNAGIN & John SCRUGGS, Executors for Rufus
M. SCRUGGS, decd. 4 Oct 1842. Mentions: Matthias CRANE, Charles BROWN, John
BOILES, John CHANDLER, Wm COOSE, James M. ROACH, Chester JARNAGIN, COCKE & NAFF,
William WILLIAMSON, Thomas BROWN, RICE & McFARLAND, Abraham FULKERSON, Samuel
C. GOWENS, E. TATE, Jeremiah JARNAGIN, Mary SCRUGGS, widow & relict, Wm P. JONES
surviving partner, Saml C. GREEN & John RENTFROW, John SHARP, John CHESNEY,
George ATKINS, Chesley RAY, John INGLES, John EDINGTON, John HARMERS, George
EZELL, Edward SHIPLEY. Recorded 12 Oct 1842 E. TATE, clerk.

p. 228   Noncupative Will - James MAYES, decd. Made by him 17 Sep at night,
1842; my son Henry MAYES, Elika A. TAYLOR & Daniel C. CARMICHAEL to be my
Executors; all my children; money borrowed from Ethelred WILLIAMS for my son
William; money owed by William to Daniel C. CARMICHAEL. Signed 10 Oct 1842

A. H. TARR & Hughs W. TAYLOR. Recorded 8 Nov 1842 E. TATE, clerk.

Guardian Report - Mary SHIELDS, Guardian of James T. SHIELDS minor heir of John SHIELDS, decd. Signed Mary SHIELDS, Guardian 5 Oct 1842.

Guardian Report - Mary SHIELDS, Guardian of E. J. SHIELDS minor heir of John SHIELDS, decd. Signed Mary SHIELDS, Guardian 5 Oct 1842.

Recorded 8 Nov 1842 E. TATE, clerk.

p. 229   Settlement - John HUBBS & Stephen FROST, Executors for the Estate of John HILL, decd. 27 Oct 1842. Mentions: Genl John COCKE, Atto; Wm T. CARDIN; E. TATE; Wm HUBBS; Joseph HILL, Constable; Wm HICKLE for Crying Sale; Wm T. TATE; Wm P. JONES; Nath. PETERS, Dpt Shff; Joseph HILL, Dpt Shff; Nancy HILL, widow; Martin CLEVELAND, Guardian for minor heirs. Recorded 8 Nov 1842 E. TATE.

p. 230   Guardian Report - Robert CARDWELL, Sr., Guardian of the minor heirs of Andrew CHAMBERLAIN, decd. 5 Nov 1842. Mentions: last report 3 Apr 1840; rents for 1840; Charles GOWFORTH note; James HAGGARD; Jeremiah, a ward; Jane, a ward; E. THOMASEN, Shff for taxes 1841; money due widow. Recorded 10 Nov 1842.

p. 231   Guardian Report - Elizabeth HODGES, Guardian of minor heirs of Eli HODGES, decd. 11 Oct 1842. Mentions: last report 7 Jun 1841; Eli HODGES, a ward; Jacob E. HODGES, a ward; Louisa Caroline & Elizabeth HODGES, two of her younger wards. Signed Elizabeth x HODGES, Guardian. Recorded 10 Nov 1842.

Second Settlement - Mark MONROW, Adm of Nathan ATKINS, decd. 6 Oct 1842. Mentions: last settlement 3 Jun 1842; Hiram VITTITO who intermarried with Ann ATKINS, widow & relict of Nathan ATKINS, decd, and Guardian of minor heirs of Nathan ATKINS, decd. Recorded 10 Nov 1842 E. TATE, clerk.

p. 232   Account of Sale - John DEVAULT, decd. 20 Oct 1842. Mentions: Thomas MYNATT, G. P. MYNATT, Samuel SHARP, Isaac M. LOWE, Andrew CLOWER, Jacob HARRIS, Wm PETERS, Joseph JACKSON, John ZEACHERY, John SAWYERS, John TROUT, Mary DEVAULT, Silas MYNATT, Martin E. MYNATT, Jonathan JACKSON, John McCRARY, J. C. H. SAWYERS, David BALLINGER, Andrew FURGASEN, Nathaniel PETERS, Lawson DAMEWOOD. Signed John F. ZACHERY, Executor. Recorded 10 Nov 1842 E. TATE, clerk.

p. 233   Inventory - James McANALLY, decd. Mentions: notes on Hamilton EVANS, John PERSON on Mahala MITCHEL now the widow of the decd, John WEST, William WOLF, Mefy BOSHEY, George W. THOMPSON, George WARD & Lucis DAY, Marvel NASH, C. McANALLY, Enoch MACKEY, Thos McANALLY; a suit in Claiborne Co. George BA____ vs Jeremiah YOUNG; accompts on Aquilla PAYNE, William IMES, Clabourn LATHIM, Enoch MACKEY, Thos McANALLY, Drew MATHIS, Wm NASH, Austus JENNINGS, Wm HARREL, Marvel NASH, Ryal PEARSON, Bosha HARVEY, Chesley WEST, Richard SINGLETON, Pleasan HOLT, Anderson MALLICOAT, Clabourn BULL, Wm SMITH, Doctor PARKER, Thomas JONES, Crispin COLLINS, James K. McANALLY, John ELROD, Jackson HELTON, Rease WILLIAMS, Jeremiah SINGLETON, John MALLICOAT, Green BUNDIN, Jonathan VAUN, Robert MURPHY, Samuel PARKER, Edmund COLLINS, Thomas HAYES, Hiram BUNDEN, Washing LANE, Andrew McGINNIS, George LANE, John ALLEN. Signed Chas McANALLY, Adm. 30 Sep 1842. Recorded 10 Nov 1842 E. TATE, clerk.

p. 234   Account of Sale - James M. McANALLY, decd, sold 25 & 28 Oct 1842.
Mentions: Wm HARREL, John MALLICOAT, Manilla McANALLY, widow of decd, Charles
W. F. McANALLY, James K. McANALLY, Thos P. McANALLY, J. M. HAYES, Samuel PARKER,
Wm HARRELL, Sr., Wm R. PERSON, Sterling McANALLY, Jeremiah SINGLETON, George
BARNARD. Signed C. McANALLY, Adm 28 Oct 1842. Recorded 10 Nov 1842 E. TATE.

p. 235   Administrators Report - John COCKE, Adm for Peter GODWIN, decd.
Mentions: Estate used and squandered by widow & children; filling a bill of
recovery. Signed John COCKE, Adm. Recorded 10 Nov 1842 E. TATE, clerk.

        Commissioners Report - John D. HICKMAN, decd. 1 yr support for Mary
Ann HICKMAN, widow, and family. Signed 22 Sep 1842 Jacob BEELAR, Wm SHARP,
Joseph HILL. Recorded 9 Dec 1842 E. TATE, clerk.

p. 236   Settlement - Wm M. MOODY & John MOODY, Executors of George MOODY, decd.
30 Nov 1842. Mentions: sales 11 Nov 1840 & 7 Jan 1841; M. N. JEFFREYS; RICE &
McFARLAND; A. P. & D. GREEN; Wm T. TATE; Henry GROVE; E. TATE; Clisbe AUSTIN;
Wm COOSE; David HEMER, Wm C. COCKE, Jacob P. CHAISE, G. C. HASKINS; note to
Wm E. COCKE & Ruse BOWEN; F. B. S. COCKE; Reese BOWEN who intermarried with Mary
MOODY a legatee; James LACY who intermarried with Nancy MOODY a legatee; John
MOODY a legatee; Saml THORNBURG who intermarried with Sarah MOODY a legatee;
George HASKINS who intermarried with Charlottie MOODY a legatee; Wm NEAL who
intermarried with Clitts (?) Amelia MOODY a legatee; James BOWERS who inter-
married with Rachel MOODY a legatee; Hugh JONES who intermarried with Jane
MOODY a legatee; G. P. MOODY a legatee, he having purchased their interest in
Estate & holds their deeds including their share of personal property; E. TATE
who intermarried with Lucy MOODY a legatee; Wm M. MOODY, Executor & legatee;
Wm MAYES who intermarried with Elizabeth MOODY a legatee. Recorded 10 Dec 1842.

p. 237   Additional Account of Sale - John D. HICKMAN, decd. Mentions: Pleasant STARNES, Pleasant JENNINGS, L. M. ELLIS, William MARTIN. Signed Stephen
ATKINS, Adm. Recorded 10 Dec 1842 E. TATE, clerk.

p. 238   Inventory - Robert RAY, decd. Signed Nov 1842 James T. WEST, Adm.
Recorded 5 Nov 1842 E. TATE, clerk.

        Second Settlement - Hughs W. TAYLOR & Elika A. TAYLOR, Executors for
Hughs O. TAYLOR, decd. 6 Dec 1842. Mentions: last settlement 27 Apr 1841;
Thos D. TAYLOR a legatee; Amanda S. TAYLOR a legatee; Amelia WITT a legatee;
George & Amelia WITT one of the legatees; TAYLOR, LONG & Co.; E. TATE; interest
since 1 Jan 1841. Recorded 10 Jan 1843 E. TATE, clerk.

p. 239   Inventory - Preston LOYD, decd. Signed Jesse HOWELL, Adm. Recorded
9 Feb 1843 E. TATE, clerk.

p. 240   Account of Sale - Preston LOYD, decd. Mentions: Mary LOYD, Elizabeth
HODGES, Joshua HAZELWOOD, Eli HODGES, John McAMIS, N. PATTERSON, note on Thomas
HARREL, John BANNER, clerk & M. on Charles HODGES Estate, note on Young J.
MORRIS, note H. S. KOONTZ, note John HICKY, Cable HOWEL. Signed Jesse HOWELL,
Adm. Recorded 9 Feb 1843 E. TATE, clerk.

p. 241   Inventory - James MAYES, decd. 1 Feb 1843. Mentions: notes on Elika

A. TAYLOR, Henry MAYES, John POINDEXTER, Pertman LONG, Chapman POINDEXTER, F. B.
& P. B. COBB, Wm L. ATKINSON, Ahab BOWEN, of the State of MO, Reuben LONG, Henry
WHISTTEHUNT, Wm CORUM, Wm DAVIS, Jos DAVIS, John MAYES. Signed Henry MAYES, E.
A. TAYLOR, D. C. CARMICHAEL, Adms. Recorded 9 Feb 1842 E. TATE, clerk.

p. 242   Will - Abner DAIL, decd.   Wife Jane DAIL; son Reuben M. DAIL; son Abel
DAIL; dau ELIZABETH DAIL; son Jesse F. DAIL; dau Lenah DAIL; son Henry N. DAIL
to stay with mother until full age; dau Laurith DAIL; dau Jane C. DAIL to have
"Neelin Cose Chest" when m. or becomes of age; six sons - Orvil DAIL, youngest,
Ira DAIL, William DAIL, Nicholas DAIL, John R. DAIL, Tilman A. H. DAIL.   Executors wife & friend Lewis M. ELLIS.   Signed 16 Oct 1842 Abner DAIL.   Wit: Clabourn JOHNSON, Martin CLEVELAND.   Recorded 25 Mar 1843.

p. 243   Additional Account of Sale - Wm WILLIAMS & Samuel GIL, Adms for Wm F.
WILLIAMS, decd. Mentions: 1841 sold Black boy ALFRED to Ethelred WILLIAMS; J.
GODWIN; hire GEORGE to David NOE, THOMAS to Jacob GODWIN, SILAS to Jacob NOE,
LEWIS to Thomas GILL, DICK & PHILLIS to J. RHOTON, BETSEY, FRANCIS, MATISON,
STEPHEN & some children to Ann K. WILLIAMS; 1842 hired THOS & DICK to Thomas K.
HOWELL, SILAS to Jacob NOE, LEWIS to Ethelred WILLIAMS, PHILLIS to J. RHOTEN,
MATISON, STEPHEN, BETSY, FRANCIS & several children to Ann K. WILLIAMS, GEORGE
to Charles McANALLY.   Signed Wm WILLIAMS & Saml GILL, Adms.   Recorded 25 Mar 1843.

p. 244   Account of Sale - Patsey COUNTZ, decd.   Sold 16 Jun 1842.   Mentions:
Wm E. COCKE, Jacob GODWIN, John EASLEY, John McDANIEL, John CALLISON, Wm T. TATE,
James PENNINGTON in Allabama Banknotes, note on Wm COOSE, judgement against Wm
B. HODGES.   Signed Thomas McBROOM, Adm.   Recorded 25 Mar 1843 E. TATE, clerk.

p. 245   Commissioners Report - Preston LOYD, decd.   1 yr support for Mary LOYD,
widow, & family.   Signed 10 Dec 1842 Joseph RICH, John IVY, James CARMICHAEL.
Recorded 25 Mar 1843.

        Guardian Settlement - Martin CLEVELAND, Guardian of G. W. DYER.   1 Apr
1843. Mentions: Smith STRANGE, Adm for Nicholas NICELEY, decd.   Recorded 4 Apr
1843 E. TATE, clerk.

p. 246   Account of Sale - Robert RAY, decd.   Mentions: Thomas RAY, Sarah RAY,
Daniel MORRIS, Wm P. JONES, Samuel RIGHT, Thos PASCHAL, Aquilla MITCHEL, Thomas
SMITH, Lide INKLEBARGER, Samuel WEST.   Signed 5 Nov 1842 James T. WEST, Adm.
Recorded 4 Apr 1843.

p. 247   Inventory - James SELLARS, decd, pensioner who d. 20 Dec 1842.   Signed
James SELLARS, Adm 3 Apr 1843.   Recorded 4 Apr 1843 E. TATE, clerk.

        Settlement - William NORRIS, Adm for Jarrett NORRIS, decd.   21 Apr 1843.
Mentions: Joseph HILL; R. M. SCRUGGS & Co.; Alexander HAMILTON; L. McCOLLINS;
John COCKE, John HILL; George W. ARNOLD; Wm BAKER; S & M SHIELDS; Jno A. BLACK-
BURN, Constable; Wm DENNIS; J. R. NELSEN; MYNATT & SAWYER; Wm M. MOODY; Wm HICKLE
Garland NORRIS; Wm T. CARDIN; John MYNATT; 2 judgements against Jarrett NORRIS
in his lifetime; Eli HART for making coffin.   Recorded 4 May 1843 E. TATE, clerk.

p. 248   Settlement - Isaac DANIEL, Trustee of Grainger Co. Common School Fund
received from R. P. CUMIN, Superintendent of Public Instruction.   26 Jul 1841.

Mentions: David NOE for 1st Civil District; A. G. LEVINGSTON for 2nd Civil District; Joseph RICH for 3rd Civil District; Reubin GROVE 4th Civil District; Massy COCKRUM for 5th Civil District; Thos DYER for 6th Civil District; Henry ALSUP for 7th Civil District; Preston MITCHEL for 8th Civil District; G. W. MATTOCK 9th Civil District; Jacob GODWIN for 10th Civil District; Thomas LATHIM for 11th Civil District; Wm C. MALLICOAT for 12th Civil District; Wm SHARP for 13th Civil District; Wm HILL for 14th Civil District; Christopher HETCH for 15th Civil District. Recorded 4 May 1843.

p. 249   Settlement - Isaac DANIEL, Trustee of Grainger Co. on Account of Common School Funds received from Scott TERRY, Superintendent of Public Instruction year ending 1 Jul 1842. Mentions: Jno ROBERTSON & David NOE of 1st District; Joth NOE & Jas T. CARMICHAEL of 2nd District; Joseph RICH of 3rd District; M. N. JEFFREYS of 4th District; Massy COCKRUM of 5th Distric; Thos DYER by R. LOYD of 6th District; J. G. WALKER of 7th District; Daniel VINEYARD of 8th District; A. G. SULLENBARGER of 9th Dist; Wm T. TATE of 10th District; H. WILLIAMS of 11th District; Martin CLEVELAND of the 12th District; Stephen ATKINS of 13th District; Wm HUBBS of 14th District; Allen HURST of 15th District. Recorded 4 May 1843.

p. 250   Commissioners Report - William ACUFF, decd. Lay off 1 yr support for widow & family. Signed 29 Aug 1840 Joseph CLARK, Joseph WILLIAMS, Asa EVANS. Recorded 6 Jun 1843 E. TATE, clerk.

p. 251   Settlement - John HUBBS & Stephen FROST, Executors of John HILL, decd. 5 May 1843. Mentions: last settlement 27 Oct 1842; Wm MARTIN; Wm SHARP; Wm COLVIN; John H. FROST; James VITTITO; Wm HILL; Joel FIELDS; Martin CLEVELAND, Guardian of minor heirs. Recorded 6 Jun 1843 E. TATE, clerk.

p. 252   Fourth Settlement - Henry HOLSTIN & John M. HODGES, Adms of Eli HODGES, decd. 25 Apr 1843. Mentions: R. LOYD, Shff, costs in case Joseph NOE, Jr. against Adms in the Supreme Court at Knoxville; James MALLICOAT in suit Adm against Joseph NOE, Jr. & C. B. IVY. Recorded 7 Jun 1843 E. TATE, clerk.

        Settlement - Preston MITCHEL, Executor for Edward CHURCHMAN, decd. 3 Jun 1843. Mentions: Edna CHURCHMAN, widow; Wm DICK; Muchant HANKINS, J. & S. McKINNY; BRAZELTON & MOFFET; S & M SHIELDS; James LAMAR; note to Giles J. BLEDSOE; A. BLACKBURN; Samuel EVANS; James MILLS; S. C. RENTFROW, Dpt Shff taxes 1840; Lewis BRADSHAW; note to Elizabeth CHURCHMAN; Levi BRADSHAW; Joab PERRIN; Lewis COLLETT; James FURGASON vs Preston MITCHEL; John MITCHEL; Neoma MILLS; John BRADLEY; James C. MOSES; Vadin PERRIN a legatee; John MITCHEL who inter-married with Delilah CHURCHMAN a legatee; John BRADLEY who intermarried with Hannah CHURCHMAN a legatee; James MILLS who intermarried with Namoma CHURCHMAN a legatee; Jefferson NANCE who intermarried with Jane CHURCHMAN a legatee; John MILLS who intermarried with Nancy CHURCHMAN a legatee; Giles J. BLEDSOE who intermarried with Mary CHURCHMAN a legatee; Lewis COLLITT who intermarried with Cynthia CHURCHMAN a legatee; Joab PERRIN who intermarried with Rebecca CHURCHMAN a legatee; William MITCHEL who intermarried with Margaret CHURCHMAN a legatee; Jno BRADLEY, Executor of Matilda CHURCHMAN, decd, a legatee; James MILLS, Guardian of John P. PERRIN a legatee; Preston MITCHEL, Executor & legatee by his marriage with Rachel CHURCHMAN an heir. Recorded 7 Jun 1843 E. TATE, clerk.

p. 254   Account of Sale - James SELLARS, decd. Mentions: Sarah SELLARS, James

SELLARS. Signed James SELLARS, Adm. Recorded 5 Jul 1843.

Inventory - Hannah WILLIAMS, decd. Mentions a pension certificate.
Signed Joseph WILLIAMS, Adm. Recorded 5 Jul 1843 E. TATE, clerk.

p. 255   Will - Lemuel McBEE, Senr, decd. Formerly of Knox Co., TN; wife Sarah;
land bought from Samuel GILL & Diannah Y. GILL, his wife; my eldest son William
C. McBEE; my youngest son James A. McBEE; Negros JAMES, DICK, FILL, HENRY, CLOE,
LUCY, LIZE, LINDY, MARIAH, NATTY, REAR, ANDY, JOHN, RACHEL, RODA, HANNAH, ADALINE
CHARLES, MAJOR, JEFF, TOM, MANUEL, JURDAN, JOSEPH, FRANK JUPATIN, ALFRED; land on
McKINNEY Road toward Sally HODGES, the CARRUTHERS place; my second son Adam H.
McBEE; 245 acres lying in Jefferson Co., TN; my third son Isaac M. McBEE; land
brought from Pleasant JARNAGIN in Jefferson Co., TN; my 4th son Ganum C. McBEE;
the heirs of Wm McBEE, decd, agreeable to a decree of the Chancey Court at
Knoxville; my 5th son Lemuel J. McBEE; land bought from Thomas HANKINS lying in
Jefferson Co.; my 6th son Milo McBEE; my 7th son Daniel McBEE; land bought from
James HANKINS a part known as DAVISES Island; my 8th son Calleway McBEE; my dau
Patsey; dau Mary Ann; land bought from Stephen GROVES; drawing of SLAVES belonging to estate of Wm McBEE, decd, which is to take place at Knoxville between this
& next Oct; sons Isreal M. McBEE & Ganum C. McBEE, Executors. Signed Lemuel
McBEE 21 Apr 1843. Wit: G. C. McBEE, T. D. THORNTON, Samuel SHIELDS. Recorded
5 Jul 1843 E. TATE, clerk.

p. 257   Guardian Report - Martha M. FORT, Edwin R. FORT & Jacob H. FORT heirs at
law of Jacob H. FORT, decd, late of Hinds Co., MS. Josiah RHOTON & Wm A. BROWN,
Guardians. Mentions: Georg W. MATLOCK, agent for Josiah RHOTON; Owen D. BATTLES
former Executor of the will of Jacob H. FORT & Guardian of his children appointed
by Court in Hinds Co., MS; Messrs LEA & LEA, Attos, of Jackson, MS; land sold in
MS to William C. ELLIS a trustee of decd; notes on William MILLAR, Upton MILLAR
& Wm J. DULANY (1837 & 1839), Wm H. YOUNG, R. A. PATRICK, John M. N. A. SMITH
(1839), J. B. HADLEY in the hands of Daniel MAYSE (1839), Wm ATKINSON, Henry
ATKINSON & Alsa ATKINS in the hands of George WORK (1839), Esuam SERVICE & John
A. COTTON (1837), Nelson BLANCHARD, E. H. STONE & Jesse ANDREWS (1837), ROSS vs
Others against heirs of Jacob H. FORT at Nashville; tuition of Martha M. FORT at
Knoxville in Oct 1842. Recorded 17 Aug 1843.

p. 259   Commissioners Report - Henry BOATMAN, decd. 1 yr support to Mary
BOATMAN, widow. Mentions: note on Alexander HELTON. Signed 22 Jul 1843 Joseph
RICH, John OLLIVER, D. C. CARMICHAEL. Recorded 17 Aug 1843 E. TATE, clerk.

p. 260   Settlement - Jesse RIGGS, Adm of John ESTES, decd. 4 Jul 1843.
Mentions: notes to Clisbe AUSTIN, Russel RIGGS, TALOR, LONG & Co., John M.
COFFIN & Co., Lindsey WRIGHT; Melton SHIELDS & Co.; Isaac BARTON, Adm of David
BARTON, decd; G. B. MAYES, Dpt Shff taxes for 1838 to 1841; Mary ESTES, widow.
Recorded 17 Aug 1843 E. TATE, clerk.

Will - James COOK, decd. Wife Ailsy COOK; my son Enoch, being under
age, a certain mare which I have sent to him in MO; the children. Signed James
(his mark $\mathcal{J}$) COOK 8 Jun 1843. Wit: Carlisle HAYNES, James BRADEN, Martin
COOK. Recorded 17 Aug 1843 E. TATE, clerk.

p. 261   Guardian Report - Hiram VITTITO, Guardian of the minor heirs of Nathan

ATKINS, decd. 24 Jun 1843. Mentions: Mark MONROW, Adm of the Estate of Nathan ATKINS, decd, receipt of 6 Oct 1842. Recorded 17 Aug 1843 E. TATE, clerk.

Guardian Report - James MILLS, Guardian of John P. PERRIN. 29 Aug 1843. Mentions: last report 28 May 1842. Recorded 15 Sep 1843 E. TATE, clerk.

p. 262 Inventory - James COOKE, decd. 1 Sep 1843. Mentions: notes on Allen HURST & John CAPPS; accompt against John BLACKBURN; claims against the Estate of Jacob SHARP, Thos HARDING, Nicholas GIBBS, James ROBERTSON, Martin COOK, Robert SMITH; $13 in Alabamy money; Hugh GRAHAM. Signed Alsy x COOK, Executrix. Recorded 15 Sep 1843 E. TATE, clerk.

p. 263 Will - James HINES, decd. Having become old & infirmed in body; sons William HINES, Zachariah HINES, Zepaniah HINES & Mikajah HINES; my five daus Jane, Martha, Parthena, America & Sarah; my wife Sarah HINES & my dau Mary; Samuel SHIELDS, Executor. Signed James HINES 17 Jun 1842. Wit: Harmon G. LEA, Balis E. GAINS. No recording date.

Guardian Report - Benjamin SMITH, Guardian of Mary SMITH, Frances SMITH, Alexd SMITH & Taby SMITH. 28 Aug 1843. Mentions: Samuel D. SMITH, Adm of Martha SMITH, decd, receipt 28 Mar 1843; Guardian traveling to Cocke Co. collecting money. Recorded 15 Sep 1843 E. TATE, clerk.

p. 264 Third Settlement - John HUBBS & Stephen FROST, Executors of John HILL, decd. 25 Aug 1843. Mentions: Abel HILL; James VITTETO; Martin CLEVELAND, Guardian of the minor heirs of Jno HILL, decd; rifle sold 1st to Joel FIELDS & then to Levi DENNIS. Signed E. TATE, no recording date.

p. 265 Settlement - Bean Station Turnpike Comms. for 1842. Mentions: Henry WILLIAMS, overseer; Wm MURPHY; Wm HOUSTON; Isaac TOWNSLEY; Wm HIPSHEAR; Gray GARRETT; Wm SMITH, overseer; Henly HURST; Thos McANALLY; B. SEWELL. Signed Wm T. TATE, B. T. McFARLAND, John EASLEY, Comms. 30 Aug 1843. No recording date.

p. 266 Settlement - James JONES, Adm of the Estate of Henry BOATMAN, decd, who was Adm of the Estate of Nenian RIGGS, decd, done for the Estate of Nenian RIGGS, decd. 28 Sep 1843. Mentions: last settlement 19 Aug 1841; Elizabeth RIGGS, Guardian of the minor heirs of Nenian RIGGS, decd; laying off Widow RIGGS dower by Jacob LIVINGSTON 9 Feb 1842. Recorded 17 Oct 1843 E. TATE, clerk.

p. 267 Account of Sale - John HILL, decd. Beginning 20 Jan 1843. For minor heirs of decd. Mentions: Franklin SANDERS, Lewis ELLIS, Wm SHARP, Levi DENNIS, Wm DENNIS, Wm BROCK, James VITTITOE, Allen HURST, Anderson DYER, John HILL, Wm T. CARDIN, Wisener DYER, Jno HUBBS, Wm DAVIS, Thos McBROOM, Wm WOLFINBARGER, Andrew BOWER, Pryor DYER, Harvey DIAL, Jesse F. DIAL, John M. GRIGSBEE, Joel FIELDS, Eli DENNIS, Joseph HILL, James DYER, Sr., Pleasant STARNES, John STARNES, B. F. McFARLAND, Wm HILL, Levi MONROW, Goldman CARDIN, Charlten DYER, Charles SKAGGS, Wm P. McBEE, Green SATTERFIELD, Wm MARTIN, Wm DONAHOO, Abigal FIELDS, Booker DYER, George GRAVE. Signed Martin CLEVELAND, Guardian. Recorded 17 Oct 1843 E. TATE, clerk.

p. 268 Guardian Settlement - Martin CLEVELAND, former Guardian of G. W. DYER. 20 Sep 1843. Mentions: Willie B. DYER, present Guardian. Recorded 17 Oct 1843.

Account of Sale - Robert HARRIS, decd. Hiring slaves: ISBEL to Henry ALSUP, JAMES to S. W. INMAN, PATSEY to E. HARRIS, widow, SUSAN to Henry ALSUP, SARAH to S. W. INMAN. Signed Reuben HARRIS, Isaac HARRIS, Adms. Recorded 17 Oct 1843 E. TATE, clerk.

p. 269	Inventory - Lemuel McBEE, decd. Mentions: Tennessee & Alabama bank notes; notes on George GRAVES, Aaron HARBINSON, Daniel GRAVES, H. G. LEA, Joseph JACKSON, Samuel SHIELDS, James KENNON, Jno McKINNEY, M. I. PARROTT, A. P. CALD-WELL, James CLARK, P. LOVELACE, A. M. SHIPE, D. McCOLLUM, Jacob DICK, Isaac McBEE, A. G. JACKSON; Negro men JAMES, DICK, FILL & HENRY; Negro women CLOWE, LIZE, MARIAH, REARS; Negro girl LUCY; Negro children LINDY, NUTTY; household & kitchen bequeathed to Sarah McBEE; Negro man JOHN bequeathed to Wm C. McBEE; Negro JOSEPH & FRANK bequeathed to Milo McBEE; Negro boy JUPATER bequeathed to Daniel McBEE; Negro boy ALFRED bequeathed to Callaway McBEE; Negro boy MAJOR bequeathed to James A. McBEE; Negro woman RHODY & 2 Negro children HANNAH & ADALINE bequeathed to Patsy; Negro woman PRISCILLA, aged 55 to 60; Negro girl AMANDA, age c2 mos. Signed Isaac & G. C. McBEE, Executors, Jul 1843. Recorded 19 Oct 1843.

p. 270	Account of Sale - Lemuel McBEE, decd. 30 Sep 1843. Mentions: Sarah McBEE, John S. WATERS, John NANCE, Jr., A. H. McBEE, C. B. NANCE, Jacob DICK, Milo McBEE, L. J. McBEE, Silas MYNATT, Wm C. McBEE, John NANCE, Jas McBEE, H. CREWS. Signed Isaac M. & G. C. McBEE, Executors. Recorded 19 Oct 1843 E. TATE.

p. 271	Inventory - Henry BOATMAN, decd. Mentions: notes on Jacob NOE, James JONES, Lewis BELL, Abram TOWERY, Thos ROBERTSEN, Jesse RIGGS, David McANALLY, Lucinda KEETON; accompts on David COUNTZ. Signed James JONES, Adm. Recorded 19 Oct 1843 E. TATE, clerk.

p. 273	Account of Sale - Henry BOATMAN, decd. 25 Jul 1843. Mentions: Alxd HETTON, Ezhl BOATMAN, Elias WESTERN, Jas A. LAFFERTY, Elizabeth RIGGS, Widow, Ezk BOATMAN, Marene DEVAULT, Pleasant WESTERN, Warham EASLEY, Marcus (?) L. DANIEL, Joseph LYNN, note on Jacob NOE. Signed James JONES, Adm. Recorded 20 Oct 1843 E. TATE, clerk.

p. 274	Commissioners Report - Wm HAYNES, decd. 1 yr support for widow Sarah HAYNES. Signed Joseph CLARK, Wm SHARP, Joseph YADON 7 Sep 1843. Recorded 20 Oct 1843 E. TATE, clerk.

p. 275	Commissioners Report - The support of the WITHERS (?) Widow & family for rest of yr. Signed Henry x HIPSHEAR, Wm x McCOY, William IMES, Comms. Recorded 20 Oct 1843.

Will - Thos HOWELL, decd. My mother all of my land No. Side of Holsten River & profits from mill, at her d. to Samuel CARMICHAEL, son of Dennis & Prudence CARMICHAEL; will my mother my boy JACOB & my girl RHODA & her children, at her d. to Prudence CARMICHAEL; land on So. Side of river divided in 5 parts amongst Elizabeth COUNTS & Jane COUNTS (one part), James CARMICHAEL, Susan CARMICHAEL, Daniel T. CARMICHAEL & John T. CARMICHAEL, children of Daniel & Prudence CARMICHAEL; a coult now at Eliha A. TAYLOR's; Jane MOODY formerly Jane COUNTS mare bought from Joel DENISON; my boy GEORGE; my sister Prudence; Gowens farm sold & money for use of Nancy HILL & two of Caroline DYERS children, Susan

& Oliver; Daniel CARMICHAEL & Robert J. McKINNY, Executors. Signed 26 Sep 1843
T. K. HOWELL. Wit: N. M. JEFFREYS, David x COUNTS. Recorded 8 Nov 1843.

p. 276   Settlement - Joseph WILLIAMS, Adm of Hannah WILLIAMS, decd. 5 Oct 1843.
Mentions: Hannah WILLIAMS pension; Alnd RAY; Reece WILLIAMS an heir; John
WILLIAMS an heir; Saml DOTSEN who intermarried with Mary WILLIAMS an heir;
Joseph CLARK; Joel DOTSEN; Wm MALLICOAT; Wm T. TATE; Joseph WILLIAMS, Adm, an
heir. Recorded 13 Nov 1843 E. TATE, clerk.

p. 277   Settlement - Nathl MALLICOAT, Adm of Dedman MALLICOAT, decd. 20 Oct
1843. Mentions: notes to Wm THOMPSON, James DAY, Wm MALLICOAT, Jno P. JENNINGS,
LAFFERTY & WHITESIDE; Jacob SHOULTZ; Wm T. TATE; Ethelred WILLIAMS; Martin
CLEVELAND; Hamilton EVANS; E. THOMASON, Shff, tax 1838; RICE & McFARLAND; Henry
HIPSHEAR; James MALLICOAT; Cleveland COFFEE; Peter BUNDEN. Recorded 13 Nov 1843.

p. 277   Second Settlement - Rice COFFEE, Adm of Meredith COFFEE, decd. 9 Oct
1843. Mentions: last settlement 25 May 1841; John COFFEE a legatee; Esther
COFFEE, widow; Harden SPARKMAN who intermarried with Miriam COFFEE a legatee.
Recorded 13 Nov 1843 E. TATE, clerk.

p. 278   Inventory - Nathan P. WHITSETT, decd. Mentions: accompts on Jno
LATHIM, James LATHIM, C. W. LATHIM, Green BUNDEN, Wm HIPSHEAR, Lewis TILLY, A.
McGINNIS, Marvel NASH, H. WILLIAMS, E. WALKER, William COFFEE, Harmon HAYES,
Jno P. JENNINGS, Rebecca MOBLEY, Cleveland COFFEE, Thomas HAYES, Jr., Tenth
VAUGHN, James BULLIN, Pendleton TAYLOR, Henry WILLIAMS, David WOLF, B. COFFEE,
Delpa DOLTON, Jno HIPSHEAR, Thos DOLLEN, Jr., Jas HAYES, Jr., Jno COFFEE, Jr.,
Reuben DOLLEN, Sr., Thos HAYES, Sr., Needham COLLINS, Wm COFFEE, Joseph FURGASON,
A. TUCKER, S. M. EPPERSON, James H. GORDEN, George HAYES, Moses McGINNIS, James
HAYES, John RAINS, Joseph RADER, Ezekiel HUDDLESTONE, John WOLF, Wm WALKER, A.
P. McCARTY, Solomon MILLIKAN, F. ROW, George TUCKER, L. D. WEBB, Jacob WOLF, A.
McCOY, Willie HIPSHEAR, H. TUCKER, Jonathan TRAIL, David McCOY, Margaret TURN-
MIRES, William WALKER, James HAYES, J. MILLS, W. WEBB, John PERSEN, Enoch
MOBLEY, Madison HAYES, C. TAYLOR, D. HUDDLESTONE, Wm GORDEN, Susan WEBB; notes
on Jno COFFEE, S. M. EPPERSON, Enoch JORDAN, A. COFFEE. Signed A. COFFEE, Adm.
Recorded 13 Nov 1843.

p. 279   Account of Sale - Nathan P. WHITSETT, decd. Mentions: Wm HIPSHEAR,
Elizabeth WHITSETT, Jno RUCKER, George HAYES, John RUCKER, C. W. LATHIM, A. G.
SULLENBARGER, Wm RUCKER, Jno COFFEE, Sr. Signed 7 Nov 1843 A. COFFEE, Adm.
Recorded 13 Nov 1843 E. TATE, clerk.

p. 280   Inventory - Wm HAYNES, decd. Mentions: one note of hand on Benj.
SEWELL, Jr. Signed Sarah HAYNES, Admx 6 Nov 1843. Recorded 13 Nov 1843 E. TATE.

p. 281   Commissioners Report - Set apart for the widow & family of N. P.
WHITSETT, decd, until 18 Jan next. Signed Henry HIPSHEAR, Wm x McCOY, William
IMES, Comms. Recorded 14 Nov 1843 E. TATE, clerk.

          Commissioners Report - Robert RAY, decd. 1 yr support for widow &
family of small children. Signed Urijah KEY, Robert MASSENGILL, Comms 27 Nov
1843. Sworn before D. McKINNEY, JP. Recorded 14 Dec 1843 E. TATE, clerk.

p. 282   Report - Edward TATE, Clerk, Pro Ratio Division of the Estate of Robert
RAY, decd. Mentions: James T. WEST, Adm; Wm T. TATE & Co. for srouding; James
TROTT for coffin; Lide INKLEBARGER for gathering corn; James E. MOSES for print-
ing & advertising; Saml WEST for getting out wheat; creditors Wm P. JONES, Joseph
KERSEY, George EZELL, Angeline RAY, Joseph DYER, James T. WEST, James A. KLINE,
Thos & Saml SMITH, Jesse EZELL, Lewis KINNY, RICE & McFARLAND, Jubal MITCHELL,
Saml RIGHT, Thomas RAY, James TROTT, Thos WALKER, Wm T. TATE & Co., James WALKER.
Recorded 14 Dec 1843 E. TATE, clerk.

p. 283   Inventory - Jane TAYLOR, decd.   31 Oct 1843.   Mentions: James TAYLOR.
Signed David McANALLY, Daniel TURLEY, Adms.   Recorded 14 Dec 1843 E. TATE, clerk.

p. 284   Inventory - Thomas K. HOWELL, decd.   28 Dec 1843. Mentions: notes on
hand on John SPOON & Jesse LIVINGSTON, R. LONG & Jehu MORRIS, John NOE, Jr. &
John F. NOE, Isaiah REECE & Elika BULL, R. RAY & Levi CAMPBELL, Robert LONG,
Russel CROW & John CROW, S. B. STEVENS, Wm HILL (who is a minor), Alfred HOWELL
(absconded & not know where departed), notes due 1837; due bills on Godwin PRICE,
Thos HILL; notes on John HICKSON, John HOLT & Joseph NOE, James SHIELDS & Chesley
BURNETT, Jacob NOE & John F. NOE, Wm BROWN, N. LONG & S. B. STEPHENS, Wm R.
SUMMERS, P. MILLIKAN & Lewis RIGGS, N. BROWN & John SPOON, Nicholas LONG & R.
RIGGS, Pharaoh PRICE & John SPOON, Robt LONG, Hugh LONG & Russel RIGGS, E. BULL,
J. W. PATTERSON & John COX, Saml SETZLER & Russel RIGGS, Pascal TURNER & N.
BROWN, David HOLT, Isaac PERKAPILE, John DYER, Elvin KARK (moved off & not known
where, notes due 1838), Pleasant WILLIAMS (run away, due 1833), Joseph HODGES
(run away, note due 1835), James BRYANT (due 1833, moved away & rumer says killed
in the Florady War), James JOICE, R. D. EATEN, Wm G. EATEN, Wm P. JONES; accompts
Joseph NOE, Jr., T. D. KNIGHT, W. JOICE, H. W. DANIEL, W. E. COCKE, Dr., John
HOLT, Warham EASLEY, Levi CAMPBELL, A. P. GREEN, Berry MAYES, James PRICE, Joseph
VAUGHN, Wm TURNER, Dr., John & James DENNISON (for building mill for HOWELL);
tools under lease to John HICKSON; Jane HOWELL, mother of decd; Elizabeth COUNTZ
an heir. Signed D. C. CARMICHAEL, Executor.   Recorded 4 Jan 1844 E. TATE, clerk.

p. 286   Settlement - Reece WILLIAMS, Adm for Joseph LEFFEW, decd.   9 Dec 1843.
Mentions: last settlement 22 Apr 1842; Benj. BRANSON; Thos LATHIM; Royal
JENNINGS; E. THOMASON, Shff, tax 1841.   Recorded 7 Mar 1844 E. TATE, clerk.

p. 287   Settlement - John F. HUDDLESTONE, Executive of Robert HUDDLESTON, decd.
26 Dec 1843. Mentions: notes on Elijah HURST, Lewis ELLIS, Elisha SAVAGE,
John McCRARY; accompt on estate of B. C. McCRARY; one judgt on R. H. SAVAGE;
accompts on Ezra BUCKNER, John F. HUDDLESTONE, John A. BLACKBURN; Robt HUDDLE-
STON, decd, note to Stephen FROST & Jno HUBBS, John SWAFFORD, Calvin HUDDLESTONE,
P. YADON; Ezra & Elizabeth BUCKNER legatees; James SMITH & Sarah Ann SMITH,
legatees; James SMITH a legatee; James SALLING, Dpt Shff taxes 1842; accmpts
William DOTTRY, John BULLARD, Wm GREEN, a certificate The State vs George H.
McBEE, John & George TURNER.   Signed 26 Dec 1843.   Recorded 7 Mar 1844 E. TATE.

p. 288   Account of Sale - James HINES, decd.   Samuel SHIELDS, Executor 22 Sep
1843.   Recorded 7 Mar 1844 E. TATE, clerk.

p. 289   Guardian Report - Isaac LEBOW, Guardian of Pheba BASSETT.   29 Jan 1844.
Mentions: Wm GRAY, Executor of the Estate of John LEBOW, decd, cash received
4 Nov 1840, 22 Dec 1841, 24 Mar 1842, 1 Jun 1843.   Recorded 7 Mar 1844 E. TATE.

Inventory - Nancy RUNNOLDS, decd. Signed William T. CARDIN, Adm. Recorded 7 Mar 1844 E. TATE, clerk.

p. 290   Guardian Report - Elizabeth HODGES, Guardian of the minor heirs of Eli HODGES, decd. 25 Jul 1844. Mentions: last report 11 Oct 1842; taxes for wards land 1839 through 1843; Jacob A. HODGES a ward. Signed Elizabeth x HODGES. Recorded 7 Mar 1844.

Guardian Settlement - John HIPSHEAR, Guardian of the minor heirs of John BARNARD, decd. 1 Feb 1844. Mentions: George BARNARD, former Guardian; cash pd S. J. BARNARD an heir in full of his share, 31 Dec 1838; pd Wm H. CONDRAY who intermarried with Louisa BARNARD an heir, in full of their share, 11 Feb 1840; pd Chesley WEST who intermarried with Sarah BARNARD, an heir, in full of their share, 27 Oct 1840. Recorded 7 Mar 1844 E. TATE, clerk.

p. 291   Account of Sale - William HAYNES, decd. Mentions: Daniel HAYNES, Calvin HUDDLESTONE, Wesley McBEE, Martin CLEVELAND, Joseph M. YADON. Signed 5 Feb 1844 Sarah x HAYNES, Admx. Recorded 8 Mar 1844 E. TATE, clerk.

p. 293   Will - Thomas JOHNSON, decd. My son Larkin JOHNSON; the grave of my wife Barbary JOHNSON; my dau Sally JOHNSON; my dau Lucy EATON; a book of accompts I have given my children at different times; my son Sanford JOHNSON; my son James JOHNSON; two old Negros JACK & SIRS, young Negro man JACK, Negro girl MARTHA; my grdau, dau of Martha CARTER; Negro girl ELVIRA; Executors sons Sanford, James & Larkin JOHNSON. Signed 27 Jul 1842 Thomas x JOHNSON. Wit: James MOORE, Saml GILL. Recorded 9 Mar 1844 E. TATE, clerk.

p. 294   Will - Daniel CHANDLER, decd. My son John CHANDLER; my wife Margaret CHANDLER; son John CHANDLER, Executor. Signed 8 Jul 1843 Daniel x CHANDLER. Wit: Martin CLEVELAND, Tandy WOLFINBARGER. Recorded 9 Mar 1844 E. TATE, clerk.

p. 295   Second Settlement - Wm GRAY, Executor for John LEBOW, decd. 25 Mar 1844. Mentions: last settlement 15 Apr 1842; note of Jesse RIGGS due 29 Dec 1838; Katherine LEBOW, widow; Isaac LEBOW, agent for Jacob LEBOW & Joseph LEBOW, heirs; Albert SULLENBARGER who intermarried with Lucretia LEBOW an heir; Sanford JOHNSON who intermarried with Louisa LEBOW an heir; Isaac LEBOW, Guardian of Pheba BASSETT an heir; Isaac LEBOW an heir; Lucinda LEBOW an heir; Wm GRAY who intermarried with Mary LEBOW an heir; Thos WHITESIDE. Recorded 15 Apr 1844 E. TATE, clerk.

p. 296   Account of Sale - Millar W. EASLEY, decd. 5 Jan 1844. Mentions: John EASLEY, A. P. GREEN, Warham EASLEY, Negro girl & child named AGNESS, Negro woman JANE, Jacob KLINE, Jacob GODWIN, Isaac PHILLIPS, Parrott GODWIN, James MALLI-COAT, Richard RAY, Edward PEMBERTON, James A. KLINE, Slave PRIMUS, Slave ABRAHAM, Slave NELSON, Wm E. COCKE, Francis EPPS, Eli GREENLEA, Elisha OWENS, John GREENLEA, Constand PEMBERTON, Thos J. YOUNG, Thos POLLARD, William PHILIPS. Signed Warham EASLEY, Sr., Executor. Recorded 16 Apr 1844 E. TATE, clerk.

p. 297   Guardian Report - Elizabeth RIGGS, Guardian of the minor heirs of Nenian RIGGS, decd. 8 Mar 1844. Mentions: last report 2 Aug 1842; rent of wards lands 1842 & 1843; Henry BOATMAN, Adm of Nenian RIGGS, decd, rents for 1844 through 1848; taxes 1842 & 1843; schooling & Dr. fees for Mahaly RIGGS a ward;

coffin & shrouding for Mahaly RIGGS a ward; clothing & boarding Elizabeth & Keziah RIGGS, wards. Recorded 16 Apr 1844 E. TATE, clerk.

p. 298   Account of Sale - Nancy RUNNOLDS, decd. Sold 15 Mar 1844. Mentions: G. B. CARDIN, Martin WYRICK, William BALES, A. T. DYER, Abel HILL, Lawson DAMEWOOD. Signed Wm T. CARDIN, Adm. Recorded 14 May 1844.

p. 299   Guardian Report & Settlement - James JOHNSON, Guardian of M. E. C. WACTKINS. 10 Apr 1844. Mentions: rents of wards lands from McAOVIES; amt reported on 10 Jul 1834; T. COONEY for goods; John UPCHURCH acct; T. L. DANIEL acct; Thos BANKS, Shff, taxes 1834 & 35; Andrew NEELY, Shff, taxes 1836, 37; John NORMAN, Shff, taxes 1839, 40, 41 & 42; C. W. PATTERSON; travel expenses from Sumnerville in 1835 to Carrol Co. on business re: land of Widow WATKINS & ward; 1837 expenses in attending business of Widow & ward; E. TATE; Sterling COCKE. Recorded 14 May 1844 E. TATE, clerk.

p. 300   Settlement - Calvin HUDDLESTONE, Adm of Estate of B. C. McCRARY, decd. 28 Apr 1844. Mentions: notes due ROSE & McCRARY in hands of George ROSE; Hugh GRAHAM; Isaac SMITH; Sterling HAYNES; Jesse WAGGONER; John LAMBDIN; Gray GARRETT; George JOHNSON; Calvin HUDDLESTON vs Dyer TUCKE; Robert HUDDLESTONE, Guardian of Campbell WILLIAMS; Jacob SHARP; John NETHERLAND fee in case George ROSE against B. C. McCRARY; H. A. & A. M. WHITE; Shff Lewis M. ELLIS; Abel KESTERSON; Asa TOLLIVER; Z. HODGES; John COX; Solomon DRAPER; J. D. GIST; Alan HURST; Wm THARP; Wm P. McBEE; Jno F. JOHNSON; N. A. EVANS; Allen HURST; Christopher HITCHES; Wm CARTER; E. TATE; Owen DYER; Wm COLVIN; Saml AILER; Robert McBEE. Recorded 14 May 1844 E. TATE, clerk.

p. 301   Inventory - Estate of Joseph YADEN, decd. Mentions: Arrears of his Pension to 6 May 1844 of $43.27. Signed John McBEE, Adm. Recorded 14 May 1844.

p. 302   Settlement - Smith STRANGE, Adm of Nicholas NICELY, decd. 29 Apr 1844. Mentions: Benjamin BRANSON note; Jeremiah BOWMAN note; Isaac M. LOWE note; John B. GRIGSBY; Alfred NOE; J. P. EVANS; Joseph BOYERS note; John CHANDLER; A. P. GREEN; Martin CLEVELAND; Anderson ACUFF; RICE & McFARLAND; Robt FRY note; John BROCK; Lewis M. ELLIS, Shff, taxes 1842 & 43; E. TATE; Elizabeth NICELY, widow; Wm T. TATE. Recorded 14 May 1844 E. TATE, clerk.

p. 303   Will - Charlton DYER, Jr., decd. My sister, Mary BEELAR use of 2 Negro boys JOHN & WILLIAM; Willie B. DYER (no relation given); my friend Martin CLEVE-LAND, Executor. Signed Charlton DYER 7 Mar 1844. Wit: Wm H. ODEL, Jacob x BEELAR. Recorded 14 May 1844 E. TATE, clerk.

p. 304   Will - Elisha CARBACK, decd. Beloved wife Sarah CARBACK; beloved son-in-law George COLLINS; beloved son John CARBACK; George COLLINS, Executor. Signe 27 May 1844 Elisha CARBACK. Wit: Daniel McKINNY, James DAVIS, Solomon NOE. Recorded 5 Jun 1844 E. TATE, clerk.

Inventory - Adam CABBAGE, decd. Mentions: note on Thos WAGGONER. Signed George NICELY, Adm. Recorded 5 Jun 1844 E. TATE, clerk.

p. 305   Account of Sale - Adam CABBAGE, decd. Mentions: Sarah CABBAGE, B. CAVENDAR, David YADON, Joseph YADEN, James NICELY, Jr., John McBEE, Thos

WAGGONER, Jacob CABBAGE, George SELLERS, Joseph PRIDDY, Archibald MULLINS, David
NICELY, Sr., Fielding L. MORE. Signed George NICELY. Recorded 5 Jun 1844.

p. 306   Settlement - G. B. MITCHEL, Adm of James WHITLOCK, decd. 5 May 1844.
Mentions: Saml SHIELDS; Wm P. JONES; James G. WALKER, James WHITLOCK note;
Jeremiah JARNIGAN; T. & L. SMITH; Aquilla MITCHEL, Jr.; E. TATE; Preston
MITCHEL, Dpt Shff taxes 1839; Henry ALSUP; S. C. RENTFRO, Dpt Shff taxes 1840 &
1841; Preston MITCHEL; B. E. GAINS; Katherine WHITLOCK, widow; R. LOYD, Shff
taxes 1842 & 1843; Solomon TREGDIN; Jno STALSWORTH; Pleasant WHITLOCK an heir;
James P. GAINS who intermarried with Lucinda WHITLOCK an heir; John DYER who
intermarried with Paulena WHITLOCK, an heir; James G. WALKER, Guardian of minor
heirs. Recorded 6 Jun 1844 E. TATE, clerk.

p. 307   Guardian Report - Isaac HARRIS, Guardian of minor heirs of Saml RAY,
decd. 25 May 1844. Mentions: last report 28 May 1842; E. TATE; Aquilla
MITCHEL for schooling heirs; Nancy BUTLER for schooling heirs; Henry RIGHT who
intermarried with Mary RAY, a ward, asking for her share of estate. Signed Issac
HARRIS, Guardian. Recorded 6 Jun 1844 E. TATE, clerk.

p. 308   Second Settlement - Preston MITCHEL, Executor for Edward CHURCHMAN, decd.
25 May 1844. Mentions: last settlement 3 Jun 1843; Joab PERRIN who intermarried
with Rebecca CHURCHMAN an heir; Giles J. BLEDSOE who intermarried with Mary
CHURCHMAN an heir; John MITCHEL who intermarried with Delilah CHURCHMAN an heir;
Jno BRADLEY who intermarried with Hannah CHURCHMAN an heir; John BRADLEY, Executor of Matilda CHURCHMAN, decd; Lewis COLLET who intermarried with Leynthice
CHURCHMAN an heir; James MILLS, agent for John MILLS & Wm MITCHEL who intermarried with Nancy CHURCHMAN & Margaret CHURCHMAN two heirs; E. TATE. Recorded
6 Jun 1844 E. TATE, clerk.

p. 309   Guardian Report - William HUBBS, Guardian of Kenady HILL. 15 May 1844.
Mentions: John HILL, Executor of the Estate of James HILL, decd; rent of wards
land 1842, 1843; pd Abel HILL for shingling house; taxes 1842, 1843; interest
from 7 Jun 1842 to date. Signed William HUBBS, Guardian. Recorded 6 Jun 1849.

        Additional Account of Sale - Estate of James WHITLOCK, decd. G. B.
MITCHEL, Adm. Mentions: first sale 25 May 1844. Recorded 6 Jun 1844 E. TATE.

p. 310   Guardian Report - G. B. MITCHEL, Guardian of the minor heirs of Wm
HANKINS, decd. 25 May 1844. Mentions: last report 28 May 1842. Recorded
7 Jun 1844 E. TATE, clerk.

        Guardian Report - G. B. MITCHEL, Guardian of Russell SMALLWOOD's heirs.
25 May 1844. Mentions: last report 28 May 1842. Recorded 7 Jun 1844 E. TATE.

p. 311   Guardian Report - Aquilla MITCHEL, Guardian of Elizabeth ARMSTRONG.
25 May 1844. Mentions: last report 28 May 1842. Signed Aquilla x MITCHEL, Jr.,
Guardian. Recorded 7 Jun 1842 E. TATE, clerk.

        Settlement - Beanstation Turnpike Commissioners. Year ending 1 Jan 1844.
Mentions: Henry WILLIAMS, overseer; Thos P. McANALLY; Wm SMITH; Jacob SHOULTZ;
Joshua COX; Hughs O. TAYLOR; Manuel NASH. Signed Wm T. TATE, B. F. McFARLAND,
John EASLEY. Recorded 7 Jun 1844 E. TATE, clerk.

p. 312   Suggestion - David C. CARMICHAEL suggests to the Court of Grainger Co.
the insolvency of the personal Estate of Thomas K. HOWEL, decd, of which
he is sole Executor. The debits against said Estate greatly exceeding the assets
which have come to his hands 27 Apr 1844. Signed D. C. CARMICHAEL, Executor.
Recorded 7 Jun 1844 E. TATE, clerk.

         Inventory - Estate of Charlton DYER, decd. Signed Martin CLEVELAND,
Executor. Recorded 5 Jul 1844 E. TATE, clerk.

p. 313   Guardian Report - Hiram VITTITOE, Guardian of the minor heirs of Nathan
ATKINS, decd. 27 Jun 1844. Mentions: last report 24 Jun 1843. Recorded 5
Jul 1844 E. TATE, clerk.

         Guardian Report - Willie B. DYER, Guardian of George W. DYER. 20 Jul
1844. Mentions: Martin CLEVELAND former Guardian; Wm T. TATE & Co.; Jonas
MILLS; John CHANDLER for repairing cart; Elizabeth NICELY; the Widow RANDOLPH;
grain for the support of ward & his family; Dpt Shff L. M. ELLIS taxes 1842,
1843; Smith STRANGE, Adm of Nicholas NICELY, decd; debts by Estate of Wm DYER,
decd. Signed 30 Jul 1844 Willie B. DYER, Guardian. Recorded 16 Aug 1844.

p. 314   Account of Sale - Charlton DYER, decd. Sold 29 Jul 1844. Mentions:
Willie B. DYER, John WILLIAMS, Jacob BEELAR. Signed Martin CLEVELAND, Executor.
Recorded 16 Aug 1844 & on p. 321 11 Sep 1844.

p. 315   Guardian Report - Thomas DYER, Guardian of minor heirs of Nelson ORE,
decd. 15 Jul 1844. Mentions: John SMITH, Adm for the Estate of Nelson ORE,
decd; Widow of Nelson ORE, decd, now the wife of Thomas DYER; rents from lands;
traveling to Louisville & to Jefferson Co. on wards business; James FULLER for
registering 3 deeds; I. D. PARROTTS, Dept Shff, taxes 1841 & 1843; schooling of
ward Elizabeth ORE, Calvin ORE & Amanda ORE; Sarah J. ORE a ward. Signed Thomas
DYER, Guardian. Recorded 16 Aug 1844 E. TATE, clerk.

p. 316   Account of Sale - 28 Nov 1842, property of James MAYES, decd. Mentions:
John MAYES, Christopher STROUD, Thomas COCKE, Robert TURLEY, David NOE, Thomas K.
HOWEL, Ayers NEWMAN, Thomas WHITESIDE, H. W. TAYLOR, Archabald SULLENBARGER,
Walter SHOPSHIRE, Malin HARRIS, Solomon SHIPLEY. Signed Henry MAYES, E. A.
TAYLOR, D. C. CARMICHAEL, Adms. Hughs W. TAYLOR, Clerk.
         Additional: Jacob GODWIN, Reuben GROVE, Jr., Hughs W. TAYLOR, Larkin
JOHNSON, David McANALLY, Daniel TURLEY, Jane MAYES, Thomas D. TAYLOR, John
MAYES, J. J. McBEE, Henry MOODY, John GREENLEA, H. O. TAYLOR, Henry O. HYNSON,
Henry WILLIAMS, J. J. BELL, Robert LOYD, Pleasant SENTER, John CALLISON, E. D.
CALLISON, Russel WYATT, John GREENLEA, Jr., James MAYES. Sold 27 Dec 1843
George PETTY, Wm M. MOODY, J. B. HOMER (?), Henry MAYES. Signed D. C. CAR-
MICHAEL, Henry MAYES, E. A. TAYLOR, Adms. Recorded 17 Aug 1844 E. TATE, clerk.

p. 320   Will - Edward HANKINS, decd. Beloved wife Elizabeth; Negro girl NANCY;
Negro boy LEWIS; land in Jefferson Co.; my mother Phoebe HANKINS; my son John
H. HANKINS; my dau Eda HANKINS; my son Daniel L. HANKINS; my 6 daus Rebecca
Emaline, Eda, Pheba, Anna Jane, Susan Elizabeth & Debarah Angeline; my 8 ch:
Rebecca Emaline, John H., Eda, Pheba, Anna Jane, Susan Elizabeth, Daniel L., &
Deborah Angeline; my friends John A. McKINNY & Eli SKAGGS, Executors. Signed
18 Jul 1844 Edward HANKINS. Wit: James HANKINS, John WEBSTER, Thomas C. HANKINS

Recorded 10 Sep 1844 E. TATE, clerk.

p. 321   Will - Dudley MAYES, decd. To Jane KIDWELL $5.00; Scytha Caroline
McCARTY $5.00; Green Berry MAYES 100 acres land joining HOWELS, DANIELS &
KIDWELLS & also interest in my fathers land yet undivided; to Anna BURNETT
$5.00; Edward MAYES & William MAYES land where I now live; my two sons Edward &
William; Green Berry MAYES, Executor. Signed 2 Aug 1844 Dudley x MAYES. Att:
Isaac DANIEL, Goodwin MAYES. Recorded 10 Sep 1844 E. TATE, clerk.

p. 322   Guardian Report - James MILLS, Guardian of John P. PERRIN. 27 Aug 1844.
Mentions: last report 29 Aug 1843; John BRADLEY, Executor of the Estate of
Matilda CHURCHMAN, decd. Signed James MILLS, Guardian. Recorded 27 Aug 1844.

        Guardian Report - Thomas McBROOM, Guardian of the minor heirs of John
DENNIS, decd. 29 Aug 1844. Mentions: last report 26 Jul 1842; pd Wm T. TATE
for wine for one of wards when sick. Recorded 11 Sep 1844.

p. 323   Fifth Settlement - Henry HOLSTIN & John M. HODGES, Adms for the Estate of
Eli HODGES, decd. 10th & 29 Aug 1844. Mentions: last settlement 25 Apr 1843;
lawsuit with Joseph NOE, Jr. & H. B. IVY; case of Eli HODGES Adms vs Joseph NOE;
judgement on Joseph NOE, Jr; judgement on C. B. IVY; John A. & Robt J. McKINNY,
Attos; Wm M. COCKE, clerk; N. A. SENTER a witness; Jno M. HODGES an heir; Lucenda
HODGES an heir; Jesse HOWEL, Adm of the Estate of Preston LOYD, decd, who intermarried with Mary HODGES an heir; Elizabeth HODGES, Guardian of the minor heirs
and herself an heir; James HODGES an heir; D. P. ARMSTRONG assignee of bank-
ruptcy receipt for balance of James D. HODGES an heir. Recorded 11 Sep 1844.

p. 324   Settlement - Isaac HARRIS & Reuben HARRIS, Adms of Robert HARRIS, decd.
6 Sep 1844. Mentions: hiring of SLAVES; Jonah P. SLADE; Robert HYNAS; Saml
JOHNS; John McKINNY; Robt BLAIN; C. M. GOODLIN; Jacob PECK; William SAWYERS; John
MYNATT; ROGERS & ROSS, Attos; Wm C. GROVES; Elizabeth HARRIS, widow, 1 yr allow-
ance; R. LOYD, Shff, taxes 1842-1843; T. TATE; Henderson DYER; Mary HARRIS an
heir; E. K. McCORKLE & Reuben HARRIS receipts for N. A. TABLES, G. R. LOWRY &
Evaline HARRIS 3 of the heirs; Stephen HARRIS an heir; Elizabeth HARRIS an heir;
Saml JOHNS an heir; Jos A. ALSUP an heir; Evan HARRIS an heir; Wm P. JONES, Atto
in fact for the Bank of Alabamy, receipt for McNarie HARRIS an heir; Jacob NUTTY.
Recorded 19 Sep 1844 E. TATE, clerk.

p. 325   Settlement - Margaret CAMPBELL, Extx of the Estate of Jane CAMPBELL,
decd. 27 Aug 1844. Mentions: judgement against Jacob P. CHASE & others; Jacob
PECK; Dr. G. W. ARNOLD; Wm & Jane CHASE, legatees; John & Nancy CHASE, legatees;
M. H. STONE, Guardian of minor heirs of Sarah STONE, decd, a legatee; Alxd CAMP-
BELL a legatee; Matthew CAMPBELL a legatee; Margary CAMPBELL a legatee; a legacy
to John CAMPBELL by Jane CAMPBELL & by him bequeathed to Margaret CAMPBELL, Extrx;
Jacob PECK receipt for Atto in the case Jane CAMPBELL, decd, Extrx vs Jacob P.
CHASE & others; James CAMPBELL & family. Recorded 19 Sep 1844 E. TATE, clerk.

p. 326   Account of Sale - Daniel CHANDLER, decd. 31 Aug 1844. Mentions:
Pleasant STARNES, William HARREL, James H. STARNES, Margaret CHANDLER, Jonas
NICELY, Daniel WIDERS, Martin CLEVELAND. Signed John CHANDLER, Executor.
Recorded 20 Sep 1844 E. TATE, clerk.

p. 327   Guardian Report - Benjamin SMITH, Guardian of Mary SMITH, Frances SMITH, Alexander SMITH & Jubal SMITH. Mentions: last report 28 Aug 1843. Signed Benjamin SMITH, Guardian. Recorded 20 Sep 1844 E. TATE, clerk.

        Nuncupative Will - We, Samuel SHIELDS, William HICKLE & William T. CARDIN, state the noncupative will of Anderson DYER was made by him 2 Sep 1844 during last illness; wife Rachel DYER; all his children now born or may be born, his wife now being in a pregnant condition; all his children now born Leroy Alfred & Marion Harrison; his father James DYER, Sr., Executor. Signed 9 Sep 1844 Samuel SHIELDS, Wm HICKLE, Wm T. CARDIN. Recorded 22 Oct 1844 E. TATE, clerk.

p. 328   Will - John HUBBS, Sr., decd. My four sons William HUBBS, Stephen HUBBS, Willis HUBBS & Joshua HUBBS; my 4 daus Rutha, Sally, Polly & Rachel; the forgoing children of my 2nd wife except William HUBBS who is the son of my 1st wife; the 4 children by my 3rd wife Mary HUBBS, to wit Dorcus HUBBS, James HUBBS, Hugh HUBBS & Martin HUBBS, all now under age, I give $1.00 ea in addition to what each one of them are entitled to draw at the death of their mother, Mary HUBBS, as they become of age, by deed of trust adm. by Hugh JONES, said deed registered 15 Mar 1834 Knox Co., TN; my son John, son of my second wife; Negro girl named NELLY c20 yrs; Samuel SHIELDS, Executor. Signed 5 Sep 1843 John x HUBBS. Wit: John A. McKINNEY, Silas MYNATT.
        Exhibit A - Deed. Indenture Feb 1834, John HUBBS, Sr. of Knox Co., TN & Hugh JONES of Grainger Co., TN. John HUBBS for & in consideration of the sum of $1.00 to him in hand paid the receipt is acknowledged & also for & in considera- tion of the claim of his wife Mary HUBBS to alimony & in bar of her right of Dower has granted, bargained, alieneted _____ unto Hugh JONES in trust for the use of the said Mary during her natural life & at her d. to Dorcas, James, Hugh & Martin, infants under 21; gives land description. Wit: A. LOONY, Jos L. WILLIAMS. Signed John x HUBBS. Registered Knox Co., TN 24 Jan 1843, Book H, p. 410,11,12. Recorded 22 Oct 1844 E. TATE, clerk.

p. 331   Account of Sale - Robt L. WRIGHT, decd. Mentions: Mrs. WRIGHT, widow, H. O. TAYLOR, D. McANALLY, Elizabeth ESTES, Benjamin DAVIS, Isaac WRIGHT, John EASTERLY, Ellis RIGGS, L. LONG, I. LIVINGSTON, H. YOUNG, John WRIGHT, Wm THOMPSON. Signed J. W. PATTERSON, Adm, 20 Aug 1844. Recorded 23 Oct 1844.

p. 333   Inventory - 5 Sep 1844, Anderson DYER, decd. Signed James DYER, Sr., Executor. Recorded 23 Oct 1844 E. TATE, clerk.

        Settlement - Jesse HOWEL, Adm, Estate of Preston LOYD, decd. 23 Sep 1844. Mentions: Henry HOLSTIN, Adm of Estate of Eli HODGES, decd; Elizabeth HODGES; Robt GRAY; Joshua HAZELWOOD; note to O. R. _____; John McAMIS; note to Jesse HOWEL; C. S. HARRIS; G. B. MAYES, constable; D. McANALLY, Dpt Shff, taxes 1842; E. TATE; last report 22 Dec 1843. Recorded 23 Oct 1844 E. TATE.

p. 334   Guardian Report - Jeremiah JARNAGIN, Guardian of the minor heirs of Joseph H. DAVIS, decd. 30 Sep 1844. Mentions: money received 19 Jan 1843 & 11 Oct 1843; rents for 1843 & 1844; A. P. GREEN for hire of NEGRO girl; paid at Dandridge 1844 Dr. bills & shoes for BEN, a Slave; Wm TATE & Co.; A. P. GREEN, Shff taxes on SLAVES; JAMES & RHEA; James SCRUGGS for surveying; J. B. JACKSON; M. H. DAVIS for sewing for GILBERT, a Slave; NEWMAN, Shff of Jefferson Co., taxes; Dr. P. JARNIGAN medical aid to J. H. DAVIS, a ward; A. M. DAVIS clothing for J. H. DAVIS, a ward; J. B. GRIGSBY medical aid 1843 & 1844 to wards; WALLER & KENNON. Recorded 23 Oct 1844.

p. 335   Account of Sale - William P. JONES, Guardian of minor heirs of Rufus M. SUGGS, decd. 31 May 1844. Signed Wm P. JONES, Guardian 2 Dec 1844. Recorded 8 Dec 1844 E. TATE, clerk.

Inventory - Amos STATSWORTH, decd. Signed 29 Nov 1844 Aquilla MITCHEL, Adm, P. S. accompts on Henry ALSUP & Wm MARTIN. Recorded 8 Dec 1844 E. TATE.

p. 336   Inventory - Notes & Judgements & Accompts belonging to the Estate of Rufus M. SCRUGGS, decd, as handed to the Executor by Wm P. JONES surviving partner of firm M. SCRUGGS & CO. 1 Jul 1844. Names: Claiborne ACUFF, Moses ATKINS, Elijah ATKINS, Henry ALSUP, Harrison BROWN, Isaac BEELAR, John BEELAR, James BROWN, John BOILES, Samuel BUNCH, John BULLARD, Moses BROCK, Elijah BECKAM, David BRONSON, Martin CLEVELAND, Wm T. CARDIN, James COLVIN, Wm & John CLARK, Wm CLARK & James MALLICOAT, John CHANDLER & Isaac BEELAR, Philip COTNER, Joshua D. CURLE, John I. COTNER, Samuel CALLISON, Thorton CORUM, John COLVIN, Thomas CHESHIRE, Elizabeth CLARK, Pleasant CLARK, Elizabeth & John COTNER, Edward CLARK, Joel COFFEE, Sterling COTNER, William COOSE, Andrew COLLINS, Wm DYER & others, Wm & Thos DYER, Pryor H. DYER, Anderson G. DYER, John DAVIS, Wm DENNIS, Jr., Wm DAVIS, James W. DAVIS, Levi DENNIS, Isaac B. DYER, Robert DUFF, Carter T. DOLTON, John DUGLAS, Thos DYER, James DYER, Jr. & Wm T. CARDIN, Lewis M. ELLIS, Warham EASLEY, Robert D. & Jennitt EATON, Joseph P., R. D. & Wm G. EATON, Mary FURGASON, James FURGASON, Henry & Hickle FROST, Lorenzo D. FROST, Abraham FULKERSON, Hugh GILMORE, Samuel C. GOWENS, Balis E. GAINS, Robert C. GAINS, Wm GILMORE, Joshua HINSHEW, John HITCH, Aaron & Alex HAMILTON, Ann HINSHEW, Jesse HILL & others, Joseph HILL & R. ATKINS, James HUBBS, Abel HILL & I. COLVIN, John HICKMAN, decd, Isaac HARRIS, Epaphsoditus HIGHTOWER, Joseph HILL, James HANCOCKE, Paschal L. & Noah JARNAGIN, Noah & Asa JARNAGIN, Clabourn JOHNSON, Lide INKLEBARGER, James H. JONES, Jr., Chester JARNAGIN, Uriah KEY, Sarah KERSEY, Alfred KEY, Agness KERSEY, Harmon G. LEA, Thomas MAPLES, Joberry MITCHEL, David & Thomas M. MILLIN, Mary MAPLES, Theophilus MALONE, Anderson NICELY, William NICELY, Alfred & Cleveland NOEL, Alfred NOEL & N. NICELY, Stephen C. RENTFRO, James SELLARS, John STALWORTH, David SMITH, James SMITH, Nathaniel SPENCER, Susanna SANDERS, Sarah SIMMONS, James VITTITOE, Thomas WAGGONER, Benjamin WILSON & others, William WYRICK, Jr., Thomas L. WILSON & others, Alexd WEST, Jos WOLFENBARGER & others, Robert M. WEST, James G. WALKER, Israel & G. W. V. WALTERS, Pleasant D. WATSON, William WILLIAMSON, Solomon WYRICK, Hardin WATSON, John YATES, John B. GRIGSBY, Charles BROWN, Nance & J. Nance DEDMAN, Hiram YATES, Israel WALTERS, Meredith YATES, Reuben YATES, George W. SPARKMAN, James SPARKMAN, Calvin COTNER, William M. MITCHEL, Anderson THOMAS, in the hands of James JONES, George VANDAGRIFF, a bill on A. FULKERSON's land, a bill on Isaac VITTITOE lands. The following notes due between 6 & 28 Nov 1844: James VITTITOE, William SHARP, Levi DENNIS, John CLARK (Buffelowg), Noah JARNEGIN, Jr., Calvin COTNER, Clark EDWARDS, Benjamin ACUFF, Thomas DYER, Lide INKELBARGER, James KENNON, John CHANDLER, Lewis M. ELLIS, Jonas NICELEY, Hiram YATES, William HUBBS, William DYER (red head), Solomon WYRICK, William WYRICK, Eli & Wm DENNIS, Elizabeth CLARK. Accompts supposed to be Good: John CARDIN, Abraham JARNAGIN, Isaac PHILIPS, Israel WALTERS, Robert EATON, Martin VINEYARD, Sarah SIMMONS, Philip WYRICK, Charles LEA, Alfred ARMSTRONG as signed by A. FULKERSON, James SPARKMAN, Thomas PATTERSON, Mary COATS, Jacob VANDAGRIFF, Sr., Absalom MENLY, Robert C. GAINS, Joseph HILL, Pleasant STARNES,

James G. WALKER, James ROACH, Elijah BECKAM, John B. GRIGSBY, Robert LOYD,
William COLVIN, Angey RAY, Calvin M. ORE, Carter T. DOLTON, Jaberry MITCHEL,
Stephen ATKINS, Bales G. GAINS, L. & M. SHIELDS, Abraham FULKERSON, Levi SATTER-
FIELD, Chesly JARNAGIN, Samuel RIGHT, Thomas RAY, Martin COTNER, James W. DAVIS,
James H. JONES, Benjamin WALKER, Samuel SMITH, Clabourn JOHNSON, George W. VIT-
TOTOE, Meredith YATES, Isaac B. DYER, Olliver FIELDS, Winney WICKLIFF, William
CHESHIRE, Thomas McBROOM, Wm DONAHOO, C. M. GODWIN, Joseph BRYAN, James FURGESEN,
E. Balis & R. C. GAINS Guardians of John PARROTT, William HINCKLE, Abjah SCRUGGS,
Hannah CHANDLER, Dotson MORGAN, William YADON. Doubtful notes with interest up
to 1 Jul 1844: Charles ACUFF, Anderson ACUFF, James BARTON, Preston BURNETT,
Martin BAKER, Augustus BOWERS, Daniel CHESHIRE, Fredarick COFFMAN, James DUNN,
Asa EVANS & A. ACUFF, Ezekiel GOWFORTH, Peter KITTS, Jacob JOHNSON, George W. MOYERS
Wm P. McBEE, John MORGAN, Jr., Lea A. MONROW, Mary A. MAPLES, Robert MARTIN, Levi
MONROW, Ira NEEDHAM, Wm H. ODEL, Lucy PASCHAL, William PETERS, Moses RIGHT,
Sampson SHARP, Cardwell SEAMORE, Perrin SATTERFIELD, Joseph SMITH, James VANDA-
GRIFF, William WATSON, Stephen FROST, Carney SIMMONS, Henry JARNAGIN, Abel DALE,
Sterling MALLICOAT, William MORGAN, Milburn RUSSEL, Isaac JANUARY, Wm McDOWEL,
Lewis R. MILLIKAN, James RICE, Caldwell SEAMORE, John BRABSON, John DUNVANT.
Notes desperate with interest to 1 Jul 1844: William ARNETT, Clarysa CHESHIRE,
Julian FRAZIER, John M. GREEN, George W. GRAHAM, Barnett L. MULLINS, James NEED-
HAM, John SELLERS, Alfred ROACH. Accompts desperate: James NEEDHAM, Joseph
HIGHTOWER, William SNODGRASS, Caleb PUTNAM, Isaac BUTCHER, David WILLIS, Moses
CATES, John DAVIS, Jesse HILL, Bob JARNAGIN, George W. GRAHAM, Nancy CORUM,
Letitia HIGHTOWER, Herndon HIGHTOWER, Cheney HIGHTOWER, Aaron HIGHTOWER, Nancy C.
JARNIGAN, Little Jin HIGHTOWER, Jude HIGHTOWER, Elias JARNAGIN, Selburn WILLIAM-
SON, Ran WALKER, Park WILLIAMSON, Braddock CLAY, Pad JARNAGIN, Nancy SOUTHERLAND,
Joe WALKER, John H. KERSEY, Toney HIGHTOWER, Old Jin HIGHTOWER, Harriet JARNAGIN,
Valentine SHIRLEY or Shirley VALENTINE, Joseph KITTS, Franklin HICKMAN, Moses
SHARP, Mary WYRICK, Davis CRANE, Gilbert PATTERSON, Samuel LAIN, John SHARP, John
MORGAN. Property to be divided belonging to partners of SCRUGGS & JONES: 5
Negroes - MARTHA age 12 (about whom there is a lawsuit), BETS age 10, ELIZABETH
age 10, GEORGE age 7, PETER age 6; a claim on A. CARTER; land called the BECKAM
place. Signed John SCRUGGS, Executor. Recorded 9 Dec 1844.

p. 340   Inventory - William CORUM, decd. Signed John S. CORUM, Adm. Recorded
6 Jan 1845.

p. 341   Commissioners Report - Set apart to Susan STONE & family, widow of Rober
STONE, decd, support for 1 yr, including salt in the hands of Wm STONE. Signed
5 Nov 1844 Aquilla MITCHEL, Jr., G. B. MITCHEL, James T. WEST, Comms. Recorded
15 Jan 1845 E. TATE, clerk.

        Inventory - Robert STONE, decd. Mentions: 4 Negroes - REUBEN c35,
FRANK c35, STEPHEN c27, DORCAS c65; lot of corn & fodder which Everett STONE
claims; notes on Michael STONE, James S. TALBOTT payable to William GOLDEN, Henry
ALSUP, James S. BOYD, James KENNON, Amos STALSWORTH, Wilbert T. REECE (1831),
Hardaman STONE (1797), James MASSINGILL, William x GRIFFIN (1824), Varden x
PERRIN (1832), William LEWIS (1831) and resigned by Robt BLAIR (1832), Bannister
MILES (1833), Daniel x SOUTHERLAND (1811), Spencer x GRIFFIN (1806), George
BEEN (1796), John RICHARDS (1811), Uriah x JOHNSON (1809), William COLE (1800).
Signed Henry ALSUP, Adm 6 Jan 1845. Recorded 15 Jan 1845 E. TATE, clerk.

p. 343   Account of Sale - Thomas K. HOWEL, decd. D. C. CARMICHAEL, Executor,
6 Dec 1843. Mentions: Wartham JOICE, Wm TURNER, John H. IVY, James T. CAR-
MICHAEL, Marcus DANIEL, John CALLISON, Benj. IVY, Jacob GODWIN, Reuben GROVE,
Jno HOLT, Warham EASLEY, John NOE, Richd RAY, John MAYES, Wm DAVIS, David NOE,
Pleasant M. SENTER, John WALKER, A. P. GREEN, Nelson BOWEN, Charles SMITH, T. M.
ANDERSON, John DANIEL, Saml GILL, Jane HOWEL, Robert TURLEY, James BARTON, Hardy
LONG, Ezekiel BOATMAN, Joshua KIDWELL, Thos WHITESIDE, Wm LONG, S. S. SHIPLEY,
A. M. WINSTON, Jesse LIVINGSTON, Thos GEORGE, David COX, Hutson PEMBERTON, James
M. PRICE, John SPOON, Joseph NOE, E. THOMASON, Marlin HARRIS, John WALKER, P. J.
JERRERIES, Nicholos LONG, Richd PEMBERTON, Wm P. ATKINSON, George PETTY, Joseph
N. RICH, Wm SPOON, Wm TURNER, Wortham IVIE, E. MAYES, J. B. ELLEDGE, G. P. MOODY,
E. PEMBERTON, Robert LOYD, E. WESTER, John HICKSON, F. B. S. COCKE, M. N. JEFFERES,
Wm M. MOODY, Josiah HOLDER, James LACY, Walter SHROPSHIRE, Thomas HILL, Anderson
HOPPER, John HORNER, Daniel TURLEY, John WILLIAMS, Ben P. TURNER, David McANALLY,
Thos H. ELLEDGE, G. B. MAYES, Paschal TURNER, John GRIFFIN, James MAGEE, John
HOLT, Edmund PEMBERTON, John MATHIS, Wilbourn HOLT, W. H. DANIEL. Signed D. C.
CARMICHAEL 5 Aug 1844. Recorded 15 Jan 1845 E. TATE, clerk.

p. 345   Account of Sale - Thos HENDERSON, decd. Mentions: Mary HENDERSON rents
for 1839, oats 1843, hire of NEGROS 1844; David HARRIS; Eli JONES; John SHELTON;
Wm Y. HENDERSON hiring 3 NEGROS; Wm GODWIN; John HICKS hiring one NEGRO woman;
David SHELTON. Signed James MOORE, Executor. Recorded 16 Jan 1845.

p. 346   Settlement - John IVY, Adm of Isaiah MIDKIFF, decd. 31 Dec 1844.
Mentions: note to Wm LINE; David BENTON, Atto; note to Benj. CRAIGHEAD; 2 notes
to Henry ALSUP; note to LAFFERTY & WHITESIDE; Walter D. COWEN; C. S. HARRIS.
Recorded 16 Jan 1845 E. TATE, clerk.

        Guardian Report - Benjamin BRAY, Guardian of Polly OGAN. 6 Dec 1844.
Mentions: last report Dec 1840; E. THOMASON, Shff, taxes 1844; A. M. FLETCHER,
Dpt Shff of Clabourn Co., taxes 1841; Wm BEGLEY who intermarried with Polly OGAN.
Signed Benjamin BRAY, Guardian. Recorded 17 Jan 1845.

p. 347   Second Settlement - John F. HUDDLESTONE, Executor of the Estate of Robert
HUDDLESTONE, decd. 31 Dec 1844. Mentions: last report 26 Dec 1843; collected
from William DETHERY, John BALLARD, William GREEN, a cert. the State vs George H.
McBEE, John & George TURNER; Evan HARRIS; James C. MOSES; John WESTERFIELD; Pheba
McCUBBINS a legatee; John C. BAKER & Leah BAKER, legatees; John C. BAKER who
intermarried with Leah C. HUDDLESTONE, a legatee; J. B. SMITH who intermarried
with Sarah Ann HUDDLESTONE, a legatee; D. F. HUDDLESTONE, a legatee. Recorded
17 Jan 1845 E. TATE, clerk.

p. 348   Third Settlement - Issac HARRIS & Preston MITCHEL, Adms of Samuel RAY,
decd. 29 Nov 1844. Mentions: last report 28 May 1842; Hardin CAMRON & Elizabeth CAMRON; Wm M. MITCHEL & Eliza MITCHEL, his wife; Henry CARBACK who intermarried with Anna RAY, a legatee; Isaac HARRIS, Guardian of 3 minor heirs; Henry
RIGHT who intermarried with Mary RAY, a legatee; Hardin CAMRON who intermarried
with Elizabeth RAY, an heir. Recorded 17 Jan 1845.

        Guardian Report - Joshiah RHOTEN & Wm A. BROWN, Guardians of the minor
heirs of Jacob H. FORT, decd. 26 Dec 1844. Mentions: cash rec'd 23 Oct 1843
belonging to heirs; Josiah RHOTEN, Guardian, who intermarried with Mary C. FORT,

an heir; Wm A. BROWN, Guardian, who intermarried with Cynthia C. FORT, an heir;
Cynthia C. COX, late widow of Jacob H. FORT, decd; Martha M. FORT, Edwin R.
FORT, Jacob H. FORT, wards, for board, clothing & schooling. Recorded 17 Jan
1845. E. TATE, clerk.

p. 349   Second Settlement - John SCRUGGS, Executor of R. M. SCRUGGS, decd.
2 Dec 1844. Mentions: Wm P. JONES who intermarried with Mary C. SCRUGGS, widow
of R. M. SCRUGGS; Wm P. JONES, Guardian of minor heirs; will dated 2 Dec 1844.
Recorded 17 Jan 1845 E. TATE, clerk.

p. 350   Inventory - John HUBBS, decd. Mentions: John HUBBS, Jr. with whom the
decd lived some yrs; one Negro girl NELLIE; 3 notes on Wm HUBBS (1837 & 1840).
Signed 10 Sep 1844 Samuel SHIELDS, Executor. Recorded 6 Feb 1845.

          Inventory - Lettiticia McGINNIS, decd. Mentions: Negro boys TIM, TOM,
PENDLETON, ANDERSON, IRVIN, AARON, CUPID; Negro girls RACHEL, HANNAH, NEL, UNITY
& SUSANNA. Signed Andrew McGINNIS, Adm. Recorded 6 Feb 1845 E. TATE, clerk.

p. 351   Account of Sale - Anderson T. DYER, decd. Sold Oct & Nov 1844.
Mentions: Pryer H. DYER, Widow Rachel DYER, William DENNIS, Harmon LEA, Owen
DYER, Alfred ACUFF, Wm T. CARDIN, G. B. CARDIN, James HUBBS, Martin WYRICK,
Robert McBEE, Lawson DAMEWOOD, Silas MYNATT, Nathaniel POPEJOY, Rachel HUBBS,
Hiram VITTETOE, James DYER, Sr., Wm P. McBEE. Signed James DYER, Sr., Executor.
Recorded 6 Feb 1845.

p. 352   Settlement - James SUNDERLAND, Adm of George BURKET, decd with a nun-
cupative will. 24 Jan 1845. Mentions: sale 22 Dec 1840, Wm WILLIAMS; Jon-
athan WILLIAMS for coffin; Pierce COODY; E. TATE & Wm M. MOODY; N. M. JEFFERES;
Mary BURKET a legatee; George BURKET note to Wm WILLIAMS; A. P. GREEN; Wm E.
COCKE; Moses MILLAR; Isaac PRATT; James JAMES; Massy COCKRUM; Thomas WEST, Sr.
Recorded 6 Feb 1845 E. TATE, clerk.

p. 353   Settlement - James JONES, Adm of Henry BOATMAN, decd. 14 Jan 1845.
Mentions: notes on Jacob NOE, James JONES, Lewis BELL, Leucinda KEETON; J & J
LAFFERTY; Ezekill BOATMAN; Samuel GILL; A. R. SULLENBARGER; John L. OLLIVER;
Wm McDANIEL; Mary BOATMAN, widow; Alexander HETTON; note to Thos WHITESIDE, N. A.
SENTER, James CARMICHAEL; Levi RIGGS who intermarried with Sarah BOATMAN, an heir
Elias WESTER who intermarried with Keziah BOATMAN, an heir; Alexander HELTON who
intermarried with Nancy BOATMAN, an heir; Ezekial BOATMAN who intermarried with
Polly BOATMAN, an heir; D. McANNALLY, Dpt Shff, taxes 1842 & 43; James JOICE,
Constable; A. P. GREEN, Shff, taxes 1843; Pleasant WESTERN; W. H. DANIEL; Marcus
DANIEL. Recorded 7 Feb 1845 E. TATE, clerk.

p. 354   Second Settlement - Jesse HOWEL, Adm of Preston LOYD, decd. 13 Jan 1845
Mentions: cash on hand 23 Sep 1844 last report; note to Elizabeth HODGES; Mary
LOYD, Guardian of minor heirs. Recorded 7 Feb 1845 E. TATE, clerk.

p. 355   Settlement - Henry MAYES & Daniel C. CARMICHAEL, Adm of James MAYES,
decd. 11 Jan 1845. Mentions: notes to Reuben GROVES, James DAVIS, Wm FREE-
MAN, Jacob KINDAL; David McANALLY, tax 1842; Hughes O. TAYLOR; James READKIN (?);
S. S. SHIPLEY; J. J. LAFFERTY; Wm MURRY, John BIGGS; C. A. JONES; Malin HARRIS,
Daniel FLORA; John HICKSON; R. LOYD; Elika A. TAYLOR & Henry MAYES note; notes

on John POINDEXTER, Pestiman LONG, Chapman POINDEXTER, F. B. & P. B. COBB, Wm
L. ATKINSON; Ahab BOWEN, Reuben LONG, Henry WHISTEHUNT; Wm CORUM, Wm & James
DAVIS; John MAYES note. Recorded 7 Feb 1845 E. TATE, clerk.

p. 356   Second Settlement - James JONES, Adm of Henry BOATMAN, decd, who was
Adm of Nenian RIGGS, decd. On account of Estate of Nenian RIGGS, decd. 14 Jan
1845. Mentions: last report by Henry BOATMAN 23 Sep 1843; note due Estate by
James HODGES an heir of Nenian RIGGS, decd. Recorded 7 Feb 1845 E. TATE, clerk.

p. 357   Inventory - Wilson A. CORUM, decd. Signed D. P. MYNATT, Adm. Recorded
23 Mar 1845.

        Account of Sale - Wilson A. CORUM, decd. 17 Jan 1845. Mentions: John
S. CORUM, Pryor NANCE, Wm HALL, Balis GAINS, Robt N. CORUM, Martha T. CORUM,
Elizabeth CORUM, Jesse MITCHEL, Jno A. McKINNEY, Willis PATE, Washington WRIGHT,
Calvin HOWEL, Calvin MAGGOT, James CANADAY. Signed D. P. MYNATT, Adm. Recorded
23 Mar 1845 E. TATE, clerk.

p. 358   Guardian Report - Mary FURGASON, Guardian of minor heirs of John FUR-
GASON, decd. 21 Feb 1845. Mentions: last report 29 Jul 1842; Martha FURGASON,
a ward, full age as of 12 Dec 1842; John FURGASON, a ward, full age as of 5 Apr
1844; James FURGASON, a ward; Rabeeka FURGASON, a ward; William FURGASON, a ward;
Mary FURGASON for her services as Guardian from the time of her appointment to
this date for 9 years. Signed Mary x FURGASON. Recorded 23 Mar 1845.

        Certificate of the Contents of the Last Will & Testament of John CAMP-
BELL, decd. March term 1845. The will of John CAMPBELL was presented in court
1839 or 1840 and proved in open court by Julian FRAZIER a subscribing witness.
Will has been lost or misplaced. According to E. TATE, clerk, there was only one
heir, Margaret CAMPBELL, his mother. Signed E. TATE, James LAY, Chairman pro tem.
Recorded 23 Mar 1845.

p. 359   Settlement - John ZACHARY, Executor of John DEVAULT, decd. 18 Mar 1845.
Mentions: Morris ADKINS; C. M. GOODWIN; Wm BOOKER; note to Henry WHITNER; Wm C.
GROVES; Wm SAWYERS; J. & S. McKINNEY; John WHITEFIELD; E. R. GROVES; Saml
SHIELDS; Jesse HOWERTON; Wm HOWERTON; John S. WOLLINGTON; Wm MYNATT; D. McCOLLIER;
John BAKER; Ira HOWERTON; note to D. McCOLLIER; N. PETERS, Dpt Shff, taxes 1843;
James SALLING, Dpt Shff, taxes 1844; James ZACHARY. Recorded 16 Apr 1845 E. TATE.

p. 360   Settlement - Stephen ADKINS, Adm of John HICKMAN, decd. 24 Mar 1845.
Mentions: sale 17 Sep 1842 & 6 Nov 1842; note to Wm JONES; Jno MYNATT; Dr. Jno B.
GRIGSBY; Lewis M. ELLIS; note to Paschal HOLT; Joseph HILL; Mary Ann HICKMAN,
widow, 1 yr support; Wm SHARP; Francis HICKMAN's note. Recorded 16 Apr 1845.

p. 361   Inventory - Josiah SMITH, decd. Mentions: Negros SAM, CHARLES &
GRACIE, Nancy SMITH holds them during life or widowhood under the will; notes on
Owen DYER & Lewis MILLAR. Signed Jno A. SMITH, Adm. Recorded 16 Apr 1845.

        Inventory - Edward HANKINS, decd. 5 Oct 1844. Mentions: Negro boy
LEWIS, Negro girl NANCY, notes on John A. McKINNEY, J. & S. McKINNEY, John
WEBSTER, Henry CREUES, Jacob JESSEE, James BOYD, C. M. GOODLIER. Signed John
A. McKINNY, Executor. Recorded 16 Apr 1845 E. TATE, clerk.

p. 362   Will - Michael PERKYPILE, decd.   Son John PERKYPILE; heirs of my dau
Caty NOE, decd; dau Betsey ESTES; dau Polly NOE; son Isaac PERKYPILE; dau Sary
PERKYPILE; son David PERKYPILE; one saddle for Sarah equal in value to Margaret's
saddle; land when David comes of age & 1 yr schooling; Isaac PERKYPILE & Jonathan NOE, Executors. Signed 15 Feb 1840 Michael x PERKYPILE. Wit: John
EASTERLY, Joseph W. PATTERSON. Acknowleged before me, Milton SHIELDS, 24 Jan
1845.
        Codicil - $1.00 to John PERKYPILE, children of Caty NOE, Betsy ESTES &
Polly NOE, in addition to what I have already given them; dau Margaret PERKYPILE
now Margaret CROSLEY; Sarah PERKYPILE; land given Isaac & David PERKYPILE have
become incumbered by a judgement by the Bank of TN; Executor to be soley Isaac
PERKYPILE. Signed 25 Jan 1844 Michael PERKYPILE. Wit: John EASTERLY, Milton
SHIELDS, Isaac REECE. Recorded 17 Apr 1845.

p. 365   Account of Sale - Andrew McGINNIS, Adm of L. M. McGINNIS, decd.
Mentions: James K. McANALLY, C. W. LATHIM, Robert MITCHEL, Mr. L. McGINNIS, John
RUCKER, Wm IMES, A. G. SULLENBARGER, C. COFFEE, Capt. RUCKER, B. B. BRAY, Wm
HARREL, H. ADKINS, Joseph McGINNIS, E. P. HARREL, Miss Polly MOBLEY, Henry
HIPSHIER, H. MILLAR, Michael FARMER, Wilborn TAYLOR, Jonathan VAUGHN. Signed
Andrew McGINNIS, Adm 21 Feb 1845. Recorded 6 May 1845 E. TATE, clerk.

p. 367   Account of Sale - Michael PERKYPILE, decd. 1 May 1845. Mentions: Wm
HAUN, Elizabeth ESTES, Joseph VAUGHN, Alfred H. TARR, William BASSETT, Carrol
BAKER, David PERKYPILE, Hughs W. TAYLOR, Chesley ROGERS, Berry MAYES, Sarah
PERKYPILE, Isaiah REECE, John McDANIEL, Jos HUTCHENS, Alexander WILLIAMS, Jesse
RIGGS, Nathaniel COX, William LEA, Willie I. REECE, Henry ROBERTSON, John PERKY-
PILE, Felps RIGGS, Isaac JOHNSON, Clisler (?) RIGGS, Caleb CROSLEY. Signed Isaac
PERKYPILE, Executor. Recorded 7 May 1845.

p. 369   Third Settlement - James MOORE, Executor of Thomas HENDERSON, decd.   30
Apr 1845. Mentions: last settlement 26 Aug 1841; sale & hire of SLAVES Jan
1845; Joseph RHOTIN dr. bills & medicine for 1 Slave; Wm GODWIN repair a fence;
Mary HENDERSON repair fence on plantation (1839); A. P. GREEN, Shff, taxes 1842,
43 & 44. Recorded 7 May 1845 E. TATE, clerk.

        Guardian Report - Mary HENDERSON, Guardian of Mary S. HENDERSON. 27 May
1845. Mentions: care, raising, clothing & boarding the ward, she being Deaf &
Dumb for the term of 6 yrs against the 1 Jul next. Recorded 4 Jun 1845 E. TATE.

p. 370   Guardian Report - G. B. MITCHEL, Guardian of minor heirs of William
HANKINS, decd. 31 May 1845. Mentions: last report 25 May 1844; James SALLING,
Dpt Shff, taxes 1844. Recorded 4 Jun 1845 E. TATE, clerk.

        Guardian Report - G. B. MITCHEL, Guardian of Russell SMALLWOOD's heirs.
31 May 1845. Mentions: last report 25 May 1844; taxes 1844. Recorded 4 Jun
1845.

p. 371   Guardian Report - James G. WALKER, Guardian of minor heirs of James
WHITLOCK, decd. 31 May 1845. Mentions: cash received from G. B. MITCHEL, Adm;
rents of wards land 1844 & 45. Recorded 4 Jun 1845.

        Guardian Report - Isaac HARRIS, Guardian of minor heirs of Saml RAY, decd. 31 May 1845. Mentions: last report 25 May 1844; Thos SMITH for goods for Tabitha RAY; paid Angeline RAY for schooling Tabitha RAY & Samuel RAY, two wards. Recorded 4 Jun 1845 E. TATE, clerk.

p. 372   Guardian Report - Aquilla MITCHEL, Guardian of Elizabeth ARMSTRONG. 31 May 1845. Mentions: last report 25 May 1844; John DUGLAS, Dpt Shff, taxes 1844; Guardian chargeable with interest from 25 May 1844 to 25 Feb 1845 the time his ward became of full age; satisfied & paid in full. Signed Aquilla x MITCHEL, Guardian. Recorded 4 Jun 1845 E. TATE, clerk.

Commissioners Report - Supplies & provisions for Widow CORUM & family for 1 yr from d. of husband Wm CORUM, decd. Signed 11 Jan 1845 G. B. MITCHEL, James MILLS, John x LARGE. Recorded 4 Jun 1845.

p. 373   Settlement - Samuel SHIELDS, Executor of John HUBBS, decd. 29 May 1845. Mentions: Wm HUBBS a legatee; Mary HUBBS, Widow & legatee; Dorcas PHIPPS, a legatee; James HUBBS, a legatee; John HUBBS, Jr., a legatee; Legatees - Stephen HUBBS, Willis HUBBS, Joshua HUBBS, decd, Rutha, Sally, Polly, Rachel, Hugh HUBBS & Martin HUBBS, children & heirs. Recorded 4 Jun 1845 E. TATE, clerk.

Guardian Report - Robert CARDWELL, Guardian of the minor heirs of Andrew CHAMBERLAIN, decd. 30 May 1845. Mentions: last report 5 Nov 1842; rents from lands 1842 to 45; E. THOMSON, Shff, taxes 1838; A. P. GREEN, Shff, taxes 1842; R. LOYD, Shff, taxes 1843; John DUGLAS, Dpt Shff, taxes 1844; pd David N. TATE for plank to build a house; Dr. M. N. JEFFERS for attention on Jeremiah, a ward; James MAYES 1842 for wheat. Recorded 4 Jun 1845 E. TATE, clerk.

p. 374   Settlement - Nelson A. SENTER, Adm of Stephen W. SENTER, decd. 4 Feb 1845. Mentions: John C. HALEY accompt & postage; J. W. LIDE; T. D. KNIGHT; C. McANALLY; John McGEE; P. B. COBB; Cleon MOORE; C. W. LATHIM, Dpt Shff, taxes 1839; James WILLIAMS; Pryor HANECY (?); Willson C. DUNAVANT; Daniel HUTCHESON; Harmon HAYES; F. BOYD; Samuel BUNCH, Shff; Elizabeth JACK; David HOTTS; Jacob NOE; Wm T. TATE for amt of E. WILLIAMS accompt; John B. PROFFITTS; F. S. HEISKLE; S. BUNCH; Pleasant COCKE, clerk; James R. COCKE, Dpt Clerk; Gray GARETT, Atto fee; Sterling COCKE, Atto fee; Elizabeth SENTER, Guardian of Pleasant, James, Leaburn, Elizabeth & Joanna SENTER & herself, dated 16 Sep 1841; N. A. Senter; C. W. LATHIM, Dpt Shff, taxes 1830; S. BUNCH, Shff taxes 1831; F. BOYD, Dpt Shff, taxes 1832; R. LOYD, Dpt Shff taxes 1833, 34, 35, 36, 37; E. THOMASON, Shff, taxes 1838, 39, 40, 41; A. P. GREEN, Dpt Shff taxes 1842 & 43; N. A. SENTER Probate of last Receipt of Peter GODWIN; Samuel TATE who intermarried with Caroline SENTER, an heir; Elizabeth SENTER; Abraham McCONNEL for Crying Sale; Harmon G. LEA; C. McANALLY; Insolvency of the Estate of Thos TURLEY, decd; Martha THOMASON for attending two BLACK GIRLS; N. A. SENTER, an heir & Adm. Recorded 6 Jun 1845.

p. 376   Will - James SPARKMAN, decd. My youngest son Henry SPARKMAN; land on Jubal MITCHEL's line, Benjamin WALKERS line; wife Fanny; son James SPARKMAN; my dau Nancy JANUARY; my dau Angeline RAY; my dau Martha RITE; my dau Narcessa MORRIS; my son John SPARKMAN; son Hardin SPARKMAN; George SPARKMAN; my son William SPARKMAN; my grandson John SPARKMAN son of my son John SPARKMAN; Henry SPARKMAN, Executor. 3 Sep 1844 Signed James x SPARKMAN. Wit: Aquilla MITCHEL, Jr., Henry ALSUP. Recorded 12 Jul 1845.

p. 377   Second Settlement - Margaret CAMPBELL, Exetrix of Jane CAMPBELL, decd.
8 Jul 1845. Mentions: last settlement 27 Aug 1844; Margary CAMPBELL, a legatee;
Margary CAMPBELL the full amt of her legacy of $50 dated 4 Jul 1845; Alexd
CAMPBELL, a legatee, the full amount of his legacy dated 4 Jul 1845; Wm CHASE &
Jane CHASE, two legatees, full amount of their legacy dated 5 Jul 1845; John
CHASE & Nancy CHASE, two legatees, full amount of legacy dated 5 Jul 1845.
Recorded 12 Jul 1845 E. TATE, clerk.

p. 378   Third Settlement - William GRAY, Executor of John LEBOW, decd.   3 Jun
1845. Mentions: last settlement 23 Mar 1844; note of Jesse RIGGS due 29 Dec
1839; James TAYLOR note; Albert SULLENBARGER who intermarried with Lucietee LEBOW
a legatee; Sanford JOHNSON who intermarried with Louisa LEBOW a legatee; Isaac
LEBOW a legatee; Isaac LEBOW agent for Pheba BASSETT, Jacob LEBOW & John LEBOW,
all legatees; John RICE who intermarried with Senah LEBOW, a legatee; Lucinda
LEBOW a legatee; Catherine LEBOW, widow, a legatee; Wm GRAY, being a legatee by
his marriage with Mary LEBOW. Recorded 12 Jul 1845 E. TATE, clerk.

p. 379   Guardian Report - Hiram VITTITOE, Guardian of minor heirs of Nathan
ATKINS, decd. 5 Jul 1845. Mentions last report 27 Jun 1844. Recorded 12 Jul
1845 E. TATE, clerk.

       Account of Sale - Thomas HENDERSON, decd. Hiring Negros: woman LUCY,
boy HANNIBAL, girl RHODA. Signed A. J. McANALLY, Adm. Recorded 12 Aug 1845.

p. 380   Guardian Report - Edward TATE, Guardian of Wm M. GRAY. Mentions: last
report 1 Aug 1842; rent of lands; hiring of SLAVES belonging to heirs of John
STIFFY, decd, his ward being one; Isaac DANIEL for schooling; RICE & McFARLAND
for goods; Allen MATHIS for tuition at Holstin College; George HASKINS for
board; D. N. TATE; Wm H. & J. S. MOFFIT for goods; Mary AUSTIN for a horse;
taxes 1843 to 1845; Marriage License for ward; Mrs. Mary AUSTIN in exchange for
James MAYES note; judgement against Wm MAYES & Isaac DANIEL; James MALLICOAT
for shoes. Recorded 12 Aug 1845 E. TATE. Sworn in Open Court, James LACY,
Chairman protem.

p. 381   Guardian Report - 1 Aug 1845. Calliway McBEE one of the children &
heirs at law of Lemuel McBEE, decd. Mentions: Negro boy ALFRED, age 16; J. M.
& G. H. HOUSLEY hiring a SLAVE. Signed Isaac M. McBEE, Guardian. Recorded
12 Aug 1845.

       Guardian Settlement - Elizabeth WEST, Guardian of the minor heirs of
Samuel WEST, decd. 19 Jun 1845. Mentions: money received from Executor of
Saml WEST, decd, 3 Oct 1836; Sterling COTNER & Narcessa COTNER (1837); Jno
F. THOMPSON, agent for Jane A. THOMPSON, a ward (1837); Patrick NEAL who inter-
married with Elizabeth WEST a ward (1842). Recorded 12 Aug 1845 E. TATE, clerk.

p. 382   Account of Sale - Robert STONE, decd. Mentions: William STONE, Susan
STONE, Alice MASSENGILL, Charles CAMPBELL, Michael STONE, hiring REUBEN &
DORCAS for 6 mos, Thomas E. STONE. Signed 4 Sep 1845 Henry ALSUP, Adm. Recorded
12 Aug 1845 E. TATE, clerk.

p. 384   Division of the Estate of Lillitea McGINNIS, decd.   27 Mar 1845.
Mentions: present C. H. McGINNIS, Andrew McGINNIS, Joseph McGINNIS, C. W.

LATHIM & his wife Mariam, Henry MAYES & his wife Nancy M., absent Noble T.
McGINNIS & William P. McGINNIS; valuation of SLAVES was made & agreed to by all
legatees; Slave TIM a man 25 yrs to C. H. McGINNIS, TOM a man 22 yrs to Wm P.
McGINNIS, PENDLETON a man 19 yrs to Noble T. McGINNIS, RACHEL a girl 16 yrs to
Henry MAYES & wife Nancy M., IRWIN a boy 14 yrs, ANDERSON a boy 14, HANNAH a girl
10 & CUPID a boy 8 to Andrew McGINNIS, AARON a boy 12 yrs to Joseph McGINNIS,
CORNEILY a girl 4 yrs & SUCKY a blind woman 43 yrs to C. W. LATHIM & wife Mariam,
UNITY a woman 41 yrs to Andrew McGINNIS. Recorded 12 Aug 1845 E. TATE, clerk.

p. 386   Inventory - James MOORE, decd. Mentions: a list of goods in the
possession of Wm GODWIN which he claims as partnership between himself & the decd;
bill of John PROFFIT; County claims; state contract; acc against Odly GILLWATH.
Signed A. I. McANALLY, Adm. Recorded 15 Apr 1845 E. TATE, clerk.

p. 388   Second Settlement - Calvin HUDDLESTONE, Adm of B. C. McCRARY, decd. 4
Aug 1845. Mentions: 1st settlement 28 Apr 1844; Wm M. COCK, Clerk of Circuit
Court for part of the juget against said Adm by George W. ROSE; Lewis A. GARRETT,
clerk; E. WARWICK; notes on A. HOPKINS, David PARKEY, Robert CARDIN, John
SATTERFIELD, Roddy H. SAVAGE, George FIELDS, Edward MERRIT, Joth. POWEL, Andrew
E. ELLIS, Thos SHUMACK; accompts on Daniel B. CAPPS, Obadiah TUCKER, George
FIELDS, Lewis HARREL, Thos WILLSON, David PARKY, Abel DALE, Wm ROGERS, Nancy ELI,
Joseph WYRICK, Isaac HAMPTON, Andrew I. CARTER, Stephen WILLIS, Thomas HARDIN,
Jeremiah SELVAGE, John MULLINS, John MOORE; insolvent accpts: Henry PICKARD,
Ira NEEDHAM, Georg McCRARY, George TURNER, Charles BERRY, Wm GREEN, Isaac BUTCHER,
Martin COOK, Wm SNODGRASS, Mary WILLIS, Benjamin PIKE, Robert SMITH; George
McCRARY's land on N. A. EVANS receipt. Recorded 16 Aug 1845.

p. 389   Inventory - William GODWIN, Adm of Mariah S. GODWIN. Mentions: her
undivided share of the Estate of Thomas HENDERSON, decd, her father, in the hands
of A. I. McANALLY, Adm of James MOOR, decd, who has been Executor of Thomas
HENDERSON. All of which I claim in right of my former wife the said Mariah.
Recorded 3 Sep 1845 E. TATE, clerk.

p. 390   Account of Sale - Hiring Slaves belonging to Estate of Wm F. WILLIAMS,
decd. 13 Nov 1843. Mentions: boy GEORGE to Charles McANALLY; boy TOM to John
WALKER; boy MADISON, boy STEPHEN, woman FELLIS, woman BETSY, woman FRANCES to
Ann K. WILLIAMS; boy SILAS to Jacob NOE; boy DICK to Wm GODWIN; sold boy LEWIS to
Ethelred WILLIAMS; sold corn to David HOLT. Signed Wm WILLIAMS, Saml GILL, Adms.
Recorded 3 Sep 1845 E. TATE, clerk.

          Account of Sale - Hiring of Slaves belonging to the Estate of Wm F.
WILLIAMS, decd. 13 Nov 1844. Mentions: boy THOMAS to John WALKER; boy DICK to
Wm GODWIN; boy SILAS to Albert SULLENBARGER; boy GEORGE to Isaac LEBOW; boy
MADISON, boy STEPHEN, girl BETSY, girl FELLIS to Ann K. WILLIAMS; girls FRANCES
& JANE to John RHEA; 1 lot corn to John WALKER. Signed Wm WILLIAMS, Saml GILLS,
Adm. Recorded 3 Sep 1845 E. TATE, clerk.

p. 391   Settlement - William WILLIAMS & Saml GILL, Adm of Wm F. WILLIAMS, decd.
12 Aug 1845. Mentions: sale 12 Nov 1840; hiring of SLAVES 7 Dec 1840, 12 Nov
1841, 12 Nov 1842, 13 Nov 1843, 13 Nov 1844; notes on Moses DUNSMORE, Coonrod
STALEY, Levi CAMPBELL; note to John OLIVER; Wilson OLIVER; E. THOMASON, Shff,
taxes 1840 & 41; John PHILIPS; Welcom HODGES; James HODGES; John LAFFERTY; P. M.

SENTER; Jacob KLINE; Wm M. COCKE, Clerk of Circuit Court for cost of case Wm
F. WILLIAMS, Lessee vs Jno PRINCE; Thos WHITESIDE; A. P. GREEN, Shf, taxes 1842
to 1844; Thos S. COCKE, Atto; Joseph COBB; Wm T. TATE & Co.; Saml GILL; Wm M.
MOODY; Henry GROVE; James LACY; Solomon S. SHIPLEY; C. McANALLY; Wm E. COCKE; Wm
MURRY; Nathan PERRY; Thomas WEST; LAFFERTY & WHITESIDE; note to Ethelred WILLIAMS
doubtful notes Winsten PARTEN, Thos BURCHEL, L. A. LONG, James IVY, Frank RAIL,
Matthew WILLIAM, Robt R. CORBAN, Moses DUNSMORE, James LYNN, Lewis BELL, Jesse
EVANS, Joseph MAGEE; Jno BARTON, Ato; notes sold on Thos BURCHIL, Robert MITCHEL;
Ann K. WILLIAMS, Guardian of minor heirs. Recorded 3 Sep 1845 E. TATE, clerk.

p. 393   Settlement - Charles McANALLY, Adm of the Estate of James M. McANALLY,
decd. 27 Aug 1845. Mentions: Jeremiah HUTCHESON, Saml GILL, Bosha HARVEY;
J & J LAFFETTY; L. M. ELLIS, Dpt Shff, taxes 1432; note to E. WILLIAM; Wm
HIPSHEAR; Green BURDEN; Henry WILLIAMS, Esq; C. W. F. McANALLY; John CREECH;
Elitha HUTCHASON; Jonathan VAUGHN; note to James C. MOSES; Wm HOUSTON; Thos P.
McANALLY; James K. McANALLY; Zorababel HARVEY; A. G. HELTON; note to Thos
WHITESIDE; Eli HENRY; Wm IMES; Thos JONES accmpt which was sued for & not
collected; notes on George WARD & Lewis DAY, both insolvent. Recorded 8 Sep 1845

p. 394   Settlement - Clabourn BULL, Executor of George BULL, decd. 27 Aug 1845.
Mentions: Hugh HOUSTON; notes to Ethelred WILLIAMS, John RUCKER, Jacob SHULTZ,
J. LAFFERTY & WHITESIDE, Peter OGAN, James KENNER; John EPPERSON. Recorded 8 Sep
1845 E. TATE, clerk.

p. 395   Settlement - Bean Station Turnpike Road Commissioners. Year ending,
1 Jan 1845. Mentions: Willie SANDERS, overseer; Hugh CAIN; Thos HOLLANDS; Thos
P. McANALLY; W. R. PEARSON; Henry WILLIAMS, overseer; Marvel NASH, overseer; Wm
HIPSHEAR; Wm SMITH. Signed Wm T. TATE, B. F. McFARLAND, Warham EASLEY, Jr.
Recorded 8 Sep 1845.

p. 396   Guardian Report - Benjamin SMITH, Guardian of Mary SMITH, Frances SMITH,
Alexander SMITH, Juba SMITH & Rachel SMITH. 27 Aug 1845. Mentions: clothing &
care of Mary SMITH, a ward, she being Dumb & not being able to do any thing for
the Term of two years & six months; taxes 1845. Recorded 8 Sep 1845 E. TATE.

p. 397   Account of Sale - 21 Aug 1845. Estate of Andrew COFFMAN, decd. Mention
James CARMICHAEL, David McANALLY, James MOORE, James D. KENNER, Wm G. McDANIEL,
Octavus YOE, Jno RAMSEY, Algenon JEFFREYS, Russel RIGGS, Jacob LIVINGSTON, David
N. RICH, James LONG, John M. WILLIAMS, Alexander HELTON, Thos COFFMAN, Levi
LONG, Thos H. ELLEDGE, Reuben LONG, Jno LONG, Sr., George MILLEKAN, Wm DAVIS,
Ashley MILES, Jno BROOKS, Joshua KIDWELL, Jos POINDEXTER, Thos BROOSE, Elisha
BULL, Wm GODWIN, Wm COLLINS, Jno BIGGS, James MOORE, David NOE, Drury MORRIS,
Nathl BROON, NEGRO woman & two children hired to George MILLIKAN, one NEGRO boy
hired to Wm A. HARRIS, one boy RALPH to Wm A. HARRIS, 1 woman ALICE hired to
Wm G. McDANIEL, 1 woman DELILAH & 3 children to John BIGGS. Signed Ellis RIGGS,
Adm. Recorded 14 Oct 1845 E. TATE, clerk.

p. 400   Fourth Settlement - John HUBBS & Stephen FROST, Executors of John HILL,
decd. 3 Oct 1845. Mentions: last settlement 25 Aug 1843. Recorded 14 Oct 1845

p. 401   Guardian Report - Martin CLEVELAND the former Guardian of the minor heir
of John HILL, decd. 9 Sep 1845. Mentions: cash received from John HUBBS &

Stephen FROST, Executors; rents, sale of lands and hiring of SLAVES 1842 to
1846; Alfred ACUFF labor on lands; J. F. ZACHARY, Dpt Shff, taxes 1843; James
SALLING, Dpt Shff, taxes 1844; Eli DENNIS labor on lands; Wm SHARP & Alfred ACUFF;
L. M. ELLIS; Aleck HILL; Andrew BOWER; L. A. GARRETT; shoes for STEPHEN a Slave;
Andrew BOWERS the present Guardian. Recorded 14 Oct 1845 E. TATE, clerk.

p. 402   Settlement - Martin CLEVELAND, Executor of Charlton DYER, decd. 9 Sep
1845. Mentions: sale of SLAVE; Joseph COMBS; Gray GARRETT, Atto. Recorded 15
Oct 1845 E. TATE, clerk.

p. 403   Account of Sale - Amos STATSWORTH, decd. Mentions: Katherine STATS-
WORTH, widow of Amos STATSWORTH, Joel COFFEE, John NANCE, Joseph PARROTT, Bales
E. GAINS, Theophelus MALONE, Pryor NANCE, Eliza DAVIS, Wm TOWNSLEY, Lide
INKLEBARGER, Willis FIELDING, James T. WEST, James DAVIS, Jesse MITCHEL, James
S. TALBOTT, Pleasant VINEYARD, Calvin NANCE, Caswell BOX, George SPARKMAN.
30 Nov 1844, Aquilla MITCHEL, Jr., Adm. Recorded 15 Oct 1845.

p. 405   Inventory - John BRYAN who d. 20 Sep 1845. Signed Wm BRYAN, Adm.
Recorded 15 Oct 1845 E. TATE, clerk.

        Inventory - Thos HAYES, decd. Signed Mary x HAYES, Adm. Recorded 15
Oct 1845 E. TATE, clerk.

p. 406   Second Settlement - Royal JENNINGS, Jr., Adm of Wm D. JENNINGS, decd.
26 Oct 1845. Mentions: notes on Royal JENNINGS, Sr., Wm POSEY, John COCKE,
___ PENDLETON, John ROBERTSON, John PRINCE; accompt due by Estate of Wm CLARK,
decd; Wm McCOY; Harrison LOGAN; N. A. SENTER; E. THOMASON; Jacob PECK, Atto.;
R. J. McKINNEY, Atto.; A. P. GREEN, Shff; expenses of Adm from 1837; John COCKE
who was sued; Wm POSEY who was sued. Recorded 13 Nov 1845 E. TATE, clerk.

p. 407   Guardian Report - Wm M. COCKE & Wm T. TATE, Guardians of Martha &
Evalina LATHIM, minor heirs of John LATHIM, decd. 31 Oct 1845. Mentions: last
report 29 Jul 1842; C. W. LATHIM; hire of SLAVES & rents of land 1843 to 1846;
judgement in Chancery Court at Tazwell against C. W. LATHIM, Henry WILLIAMS,
Andrew McGINNIS & James LATHIM; L. M. ELLIS, Dpt Shff, taxes 1842 & 43; Thos
LATHIM, Dpt Shff, taxes 1844; A. P. GREEN, Shff, taxes 1842 to 1845; C. McANALLY
for surveying lands; Jno DUGLAS, Esq, for taking disposition; A. G. SULLENBARGER,
Esq, for taking 6 dispositions; Colbert HAYES 2 days witness in case Guardians
vs C. W. LATHIM, Adm; R. J. McKINNEY, Atto; registering deed from James LATHIM
to John LATHIM, decd; shoes for Negro girl MATILDA, Slave of wards; Harriett
STRAW ? for tuition; Samuel GILL for boarding Evaline; JAMES & RHEA for goods;
RICE & McFARLAND for goods; James LATHIM for clothing & board; Wm T. TATE & Co.
for goods; James LATHIM board & clothing Martha; Wm T. TATE & Co. clothing &
schooling Martha. Recorded 13 Nov 1845 E. TATE, clerk.

p. 408   Commissioners Report - John BRYAN, decd. Support of widow for 1 yr
from d. of husband. 25 Oct 1845 N. A. SENTER, S. B. TATE, John RICE, Sr.
Recorded 14 Nov 1845 E. TATE, clerk.

p. 409   Account of Sale - John BRYAN, decd. Sold 25 Oct 1845. Mentions: Nancy
BRYAN, Thos JONES, George M. MATLOCK, Wm GODWIN, Jeroam B. JONES, Hiram SHAVER,
John RICE, Rice BRYAN, Wm BRYAN, Aquilla JONES, Albert SULLENBARGER, Wm JONES,

Larkin GRAY, Clinton A. JONES, Thos JONES, George MEDLOCK. Signed Wm BRYAN, Adm.
Recorded 15 Mar 1845 E. TATE, clerk.

p. 410   Account of Sale - James MOORE, decd. Sold 18 Sep 1845. Mentions: Wm
GODWIN, Thos DODSON, Parrott GODWIN, A. I. McANALLY, Jos L. ETTER, David McANALLY,
Wm JONES, David HARRIS, Mrs. Rhoda MOORE, P. M. SENTER, Wm JOHNSON, James LONG,
Sr., A. SULLENBARGER, Charles McANALLY, S. W. SENTER, A. NEWMAN, Isaac LEBOW,
John DETHRIDGE, Wm JOHNSONSEN, Thos JOHNSON, R. P. MOORE, Dr. JONES. Signed A. I.
McANALLY. Recorded 15 Nov 1845 E. TATE, clerk.

p. 412   Account of Sale - James MOORE, decd. Done 18 Sep 1845. Mentions:
Thomas DOTSON, Wm JOHNSON, Richard BRAGG, Wm GODWIN, A. I. McANALLY, A. NEWMAN,
Isaac LEBOW, Robert MOORE, S. JOHNSON, John RICE, Joseph GRAY, John LONG, R.
WYATT, Mrs. R. MOORE, H. L. SHAVER. Signed A. I. McANALLY, Adm. Recorded 17
Nov 1845 E. TATE, clerk.

p. 414   Will - John McDANIEL, decd. My son Lea McDANIEL; my present wife (not
named); fence the grave of my children Jane, Elizabeth & Margaret; my daus Susan
& Adaline when they come of age or marry; my dau Polly MORGAN; my son Eli
McDANIEL; Susan, Adaline & Orlenia children of my first wife; Orleania must
remain with my present wife on the place; Robert LOYD & Eli McDANIEL, Executors.
Signed 29 Mar 1845 John McDANIEL. Wit: Wm M. COCKE, B. F. McFARLAND. Recorded
4 Dec 1845 E. TATE, clerk.

p. 415   Inventory - James MALLICOAT, decd. Wm T. TATE, Adm. 1 Dec 1845.
Mentions: yr support of widow & family; notes on David KOLT, John GRAY, Berry
GATEWOOD; order from Godwin SOLOMON to Abraham FULKERSON; account on Isaerl
PHILIPS. Wm T. TATE, Adm. Recorded 4 Dec 1845 E. TATE, clerk.

          Commissioners Report - James MALLICOAT, decd. Support of Widow & family
for 1 yr. Signed Saml BUNCH, Joseph BRYAN, Benjamin PECK. Recorded 4 Dec 1845.

p. 416   Second Settlement - James JONES, Adm of Henry BOATMAN, decd, who was
Adm of Nenian RIGGS, decd, on account of Estate of Nenian RIGGS, decd. 8 Nov 1845
Mentions: last settlement 14 Jan 1845. Recorded 4 Dec 1845 E. TATE, clerk.

          Guardian Report - James MILLS, Guardian of John P. PERRIN. 15 Nov 1845.
Mentions: last report 27 Aug 1844. Recorded 4 Dec 1845 E. TATE, clerk.

p. 417   Guardian Report - Joseph BRYAN, Guardian of Tenny Ann & Armenia BRYAN.
14 Nov 1845. Mentions: Aquilla E. JONES who intermarried with Armenia BRYAN &
Larkin GRAY who intermarried with Tenny Ann BRYAN. Recorded 5 Dec 1845 E. TATE.

          Guardian Report - Wm HUBBS, Guardian of Kenada HILL. 14 Nov 1845.
Mentions: last report 15 May 1844; Jos SALLING, Dpt Shff, taxes 1844 & 45.
Recorded 5 Dec 1845 E. TATE, clerk.

p. 418   Guardian Report - Isaac LEBOW, Guardian of Pheba BASSETT. 30 Dec 1845.
Mentions: last report 29 Jan 1844; Wm GRAY, Executor of John LEBOW, decd.
Recorded 22 Jan 1846 E. TATE, clerk.

          Inventory - Keziah BARTON, decd. Mentions: notes on James BARTON,

Isaac B. McFARLAND, Martha JARRAGIN, decd, & Robert McFARLAND, decd, Henry
COUNTZ. Signed James BARTON, Adm. Recorded 23 Jan 1845.

p. 419   Inventory - John McDANIEL, decd. 12 Jan 1846. Mentions: property
belonging to widow & children; notes on Hugh GILMORE, Chesley JARNAGIN, Nicholas
NOE, Thos McBROOM, R. D. GRAY; Nancy McDANIEL, widow of decd. Signed Eli
McDANIEL, Robert LOYD, Executors. Recorded 23 Jan 1845 E. TATE, clerk.

        Commissioners Report - 8 Nov 1845. Polly HAYES, widow of Thos HAYES,
decd, 1 yr support for her & family. Signed C. McANALLY, Hamilton EVANS, Jno P.
JENNINGS. Recorded 23 Jan 1846 .

p. 420   Second Report - Booker DYER, Executor of Wm DYER, Sr., decd. 23 Dec
1845. Mentions: last report 14 May 1842; Martin DONEHOO who intermarried with
Cynthia DYER a legatee; Elizabeth McHAFFY who was formerly Elizabeth DYER a
legatee; notes on Reubin SELLARS, decd; judgement against Samuel WAGNER. Recorded
23 Jan 1846 E. TATE, clerk.

        Account of Sale - Thos HAYES, decd. Mentions: Thos WALKER, I. K.
McANALLY, T. P. McANALLY, Thos WATKIN. Signed Mary x HAYES, Adm. Recorded 23
Jan 1846 E. TATE, clerk.

p. 421   Account of Sale - 21 Aug 1845. Andrew COFFMAN, decd. Mentions: James
CARMICHAEL, David McANALLY, James MOORE, James D. KENNER, Wm G. McDANIEL, Octavus
YOUR, Algenon JEFFRES, Russel RIGGS, John RAMSEY, David N. RICH, Jacob LIVING-
STON, James LONG, John WILLIAMS, Alexander HELTON, Thomas R. COFFMAN, Levi LONG,
Thos H. ELLEDGE, Reuben LONG, John LONG, Sr., George MILLIKAN, David HELTON,
William DAVIS, Ashley MILLS, John BROOKS, Richard PEMBERTON, James POINDEXTER,
William RAMSEY, Alexander HELTON, Sr., Thomas BROOKS, Elisha BULL, William
GODWIN, William COLLINS, John BIGGS, John COLLINS, David NOE, Drury MORRIS,
Nathaniel BROOKS, Joshua KIDWELL; 2nd sale 22 Nov 1845 mentions: Thomas
GLASGO, David NOE, Solomon SHIPLEY, John WALKER, Pleasant M. SENTER, James DAVIS,
John MONTGOMERY. Signed Ellis RIGGS, Adm. Recorded 23 Jan 1846 E. TATE, clerk.

p. 424   Account of Sale - Jane TAYLOR, decd. 30 & 31 Oct 1843. Mentions:
Jos NICHOLSON, Wm CREED, Geo MATLOCK, Wm RODDY, Daniel TAYLOR, Joseph GRAY,
Henry LONG, Thos COCKE, Warham EASLEY, R. L. TAYLOR, J. GOODWIN, A. I. McANALLY,
Wm LEA, P. G. YOE, James HEDSTON, Russel WYATT, H. O. HYNSON, G. G. TAYLOR,
Richard STUBBLEFIELD, John HARRIS, Elizabeth TAYLOR, Thomas GLASSGO, Wm TURLEY,
Destimony TURLEY, Wm McANALLY, I. M. TAYLOR, Grensfield TAYLOR, Mrs. RODDY, Henry
PECK, Christopher STROUD, J & J LAFFERTY, J. SEVERS, H. O. TAYLOR. Signed David
McANALLY, Daniel TURLEY, Adms. Recorded 24 Jan 1846 E. TATE, clerk.

p. 426   Will - Anna HAWKINS, decd. My dau Priscilla B. HAWKINS; Negro boy JOR;
my dau Harriett L. REEDER; Negro girl MARY; my son Thomas I. M. HAWKINS; Negro
boy SAM; negro girl LILA & her child JINY; my sons children Elizabeth N. CAMPBELL,
Martha BROWN, Sally HUFFORD, Henry S. HAWKINS, Susan McBEE & William P. HANKINS;
my son-in-law William BROWN who now lives in MO, my sole Executor. Signed 31
Oct 1843 Anna x HAWKINS. Attest: Samuel SHIELDS, Harmon G. LEA. Recorded 24
Jan 1846.

p. 427   Will - Thos GILL, decd. My son Samuel GILL all of Estate including

NEGROES; each of my 3 daus Elizabeth KNIGHT wife of Trestian Day KNIGHT, Mary
SHIELDS, widow of John SHIELDS, & Martha JARNAGEN, wife of Chesley JARNIGAN;
my son Samuel GILL, Executor. Signed 29 May 1843 Thomas GILL. Wit: Wm
WILLIAMS, Warham EASLEY, Sr., Jacob NOE. Recorded 10 Feb 1846 E. TATE, clerk.

p. 428   Second Settlement - James JONES, Adm of Henry BOATMAN, decd. 3 Feb
1846. Mentions: last report 14 Jan 1845; Ezekiel BOATMAN who intermarried with
Mary BOATMAN an heir; Mary BOATMAN, widow; Alexander HELTON who intermarried
with Nancy BOATMAN, an heir; Elias WESTER who intermarried with Keziah BOATMAN an
heir; Robert BARTON, Atto, fee; judgement against Jacob NOE for note; amount
pd heirs of Nenian RIGGS, decd, in the hands of Henry BOATMAN, decd, Adm of
Nenian RIGGS, decd. Recorded 10 Feb 1846 E. TATE, clerk.

p. 429   Guardian Report - Wm M. MOODY, Guardian of James MAYES a minor, heir of
James MAYES, decd. 31 Jan 1846. Mentions: rents & hire of SLAVES 1843 to 1845;
wards expenses in Monroe Co.; H. O. HYNSON for schooling. Recorded 10 Feb 1846.

          Commissioners Report - 27 Jan 1846. Hamilton EVANS, John P. JENNINGS
& Samuel x DODSON, Jr., Commissioners. Support of widow & family 1 yr from time
of d. of John COFFEE, decd. Recorded 4 Mar 1846.

p. 430   Third Settlement - John F. HUDDLESTONE, Executor of Robert HUDDLESTONE,
decd. 4 Feb 1846. Mentions: last report 31 Dec 1844; Calvin HUDDLESTON a
legatee; James B. SMITH who intermarried with Sarah Ann HUDDLESTON a legatee;
Letty McCRARY a legatee; John C. BAKER & his wife Leah E. BAKER a legatee; D. F.
HUDDLESTONE a legatee; Pheba McCUBBINS; Jemima O. HUDDLESTONE being a legatee &
Executor; accompt against Wm DETHERY & Wm GREEN, doubtful. Recorded 4 Mar 1846.

p. 431   Settlement - James DYER, Sr., Executor of Anderson T. DYER, decd. 26
Feb 1846. Mentions: note to Wm D. TATE & Co.; Samuel SHIELDS; note to Wm T.
CARDIN; Alfred ACUFF; Pryor H. DYER; Jno F. HUDDLESTONE; Martha HILL. Recorded
4 Mar 1846 E. TATE, clerk.

          Guardian Report - Guardian of Martha M. FORT, Edwin R. FORT & Jacob H.
FORT minor heirs of Jacob H. FORT, decd. Mentions: by letter from John M. LEA
of LEA & LEA, Attos, of Nashville, dated 5 Apr 1845, for the undersigned at
Jackson, MS, the sum of which we have distributed to Martha M. FORT, Edwin R.
FORT & Jacob H. FORT and also Cynthia C. COX late the wife of Jacob H. FORT,
decd & Isiah RHOTEN & William A. BROWN acting for their wives all of whom are
legatees in equal interest; William WILLIAMS; Wm T. TATE & Co.; accompts at New
Market for board & tuition for Edwin; expenses to Panther Springs; E. WILLIAMS;
LOWERY BOOM & Co.; funds loaned to Elisha S. RHOTEN with Massey HILL & James
THOMPSON as security; board, merchandise & tuition for Elisha RHOTEN, F. & H.
BOYD & Massy HILL. Signed 2 Mar 1846 William A. BOWEN & Josiah RHOTEN,
Guardians. Recorded 4 Mar 1846 E. TATE, clerk.

p. 433   Will - Joseph BEELER, decd. Beloved wife Ann BEELAR; land on WILLIAMS
Creek; Negro man DICK; sons Isaac BEELAR, Daniel BEELAR, John BEELAR, Henry
MOYERS & John LONG; Negro girl PATS; son Jacob BEELAR; my dau Margaret ODEL; note
on James BROCK shall not be collected, but given to the children of Elizabeth
BROCK as a part of their portion of my estate; my dau Esther WATSON; my grch
ch of David BEELAR namely George W. BEELAR, Joseph BEELAR, Catharine BEELAR &

Margaret BEELAR; sons Jacob BEELAR & John BEELAR, Executors. Signed 22 Aug 1845.
Recorded 5 Mar 1846 E. TATE, clerk. Wit: Martin CLEVELAND, John x CARTER,
Joseph x GLASSCLOW.

p. 434   Will - William LANE, decd. Beloved wife Sarah LANE; my son John LANE;
when wife dies all money to be given to son John LANE; "Ex perform with the article that I am bound in unto Polly KITTS & Her son Henry KITTS that is now in
the hands of Stephen FROST for safe keeping, if said Henry KITTS should live
with untill he is twentyone years of age agreeable to the said article turned
over."; John LANE, Executor. Signed 22 Sep 1841 William LANE. Wit: John H.
FROST, Henry FROST. Recorded 21 Apr 1846.

p. 435   Account of Sale - John COFFEE, decd. Mentions: John COFFEE, Benjamin
COFFEE, Cleveland COFFEE, Harmon HAYES, John RUCKER, George W. HAYES, Enos SHOCK-
LEY, Lucinda COFFEE, Wm HARREL, Wm ADAMS, Thomas I. COFFEE, Timothy DALTON, Thos
DALTON, Wm COFFEE, Eliza COFFEE, James K. McANALLY, Duncan COLLINS, Henderson
LATHIM, Wm IMES, Green BURDEN, Wm T. ASBEA, Azariah DOLTEN, Andrew COLLINS, John
HAYES, Cobby HAYES; aptes against C. W. LATHIM 1840-1843 doubtful. Signed A.
COFFEE, Elizabeth x COFFEE, Adms. Recorded 21 Apr 1846 E. TATE, clerk.

p. 436   Account of Sale - Keziah BARTON, decd. Sold Wed., 28 Jan 1846. Mentions:
Isaac BARTON, Edmond CLUCK, John H. MILLAR. Signed James BARTON, Adm. Recorded
21 Apr 1846 E. TATE, clerk.

        Guardian Report - Edward TATE, Guardian of Joel Noel MILLAR, a minor.
Mentions: appointment 7 Apr 1845. Sworn before Warham EASLEY, Chairman of the
Circuit Court. Recorded 21 Apr 1846.

p. 437   Guardian Report - Jesse F. BEELAR, Guardian of minor heirs of David
BEELAR, decd. 4 Apr 1846. Mentions: rents & taxes 1841 to 1845; last report
5 Jan 1841; his 4 wards. Recorded 21 Apr 1846 E. TATE, clerk.

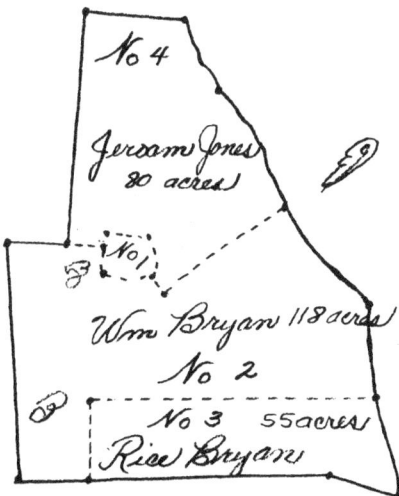

Comissioners Report - This platt of the
land that John BRYAN, decd, had. Asking the
Commissioners to make partition & distribute
to heirs: Nancy BRYAN, Lot No. 1, widow &
relict; Wm BRYAN, No. 2; Rice BRYAN, No. 3;
Polly JONES, formerly Polly BRYAN who intermarried with Jeroam JONES, Lot No. 4.
Mentions: Joseph BRYAN's line, James BRYAN's
line, Isaac LEBOW's corner, state road near
the Hawkins Co. line, Henry LEBOW's old
corner, old field at Isaac LEBOW's. Signed
4 Mar 1846 G. McCROW, Spencer BASSETT,
Isaac LEBOW, Joseph BRYAN. Recorded 21 Apr
1846 E. TATE, clerk.

p. 439   Bean Station Turnpike Commission ending 31 Dec 1845. Mentions: J. P.
JENNINGS, gatekeeper; C. W. LATHIM, gatekeeper; Charles McANALLY, former treas-
urer, I. SHOULTZ, Marvel NASH, Willie SANDERS; Thos WHITESIDE, present treasurer;
Daniel G. MILLAR, overseer; Henry WILLIAMS, overseer; a new ford on Powell's
River; Jacob CLOUD. Signed B. F. McFARLAND, W. B. CUNNINGHAM, J. GODWIN, Comms.
Recorded 22 Apr 1846.

p. 441   Inventory - Joseph BEELAR, decd. Mentions: notes on George SEAMORE,
John BEELAR, Benjamin CAVENDAR, L. M. ELLIS, James SHIELDS & Daniel NELSON, John
SELLARS & Joseph CHANDLER, John PERRIN, James STARNES, Martin CLEVELAND, John
BEELAR, Sr., Robert FRY, Edward & Joseph CLARK, Smith STRANGE, COCKE & MASSINGILL
Daniel BEELAR, John CHANDLER, John LONG, Charles JONES (1830), Haluim OBRIAN
(1831), Wm H. ODEL (1830 & 1839), Daniel McVEY (1832), Wm HOLLINSWORTH (1836 &
1843), Joseph SMITH (1836, 1837 & 1839), Elizabeth COFFMAN (1836), Julies HACKER
(1841), Eli SHELTON (1828), Caleb SHOCKLEY, Wm NAPER (1816), James BROCK, Richard
BRAGG, John CHANDLER, Sr.; suit Daniel McVEY vs Gideon HARRIS; Jonathan BRANSEN
collecting notes on Abraham BEELAR, John STEWART; hides at Martin CLEVELAND's to
be tanned; 7 NEGROES; 645 acres of land. Signed Jacob BEELAR, Executor. Recorded
8 May 1846 E. TATE, clerk.

p. 443   Account of Sale - Joseph BEELAR, Sr., decd. Mentions: Martin CLEVELAND
Moses BLACK, Daniel BEELAR, Clabourn ACUFF, William HARREL, Sr., Samuel DODSON,
Jr., John BEELAR, Jr., William WOLFINBARGER, Hanecy DALE, Wm JEFFERES, Elijah
JONES, Jacob SHELTON, John AREWINE, Thos WAGNER, L. M. ELLIS, Robert CARDWELL,
John COX, John DODSON, Richard WADE, Daniel WIDDERS, Alfred BUNCH, Alvis McMILLIN
Thos. WILSON, Andrew GREST, Nathan N. MOORE, Pleasant STARNES, William HIPSHEAR,
Augustus F. JENNINGS, Joseph SHELTON, Green BURDEN, Wm BOWER, G. W. DYER, John
CHANDLER, Allen HURST, Ann BEELAR, John CLARK, Henry MYERS, John LONG, James
HARREL, James BROCK, Joseph GROSECLOSE, G. W. VITTETOE, John NANCE, George SELLERS
John WALTERS, John B. GRIGSBEE, Joseph BROCK, Martin COOK, William WAGNER,
Michael GOLDMAN. Signed 28 Mar 1846 John CLARK, John A. CLEVELAND, clerks.
Recorded 8 May 1846 E. TATE, clerk.

p. 446   Settlement - David McANALLY & Daniel TURLEY, Adms of Jane TAYLOR, decd.
7 Apr 1846. Mentions: H. O. HYNSON, John GIBBS, R. S. TAYLOR, George W. MATTOCKS,
taxes 1843. Recorded 12 May 1846 E. TATE, clerk.

          Second Settlement - Martin CLEVELAND, former Executor of Charleton DYER,
Jr., decd. 28 Apr 1846. Mentions: last report 9 Sep 1845; Jesse F. BEELAR, the
Adm. Recorded 12 May 1846.

p. 447   Settlement - Wm T. CARDIN, Adm of Nancy REYNOLDS, decd. 29 Dec 1845.
Mentions: G. B. CARDIN, James DYER, Sr. Recorded 12 May 1846 E. TATE, clerk.

          Inventory - Charleton DYER, Jr., decd. Mentions: notes on Jesse F.
BEELAR, David BEELAR & Willie B. DYER; account against Charles INGRUM of Pulaski
Co., KY; one negro boy JOHN bequeathed to sister Mary BEELAR. Signed Jesse F.
BEELAR, Adm., 4 May 1846. Recorded 12 May 1846 E. TATE, clerk.

p. 448   Inventory - Thomas HENDERSON, decd. May 1846. Mentions: Negroes:
woman LUCY, girl RHODA, girl LUIZA; notes on Wm Y. HENDERSON, Mary HENDERSON, Wm
GODWIN, David HARRIS, John DUEER, A. I. McANALLY, William McCRAW, William MURRY,

Joseph HICKS & Pleasant WHITLOW. Signed William GODWIN, Adm. Recorded 12 May 1846 E. TATE, clerk.

Will - Andrew COFFMAN, decd. My four sons, David, Thomas, Andrew & Barton COFFMAN; my dau Betsy MILLIKAN; my grandson David KNOX, son of David & Nancy KNOX, if he applies part within 5 yrs of d.; all SLAVES set free; trusty friends Ellis RIGGS & James CARMICHAEL, Jr., Executors. Signed 30 Apr 1844. My Slaves are now SARAH, LIZA, ELSE, RALPH, HOUSTON, ANNA, BETSY, JANE, JEMIMA & STERLING. Signed Andrew COFFMAN. Wit: C. M. McANALLY, Edwd TATE. After this will was written it was apertained that David COFFMAN named in will is dead & his part is to go to his heirs. Signed 30 Apr 1844, Andrew COFFMAN. Recorded 12 May 1846.

p. 450   Affadavit attached - James DAVIS swears before R. P. MOORE, Co. Court Clerk, that Rafe COFFMAN, a boy of color, is one of the Slaves that was freed by the will of Andrew COFFMAN by his will dated 30 Apr 1844. Signed James DAVIS 7 Jun 1860.

Receipt - Received of John LANE, Executor of my husband, William LANE, decd, my legacy in full, received 15 May 1846. Signed Sarah x LANE. Wit: John H. FROST, Michael GOLDMAN. Recorded 8 Jun 1846.

Commissioners Report - 1 yr supplies to Lucy PEMBERTON, widow of Hutsen PEMBERTON, decd, & family. 22 May 1846 Robert D. GRAY, Alexander x JOICE, M. L. DANIEL, Commissioners. Recorded 8 Jan 1846.

p. 451   Settlement - George NICELY, Adm of Adam CABBAGE, decd. 16 May 1846. Mentions: note on Thos WAGNER; Martin CLEVELAND; John LONG, A. P. GREEN, Shff, taxes 1844-45; Sarah CABBAGE, an heir; Elizabeth KIRBY, an heir; George NICELY, Adm., who intermarried with Hannah CABBABE, an heir. Recorded 16 May 1846.

Will - Richard GRANTHAM, decd. My beloved wife Frances GRANTHAM; my black boy SIMON; my 1st dau Penelope advanced in age; my dau Tabitha ROBERTSON; the children of my dau Mary, decd, who intermarried with George SANDERS; the children of my dau Anna, decd, who intermarried with Hezekiah ROBERTSON; my son Amos; my dau Rachel; my dau Rhoda; my son John GRANTHAM; my son James GRANTHAM; my dau Alice; my son Richard GRANTHAM; my son Willis GRANTHAM; James GRANTHAM & Hughs W. TAYLOR, Executors. Signed 6 Dec 1845 Richard GRANTHAM. Wit: George G. TAYLOR, Jacob P. KIRKHAM, James H. GRAY. Recorded 18 Jul 1846.

p. 453   Account of Sale - 22 May 1846. Hutson PEMBERTON, decd. Mentions: George BUNDEN, Richard B. PEMBERTON, Richard RAY, R. D. GRAY, Constant PEMBERTON, W. H. DANIEL, Wm E. COCKE, Anderson HOPPER, Jennings PEMBERTON, Ezekill BOATMAN, Richard RAY, John W. PEMBERTON. Signed 6 Jul 1846 E. THOMASON, clerk. Edmond x PEMBERTON, Adm. Recorded 20 Jul 1846 E. TATE, clerk.

p. 454   Commissioners Report - Mary TROTT, widow of James TROTT, decd, 1 yr support of family. Signed 2 May 1846 Hugh GILMORE, Saml SMITH, John x TALLY. Recorded 20 Jul 1846 E. TATE, clerk.

Inventory - James TROTT, decd. Mentions: lumber at J. S. TALBOT's; timber on Indian Ridge, timber in Jefferson Co.; accts in hands of James G.

WALKER, Jesse MITCHEL, A. Q. MITCHEL, Jr., George SPARKMAN, David LIVINGSTON, James H. DYER, John TALLY, Jr., Absalom MANLY, Abner LOWE, Thomas RAY, George KEY for S. WATSEN, Lide INGLEBARGER, Wm LOWE, Thos DAVIS, Hugh GILMORE, Chesley RAY, James ROACH & John STALWORTH. Signed 6 Jul 1846 James H. DYER, Adm. Recorded 20 Jul 1846 E. TATE, clerk.

p. 455   Guardian Report - Hiram VITTETOE, Guardian of the minor heirs of Nathan ATKINS, decd. 4 Jul 1846. Mentions: last report 5 Jul 1845. Recorded 20 Jul 1846 E. TATE, clerk.

p. 456   Guardian Report - Isaac HARRIS, Guardian of the minor heirs of Samuel RAY, decd. 20 Jul 1846. Mentions: last report 31 May 1845; A. WILHITE for tuition for Saml & Abner RAY, 2 wards. Recorded 8 Aug 1846.

Guardian Report - Thomas DYER, Guardian of the minor heirs of Marvel WICKLIFF, decd. 10 Jul 1846. Mentions: last report 29 Jul 1842; John DUGLAS, Dpt Shff, taxes 1844 & 45; Wm HARRIS clothing for Mary & Matilda WICKLIFF, 2 wards. Recorded 8 Aug 1846 E. TATE, clerk.

p. 457   Guardian Report - Andrew BOWER, Guardian of the minor heirs of John HILL decd. 10 Jul 1846. Mentions: cash received from former Guardian Martin CLEVE-LAND on 9 Sep 1845; hire of SLAVES & rents; R. J. McKINNEY, Atto, fee; C. RAGEN Tuition for Ramsey HILL, a ward; James SALLING, Dpt Shff, taxes 1845; L. M. ELLIS to renew note. Signed Andrew x BOWER, Guardian. Recorded 8 Aug 1846 E. TATE.

p. 458   Guardian Report - Thomas DYER, Guardian of the minor heirs of Nelson ORE, decd, taken 10 Jul 1846. Mentions: last report 15 Jul 1844; note on KEELAR due 10 Feb 1843; note on Anderson PATE due 10 Sep 1844; rents of wards lands 1844 & 45; cash paid Joseph ORE for title to land in dispute; Jacob PECK, Atto; A. BLACKBURN for medicine & medical attendance for wards; board & tuition for Calvin ORE, Amanda ORE & Sarah Jane ORE, his wards; tuition for Elizabeth ORE, his ward; clothing for Elizabeth ORE & Amanda ORE, his wards; lawsuits; boarding & clothing wards for 4 years. Signed E. TATE. Recorded 9 Aug 1846.

p. 459   Account of Sale - Sarah HAYNES, Admix of the Estate of William HAYNES, decd. Mentions: lands rented to Carlisle HAYNES for 1845; minor heirs Wm, Catherine, Anna, Rachel & Zelpha; oats sold to Daniel HAYNES; eight heirs at law who were not minors & 5 minor heirs; produce sold to David YADON & John YADON. Signed Sarah x HAYNES, Admix. Recorded 9 Aug 1846.

Commissioners Report - Set aside for Omy MITCHEL, widow of Aquilla MITCHEL, Jr., decd, 1 yr support for her & family. Signed 18 Sep 1846 Henry ACUFF, James T. WEST, James YATES, Comms. Recorded 17 Sep 1846 E. TATE, clerk.

p. 460   Inventory - Cynthy C. BROWN, decd, wife of William A. BROWN, Adm. Mentions: 1/6 interest in the undivided Estate of Jacob H. FORT, consisting of claims on individuals in TX & MS; Dr. Josiah RHOTON, representative of the heirs of Jacob H. FORT; Joseph H. BROWN only surviving heir of Cynthia C. BROWN. Signed William A. BROWN, Adm. Recorded 17 Sep 1846 E. TATE, clerk.

Guardian Report - Benjamin SMITH, Guardian of Mary SMITH, Frances SMITH, Alexander SMITH, Juba SMITH & Rachel SMITH. From 26 Aug 1845 to date 7 Sep 1845.

Mentions: board, clothing & care of Mary SMITH, a ward, being Dumb & not to do anything for herself; taxes for 1846. Signed Benjamin SMITH, Guardian. Recorded 17 Sep 1846 E. TATE, clerk.

p. 461   Guardian Report - Robert CARDWELL, Guardian of the minor heirs of Andrew CHAMBERLAIN, decd, taken 20 Jul 1846. Mentions: last report 30 May 1845; rents of lands 1844 & 1845; clothing for Jeremiah CHAMBERLAIN, a ward; clothing for Jane CHAMBERLAIN, a ward; A. P. GREEN for taxes 1845. Signed Robert CARDWELL, Guard. Recorded 17 Sep 1845 E. TATE, clerk.

Will - Eli HODGES, decd. Wife Emalue; note on hand on Daniel & Joseph NOE due 14 Sep 1845; note on hand on Drury MORRIS due Aug 1846; note on Hannah MORRIS due Dec 1846; note on H. BEAR due Sep 1846; my sisters Elizabeth, Lavince (?) & Cornelia entire interest in land belonging to the Estate of Eli HODGES, decd; my mother Elizabeth HODGES note on John HUNT due Jan 1847; note on Y. I. MORRIS; note on John GARRISTON; my bros Jos D., John M., Jacob E., Isaac B. & Thos C. HODGES; my sisters Lucinda HUNT & Mary Ann McBRIDE; good friend Hughs W. TAYLOR & Ellis RIGGS, Executors. Signed 5 Sep 1846 Eli x HODGES. Att: John M. PATTON, Francis Y. WILLIAMS, Jr. & James M. PATTON, Jr. Recorded 20 Oct 1846.

p. 462   Inventory - 2 Oct 1846. Eli HODGES, decd. Mentions: notes on James E. HOLSTEN, Harmon COX, Marcus McBRIDE, Y. I. MORRIS & Russel RIGGS, Nicholas McBRIDE, P. I. JONES & Wm EVANS. Signed Hughs W. TAYLOR & Ellis RIGGS, Executors. Recorded 21 Oct 1846 E. TATE, clerk.

Inventory - John KIDWELL, decd. Signed John IVY & Josiah KIDWELL, Adms. Recorded 22 Oct 1846 E. TATE, clerk.

p. 463   Account of Sale - Estate of John KIDWELL, decd. Signed John IVY & Josiah KIDWELL, Adm. Recorded 22 Oct 1846 E. TATE, clerk.

Guardian Report - Mary A. McBRIDE, Guardian of Elizabeth C. LOYD & Lucinda J. LOYD, minor heirs of Preston LOYD, decd. Mentions: Mary McBRIDE & Nicholas McBRIDE, Guardians; Jesse HOWEL, Adm of the Estate of Preston C. LOYD, decd, as per receipt dates 18 Oct 1844; rent of wards lands 1845 & 46; boarding & clothing ward for 2 yrs; D. McANALLY, Dpt Shff, taxes 1844 & 45 on lands; John J. NOE, Dpt Shff taxes 1846. Signed Nicholas x McBRIDE & Mary x McBRIDE, Guards. Recorded 22 Oct 1846 E. TATE, clerk.

p. 465   Guardian Report - Elizabeth HODGES, Guardian of the minor heirs of Eli HODGES, decd. Mentions: last report 25 Feb 1844 to date 19 Sep 1846; Henry HOLSTEN, Adm of the Estate of Eli HODGES, decd, recpt dated 20 Aug 1844; taxes 1845 & 46; Eli HODGES, a ward, cash 16 Oct 1844; saddles for Isaac HODGES, a ward & Thos C. HODGES, a ward, also horses, blankets & bridles. Signed Elizabeth x HODGES, Guardian. Recorded 22 Oct 1846 E. TATE, clerk.

Commissioners Report - Catherine WYRICK & family, widow of William WYRICK, decd. 1 yr support. Signed 2 Oct 1846 Wm SHARP, Thos McMILLINS & Joseph HILL, Comms. Recorded 22 Oct 1846.

p. 466   Settlement - Isaac M. & G. C. McBEE, Executors of the Estate of Lemuel McBEE, decd, done 28 Sep 1846. Mentions: notes on George GRAVES, Aaron

HARBERSON & Daniel GRAVES due 17 Sep 1841; note on George GRAVES due 17 Sep 1842;
M. J. PARROTT, Shff for taxes 1843; Wm C. McBEE, a legatee; L. J. McBEE, a leg-
atee; Sarah McBEE, the widow; A. H. McBEE, a legatee; Sarah McBEE, the widow, as
Guardian of James A. McBEE, a legatee; Jesse RENEW (?), Atto; Daniel McBEE; L.
J. McBEE, a legatee; A. H. McBEE, a legatee; John WALTERS who intermarried with
Mary Ann McBEE, a legatee; Lemuel McBEE, decd, order to Joseph JACKSON; Milo
McBEE, a legatee; Robt LOYD, Shff, taxes 1843; Jacob DICK & Martha M. DICK,
legatees; Isaac M. McBEE, Guardian of Calleway McBEE, a legatee; Daniel McBEE,
a legatee; G. C. McBEE, a legatee; Jacob DICK who intermarried with Martha McBEE,
a legatee; J. C. SMITH; Wm MURRY for Tomb Stone; Henry CREWS: Sarah McBEE,
Guardian of James & Danial McBEE, two legatees; James SAWYER, Atto; John H.
CROZIER, Atto; James C. MOSES, printer; Wm H. & J. S. MOFFETT; A. BLACKBURN; M.
J. PARROTT, Dpt Coroner; Harvy GASS, M.G. Signed E. TATE, clerk. Recorded 22
Oct 1846.

p. 467   Commissioners Report – Saml GILL, Wm MINCY (?), A. J. SULLENBARGER,
Comms. 27 Sep 1846. 1 yr support for widow of Nelson A. SENTER, decd. Recorded
5 Nov 1846.

p. 468   Inventory – Aquilla MITCHEL, Jr., decd. Mentions: 1 BLACK GIRL; accoun
against John STATSWORTH; one account against Thos SMITH. Signed G. B. MITCHEL,
Adm. Recorded 5 Nov 1846 E. TATE, clerk.

          Account of Sale – Aquilla MITCHEL, Jr., decd. Done 22 Aug 1846. Men-
tions: Widow, James YATES, Jas T. WEST, Henry ALSUP, Preston MITCHEL, Calvin
MITCHEL, John MITCHEL, John T. MITCHEL, M. FURGASON, A. MITCHEL, Sr., Jno T.
MITCHEL, Joel COFFEE, Jas S. TALBOTT, David JANUARY, Thomas SMITH, Aquilla
MITCHEL, Sr., George EZELL, John B. GRIGSBEE, William MITCHEL, Thomas RAY,
Theophilus MALONE, James WALKER, William MALONE. Signed G. B. MITCHEL, Adm.
Recorded 5 Nov 1846 E. TATE, clerk.

p. 469   Will – Enos HAMMERS, decd. Zachariah HAMMERS, William HAMMERS, Abraham
HAMMERS & Enos HAMMERS, sons; dau Elizabeth HAMMERS; Martha ACUFF, formerly
Martha HAMMERS; Robert LOYD, Executor. Signed 19 Sep 1846 Enos x HAMMERS.
Att: Isaac DANIEL & Henry M. MOODY. Recorded 5 Nov 1846.

p. 470   Account of Sales – Estate of William CORUM, decd. Mentions: Mrs.
CORUM, A. DOLIN, C. JACKSON, J. A. McKENNY, Willson CORUM, E. HANKINS, P.
MITCHEL, Jesse MITCHEL, George GROVES, Widow CORUM, Ed HANKINS, D. P. MYNATT,
H. S. HAWKINS, John NANCE, Jane ALLEN, M. H. STONE, Wm G. GROVES, C. MITCHEL,
David WELDEN, Jos DALE, Edward CROFFORD, Anderson DOLIN, Willson A. CORUM, Robert
BLAIR, C. B. NANCE, G. B. MITCHEL, P. P. NANCE, Rend CLOWERS, James HAWKINS,
And. CLOWERS, James ZACKS, Saml COBLE, Pryor NANCE. Signed 2 Nov 1846 John S.
CORUM, Adm. Recorded 6 Nov 1846 E. TATE, clerk.

p. 473   Settlement – Henry ALSUP, Adm of the Estate of Robert STONE, decd. Done
15 Oct 1846. Mentions: Widow of decd for 1 yr allowance; hire of SLAVES; Saml
SHIELDS; J. J. SMITH; Wm BRAZELTON; A. P. GREEN probate of Alfred NOELS: C. M.
GODWIN: J. S. TALBOTT who intermarried with Elizabeth STONE an heir; Alice
MASSENGILL, an heir; Wm McSTONE, trustee of Mary CAMPBELL, an heir; Wm McSTONE,
Guardian of Susan STONE, an heir; Susan STONE, widow of Robert STONE, decd; John
DOUGLAS, Dpt Shff, taxes 1845 & 46. Recorded 6 Nov 1846 E. TATE, clerk.

p. 474   Guardian Report - Wm HUBBS, Guardian of Kenada HILL. 28 Oct 1846.
Mentions: last report 14 Nov 1845; rents of lands 1846; taxes 1846; schooling
for Wm CLEVELAND; paid Kenady HILL 7 Sep 1846 since he has become of age. Signed 28 Oct 1846 Wm HUBBS, Guardian. Recorded 6 Nov 1846.

p. 475   Settlement - Sarah HAYNES, Widow and Admx of the Estate of Wm HAYNES,
decd. 11 Nov 1846. Mentions: note on Benjamin SEWEL (?); Martin CLEVELAND;
Joseph YADON; John N. YADON; Wm SHARP; Joseph CLARK. Signed E. TATE. Recorded
18 Dec 1846.

p. 476   Settlement - Warham EASLEY, Sr., Executor for the Estate of Millar W.
EASLEY, decd, done 11 Nov 1846. Mentions: notes on Jacob KLINE, Warham EASLEY,
Jr., & Wm E. COCKE; John EASLEY; R. J. McKENNY, Atto; RICE & McFARLAND; George
MYERS; John NOTHERLAND, Atto; Wm M. COCKE, clerk; George CARDWELL; Francis EPPS,
an heir; H. G. LEA, surveyor; Robert PARKS who intermarried with Nancy EASLEY,
an heir; recpt of Thomas JAMES, Atto-in-fact for Patsey JAMES, Sarah DUKE &
Pleasant DUKE, three of the heirs of Susanna DUKE, formerly Susanna EASLEY, now
decd, one of the heirs of said Millar W. EASLEY, decd, dated 22 Nov 1845; Margaret
EASLEY, Admx, an heir; John EASLEY, an heir; Jacob KLINE who intermarried with
Patsey CARDWELL, formerly Patsey EASLEY, an heir & for Wm EASLEY, decd, also
one of the heirs, recpt dated 17 Dec 1845; Warham EASLEY, Executor, & heir; Gray
GARRETT, Atto-in-fact for Mary MERIDITH, formerly Mary EASLEY an heir. Signed
E. TATE. Recorded 18 Dec 1846.

p. 477   Inventory - Nelson A. SENTER, decd. Mentions: notes on Tandy DALTON
(26 Jan 1842), C. W. LATHIM (19 Feb 1843), G. W. MOORE (25 Apr 1846), Jacob NOE
(11 Nov 1842), John PHILIPS, Sr. (10 Jul 1838), Wm PROFFITT (12 Oct 1843), John
B. PROFFETT (8 May 1838), Henry RICE (3 Oct 1843), John RENTFRO (25 Apr 1843),
Thomas WHITESIDE & S. S. SHIPLEY (2 Feb 1841), Melton TATE (13 Jul 1831), Willson
WYATT (4 Apr 1843), Russell WYATT (1 Dec 1841), William ADAMS (30 Dec 1837),
Josiah BLAIR (23 Jul 1843 & 2 Aug 1842) Redmand BIRD (20 Dec 1829), J. U. BASSETT
(17 Aug 1842), Spencer BASSETT (29 Aug 1840), Hilyard BULL (4 Jun 1840), Hugh
BASSETT (10 Nov 1841), Thomas BURCHEL (11 Feb 1842 & 8 Feb 1838), James BULL
(11 Jan 1841), Thos COFFEE (23 Jul 1841), Duncan COLLINS & A. COFFEE (2 Nov 1841),
Thos COFFEE (11 Jan 1841), Benjamin COFFEE (23 Nov 1843), James CHEEK & P. M.
SENTER (22 Oct 1841), Ausburn COFFEE (2 Feb 1841), John L. CONNER (27 Dec 1837),
F. B. COBB (25 May 1843), P. B. COBB (27 Feb 1835), C. COFFEE & E. COFFEE (24
Oct 1841), John COFFEE (21 Oct 1844), John COFFEE & A. COFFEE (no date, but
credited 21 Aug 1840), John D. & A. COFFEY (21 Oct 1841), Wm DONTY (21 Sep 1838),
Thomas DOLTON & M. B. DOLTON (8 Mar 1843), M. DOLTON (19 Nov 1845), C. J. DOLTON
16 Mar 1839), Wm DAVIS (27 Apr 1845), Enos DOLTON (16 Oct 1830), John HOWELL
(17 Jan 1840), David HARRIS (26 Jan 1844), John HARRIS (10 Feb 1842), Couley
HAYES (16 Feb 1839), Hiram HAYES (22 May 1841), Adam HOPPER (5 Mar 1846), Tom
HODGES (19 Mar 1839), Mariah DOLTON (7 Feb 1839), James HODGES (2 Apr 1844),
Mahlin HARRIS (4 Apr 1843), Abel LONG (30 Jun 1843), James LONG (4 Jan 1845),
John LONG (21 Jan 1841, 5 Jan 1841, 13 Jan 1840), Jas LONG (18 Sep 1845), Reuben
LONG (10 Feb 1846), G. McCRANE (1 Sep 1841), Thos MOODY (29 Sep 1845 & 18 Oct
1845), Harry MILLS (24 Jan 1846), David McANALLY, Jr. (26 Jul 1842), David Mc
ANALLY, Sr. (26 Jul 1842), Charles McGINNIS (19 Oct 1843), Thos McANALLY, Sr.
(28 Mar 1840), George McANALLY (30 Jan 1840), Wm H. MOORE (13 Jun 1843), Aaron
McGINNIS (25 Apr 1840), George G. MEDLOCK (Oct 1845), John NEWMAN (7 Dec 1839,
23 Feb 1840, 28 Sep 1841), R. PEMBERTON (9 Sep 1842), Richard PEMBERTON (9 Sep

1842), Richard PEMBERTON (9 Sep 1843), John SHELTON (17 Feb 1844), Richard
STUBBLEFIELD (1 Mar 1845), S. S. SHIPLEY (27 Jan 1844), P. M. SENTER (17 Apr
1843), James SHIELDS & Wm S. ATKINSON (14 Aug 1837), Lerena (?) SAMPSEL (20 Apr
1840), P. M. SENTER (25 Nov 1845), Richard BLAIR (10 Dec 1838), Benjamin BRAY
(26 Jan 1841), Thomas BRIAN (24 Sep 1839), Lewis BELL (20 Dec 1839), Prior BIBA
(9 Jun 1840), Jas BRYANT, Calvin BRYANT & Minerva BRYANT (8 Dec 1844), George
BURDEN (30 Jan 1841), J. & S. BAKSOT (2 Dec 1839), Wm BURGES (25 Apr 1842),
Charles BEANDER (27 May 1843), Wm BURGES (24 May 1834), John COCKE (13 Aug 1836),
J. COLLINS (25 Feb 1841), Charles N. COWAN (30 Aug 1835), J. COLLINS & A. COLLINS
(17 Oct 1840), Nicholas COUNTZ (10 Nov 1839), Wm CLEVER (?) (24 Oct 1837), Robert
CAMPBELL (17 Sep 1842, 20 Oct 1835), John R. CHAMBERS (20 Dec 1837, 1 Jun 1838,
18 Feb 1846), John COZART (5 Apr 1838), Thomas COTTER (25 May 1838), James COLLIN'S
(4 Aug 1840), Charles N. COWN (23 Apr 1836), John CONN (10 Jan 1840), T. CHRIS-
MAN (11 Aug 1832), R. J. COCKE (25 Sep 1841), Carpenter WILSON (29 Jul 1834), John
COUNTZ (15 Sep 1845), R. CAMPBELL & H. HAMILTON (3 Oct 1835), R. CAMPBELL (20 Oct
1835), John COLLIS (4 Dec 1830), Robert CAMPBELL (10 May 1834), C. N. COWAN (29
Jun 1836), Elijah ELLIOTT (26 Feb 1832), Wm EVANS (27 Jul 1844), Alfred EVANS
(27 Jul 1844), Jas FLANAGIN (4 Feb 1837, 18 May 1836), Daniel FLORA (16 Sep 1843)
Joab FOREST (28 Jan 1841), John A. GIPSON (19 Dec 1844), John GODWIN (27 Jan
1841), William GRIFFIN (14 Jan 1840), Abel GREENLEE (13 Sep 1845), Wm HARRIS (31
Aug 1840), John HIXON (28 Jul 1840, 7 Sep 1840), James C. HODGES (25 Apr 1843),
Wm HIPSHEAR (9 Jun 1841), J. C. HENSON (29 Aug 1839), John HARBIN (10 Jun 1840),
A. J. HELTON (25 Oct 1839), Joseph HICKS (29 ___ 1844), J. H. HOOSER (27 Aug
1830), John HURT (8 Apr 1825), James D. KENNER (18 Apr 1842), Lucy KETON (6 Feb
1843), Hardy LONG (1 Jun 1843), Thos LAYCOCKE (8 Dec 1843), Arthur LONG (20 Jan
1832), Henry LONG & Thos BRYAN (13 May 1843), Lawson LONG (22 Aug 1845), T. A. R.
LONG (2 Apr 1840), Pertiman LONG (9 Mar 1843), James F. LEA (11 Apr 1838), Henry
LONG (1 Jan 1836), Wm McCROWE (8 Jul 1840, 14 Jan 1839, Aug 1840), James Mc
GOLDRIE (2 notes 6 Jan 1846), Robert MITCHEL (11 Feb 1842), Abner MILLAR (10 Jan
1840), Thos McGOLDRIE (Dec 1843), Martin MYARS (29 May 1839), Robert MARTIN
(5 Sep 1842), Peter MYERS (13 May 1839), John MOORE (1 Sep 1836), James MILLAR
(29 May 1838, 20 Dec 1839), M. MYERS (19 Feb 1842), Wm McGILL (29 Jun 1840), Levi
McVEY (25 Oct 1837), Wm MORGAN (1 Mar 1841), Ewel MOORE (27 Sep 1837), Lemuel
MOORE (8 Jul 1837), James NASH (31 Dec 1841), J. D. NORTON (4 Dec 1837), Jas P.
NASH (15 Apr 1843), Samuel NEWMAN (16 Feb 1836), Wm QUEEN (14 Jan 1836, 31 Mar
1840, 26 Jan 1836), John OAKLEY (22 Oct 1841), Bendigo OLLIVER (11 Jan 1840),
David OWEN (22 Oct 1835), Aaron PITTKERSON (21 Feb 1836), John & Wm PUCKET (8
Oct 1833), Wm PATRICK (30 Jan 1838), Thos POLLARD (8 Feb 1840), J. W. PATTERSON
(31 Aug 1843), Samuel POLLARD (18 Dec 1840), Wm PARRICH (?) (3 Aug 1836), Wm
RUSH (26 Dec 1839), Wm ROGERS (26 Jan 1837), John ROYAL (20 Apr 1840), Sarah
THOMAS (1 Apr 1843), Pendelton TAYLOR (14 Apr 1845), John TUCKER (18 Mar 1842),
J. P. SIMPSON (25 Feb 1840), David SHOPSHIRE (24 Feb 1833), A. R. SULLENBARGER
(24 Mar 1846), Peter SPOON (1 May 1840), Peter SAMPSEL (14 Mar 1844), Joel SMITH
(2 Nov 1840), Wm SPOON (25 Apr 1842), Walter SHOPSHIRE (27 Jan 1844), Joseph
PROFFITT (9 Mar 1835), Jct. WALKER (14 Sep 1842), Joshua WALER (25 Dec 1840),
Wm WALTERS (12 Jul 1839), Jacob WILLIS (24 Sep 1840), Lewis E. WOLF (31 Nov 1837)
A. NORVELL (2 Oct 1832), N. S. WELLS (13 Jul 1844), Wm WOLF (28 Feb 1838, 6 Apr
1840), E. P. WRIGHT (13 Feb 1841), R. M. YANCY (21 Nov 1846). "Accounts that
are standing open from the year 1838 until the year 1841 that has never been
closed according to the Books." To wit: Gabriel PROFFITT, Andrew McGINNIS,
John LONG, J., Abner FAIRCHILD, Wm ROGERS, David HOLT, Wm H. BRADFORD, James
IRBY, George H. THOMPSON, John BURCHIL, William LAY, Enoch MACKEY, William

PHILIPS, Thos WATSON, Thos WHITESIDE, Simon FROST, William MORSE, Jesse T.
COFFEE, Matilda DOLTON, John SMITH, Thos SOLOMON, Aaron COLLINS, John BIGGS,
Maddison HARVEY, John HELTON, Alexander GIPSON, Charles McANALLY, Anthony HEUES,
Wm COLLINS, Paschal TURNER, William TURNER, Julian FRAZIER, John OLLIVER (2),
Charles JOURDON, Washington JOURDON, Elijah HOPPER, Bosha HARVEY, Richard
WILLIAMS, John CAMPBELL, Thos HARVEY, James PHIPPS, Simeon ACUFF, Hugh JONES,
Jacob FLORA, Wm STATTEN, W. OWENS, Wm IMES, John NEWMAN, James HARVEL, Jr., John
GODWON, S. B. TATE. "Now will follow all accounts up to the present date, which
is 1846." To Wit: Lawson LONG, S. B. TATE, A. D. HOPPER, David HARRIS, Joseph
PROFFITT, Temolian CROFFORD, Jas O. SENTER, Edward SAVRSY (?), Thos SHELTON, A. M.
WINKER, Robert SPIESS, P. M. SENTER, Harvey MILLS, John SHELTON, Elizabeth SENTER,
Henry HIPSHEAR, F. SHELTON, Aquilla JONES & Eli JONES, Pendleton SHIPSHIRE, David
SHELTON, Robert TURLEY, James BARTON. Notes on Jos. PROFFITT (28 Apr 1845),
W. L. ATKINSON & Jas SHIELDS (16 Apr 1844), John C____H (?) (19 Mar 1844), G. W.
RICH (26 Feb 1844), Richard MOORE (4 Apr 1843).

p. 484   Account of Sale - 2 & 3 Oct 1846. Estate of Nelson A. SENTER, decd.
Mentions: Green BURDEN, S. S. SHIPLEY, Abraham McCONNEL, I. Ames LYNDEMOOD,
C. JACKSON, David WHITESIDE, F. M. WALKER, James O. SENTER, Parrott GODWIN, John
RUCKER, Anderson DOLTON, Tandy DOLTON, John RICE, Wm DAVIS, Thos EPPERSON, Ausborn
COFFEE, Adam HOPPER, James DANIEL, Robert SPIERS, Hardy LONG, Jas DAVIS, L.
JOHNSON, Wm HIGHTOWER, R. LONG, John LONG, A. G. SULLENBARGER, Thos MOODY, A.
WINKLE, Albert SULLENBARGER, W. M. MOODY, John SHELTON, Marine DUVAUL, W. HODGES,
Sterling BARNETT, Jinkin McGOLDRICK, J. P. GODWIN, Sarah P. SENTER, Wm E. GOD-
WIN, hiring MARY & CHILD, Levi CAMPBELL, Peter SAMSEL, John HARRIS, Elizabeth
SENTER, O. YOE. Signed S. W. SENTER, J. E. HOGAN, Adms. Recorded 22 Dec 1846.

p. 488   Additional Inventory - Estate of Joseph BEELAR, decd. Mentions: notes
& due dates on George COFFMAN (1846), Samuel WYRICK (1836), Roger ____? (1821),
John CONN (1833), George RINEHART (1820), Aaron & Thom PIERCE (1824, 1831), Geo.
MILLAR (for 11 shillings & 3 pence due 1 Oct 1819), Abraham RAISOR (?) (1821),
Ezekial GOFORTH (1834), Wm ARWINE (1844), Esther TEAGUE & James S. ACUFF (1841);
Sales to Joseph HOLLINGSWORTH, L. M. ELLIS, Joseph WOLFENBARGER, John B. GRIGS-
BEE, Jesse F. BEELAR, Wm MALLICOAT, John SELLARS, Sr., Stephen ATKINS, Pleasant
STRANES, Ann BEELAR, Wm HEREN, Martin CLEVELAND, Willis ATKINS, trade debt on
Joseph SMITH sold to John B. GRIGSBY, Isaac BEELAR, Henry MOYER, Anderson ACUFF.
Signed 25 Dec 1846 John A. CLEVELAND, William M. CLEVELAND, Jacob BEELAR,
Executors. Recorded 15 Jan 1847 E. TATE, clerk.

p. 489   Inventory - Tandy WOLFENBARGER, decd. Mentions: notes on Lewis M.
ELLIS, Martin CLEVELAND, G. W. VITTITOE, Pleasant STARNES, James WELCH, Nicholas
SATTERFIELD, Reuben WOLFINBARGER, Joseph WILLIAMS, G. W. DYER, Peter WOLFEN-
BARGER, B. BRANSON; accompt on John CHANDLER, Joseph WOLFENBARGER, Isaac BEELAR,
William WILLIAMS, Jackson BULLEN. Signed 4 Jan 1847 Peter WOLFENBARGER, Adm.
Recorded 15 Jan 1847 E. TATE, clerk.

p. 490   Settlement - John CHANDLER, Executor for Daniel CHANDLER, decd. Done
29 Dec 1846. Mentions: Wm T. TATE & Co.; Daniel CHANDLER note to Joseph BEELAR;
Elizabeth McMILLIN. Recorded 15 Jan 1847 E. TATE, clerk.

p. 491   Settlement - John A. SMITH, Adm of the Estate of Josiah SMITH, decd.
Done 29 Dec 1846. Mentions: notes on Queen DYER, Lewis M. ELLIS; Nancy SMITH,

the Executrix; John NETHERLAND; Queen DYER; Joseph HILL; Harmon G. LEA; Jacob
PECK, Probate for last due bill; S. A. GRANT, clerk; James SALLING, Dpt Shff,
taxes 1845. Recorded 15 Jan 1847 E. TATE, clerk.

Account of Sale - Eli HODGES, decd. 5 Nov 1846. Mentions: Jacob
HODGES, John HODGES, Thos GLASGO, Emaline HODGES, A. COOTER, James HODGES.
Signed Hughs O. TAYLOR, Ellis RIGGS, Executors. Recorded 15 Jan 1847 E. TATE.

p. 492   Second Settlement - James DYER, Sr., Executor of the Estate of Anderson
T. DYER, decd. 28 Dec 1846. Mentions: last settlement 26 Feb 1846; Anderson T.
DYER note to Wm P. JONES; Wm HUBBS; Anderson T. DYER note to John HILL; Clabourn
JOHNSON; Henry NEEDHAM; Wm HICKLE; Rachel HUBBS, the widow of Anderson T. DYER,
decd. Recorded 20 Jan 1847 E. TATE, clerk.

Guardian Report - James WALKER, Guardian of the minor heirs of James
WHITLOCK, decd. From 3 May 1845 to the time of last report 31 Dec 1846.
Mentions: rents of wards lands 1845 & 46; Thos MAPLES who intermarried with
Rachel WHITLOCK, a ward, recpt dated 27 Aug 1846; W. L. LATHIM, clerk. Signed
James G. WALKER, Guardian. Recorded 20 Jan 1847 E. TATE, clerk.

p. 493   Guardian Report and Settlement - Jesse F. BEELAR former guardian of the
minor heirs of David BEELAR, decd. 15 Dec 1846. Mentions: rents of wards lands
for 1846; to the 4/9 of the hire of NEGRO girl; paid John SELLARS for building
new cabbin, clearing land & splitting rails; clearing land called the Mountain
Field. Signed Jesse F. BEELAR. No recording date, signed E. TATE, clerk.

p. 494   Will - Ethelred WILLIAMS, decd. Appoints William WILLIAMS, James
WILLIAMS, Thomas W. HUMES, John H. CROZIER, William A. BROWN & William T. TATE
executors and trustees; advancements on books up to 8 May 1846 to children as
follows: to my son William WILLIAMS $24,000.00, my son James WILLIAMS $12,778.00,
my dau Cornelia W. HUMES & her husband Thomas W. HUMES $9,348.00, my dau Mary W.
CROZIER & her husband John H. CROZIER $10,085.00, my son Joseph WILLIAMS $1,315.00
and my dau Margaret $999.00, all to have equal share to $25,000.00; store in
Rutledge now occupied by William T. TATE & Co.; land purchased from Nathan GRAY;
land sold to Isaac LEBOW on the south boundry of Thomas HENDERSON; lands purchased from COCKE; lands between the lands of the heirs of Thomas GILL, decd, &
the heirs of William F. WILLIAMS, decd, where upon James PHILLIPS now lives; land
in Poor Valley; place where I now reside called Rocky Springs, Grainger Co.; land
purchased from John W. LIDE; lots in the City of Knoxville adjoining the lot on
which the Mansion House stands; lands in the Western District of TN; lot in
Knoxville purchased from BARTHOLAMUE (I think) on Prince & Main Sts; lot on
Prince St. purchased from Robert HOUSTON; land bounded by Beanstation tract &
running north on line of Jesse BEAN's that he conveyed to James ORE & lands of
heirs of Thomas GILLS, decd; land in Knoxville, TN called White Hall where my son
James now resides; lot in the City of Knoxville adjoining John H. CROZIER dwelling house; store run by son William & William A. BROWN; SLAVES not to be sold &
families divided. Signed 6 Jun 1846 Ethelred WILLIAMS. Wit: G. McCRANE, Robt
J. McKINNEY. Recorded 26 Jan 1847 E. TATE, clerk.

p. 499   Will - William BRADON. My son James land on a conditional line made by
the said Edward BRADSON, Sr. & Edward Bradon, Jr. near foot of Lone Mountain; son
George $1.00, son Edward $1.00, dau Sarah $1.00; daus Elizabeth, Mary & Rachel

horse worth $50.00; me & my wife to have the benefit of our own maintenance
during our natural life. James BRADON, sole executor. Signed 26 Jun 1843
Edward x BRADON. Wit: Thomas WHITETED (?), Alexander x WOODWARD, William x
SEALS. Recorded 5 Dec 1847 E. TATE, clerk.

Inventory - Amos STATSWORTH, decd. Mentions: notes on George SPARK-
MAN, Wm J. LOWE, Catherine STATSWORTH, Wm TOWNSLEY, B. E. GAINS, James DAVIS,
Jos S. TALBOTT & Joel COFFEE, executed to Aquilla MITCHEL, former Adm. Signed
20 Jan 1847 R. LOYD, Adm. Recorded 5 Feb 1847 E. TATE, clerk.

p. 500   Settlement - John L. CORUM, Adm of the Estate of Wm CORUM, decd. 30
Jan 1847. Mentions: Henry CREWS; Wm STONE; James ZACHARY; E. TATE, clerk;
Robert BLAIN; B. E. GAINS; Preston MITCHEL; Elizabeth CORUM Widow of Wm CORUM,
decd; Rusha HANKINS, an heir; D. P. MYNATT, Adm of the Estate of Willson CORUM,
decd, an heir; D. P. MYNATT who intermarried with Lucinda CORUM, an heir; Wm G.
GROVE who intermarried with Sarah CORUM, an heir; John S. CORUM, an heir.
Recorded 5 Feb 1847 E. TATE, clerk.

p. 501   Settlement - Jonathan NOE, the Security of Isaac PERKAPILE, decd, the
Executor of the last will & testament of Michael PERKAPILE, decd. 22 Jan 1847.
Mentions: vouchers from John ROBERTSON; Wm HUTSON; D. McANALLY, Dpt Shff, taxes
1844 & 45; Jno F. NOE, Const., judgement vs Michael PERKAPILE, recovered by
Stephen JOHNSON before Ellis RIGGS, Esq; Caleb CROSBY; Michael PERKAPILE note
to Robert LONG; Michael PERKAPILE note to Betsy ESTES, Executrix of the Estate
of George W. ESTES, decd; note to M. SHIELDS; note to Hughs TAYLOR; John PERKA-
PILE; note to Jesse RIGGS. Recorded 5 Feb 1847 E. TATE, clerk.

Commissioners Report - Tandy WOLFINBARGER, decd. Support for widow &
family. Signed 21 Jan 1847 Martin CLEVELAND, Joseph CLARK, Pleasant STARNES.
Recorded 5 Feb 1847.

p. 502   Final Settlement - James T. WEST, Adm of the Estate of Robert RAY, decd.
28 Jan 1847. Mentions: vouchers from Wm P. JONES, Sarah KERSEY, George EZELL,
Angeline RAY, Joseph DYER, James T. WEST, James A. KLINE, Thos & Saml SMITH,
Henry ALSUP for Jesse EZELL & Lewis KENNY, RICE & McFARLAND, Jubal MITCHEL, Saml
RITE, Samuel SMITH, Thomas RAY, James TROTT, Wm T. TATE & Co., Thomas WALKER,
James WALKER. Recorded 6 Feb 1847 E. TATE, clerk.

Inventory - Estate of Enos HAMMER, Sr., decd. Mentions: note on Edward & Wm B.
HODGES, due 8 Sep 1844; note on Jacob KLINE & Sons, due 2 Apr 1844; note on
John COLLISON due 10 Mar 1846; note on Wm HAMMER due 10 Jun 1847; note on John
GRAY due 10 Sep 1844; note on James L. CHURCHMAN & Francis YOUNG & assigned by
Thomas C. HANKINS due 18 Feb 1845; note on Pierce CODY & Robert LOYD due 15 Mar
1840; note on Elisha TOMASON & Jacob KLINE due 14 Jul 1838; note on James GALLION
& Issac FLORA due 13 Oct 1834; recpt on Elisha THOMASON, Shff, for a note on
James WILLIAMS, Thomas WILLIAMS, John GRAY & Isaac DANIEL. Signed 14 Nov 1846
Robert LOYD. Recorded 6 Feb 1847 E. TATE, clerk.

p. 503   Account of Sale - Sherad MAYES, decd. 30 Nov 1846. Mentions: John
HOLT, Wortham JOICE, John BROOSE, Thos. HILL, L. W. IVY, W. H. DANIEL, James
CARMICHAEL, Wm TURNER, Wm SUNDERLAND, Joseph LYNCH, Paschal TURNER, Joshua
KIDWELL, Elisha GLOSSUP, John CARR, Wm MAYES, James GREENLEE, Wm H. DANIEL,

G. B. IVY, Benj IVY, James MATHIS, Wm SPOON, Wm LACY, Isaac F. McCARTY, G. B.
MAYES, A. G. LIVINGSTON, Godwin MAYES.   Signed Levi SATTERFIELD, Executor.
Recorded 6 Feb 1847 E. TATE, clerk.

p. 504   Account of Sale - Tandy WOLFENBARGER, decd.   23 Jan 1847.   Mentions:
Rebecca WOLFENBARGER, Martin CLEVELAND, Pleasant STARNES, Joseph WOLFENBARGER,
John WILLIAMS, James STARNES, Augustus JENNINGS, Robert WOLFENBARGER, Samuel
DODSON, Nicholas SATTERFIELD, Joseph WILLIAMS, Robert FRY, Washington HARRIS,
Wm CLEVELAND.   Signed William CLEVELAND, clerk.   Peter WOLFENBARGER, Adm.
Recorded 6 Feb 1847 E. TATE, clerk.

p. 505   Settlement - D. P. MYNATT, Adm for the Estate of Willson CORUM, decd.
30 Jan 1847.   Mentions: the money received from John S. CORUM, Adm of the
Estate of Wm CORUM, decd, as part of the rateable share of said Willson CORUM,
decd, being one of the heirs of said Wm CORUM, decd; vouchers from E. TATE,
clerk, Robert BLAIN, Wm HALL, Elizabeth CORUM, Dr. Samuel SHIELDS; Willson A.
CORUM note to John S. CORUM, Adm of the Estate of Wm CORUM, decd.   Signed 30 Jan
1847.   Recorded 6 Feb 1847 E. TATE, clerk.

          Inventory - John WILLIAMS, decd.   Mentions: American Gold, B. Sovreigns
F. Nepoleons, N. Carolina piece, Silver, NC Bank bills, South Carolina money,
bills on Highwassy R. Road; notes on James B. BOYD, Jr., John H. COFFEE, Jesse
COX, Wm F. DANIEL, Lewis CARTER, Nimrod FARMER, John B. GRIGSBY, Joab FOREST that
is to be discharged by Black Smith work, Temple G_____, William HAYNES, John C.
HICKY, M. N. JEFFREYS due to John COCKE, Jr., Thos K. ETTER, A. T. NALL, James
McCRARY, John M. LAUGHLIN, Samuel LANE, John MANSFIELD, John McLAUGHLIN, Robertso
McKINNY, Robt P. MOORE, George PAREEVILLE, N. FAIN, Wm RUTLEDGE, R. G. FAIN,
Nathan PATTERSON, William RICE, Presley RICE (one credit by A. THACKER), John
B. STAPLES, George K. LARRIMORE & Russel RIGGS, R. L. HOWARD & Eli SPOON, Jesse
RIGGS & Wm H. RIGGS, Clesbe RIGGS by Jesse RIGGS, Thomas RUSSELL, Joseph N.
SHANNON, Toliver ROBERTSON payable to DEDRICK & ANDERSON (1 Mar 1837), A. G.
WATKINS, Wm WILLIAMS, Margaret WATKINS, Stokley D. WILLIAMS, George W. GRAHAM,
Wm REECE, const. receipt for note on James MORRIS, Wm RICE, const. recpt for note
on John CARDWELL, R. I. CHURCHMAN, E. D. HOSS, Elihu MILLIKAN, J. B. WILKERSON,
James LEWIS, Wm BREEDEN, Wm BOLES, Edmund DANIEL, Jonathan NEWMAN (Dpt Shff) 2
notes on John INMAN payable to Wm PETTY, Thos D. HICKY, const. Sunday notes on
Wm BETTIS, Eli BETTIS, Wm REECE, David GRANT, Caleb HOWEL, D. C. MAINE & James
McKENNY, John I. NOE (Dpt Shff) notes on James MATTHIS, G. B. MAYES, John M.
PATTON & John PIOTT, accounts on Philamon HODGES, Peter DHOURE (?), John WALKER,
Wm MURY & H. O. HYNSEN, 1 Negro man Slave MIKE or MICHAEL, age 27, 1 Negro woman
Slave SARAH c18, 1 Negro boy named ANDREW c10, invoice of merchandise in the
partnership between J. M. WILLIAMS, decd, & Octavus YOE.   Signed Parrott GODWIN,
Adm.   Recorded 10 Feb 1847.

p. 510   Will - David JANUARY.   My dear wife Martha E. JANUARY; my son Marcus
DeLafett JANUARY: Lewis M. ELLIS, Executor.   Signed 21 Feb 1847 David x JANUARY.
Att: John B. GRIGSBY, B. E. GAINS.   Recorded 20 Apr 1847.

p. 511   Guardian Report - Jacob P. KIRKHAM, Guardian of the minor heirs of
Robert M. YANCY.   3 Apr 1847.   Mentions rents of wards lands 1846; pasture &
clover 1846; cash paid Robert M. YANCY for the support of his wards from the
time of his appointment up to the time Mary Marinda YANCY chose as her Guardian

A. G. SULLENBARGER, 1 Monday of Nov 1846; Adna DEBORD for work. Recorded
21 Apr 1847.

        Guardian Report - Thomas McBROOM, Guardian of the minor heirs of John
DENNIS, decd. 3 Apr 1847. Mentions: last report 29 Aug 1844; Wm P. JONES for
goods for a ward; Robert CARDWELL for medicine & medical attendance. Recorded
no date.

p. 512   Settlement - Greenberry MITCHEL, Adm of the Estate of Aquilla MITCHEL,
decd, who was Adm of the Estate of Amos STALSWORTH, decd. Mentions: Joel COFFEE;
Amos STALSWORTH bill due John NANCE; B. G. GAINS; James DAVIS; John DUGLAS, Dpt
Shff, taxes 1844; A. MITCHEL; B. E. GAINS, Constable, recpt for judgt recovered
by T. & S. SMITH for the use of Jacob ARNETT against Amos STALSWORTH; Wm MITCHEL;
Amos STALSWORTH note to Madison Acadamy; Robert LOYD; James TROTT. Recorded 21
Apr 1847 E. TATE, clerk.

p. 513   Account of Sale - John M. WILLIAMS, decd. Mentions: Ezekiel BOATMAN,
George BURDEN, D. C. CARMICHAEL, John B. CREWS, Wm B. CUNNINGHAM, Nicholas COX,
Welcome H. DANIEL, M. S. DANIEL, Hugh DUFF, Manuie (?) DUVAUL, Moses DUNSMORE,
Warham EASLEY, John FLORA, Jacob GODWIN, A. P. GREEN, Samuel GILL, Robert D. GRAY,
Willie HIPSHEIR, William HIPSHEAR, Henry HARRISON, Josiah HOLDER, H. O. HYNSON,
Philip HODGES, Thomas HILL, John HOLT, Warham JOICE, D. C. JACKSON, Jacob KLINE,
Henry MOODY, Wm M. MOODY, Robert MITCHEL, Andrew McGINNIS, Abraham McCONNEL,
Jinkins McGOLDRICK, James K. McANALLY, David MILLS, Edmund PEMBERTON, Richard
PEMBERTON, Thomas POLLARD, John RUCKER, Samuel ROACH, A. G. SULLENBARGER, Solomon
SHIPLEY, Thomas TURLEY, Elisha THOMASON, Nancy STRATTON, P. G. YOR, George WILL-
IAMS, Margaret WILLIAMS, Pleasant WESTERN, Octavies YOE, John HODGE, Richard RAY,
Jacob GODWIN. Signed 5 Apr 1847 PARROTT GODWIN, Adm. Recorded 24 Apr 1847.

p. 517   Account of Sale - Merchandise supposed to belong to the partnership of
John WILLIAMS, decd. Mentions: Ezekiel BOATMAN, Reece BOWEN, Wm B. CUNNINGHAM,
Daniel CARMICHAEL, N. COOS, John B. CREWS, Jacob KLINE, Boling DUVAL, M. L.
DANIEL, Marine DUVAUL, Hugh DUFF, Hodge DANIEL, Moses DINMORE, Wm GODWIN, Samuel
GILL, R. D. GRAY, Jacob GODWIN, Henry HARRISON, Phillimon HODGE, H. O. HYNSON,
Joseph HOLDER, Willie HIPSHEAR, George HOPPER, W. JOICE, D. C. JACKSON, James
LINDAMOOD, George LACY, James LACY, A. McCONNEL, Frederick MAY, David MILES,
Oscar McCONNEL, Robert MITCHEL, Wm MOODY, Henry MOODY, James McGEE, David RICH,
Edward PEMBERTON, I. M. PRYOR, John PHILLIPS, A. G. SULLENBARGER, Jefferson
STRATTON, G. L. SHIPLEY, Thos TWILEY, E. THOMASON, Wm THURMAN, Edward TATE, E.
TAYLOR, George WILLIAMS, P. G. YOE, Octaves YOE, Robert TURLEY. Signed 5 Apr
1847 Parrott GODWIN, Adm. Recorded 24 Apr 1847 E. TATE, clerk.

p. 522   Inventory - Ethelred WILLIAMS, decd. Mentions: 19 Negro slaves named
JACOB, ANTHONY, ALFRED, ARCH, BEN, LEWIS, ANN, SALL, JANE & her 3 children viz
MELTON, ANN & ISABELLE, MATILDA & her 6 children viz BILL, NELSON, TOM, PATTERSON,
RHODA & PATRICK. Signed William A. BROWN, one of the Executors.
        Inventory of the debts due Ethelred WILLIAMS, decd. Mentions: James
ALLEN (1843), Sarah ANDERSON (2 due 1840), George W. ALLEN (1842), Frank AMIS,
decd (1839), George BASSETT (1844), William ADAMS (1836), James BRYANT (1844),
Joseph BRYANT (1845), Hugh A. BASSET note in hands of Raleigh DODSON (1842),
Henry BOWAN (old account), Clabourn BULL (1842), Arthur BOND (1844), William B.
BASSETT (1842), Thomas BRYAN (1838), Peter BEAR (1844), Milbourn BOWMAN (1840),

Benjamin BRAY in the hands of Shff THOMASON (due 1842), William BRYAN (1844),
Richard C. BLAIR (1837), Wright BOND (1838), Spencer BASSETT & John BASSETT
(1840), Josiah BLAIR & Wm WARDEN note in hands of David McANALLY (1842), Josiah
BLAIR (1842 secured by Deed of Trust), David G. BAILY (1838), Thomas BURCHELL
note given to Wm C. DUNAVAND (1839), Pryor BUBBA (1839), Thomas COFFEE note in
hands of Sheriff THOMASON (1840), John R. CHAMBERS 2 notes in hands of Dpty
DONALDSON for collection (1839 & 1836), Sterling COCKE (1842), John COFFEE &
Ausburn COFFEE (1840), James CONNER (1839), Edmund COLLINS, Richard J. COCKE,
Martin CLEVELAND (1843), Alfred M. CARTER (1845), Thomas CONNER (1842), Fred-
arick B. COBB note to David McANALLY for collection (1839), Andrew J. COOLY
(1841), Samuel H. COPELAND (1836), note to John BOYD (1837), Henry COUNTZ,
Caswell CLEVELAND note given to Joel MILLS for collection (1839), Joseph COBB
(1844 & 45), William E. COCKE (1845), Eli A. COX (1844), Timolion G. CROFFORD
(1846), B. F. CLOUD (1834), Ezekiel CREECH, Duncan COLLINS, Andrew COLLINS (1833),
Thomas DAULTON (1840), Enoch DAULTON in hands of Shff THOMASON (2 1841), William
DECKER & Alxd WILLIAMS (1842), Booker DAULTON, John DODSON (1842), James W. &
David DEDRICK (1841), Raleigh DODSON (1842), registration of Deed of Trust PARSON
& DUFF (1831), William ELROD, decd, (1840), John EASLEY (1841), Warham EASLEY,
Jr. & Warham EASLEY, Sr. (1845), Betsey EVANS (1839), John D. EASTERLY (1845),
Simeon E. FROST (1839), James FLANAGIN, James FREZEL, Abner FAIRCHILD (1841),
John FLORA in the hands of David McANALLY for collection (1837), Mrs. Cynthia
FORT (1842), James K. GRAY (1842), James GRANTHAM, Richard GRANTHAM, decd,
Duglas GRADY (1837), Reuben GROVE, Jr. (1846), Nathan GRAY & Isaac LEBOW (1846),
Samuel GILL & Wm WILLIAMS, Adm of the Estate of William WILLIAMS, decd (1845),
W. GIFFORD (1836), John HOLDER, George HAYES (old account), John HARRIS, Esq.
(1842), Wm HARREL (1843), Colbert HIPSHEAR (1843), John HARVEL, Jr. (1844),
execution returned to Esqr DODSON, Henry HIPSHEAR, Sr. in hands of Shff THOMA-
SON (1843), Wm B. HODGE & Edward HODGES (4 notes 1843) all in the hands of Shff
THOMASON, Thomas HAYES (1841), Wyatt HICKS (1844), James HOLSTIN (1841),
Macajah HAMON in the hands of R. DODSON (1838), Malan HARRIS (1846), Jacob
HIPSHEAR & Henry HIPSHEAR, Sr. note given to E. THOMASON for collection (1842),
Mrs. Gracy BOYAKIN, Thomas AMIS (1845), John GARRISON (1841), _____BURNETT
(1841), _____ HUFFMASTER (1840), _____HAMER (1840), William HARRIS, William
BENTLEY note in hands of John L. CONNER, Dpt Shff (1841), Nicholas HAYNES in the
hands of Jno L. CONNER, Dpt Shff (1842), Joshua JONES (1845) for rents, Thomas
JOHNSON, decd, William IMES note in the hands of Sheriff THOMASON (1841), Stephen
JOHNSON, Wm PICKNEY, Larkin JOHNSON (1845), Robert JONES, Chesley JARNAGIN (1843)
William JOHNSON (1844), A. & W. C. KYLE (1843), Thos JONES, Clinton A. JONES &
Juoam JONES (1846), Elizabeth JACK & others (1847), note filed with John LAFF-
ERTY, Commissioner of the Estate of John F. JACK, decd, Miss Martha JACK (1842),
James KENNON & Ahab BOWEN (1834), Tristrum D. KNIGHT, Jacob KLINE (1844), James
KENNER, James LONG, Sr. (1843), Reuben LONG, Isaac LEBOW (1844), James LAY & Wm
DANIEL (1838), John LONG, Jr. (1839), James LONG, Jr. note in hands of Elisha
THOMASON, Shff (1841), Hardy LONG in the hands of Elisha THOMASON (1841), Joseph
LONG (1840), Isaac LANE of Tazwell (1842), Abraham LAWLESS (1843), Esau LAMB
(1837), Jacob LONG in the hands of Shff THOMASON (1842); notes in the hands of
Thomas LATHIM, Constable: Enoch DOULTON (1837), John CREECH & Henry HIPSHEAR
(1837), Pleasant JENNINGS (1839), Aaron McGINNIS (1840); James R. & Robert KNOX
(1837), Archibald McCOY (1839), Thomas P. McANALLY (1840), David McANALLY, Jr.
(1847), Joseph L. MIDDLETON, William McCOY (1840); Wm MAYES, son of James MAYES,
Jacob NOE (1845) and one note jointly with Edward TATE & Wm T. TATE (1845), Wm
C. MALLICOAT (1843), David McANALLY & John BRYAN (1844); Samuel McCRAVE (1839),

James MILLAR (1844), Gabriel McCRAVE (1838), Charles McGINNIS note in the hands
of E. THOMASON, Shff, Charles McANALLY, Sr. (1844), Moses McGINNIS (1845), Wm
MILLS in the hands of R. DODSON, Constable, Wesley McANALLY (1843), William
McCRAVE (1840), Wm G. McDANIEL in the hands of David McANALLY, Constable (1841),
Wm G. McDANIEL & Thomas K. HOWELL in the hands of David McANALLY (1836),
William McCRAW (1834); Alxd McCRAW (1833), James McANALLY, Sr. (1825), James
McGEE (1837 & 1838), John MAYES (1843) & note jointly with Saml GILL (1845), James
MALLICOAT (1843), Andrew J. McANALLY (1843), Charles McANALLY & David McANALLY,
Sr. (1845), Martin MYERS note in the hands of Shff THOMASON (1841), Robert
MARTIN in hands of Sheriff THOMASON (1814), David NOE (1842), John NEWMAN, decd,
(1840), Marvel NASH & Chas McANALLY (1840), William NORTON (1835), Robert NALL
(1843), Peter OGAN in the hands of R. DODSEN, Constable, (1840), Richard MOORE
& David McANALLY & Josiah BLAIR (1842), Joseph PROFFIT in the hands of Shff
THOMASON (1843), Susanna POINDEXTER, Chapman POINDEXTER (1843), Benjamin PECK,
Jacob PECK (1820 & 1821), John POUGE & Jacob VAUGHN (1844), James PILANT balance
on old Judgement, Stephen PATE (1838), John PHILIPS, Sr. (1831), John RAINS
(1841), Josiah RHOTEN (1842), Aaron PETERSON & John NEWMAN (1835), Robert REED
(1834), Joseph B. M. RECEE & Edward DANIELS (1841), Richard T. ROBERSON (1836),
Thomas RAINS in the hands of R. DODSON, Const., (1838), James ROBINSON old acct,
William ROGES old acct, Charles REED (1831), Russel RIGGS in the hands of John
F. NOE, Constable (1845), William RUSH (1842), Saml RIGGS (1838), Isaiah REECE
in the hands of David McANALLY (1841), John PRUNER (1839), Benjamin DAVIS note
in the hands of Dpt Shff CONNER (1842), John ROBERSON (1842), Wyatt RESORT
(1840), William R. TOW (1842), Tolliver ROBINSON (1843), James O. SENTER & N. A.
SENTER (1847), Peter SAMPSEL 2 notes in the hands of David McANALLY, Constable,
(1840), John SHELTON (1844), John SMITH & Preston ROBINSON (1840), Leroy SHORTER
in the hands of Shff THOMASON (1842), Solomon S. SHIPLEY (1847), Pleasant M.
SENTER (1842), Nelson A. SENTER (1841), Levina SAMPSEL, America STUBBLEFIELD
(1844), John H. SCHOOLER note in the hands of Jno H. CROZIER, Esq. (1842),
Joseph SHANNON & Newton SHANNON (1839), Amos STROUD & others in the hands of
David McANALLY, Constable (1838), John SLATTEN in the hands of R. DODSON (1839),
James SHIELDS & Wm MURRY in the hands of David McANALLY (1835), David SHELTON
(1842), Richard STUBBLEFIELD (1842) & jointly with Wm STUBBLEFIELD (1840), Wm
STRATTON (1833), Archibald R. SULLENBARGER in the hands of Sheriff THOMASON
(1841), John TUCKER (1844) John TUCKER, Jr. (1839), James TUCKER (1844),
Pendleton TAYLOR in the hands of Shff THOMASON (1837), William THOMPSON (1841),
Nathan THOMPSON (1838), Jacob WOLF (1844), Luther WILLS (1845), George WOLF
account in 1839, Adam WOLF (1841), Thos WILLIFORD in the hands of Shff THOMA-
SON (1844), Nathaniel WOLF (1847), George WOLF (Stumpy) (1842), Jeremiah
WILLSON in the hands of John S. CONNER, D. Shff (1840), Fetty WOLF old a/c,
Ann K. WILLIAMS, William WOLF & Adam WOLF (1838), Russell WYATT (1841) & to note
due as Guardian (1844), Willson WYATT (1843), WILLIAMS & GODWIN (1843), Joseph
VAUGHN book account, John BASSETT (1845), Robert M. YANCEY (1840). These notes
put into the hands of D. McANALLY, Conts., for collection: Jacob JESSE (1842),
John BIGGS (1842), David MINSEY (1841), Joseph NOE, Jr, Joseah YOUNG, Henry
YOUNG, Thomas I. YOUNG, Wm D. JENNINGS, decd, United States Bank Stock, Union
Bank of TN stock, Hiwassy Rail Road Stock, Union Bank at Knoxville due at d.
of Ethelred WILLIAMS as per Bank book. Cash on hand at death of E. WILLIAMS.
Signed 5 Apr 1847 Wm A. BROWN one of the executors. Recorded 19 May 1847.

p. 536   Guardian Report - Mary HENDERSON, Guardian of Mary S. HENDERSON. 6
Apr 1847. Mentions: Wm GODWIN, Adm of the Estate of Thomas HENDERSON, decd;

last report 27 May 1845; the ward being Deaf & Dumb. Signed Mary HENDERSON,
Guardian. Recorded 15 May 1847 E. TATE, clerk.

Guardian Report - Isaac HARRIS, Guardian of minor heirs of Samuel RAY,
decd. 28 Apr 1849. Mentions: last report Jul 1846; John TALLY who intermarried
with Tabitha RAY, a ward. Signed Isaac HARRIS. Recorded 15 May 1847 E. TATE.

p. 537   Guardian Report - James MILLS, Guardian of John P. PERRIN.   26 Apr 1847.
Mentions: last report 15 Nov 1845. Signed James MILLS, Guardian. Recorded
15 May 1847 E. TATE, clerk.

Settlement - Thomas McBROOM, Adm of the Estate of Patsey COUNTZ, decd.
24 Apr 1847. Mentions: notes on Wm COOSE & Wm B. HODGES; RICE & McFARLAND;
George MYERS; Doctor Wm E. COCKE; Jacob KLINE & Sons; Thomas McBROOM for care
in his home & nursing in her last illness. Recorded 15 May 1847 E. TATE, clerk.

p. 538   Settlement - Wm BRYAN, Administrator of the Estate of John BRYAN, decd.
3 Apr 1847. Mentions: estate sale; Hiram L. SHAVER; Gabriel McCRAVE; J. L.
ETTER; WILLIAMS & BROWN; John McANALLY; E. THOMASON, Shff, taxes 1846; note to
J. L. ETTER; note to E. WILLIAMS; note to R. H. BRAGG; G. W. MATLOCK; Nancy
BRYAN, Mary D. JONES, Jeroam B. JONES & J. R. BRYAN, 4 heirs; Nancy BRYAN, widow
of decd. Recorded 15 May 1847 E. TATE, clerk.

p. 539   Guardian Report - Guardians for Martha M. FORT, Edwin R. FORT & Jacob H.
FORT. Report received through Genl Stephen COCKE per letter bearing date 20 Jul
1846. Mentions: power of attorney fee; Josiah RHOTEN for use of the heirs of
Cornelia RHOTON, decd; paid Cynthia C. COX, late widow of Jacob H. FORT, decd;
recd by Wm A. BROWN for the use of Joseph H. BROWN heir of Cynthia E. BROWN;
for Martha M. FORT: Mrs. Thursey JOHNSON, 1 horse 7 Aug 1846, Samuel GILL 8 Aug
1846 on account 1 gold ps for pocket money, Wm WILLIAMS on account. For Edwin
R. FORT: WILLIAMS & BROWN store, Julias J. FLEMEING for tuition at Greenville
College, pd George G. SPECK for tuition. For Jacob H. FORT: WILLIAMS & BROWN,
H. H. ATKINSON for tailoring; John POGUE. Signed Wm A. BROWN & Josiah RHOTAN,
Guardians. Recorded 15 May 1847 E. TATE, clerk.

p. 540   Settlement - Wm GOODWIN, Adm of the Estate of Thomas HENDERSON, decd.
With a will annaxed done 2 Mar 1847. Mentions: 4 notes on Wm Y. HENDERSON,
decd, due 1839, 1840, 2 1844; 3 notes on Mary HENDERSON due 1844 & 1845; 3 notes
on Wm GODWIN due 1844 & 1845; notes on David HARRIS (1844); John DEVER ? (1845);
A. I. McANALLY (1846); Wm McCRAVE (1840); Wm MURRY (1840); Joseph HICKS (1845);
Pleasant WHITLOW (1832); Mary SAMPSEL; Mary HENDERSON, Guardian of the minor heirs
of Thos HENDERSON, decd. Recorded 15 May 1847 E. TATE, clerk.

p. 541   Settlement - James JONES, Adm of the Estate of Henry BOATMAN, decd.
9 Feb 1847. Mentions: last settlement 3 Feb 1846; cash recd of D. C. CAR-
MICHAEL, Ex of the Estate of Thomas K. HOWELL, decd; Alexander HELTON who intermarried with Nancy BOATMAN an heir; Mary BOATMAN, widow of Henry BOATMAN, decd;
Levi RIGGS who intermarried with Sarah BOATMAN an heir; Ezekiel BOATMAN who
intermarried with Mary BOATMAN; Robt M. BARTON, Atto. Recorded 16 May 1847.

p. 542   Account of Sale - Elizabeth MAYES, decd. Mentions: J. H. IVY, James T.
CARMICHAEL, Jesse LIVINGSTON, Pharoah PRICE, James A. MILES, Wm TURNER, John

BROOSE, James M. PRYOR, Robert DANIEL, Wm TURNER, C. S. HARRIS, John IVY,
Benjamin IVY, Wm GLOSSUP, G. B. MAYES, W. H. DANIEL. Signed Godwin MAYES, Adm.
Recorded 16 May 1847.

Commissioners Report - Set apart to Margaret WILLIAMS, widow of John
M. WILLIAMS, decd, for 1 year support of her & family. Signed Samuel GILL, Levi
CAMPBELL, A. G. SULLENBARGER, Commissioners. Recorded 16 May 1847 E. TATE.

p. 543   Additional Account of Sale - Nelson A. SENTER, decd. Sold 15 Dec 1846.
Mentions: S. S. SHIPLEY, Henry HASLUP, Thomas HARRIS, James LINDAMOOD, Pleasant
M. SENTER, A. M. WINKLE, Edmond COLLINS, Hardy LONG, John WALKER, S. W. SENTER,
David WHITESIDES, S. B. TATE. Signed S. W. SENTER & Jas E. HOGAN, Adms.
Recorded 15 May 1847 E. TATE, clerk.

County Court Clerk
Inventories of Estates
&
Wills
Jun 1847-May1852

Indexed.

p. 1   Second Settlement - Sarah HAYNES, Adm of the Estate of Wm HAYNES, decd.
8 May 1847. Mentions: last settlement 8 Dec 1846; Martin CLEVELAND, Guardian
of the minor heirs of Wm HAYNES, decd; Mary HAYNES, an heir, for her share of
said estate. Recorded 2 Jun 1847 E. TATE, clerk.

Inventory - David JANUARY, decd. Mentions: 1 note on George SPARK-
MAN; note executed by George SPARKMAN to David JANUARY. Signed L. M. ELLIS,
Executor. Recorded 12 Jun 1847 E. TATE, clerk.

p. 2   Account of Sale - David JANUARY, decd. Sold 7 May 1847. Mentions:
Doctor John B. GRIGSBY, Anderson ADKINS, Col. Lewis ELLIS, James GAINS, Esqr,
S. WEST, James YATES, Wm BETHEL, James CHURCHMAN, Thornton CORUM, one Sorel horse
sold in SC at private sale, John STATSWORTH, B. E. & James GAINS. Signed Lewis
M. ELLIS, Executor.

p. 3   Guardian Report - Martin CLEVELAND, Guardian of the minor heirs of Wm
HAYNES, decd. 18 May 1847. Mentions: cash received from Sarah HAYNES, Adm,
recp dated 1 Feb 1847; Daniel HAYNES for work done on minor heirs land; Wm
HAYNES an heir who became of full age, recpt dates 1 Feb 1847; rent of wards
land 1846; interest chargable from 1 Feb 1847 to date. Signed Martin CLEVELAND.
Recorded 12 May 1847 E. TATE, clerk.

p. 4   Guardian Report - James JOHNSON, Guardian of M. E. C. WATKINS. 1 Jul
1847. Mentions: last report for his ward & heirs of the Estate of John K.
WATKINS, decd; pd John NORMAN, Shff for taxes of wards lands 1843; pd J. T. RUST,
Shff for taxes 1844 through 1847; pd C. M. PATTERSON for acting agent in paying
taxes 1843 through 1847; last report made 10 Apr 1844. Recorded 18 Jul 1847.

Guardian Report - Lewis ATKINS, Guardian of the minor heirs of Nathan
ATKINS, decd. 6 Jul 1847. Mentions: Hiram VITTITOE former guardian; interest

from 5 Jul 1846. Signed Lewis his _A_ mark ATKINS, Guardian. Recorded 18 Jul 1847 E. TATE, clerk.

p. 5   Account of Sale - Thomas JOHNSON, decd. Sold 25 & 26 Mar 1844. Mentions: John RICE, Albert SULLENBARGER, Thomas COCKE, L. JOHNSON, Robert MITCHEL, Alexander McCONNEL, Walter SHROPSHEAR, William MAYES, Gabriel McCRAVE, Wm BASSETT, David McANALLY, Mrs. DODSON, Gabriel McGRAVE, Sarah JOHNSON, Edmund COLLINS, Ethelred WILLIAMS, Col. J. WALKER, John LONG, A. G. SULLENBARGER, P. M. SENTER, Reuben LONG, Sanford JOHNSON, Thos THOMAS, Dowel COLLINS, James LAFFERTY, Thos. WHITESIDE, Wm GODWIN, John HARRIS, Daniel TURLEY, W. P. ATKINSON, Thomas DODSEN, Harvey MILES, James JOHNSON, Eli COX, Purtyman LONG, James BARTON, Henry LONG, Enoch DOLTON, Negro man JACK, Negro girl MARTHA. Signed Larkin JOHNSON & Sanford JOHNSON, Executors. Recorded 11 Aug 1847 E. TATE, clerk.

p. 7   Additional Inventory - David JANUARY, decd. Mentions: accounts on Ann CLEVELAND, Absalome ROACH, Martin VINEYARD & the Widow PARROTT to one coffin; notes on R. D. EZELL & Robert FIELD: account on L. M. ELLIS. Signed L. M. ELLIS, Executor. Recorded 13 Aug 1847.

p. 8   Guardian Report - G. B. MITCHEL, Guardian of the minor heirs of Wm HANKINS, decd. 31 Jul 1847. Mentions: last report 31 May 1845; Wm CARUTHERS, Atto in fact for Hannah C. HANKINS, she being arrived at full age as per recpt dated 7 Aug 1845; full settlement made. Recorded 13 Aug 1847 E. TATE, clerk.

          Guardian Report - Greenberry MITCHEL, Guardian of Russel SMALLWOOD's heirs. 31 Jul 1874. Mentions: last report 31 May 1845; taxes paid on wards land to James SALLING & B. E. GAINS, Dpt Shffs for 1845 & 46. Recorded 13 Aug 1847 E. TATE, clerk.

p. 9   Guardian Report - James L. TALBOTT, Guardian of the minor heirs of Amos STALSWORTH, decd. 27 Aug 1847. Mentions: sale of rent corn on wards plantation. Signed J. L. TALBOTT, Guardian. Recorded 10 Sep 1847.

          Settlement - A. I. McANALLY, Adm for the Estate of James MOORE, decd. 3 Aug 1847. Mentions: A. R. SULLENBARGER; D. McANALLY; William GODWIN who intermarried with Emelia MOORE, an heir; Rhoda MOORE, widow of said James MOORE, decd; A. I. McANALLY for bldg house as settled by arbetratory; A. I. McANALLY who intermarried with Nancy H. MOORE, an heir. Recorded 10 Sep 1847 E. TATE.

p. 10   Guardian Report - Andrew BOWER, Guardian of the minor heirs of John HILL, decd. 1 Sep 1847. Mentions: last report 10 Jul 1846; hire of SLAVES for 1847; rent of wards lands 1846 &47; Robert J. McKINNY, atto fee in suit in Chancery Court; W. L. LATHIM, clk of curcuit court for transcript in case Abel HILL vs Stephen FROST & John HUBBS, Executors; B. E. GAINS, Dpt Shff, taxes of wards land & SLAVES 1846 & 47; Allen HURT for extra clothing for PHILIP & STEPHEN, slaves of wards; certified copy of the testementary to Stephen FROST & John HUBBS, Executors; Joseph HILL for selling property of wards; Hiram VITTITOE for boarding & schooling Wm R. HILL, a ward; Booker DYER for selling property of wards; Andrew BOWER, Guardian for boarding & clothing Penina Palestine HILL, his ward, 5 years & Wm Ramsey HILL, his ward, 1 years. Signed Andrew x BOWER, Guardian. Recorded 13 Sep 1847.

p. 11   Guardian Report - Benjamin SMITH, Guardian of Mary SMITH, Frances
SMITH, Alexander SMITH, Juba SMITH & Rachel SMITH. Mentions: last report 7
Sep 1846; boarding, clothing & caring for Mary SMITH, she being Dumb, for 1 yr;
taxes 1847. Signed 23 Aug 1847 Benjamin SMITH, Guardian. Recorded 15 Sep 1847.

    Guardian Report - Isaac LEBOW, Guardian of Pheba BASSETT. 30 Aug 1847.
Mentions: last report 30 Dec 1845; paid Clerk & Register of Hawkins Co. on
Deed of Trust to secure debt due ward; Thos R. NELSON, atto. Recorded 15 Sep
1847 E. TATE, clerk.

p. 12   Additional Account of Sale - Joseph BEELAR, decd. Mentions: Slave
DICK to John BEELAR, $750.00. Signed Jacob BEELAR, Executor. Recorded 15 Sep
1847 E. TATE, clerk.

    Settlement - Larkin JOHNSON & Sanford JOHNSON, Executors of the Estate
of Thomas JOHNSON, decd. 17 Sep 1847. Mentions: amount charged to Larkin
JOHNSON in will of said decd for tract of land; Wm MURRY; Larkin JOHNSON pd for
walling in the graves of Thos JOHNSON & Barbara JOHNSON, decd; Sarah JOHNSON, a
legatee; Patsey DODSEN, a legatee; Lucy EATON, a legatee; taxes 1844; A. R.
SULLENBARGER for coffin; note on Joseph HICKS. Recorded 19 Oct 1847.

p. 13   Guardian Report - Isaac M. McBEE, Guardian of Calliway McBEE. 27 Sep
1847. Mentions: last report 1 Aug 1845; cash received from Executor of the
Estate of Lemuel McBEE, decd, on 19 May 1846; hiring of SLAVES for 1845 & 46; amt
of his proportional part of one NEGRO child bought for the benefit of the heirs
of Lemuel McBEE, decd; Calliway McBEE's receipt he having arrived at full age,
dated 7 Sep 1847. Signed Isaac McBEE, Guardian. Recorded 19 Oct 1847.

    Guardian Report - Joel DODSON, Guardian of Melvina MALLICOAT. 7 Sep
1847. Mentions: rents recd of wards land until she became of age; Wm STOGS-
DALE, atto in fact for ward. Recorded 19 Oct 1847 E. TATE, clerk.

p. 14   Second Account of Sale - John M. WILLIAMS, decd. Mentions: Wm M.
COCKE purchase of Negro man MICHAEL, Reece BOWEN, Marine DUVAUL, Parrott GODWIN,
Abraham McCONNEL, Richard RAY, Thomas LANE purchase of Negro girl SARAH, Elbert
TAYLOR, Margaret WILLIAMS purchase of 1 Negro boy ANDY, Octavus YOE. Signed
5 Oct 1847 Parrott GODWIN, Adm. Recorded 19 Oct 1847.

    Account of Sale - James MALLICOAT, decd. Sold 20 & 21 Nov 1845.
Mentions: Elizabeth MALLICOAT, George DARTING, James BROCK, Isaac PHILIPS,
A. P. GREEN, Wm HARREL, Jr., Benjamin PECK, John CALLISON, Wm C. MALLICOAT,
Hamilton MALLICOAT, David LIVINGSTON, Absolom THACKER, James WOOD, Edward L.
TATE, John ROACH, Jacob KLINE, George B. GRIGSBE, Wm E. COCKE, Samuel WRIGHT,
Henry ALSUP, Thos DYER, James T. WEST, Wm COX, John CURLE, J. J. HARREL,
James JAMES, George W. MYERS. Signed Wm T. TATE, Adm. Recorded 25 Oct 1846.

p. 17.   Inventory - David HORNER, decd. 6 Oct 1847. Signed Robert CARDWELL,
Adm. Recorded 3 Nov 1847 E. TATE, clerk.

p. 18   Inventory - G. C. SPECK. Mentions: notes & accounts due - H. ADKINS
(1841), John WALTERS (1832), John RYAN (1839), Turner HALE (1834), W. L. CREED
& Thos. ANDERSON (1847), Moses B. HARRIS (1845), John WALKER, John ELKINS.

Signed Thos RUSSEL, Adm.   Recorded 3 Nov 1847 E. TATE, clerk.

        Account of Sale - G. C. SPECKS, decd.   Mentions: all bought by Widow
SPECKS. Signed Thos RUSSEL, Adm. Recorded 3 Nov 1847 E. TATE, clerk.

p. 19   Commissioners Report - 1 year support for Widow & family of George C.
SPECK, decd. Signed Jas O. SENTER, John MORRIS, Wm A. HARRIS, Commissioners,
7 Aug 1847. Recorded 3 Nov 1847 Ellis RIGGS, JP.

        Inventory 29 Oct 1847.   Jonathan WILLIAMS, decd.   Signed Isaac F.
McCARTY, Adm. Recorded 3 Nov 1847 E. TATE, clerk.

        Second Account of Sale - Aquilla MITCHEL, decd.   Mentions: hiring Negro
girl CHANY to Omy MITCHEL, Calvin MITCHEL, George MOYER. Signed G. B. MITCHEL,
Adm. Recorded 3 Nov 1847.

p. 20   Settlement - Ellis RIGGS, Adm & Executor of the Estate of Andrew COFF-
MAN, decd. 4 Sep 1847. Mentions: hiring of SLAVES up to the time they were
Emancipated; John BEGGS; D. McANALLY, Dpt Shff for taxes 1845 & selling of
personal property; John RAMSEY; Wm MURRY; George MILLIKAN, one of the legatees,
keeping SLAVES that could not be hired for 3 wks; Ellis RIGGS for keeping
SLAVES that could not be hired for 1 yr & 4 mos; midwife fee for one SLAVE; minor
heirs of David & Wm COFFMAN, decd; Thos TURLEY, Atto; Jacob PECK, Atto; Caleb
W. SMITH; John F. NOE for removing NEGROS out of state of TN according to the
last will & testament of Andrew COFFMAN, decd. Recorded 3 Nov 1847.

p. 21   Settlement - Wm P. LONG, Adm of the Estate of Joseph DANIEL, decd.
7 Nov 1847. Mentions: John C. WILLIAMS; James THOMPSON; Ja & I. LAFFERTY;
James CARMICHAEL, Sr; Josiah RHOTON; Jonathan WILLIAMS; James B. BOYD; M. N.
JEFFREYS; Wm M. MOODY; G. B. MAYES, Dpt Shff taxes 1841; D. McANALLY, Dpt Shff
taxes 1842, 43, 44 & 45. Recorded 4 Nov 1847 E. TATE, clerk.

        Guardian Report - John LONG, Guardian of the minor heirs of David
BEELAR, decd. Mentions: note on A. P. GREEN & Robert MASSENGILL given for
amount due said heirs from the Estate of Joseph BEELAR, decd, the sum having
been willed to said heirs of Joseph BEELAR, decd; note on Jesse F. BEELAR, David
NICELY & Thomas WAGNER given for the portion due said heirs out of the amount
for which a Negro girl CLARISSA was sold which girl belonged in part to the
Estate of David BEELAR, decd; taxes 1847; copy of George DYER's will; dispute
regarding will of George DYER, decd, the heirs of David BEELAR, decd, may be
entitled to something; Jesse F. BEELAR, Guardian of the heirs of Polly BEELAR,
decd, & his own heirs have an Atto attending to this business. Signed 2 Nov
1847 John LONG, Guardian. Recorded 6 Nov 1847.

p. 24   Guardian Report - Henry ALSUP, Guardian of the minor heirs of David
COFFMAN & William COFFMAN, decd. 1 Oct 1847. Mentions: sale of lands of the
Estate of Andrew COFFMAN, decd, belonging to the minor heirs of David & Wm
COFFMAN, decd; W. S. LATHIM, Clerk of Curcit Court. Recorded 6 Nov 1847 E. TATE.

        Second Settlement - D. P. MYNATT, Adm of the Estate of William CORUM,
decd. 22 Oct 1847. Mentions: last report 30 Jan 1847; Martha T. CORUM, Widow,
recpt dated 2 Feb 1837; Martha T. CORUM, Guardian of the minor heirs of Wm

CORUM, decd, recpt dated 26 Apr 1847.   Recorded 6 Nov 1847 E. TATE, clerk.

p. 25   Commissioners Report - 15 Nov 1847, set aside for support of the heirs of David HORNER, decd. Signed John CLARK, Francis YOUNG, Pierce CODY, Commissioners. Recorded 9 Dec 1847 E. TATE, clerk.

Account of Sale - David HORNER, decd. Mentions: Elizabeth HORNER, Elisha OWENS, Robert CARDWELL, Sr., George HORNER, Edward L. TATE, James CHURCHMAN, Hiram COX, Francis YOUNG, Enos HAMMER, Chesley MORGAN, Isaac DANIEL, John SNIDER, John YOUNG, Albert YOUNG, George W. PRATT, William HAMMER, J. B. L. COMBS, James JAMES, Wm DONAHOO, Thomas HASKINS, Robert CARDWELL, George LACY, John MOODY, Jr., Wm POTTER, Wm B. TATE, John L. GRAY, Edward TATE, Sr., Wm CARDWELL, John CARDWELL, Thulbert MORGAN, David N. TATE, Cornelius GOWFORTH, Isaac DANIEL, E. D. SUNDERLAND, James MAYES, James WOOD, A. R. SULLENBARGER. Signed Robert CARDWELL, Adm. Recordec 9 Dec 1847.

p. 28   Second Settlement - Willie B. DYER, Executor for the Estate of Wm DYER, Jr., decd. 13 Nov 1847. Mentions: having paid out more than remained in Estate; Wm M. MOODY; Royal JENNINGS, Constable; Robert FRY; Smith STRANGE; Joseph CLARK; Executor settling Estate since 4 Aug 1841; Robert HINES, Atto, for fee in case Robert CARDWELL vs Willie B. DYER, Executor of the Estate of Wm DYER, decd; Lewis M. ELLIS, Dpt Shff. Recorded 9 Dec 1847 E. TATE, clerk.

p. 29   Settlement - Mary HAYES, Adm of the Estate of Thos HAYES, decd.   17 Nov 1847. Mentions: John RUCKER's receipt for amount of Judgt against the Estate of Thos HAYES, decd; 1 year support for widow and family that was not on hand at time of his death; she spent .87^2 cents more than received. Recorded 10 Dec 1847 E. TATE, clerk.

p. 30   Settlement - Ausburn COFFEE & Elizabeth COFFEE, Adms of the Estate of John COFFEE, decd. 17 Nov 1847. Mentions: accounts against C. W. LATHIM dated 1840, 41, 42 & 43; Wm SMITH; Elizabeth COFFEE, widow & relect of decd, 1 yr support for her & family that was not on hand at time of his death; J. & J. LAFFERTY; 1/2 of a note given by John COFFEE & Ausburn COFFEE to N. A. SENTER. Recorded 10 Dec 1847 E. TATE, clerk.

p. 31   Settlement - Wm T. TATE, Adm of the Estate of James MALLICOAT, decd. 3 Dec 1847. Mentions: notes on David KITTS, John GRAY (2), Berry GATEWOOD & Godwin SOLLOMAN; acc on Isaac PHILIPS, A. P. GREEN & B. G. SIMPSON; James MALLICOAT, decd, note to Jeremiah JARNAGIN, Madison Accadàmy & Wm P. JONES; RICE & McFARLAND; Geo W. MEYERS; Dr. Wm E. COCKE; Dr. John B. GRIGSBEE; Wm COOSE; note to Stephen J. GODSEY; Elizabeth MALLICOAT, widow, 1 yr support; A. P. GREEN, Shff, taxes 1845; Benjamin PECK; Joshua D. CURLE, Constable; note executed by Wm MAYES & James MALLICOAT, decd, to E. TATE, Executor of the Estate of John STIFFY, decd; note on Isaac PHILIPS; note to Wm T. TATE & CO. Recorded 10 Dec 1847 E. TATE, clerk.

p. 33   Guardian Report - William STONE, Guardian of Susan STONE, one of the minor heirs of Robert STONE, decd. 12 Nov 1847. Mentions: hiring of SLAVE to 12 Mar 1845 when SLAVE died; one SLAVE kept with ward; M. & J. L. MOFFITT's for goods; Williston TALBOTT for boarding ward at school; Samuel BUNCH; A. H. MATHIS for tuition. Signed Wm STONE, Guardian. Recorded 10 Dec 1847 E. TATE.

p. 34   Guardian Report - Wm M. MOODY, Guardian of James MAYES, Jr., a minor
heir of James MAYES, decd. 3 Dec 1847. Mentions: last report 31 Jan 1846;
hire of SLAVES & rent of lands 1846; Edward DANIEL boarding ward at school;
M. W. WILLIAMS for tuition; Wm T. TATE & Co.; J. & J. LAFFERTY; travel to
McMenrow County to take despositions. Signed 3 Dec 1847. Recorded 10 Dec 1847.

p. 35   Will - Henry BOYD, decd. My niece, Lucy Angeline BOYD, money for her
education under control of her grandfather Edward TATE, if she d. then goes to
her next oldest sister, Isabella Jane BOYD, dau of James B. BOYD, if both d.
then to next oldest child; my bro Francis BOYD in our partnership of T. & H.
BOYD; my wife Jane BOYD all property left her by her Father; my infant dau
Hester Isabella BOYD; Francis BOYD of McMinn Co., TN & Samuel SHIELDS of Grainger
Co. my sole executors. Signed 20 Sep 1847. Also there shall be a genteel set
of tombstones over my Father & Mothers graves. Henry BOYD. Att: John A.
McKINNY, B. E. GAINS. Recorded 10 May 1848.

p. 36   Will - Katherine LEBOW, decd. My son Joseph LEBOW, my son William GRAY,
my son Isaac LEBOW, my son Jacob LEBOW, my dau Louisa JOHNSON, my son John LEBOW
& my dau Lucinda LEBOW & Martha C. SULLENBARGER my granddau, my dau Pheba BASSETT,
my dau Senah LEBOW to have my Negro man SAM; Negro woman JUDE & Negro girl SARAH
to be sold; Isaac LEBOW & William GRAY, Executors. 20 Aug 1842. Signed
Katherine x LEBOW. Att: James MOORE, David McANALLY. Recorded 10 Mar 1848.

         Inventory - Edna E. JACKSON, decd. Mentions: money received from H. W.
TAYLOR & E. A. TAYLOR. Signed D. C. JACKSON, Adm. Recorded 10 Mar 1848 E. TATE

p. 37   Will - 12 Oct 1847, Daniel EASLEY, decd. To my wife Susan & my dau
Mary EASLEY all my property; at their d. to the children of my dau Katherine
EASLEY & Issabella HARRIS formerly Issabella EASLEY; appts Jacob P. KIRKHAM,
Executor. Signed Daniel EASLEY. Att: George G. TAYLER & Jacob P. KIRKHAM.
Recorded 10 Mar 1848.

         Will - Calvin T. BEWLEY, decd. My wife Mary Louisa BEWLEY; notes in
the State of TN & Polk Co., MO where I have formerly lived; my beloved bro John
G. BEWLEY, Executor. Signed 15 Jan 1848 Calvin F. BEWLEY. Wit: Clesbe AUSTIN,
Wm FARIS, Archibald AUSTIN, Jr., Jno W. SISK. Recorded 8 Mar 1848.

p. 38   Inventory & Sale - Jesse T. COFFEE, decd. Mentions: John HAYES, Eli
HENRY, Cleveland COFFEE, John RUCKER, Meredity HARVEL or HOWELL, A. DOLTON, C.
COFFEE, George W. HAYES, Thomas HAILLEY, C. J. DOLTON, Cleveland CREACH, M. B.
DOLTON, T. J. COFFEE, Pinkney TAYLOR, Mary COLLINS, Mr. Henry BRAY, Thomas
DOLTON, David READER, Isacer MILLS, Plenial MAYES, Carrel COFFEE, David RADER,
John CARPENTER, Eli HENRY, Ryly MILLS, M. M. WEBB, James CAMPBELL, note on Wm
GARNER, 4 notes on George CAMPBELL, James W. CAMPBELL & Jeremiah CAMPBELL.
Signed 2 Jan 1848 Edmond COLLINS, Adm. Recorded 10 Mar 1848.

p. 39   Inventory - Lea McDANIEL, decd. Signed 29 Jan 1848 John CALLISEN, Adm.
Recorded 11 Mar 1848 E. TATE, clerk.

         Commissioners Report - 1 year support for Lena Ann McDANIEL, widow of
Lea McDANIEL, decd, & family. Signed 27 Jan 1848 Daniel McKINNEY, Benjamin
MITCHEL, John CLARK. Recorded 22 Mar 1848 E. TATE, clerk.

p. 40   Inventory - John NEWMAN, decd. Signed 8 Feb 1848 Wm T. TATE, Adm.
Recorded 11 Mar 1848.

          Settlement - Beanstation Turnpike Road, Thomas WHITESIDE & Joseph CLARK,
Commissioners. Year ending 31 Dec 1846. Expenditures to: Danl G. MILLAR,
Claboun Co., TN overseer; Henry WILLIAMS, Grainger Co., TN, overseer; C. W.
LATHIM, gatekeeper; E. S. KISSING; Joseph RICH, Grainger Co., overseer; Andrew
McGINNIS for clearing. Signed Robt. LOYD, Thos McBROOM, Daniel McKINNY, Comms.
Recorded 11 Mar 1848.

p. 41   Settlement - Joseph CLARK, one of the Commissioners of the Beanstation
Turnpike, year ending 31 Dec 1847. Mentions: Thos WHITESIDE former treasurer
of the Board of Comm.; Andrew McGINNIS, gatekeeper; Henry WILLIAMS; Willie
SANDERS; Wm B. CUNNINGHAM, B. F. McFARLAND; Jacob GODWIN; Joseph CLOUD; John M.
BIRCH; Joseph CLARK; Farmers & Machanick Bank of TN at Memphis. Signed 10 Mar
1848 John A. McKINNY, Robt LOYD, Isaac DANIEL, Comms. Recorded 13 Mar 1848.

p. 42   Inventory - David TATE, decd. Mentions: notes on Hugh GILLMORE & G. H.
PECK. Signed E. TATE & Wm T. TATE, Executors. Sworn in Court Wm B. CUNNINGHAM,
Chairman. Recorded 9 May 1848 E. TATE, clerk.

p. 43   Account of Sale - David TATE, decd. 29 & 30 Jul 1841. Mentions: James
GALLIAN, Saml B. TATE, Jacob GODWIN, John CAMRON, Isaac DANIEL, John CURLE, John
C. TATE, Wm COOSE, Hugh McELHANY, Isaac PHILIPS, John CALLISON, James JAMES,
Elisha OWENS, John CREWS, Abraham McCONNEL, Eli McDANIEL, James McDANIEL, Allen
D. MORGAN, Wm HAMMER, John KIDDER, Wm FREEMAN, Sarah KERSEY, Hugh GILLMORE,
Melton TATE, Jacob KINDAR. Sworn to in Open Court Wm B. CUNNINGHAM, Chairman.
Signed E. TATE & Wm T. TATE, Executors. Recorded 9 May 1848 E. TATE, clerk.

p. 44   Will - Phillip WYRICK, decd. Land equally divided between my sons -
when youngest is 21; my dau Elizabeth HUBBS; my wife Katharine WYRICK; my son
Rowland WYRICK; my sons William WYRICK & Martin WYRICK, Executives. Signed 5
Jun 1847 Philip x WYRICK. Att: John H. FROST, John LANE. Recorded 22 May 1848.

p. 45   Settlement - Jacob BEELAR, Executor of the Estate of Joseph BEELAR,
decd. 30 Mar 1848. Mentions: 2 sales; sale of 1 SLAVE; notes due on George
SEMORE, John BEELAR (2), Benjamin CAVENDAR, Lewis M. ELLIS, James SHIELDS &
Daniel NELSON, John SELLARS & Joseph CHANDLER, John PEARIN, Luis M. ELLIS &
James STARNDS (2), Martin CLEVELAND, James SELLARS, Robert FRY (2), Edward
CLARK (2), Smith STRANGE, COCKE, MASSINGILL & Co., Daniel BEELAR, John CHANDLER,
John LONG, William HOLLINGSWORTH, Joseph SMITH, Elizabeth COFFMAN, Julia HACKER,
CRAGHEAD & MASSINGILL, George COFFMAN, George MILLAR, Pleasant STARNS, Esther
TEAGUE & James L. ACUFF; Martin CLEVELAND; John LONG; John CHANDLER; Wm
LATHIM, Dpt Shff taxes 1846 -47; R. I. McKINNY, Atto; John NANCE; Joseph GOOSE-
CLOSE; RICE & McFARLAND; John A. CLEAVLAND & John CLARK; John CHANDLER; Peter
LONG; John COX; R. FIELDING; Wm & John CLEAVLAND; DANIEL Widow; Warham EAS-
LY; Ann BEELAR, widow of Joseph BEELAR, decd; Esther WATSON, a legatee; Mar-
garet ODEL a legatee; John LONG, Guardian of the minor heir of David BEELAR,
decd; John LONG, Jesse BEELAR, Daniel BEELAR, John BEELAR, Henry MYRES & Isaac
BEELAR; John LONG, Isaac BEELAR & Daniel BEELAR each one an heir; Jacob BEELAR,
Executor & legatee. Recorded 11 May 1848 E. TATE, clerk.

p. 47   Inventory - Katharine LEBOW, decd. 16 Mar 1848. Mentions: notes on
Malin HARRIS & Wm THOMPSON (1841); 1 note on Wm GRAY (1843); note on John MAYES
& Samuel GILL, security (1845); 2 Negro slaves, JUDE aged 60 or 70 & SALLY aged
c16 or 18. Isaac LEBOW, Executor. Recorded 12 May 1848. E. TATE, clerk.

p. 48   Account of Sale - Katherine LEBOW, decd.   25 Mar 1848.   JUDE sold to
John RICE; SALLY to George BASSETT. Signed Isaac LEBOW, Executor. Recorded 12
May 1848 E. TATE, clerk.

         Account of Sale - Lea McDANIEL, decd. Mentions: Lina Ann McDANIEL,
Polly MORGAN, John ROACH, Eli McDANIEL, James McDANIEL, James F. MORGAN, Loyd
COCKRAM, Henderson KIDWELL, David LIVINGSTON, James GREENLEA, James TALLY, Eli
McDANIEL, Sr., John BOABSTON, William MORGAN, Henry M. MORGAN. Signed John
CALLISON, Adm. Recorded 12 May 1848 E. TATE, clerk.

p. 49   Settlement - Robert LOYD & Eli McDANIEL, Executors of the Estate of
John McDANIEL, decd. 1 Mar 1848. Mentions: notes on Hugh GILLMORE, Chesley
JARNAGIN, Robt D. GRAY; Pierce CODY; James M. ROACH; Wm E. COCKE; Wm T. TATE &
Co.; Henry GROVE; E. THOMPSON, Shff, taxes 1846; Joshua CURLE, Dpt Shff, taxes
1847; Wm SMITH, tuition fee; Joel DYER, tuition fee; John G. BRISBE; Nancy
McDANIEL, widow. Recorded 19 May 1848 E. TATE, clerk.

p. 50   Settlement - James BARTON, Adm for the Estate of Keziah BARTON, decd.
31 Dec 1847. Mentions: Henry COUNTZ note; LONG & TAYLOR; C. W. MILLAR; Isaac
BARTON. Recorded 19 May 1848 E. TATE, clerk.

p. 51   Third Settlement - Hughs W. & Elika A. TAYLOR, Executors of the Estate
of Hughs O. TAYLOR, decd. 8 Dec 1847. Mentions: last settlement 6 Dec 1842;
F. A. PATTON who intermarried with Amanda A. TAYLOR, a legatee; Hughs W. TAYLOR,
a legatee; Jabin L. TAYLOR, a legatee; Colman M. WITT, who intermarried with
Rachel TAYLOR, a legatee; Elbert E. TAYLOR, a legatee; D. C. JACKSON who intermarried with Edna E. TAYLOR, a legatee; Elizabeth TAYLOR, the widow. Recorded
19 May 1848 E. TATE, clerk.

p. 52   Fourth Settlement - James JONES, Adm of the Estate of Henry BOATMAN,
decd. 25 Apr 1848. Mentions: last settlement 9 Feb 1847; Elias WESTER who
intermarried with Keziah BOATMAN, an heir. Recorded 19 May 1848 E. TATE.

         Guardian Report - James MILLS, Guardian of John P. PERRIN. 24 Apr 1848.
Mentions: last report 26 Apr 1847. Recorded 19 May 1848 E. TATE, clerk.

p. 53   Guardian Report - Robert CARDWELL, Sr., Guardian of the minor heirs of
Andrew CHAMBERLAIN, decd. 26 Apr 1848. Mentions: last report 26 Jul 1846;
rents for wards lands 1846; taxes 1846 & 47; Mary Jane, a ward; Jeremiah, a
ward; Dr. John B. GRIGSBE for attending Mary Jane CHAMBERLAIN, a ward; Saml N.
TATE for schooling wards. Recorded 19 May 1848 E. TATE, clerk.

         Guardian Report - George WILLIAMS & Margaret E. WILLIAMS, Guardians of
the minor heirs of John M. WILLIAMS, decd. 24 Apr 1848. Mentions: rents of
Panther Springs lands; J. D. CURLE, Dpt Shff, taxes 1847; J. GODWIN for selling
rents on lands; Robert HINDS, Atto. Recorded 19 May 1848 E. TATE, clerk.

p. 54   Guardian Report - John LAFFERTY, Guardian of Thos MAYES & Eliza MAYES, minor heirs of James MAYES, decd. 1 Nov 1847. Mentions: hiring of SLAVES for 1843, 44, 45 & 46; dispursements for Thomas MAYES - R. GROVE for bording & schooling, J. & J. LAFFERTY for goods, 10 weeks tuition to H. O. HYNSON, paid G. G. TAYLOR 55 days tuition, 2 mos tuition pd. W. L. PACKER, R. GROVE, Jr. for 1846, Wm M. MOODY expenses & wages to McMinn Co. to attend to deposition, 41 days tuition G. G. TAYLOR, 10 weeks tuition pd. A. H. MATHIS; expenditures for Eliza MAYES - R. GROVE for boarding & schooling, 10 weeks tuition pd. H. O. HYNSON as per R. GROVE, Jr., 45 weeks tuition to George G. TAYLOR, 2 mos tuition to Wm S. PARKER, acct of R. GROVE, Jr. 1846, expenses & wages to Wm M. MOODY to Monrow Co. taking deposition, 40 days tuition paid George G. TAYLOR 1846 & 47, 10 weeks tuition A. H. MATHIS. Recorded 19 May 1848 E. TATE, clerk.

p. 55   Inventory - Calvin F. BEWLEY, decd. Mentions: notes on Joseph BOND (2), John L. HEFFINGTON, Wm B. BURNS, L. W. BLAKE, W. C. BOWLES (2), Adam A. ROGAN, Wilkerson HARRISON, Wm Y. EVANS; 1 order from A. AYERS accepted by K. H. AYERS; 1 bond on Joseph BOND to pay C. F. BEWLEY. The foregoing considered doubtful since part of them are in MO. Signed 1 May 1848 Mary Louisa BEWLEY, Extrx. Recorded 19 May 1848.

p. 56   Guardian Report & Settlement - Samuel LAIN, Guardian of Richard M. EPPS. 2 Jun 1848. Mentions: cash received from Atto BATTIE, a legaey bequested to ward from _____ EPPS of VA; the amount Richard M. EPPS rec'd having become of full age, dated 2 Jun 1848. Signed Samuel LANE, Guardian. Recorded 7 Jun 1848 E. TATE, clerk.

p. 57   Settlement - 23 May 1848. With E. TATE, clerk, & Wm T. TATE, Executors of the will of David TATE, Sr., decd. Mentions: note on Hugh GILMORE (1842) & G. H. PECK (1846); land sold 30 Jul 1841; COCKE & NAFF; Abraham McCONNEL; Willson V. BRABSEN; Jacob KINDAR; E. THOMAS, Shff, taxes; Robert RAY; Wm E. COCKE; J. NAFF; Wm FIELDING; Wm COOSE; George MYER; Wm T. TATE & Co.; James H. DYER, Constable; notes on John BROWN (1842), G. W. TATE, Wm T. TATE (3). Signed Wm B. CUNNINGHAM & John CALLESEN, Commissioners. Recorded 7 Jun 1848 E. TATE, clerk.

p. 58   Fourth Settlement - Wm GRAY, Executor of the last will & testament of John LEBOW, decd. 24 Apr 1838. Mentions: last report 3 Jun 1845; Albert SULENBARGER who intermarried with Lucretia LEBOW, a legatee; Isaac LEBOW, agent for John LEBOW, a legatee; Catherine LEBOW, widow, a legatee; John RICE who intermarried with Senah LEBOW, a legatee; Lucinda LEBOW, a legatee; Isaac LEBOW, agent for Jacob LEBOW a legatee; Isaac LEBOW, agent for Pheba BASSETT, a legatee; Isaac LEBOW, a legatee; Sanford JOHNSON who intermarried with Louisa LEBOW, a legatee; Wm GRAY who intermarried with Mary GRAY, a legatee; E. TATE, clerk, receipt for a part of said Estate belonging to John LEBOW, Jr. & Joseph LEBOW, legatees. Recorded 7 Jun 1848 E. TATE, clerk.

p. 59   Inventory - James KENNON, Adm of the Estate of Theophilus GODWIN, decd. Jun term of court 1848. Mentions: Adm being appointed at Mar term of court; accounts & notes on John C. ROBERTS, John MYNATT, Anderson DOLAND, James CARMAN, Richard COOPER, William DONAHOO, John SHARP, James HUBBS, Jesse HOWERTON & Isaac DAMEWOOD; 1 order by D. RUTHERFORD on SIMPSON; 1 yr support of widow & children. Signed 5 Jun 1848 James KENNON. Recorded 7 Jun 1848 E. TATE, clerk.

p. 60   Account of Sale - Theophilus GODWIN, decd.   19 Apr 1848.   Mentions:
H. G. LEA, Wm CROW, Pryor P. MYNATT, Wm TROUTMAN, Jno W. KENNON, Thos MYNATT,
Widow, due Estate by accounts against John C. ROBERTS, John MYNATT, Anderson
DOLAND, James CARMAN, Richard COOPER, Wm DONAHOO & John SHARP, notes on James
HUBBS & Jesse HOWERTON, order by D. RUTHERFORD on SIMPSON, note on John SHARP.
Signed James KENNON, Adm.   Recorded 7 Jun 1848 E. TATE, clerk.

p. 61   Commissioners Report - 1 yr support of Widow and family of Theophilus
GODWIN, decd.   Signed 19 Apr 1848 Saml SHIELDS, John A. McKINNY, Harmon G. LEA,
Commissioners.   Recorded 7 Jun 1848 E. TATE, clerk.

        Settlement - Peter OGAN, Adm of the Estate of John OGAN, decd.   15 May
1848.   Mentions: last report 21 Dec 1840; bill due Aquilla PAYNE; Robt McGINNIS;
Wm HIPSHEAR; Jacob SHOULTZ; Wm CLARK, Dpt Shff, taxes 1833; Jacob HIPSHEAR; John
EPPERSON; Green BURDEN; John PRATHER; James L. ETTER; note to Ethelred WILLIAMS;
Peter BURDEN; Wm BEGLEY who intermarried with Polly OGAN, an heir; joint note
between John OGAN, decd & Peter OGAN; Peter OGAN, Adm, an heir; note on J. C.
BUNCH; John PRATHER's note.   Recorded 14 Jun 1848.

p. 62   Nuncupative Will - Robert MONROW, decd.   Made 6 Feb 1848 in his own
house; his little children to remain together on his land.   Signed 24 Feb 1845
John x MONROW, Mack x KITTS & Margaret x KITTS.   Recorded 14 Jun 1848.

        Will - Sterling BLACKBURN, decd.   Much beloved sister Jemima BLACKBURN
all my money & personal property; land warrant for $100.00 in U.S. Treasury
Scrip to which I am entitled for my service in U. S. Army under act of Congress
11 Feb 1847; to Allen HURST, my fine rifle gun; my brother Salathiel BLACKBURN
my Executor; my clothing to my 2 bros., Salathiel & Green BLACKBURN.   Signed
7 Aug 1847 Sterling x BLACKBURN.   Wit: Allen HURST, William ROGERS, Richard x
WADE.

p. 63   Account of Sale - James TROTT, decd.   Mentions: Mary TROTT, Anderson
TALLY, Wm B. CUNNINGHAM, Saml SMITH, Thos SMITH, H. ALSUP. A. H. MATHIS, Chesley
TROGDEN, L. DYER, Thornton CORUM, James T. WEST, John DUGLAS, Urijah KEY, James
FAULES (?), James TALLY, Willie TALLY, Mary TALLY, Widow, Jaberry MITCHEL.
Signed James H. DYER, Adm.   Recorded 5 Jul 1848.

p. 64   Settlement - James H. DYER, Adm of the Estate of James TROTT, decd.
20 Jun 1848.   Mentions: accounts on Jesse MITCHEL, Aquilla MITCHEL, George
SPARKMAN, David LIVINGSTON, James H. DYER, Absalom MANLEY, Abner LOWE, Thomas
RAY, George KEY, Wm LOWE, Thos DAVIS, Sr., John TUCKER, James DYER on the
ridge, James DAVIS, Hugh GILLMORE, Chesley RAY, James ROACH; notes on John
TALLY, Lide INKLEBARGER, John STALSWORTH; Wm FIELDING; Mary TROTT, widow of
decd & only heir, 1 yr allowance; Chesley TROGDEN; James TROTT note to Saml
SMITH; B. E. GAINS, Dpt Shff, taxes 1846; Isaac DANIEL; James T. WEST; RICE &
McFARLAND; Thos SMITH; Alfred WILHITE; James L. TALBOTT; Abner TROGDEN; A. BLACK-
BURN.   Recorded 5 Jul 1848 E. TATE, clerk.

p. 65   Commissioners Report - Henry M. MOODY, decd.   1 yr support to widow,
Nancy N. MOODY & family.   Signed F. B. COCKE, James JAMES, John GRAY, Comm.
Recorded 17 Jul 1848.

p. 66   Guardian Report - Lewis ATKINS, Guardian of the minor heirs of Nathan
ATKINS, decd. 6 Jun 1848. Mentions: last report 6 Jul 1847; Hiram VITTETOE for
tuition for wards 1847. Signed Lewis **A** Atkins, Guardian. Recorded 17 Jul 1848.

        Commissioners Report - 1 yr support for Widow RIGGS & family. Signed
29 Jul 1848 Joseph SHANNON, Wm A. HARRIS & John COX, Comm. before J. W. PATTER-
SON, JP. Recorded 14 Aug 1848 E. TATE, clerk.

p. 67   Guardian Report - Wm T. TATE, Guardian of Evalina CARMICHAEL, formerly
Evalina LATHIM & Martha LATHIM, minor heirs of John LATHIM, decd.   6 Aug 1848.
Mentions: hiring SLAVES & rents of lands 1846 to 1848; last report 31 Oct 1845;
judgement against C. W. LATHIM, Henry WILLIAMS, Andrew McGINNIS & James LATHIM
obtained at Tazwell, Dec 1844; E. THOMASON, Shff, taxes 1846-1847; Wm LATHIM,
Dpt Shff, taxes, 1846, 1847; Octavus YOE, R. Collector, taxes 1848; James K.
McANALLY for repairing kitchen (?) on wards lands; Dr. Wm E. COCKE for attending
ALFRED, a Slave; Lewis A. GARRETT, Clerk & Master of Chancery Ct. copies of
decrees; Isaac PHILIPS for midwife fee & caring for MATILDA, a Slave; expenses
for Evalina, a ward, RICE & McFARLAND for goods; S. S. SHIPLEY for boarding
Evalina at school, 1842; Wm H. NORTON for saddle; James LATHIM for boarding
Evalina, 1846; Wm T. TATE & Co; expenses for Martha, a ward - Wm T. TATE & Co.,
RICE & McFARLAND for goods, B. K. CUNNINGHAM for tuition, Dr. Wm E. COCKE for
attendance, Wm H. NORTON for board, 39 wks, James LATHIM for board. Signed 6
Aug 1848 Wm T. TATE, Guardian. Recorded 14 Aug 1848.

p. 69   Guardian Report - Thomas DYER, Guardian of the minor heirs of Marvel
WICKLIFF, decd. Mentions: last report 10 Jul 1846; Mary E. WICKLIFF, a ward;
Matilda I. WICKLIFF, a ward; taxes on wards money loaned out 1846 & 1847;
Isaac WICKLIFF, a ward, he becoming of full age, receipt dated 5 Jul 1848.
Signed Thos DYER, Guardian, 11 Jul 1848. Recorded 14 Aug 1848, E. TATE, clerk.

p. 70   Inventory - Ellis RIGGS, decd. Mentions: notes on James THOMPSON,
James L. JENNINGS, security debt for Nathan PATTERSON, Wm H. RIGGS, Henry
RIGGS, Elisha BULL, Felps RIGGS; open a/c on Alexander CARTWRIGHT, Elisha BULL,
Russel RIGGS, Jonathan MERCLOCK, Benjamin COX, John GARRESTON, Thomas SHIPLEY,
Felps REED, Jole GARRESTON; Russel RIGGS note on James DILLARD & Jesse RIGGS;
open a/c on MORRIS & NEWEL, James L. NEAL, Mrs. Nancy REED, on Grainger Co. for
supporting D. ROGERS last quarter. Signed 4 Aug 1848 Clesbe RIGGS, Shaderick
INMAN, Adms. Recorded 14 Aug 1848.

p. 71   Inventory - Henry M. MOODY, decd. Mentions: notes on Jessee H. MOODY,
John MOODY, R. G. PUGH, MAYES & SULLENBARGER, Edward CLARK, Benjamin BRAY. Signed
6 Aug 1848 Levi CAMPBELL, Adm. Recorded 15 Aug 1848 E. TATE, clerk.

p. 72   Will - Green B. SATTERFIELD, decd. Beloved wife, Lucenda SATTEFIELD;
my children James, Elizabeth, Martha, Martin Vanburen, Thomas, Millikan, John &
Lucenda; wife Executor. Signed 5 Apr 1848 G. B. SATTERFIELD. Att: John LANE,
Isaac x DAMEWOOD. Recorded 15 Aug 1848.

p. 73   Will - Elizabeth CHURCHMAN, widow of Thomas CHURCHMAN, decd. Nancy
FURGASON, bedding; James FURGASON, corn; Meredith FURGASON, a bed; Nancy COLLET
bed & bedding; Henry FURGASON, son of Rhoda FURGASON ½ of money; Thomas FURGASON,
son of James FURGASON ½ money; Isaac McBEE, Executor, to keep money of Henry

FURGASON until age 21; Nancy I. FURGASON, dau of William FURGASON, dress; Julia Ann FURGASON, dau of Rhoda FURGASON, decd; J. L. TALBOTT & Isaac M. McBEE, Executor. Signed 3 Jan 1848 Elizabeth x CHURCHMAN. Wit: Thomas BRADSHAW, Henry L. HAWKINS. Recorded 5 Sep 1848.

p. 74   Settlement - Clisbe RIGGS & Shadrick INMAN, Executors of the Estate of Ellis RIGGS, decd, who was the Executor of the Estate of Andrew COFFMAN, decd, on account of Andrew COFFMAN, decd. Mentions: Ellis RIGGS' last report 4 Sep 1847; money for emancipating SLAVES; George MILLIKAN, a legatee; Thomas K. COFFMAN, a legatee; Clisbe RIGGS; Felps RIGS; Clisbe RIGGS, Adm of Ellis RIGGS, decd. Recorded 7 Sep 1848 E. TATE, clerk.

        Inventory - Elizabeth McCARTY, decd. Mentions: 1/5 share in a family of NEGROS containing 11 in number, now in the hands of Levi SATTERFIELD, appt by Circuit Court of Clabourn Co., TN. Signed 4 Sep 1848 Levi SATTERFIELD, Adm Recorded 7 Sep 1848.

p. 75   Second Settlement - David McANALLY & Daniel TURLEY, Adms of the Estate of Jane TAYLOR, decd. 8 Aug 1848. Mentions: last settlement 1 Apr 1846; Morgan TAYLOR, an heir; Hughs O. TAYLOR; James TAYLOR, an heir; Daniel TAYLOR, an heir; Elizabeth TAYLOR, an heir; Greenfield TAYLOR, an heir; Daniel TAYLOR, Atto. for Mourning HARRIS, an heir; Dartimony TURLEY, an heir; Franklin W. TAYLOR, Atto, for George TAYLOR, an heir; David McANALLY in right of his wife Nancy who is an heir of Jane TAYLOR, decd, has in his hands $32.00 in part of his share of Estate. Recorded 7 Sep 1848 E. TATE, clerk.

p. 76   Second Settlement - Greenberry MITCHEL, Adm of the Estate of Aquilla MITCHEL, decd, who was the Adm of the Estate of Amos STALSWORTH, decd. 28 Aug 1848. Mentions: amount received from Henry ALSUP, River Commissioner & not charged against him in former settlement; T. W. TURLEY, Atto fee; Joseph TOWN-SLEY. Recorded 7 Sep 1848 E. TATE, clerk.

        Inventory - Nancy MAYES, decd. Mentions: 1/5 share of family of NEGRO SLAVES containing 11 in number in the hands of Levi SATTERFIELD apptd by Circuit Court of Clabourn Co., TN. Signed 4 Sep 1848 John L. OLLIVER, Adm. Recorded 8 Sep 1848.

p. 77   Inventory - Harriett T. SENTER, decd. Mentions: Negros - HENRY c35, LUCINDA c25 & an INFANT child, MARTHA 11, HARRY 8, JACOB 6 & land from her father's Estate. Signed James O. SENTER, Adm. Recorded 8 Sep 1848 E. TATE.

        Inventory - Joanna A. SENTER, decd. Mentions: FANNY, Negro woman, c40, JOHN 18, MARY 15, DELILAH 13, NANCY 11, KATHERINE 9, MELTON 7, FRANCES 4, INFANT child of MARY ca18 mos & MARTHA 18 & her INFANT child ca3 wks; land received from father's Estate. Signed James O. SENTER, Adm. Recorded 8 Sep 1848.

        Guardian Report - Henry ALSUP, Guardian of the minor heirs of David & William COFFMAN, decd. 6 Sep 1848. Mentions: last report 1 Oct 1847; paid Thos B. COFFMAN, an heir, now full age, dated 18 Jan 1848. Recorded 9 Oct 1848.

p. 78   Guardian Report - James G. WALKER, Guardian of the minor heirs of James WHITLOCK, decd. Mentions: last report 31 Dec 1846; rents recd for Mary

WHITLOCK, a ward, lands for 1847; rents recd for Eliza E. WHITLOCK, a ward, 1847; Thomas SMITH for goods for Mary; B. E. GAINS, Dpt Shff, taxes 1846 & 47; Octavius YOE, Revenue Collector, taxes 1848; John WHITLOCK, a ward, having become of full age, dated 20 Sep 1848. Signed 21 Sep 1848 James G. WALKER, Guardian. Recorded 9 Oct 1848 E. TATE, clerk.

Guardian Report - Isaac HARRIS, Guardian of the minor heirs of Samuel RAY, decd. 21 Sep 1848. Mentions: last report 28 Apr 1847. Signed Isaac HARRIS, Guardian. Recorded 9 Oct 1848 E. TATE, clerk.

p. 79   Guardian Report - Greenberry MITCHEL, Guardian of Russel SMALLWOOD's heirs. 16 Sep 1848. Mentions: last report 31 Jul 1847; B. E. GAINS & Octavius YOE for taxes. Signed G. B. MITCHEL, Guardian. Recorded 9 Oct 1848 E. TATE.

Guardian Report - James L. TALBOTT, Guardian of the minor heirs of Amos STALSWORTH, decd. 2 Oct 1848. Mentions: last report 27 Aug 1847; rents of land 1847; Octavus YOE, Revenue Collector, 1848. Signed J. L. TALBOTT, Guardian. Recorded 9 Oct 1848 E. TATE, clerk.

p. 80   Settlement - Greenberry MITCHEL, Adm of the Estate of Aquilla MITCHEL, Jr., decd. 16 Sep 1848. Mentions: amt against John STALSWORTH & Thos SMITH; second sale held 3 Nov 1847; James T. WEST; B. E. GAINS, taxes 1847; Alfred WILHITE, Robert CARDWELL, Sr.; Chesley TROGDON; J. H. DYER; Thos SMITH; J. C. MOSES; Joel COFFEE; J. G. WALKER; John B. GRIGSBY; Wm HARRIS; note on Madison Academy; Octavus YOE, Rev. Collector, taxes 1848; 1 yr support for widow & family. Recorded 19 Oct 1848 E. TATE, clerk.

p. 81   Settlement - John BRADLEY, Executor of the Estate of Matelda CHURCHMAN, decd. 19 Sep 1848. Mentions: cash recd from Preston MITCHEL, Executor of the Estate of Edward CHURCHMAN, decd, it being the amt of a legacy made to the said Matelda CHURCHMAN, decd, by her father the said Edward CHURCHMAN, decd; notes on James HANKINS; John BRADLEY, Joab PERRIN, Wm DICK & John MITCHEL; Lewis BRADSHAW; note to Preston MITCHEL, Executor of the Estate of E. CHURCHMAN, decd; Wm H. MOFFIT; C. M. GODWIN; James MILLS; Edith CHURCHMAN; James MILLS, Guardian of John P. PERRIN; Preston MITCHEL; John MITCHEL recpt for one bed bequested to his dau by the Testarix; Preston MITCHEL recpt for 1 table bequeathed to his dau Jane by the Testarix; Edith CHURCHMAN recpt for 1 side saddle, bridle, chest & 2 counterpanes bequeathed to her by the Testarix; Rebecca PERRIN recpt for 1 note on hand on Joab PERRIN by the Testarix. Recorded 19 Oct 1848 E. TATE.

p. 82   Inventory - Elizabeth CHURCHMAN, decd. Mentions: notes on Daniel VINEYARD & G. B. MITCHEL (1847), Thos SHARP (1819), John WILLIS (1833); feather bed bequeathed to Meredith FURGASON; 1 feather bed & 1 set billows, sheet & counterpane bequeathed to Nancy COLLETT; dress bequeathed to Nancy J. FURGASON; cow & calf, 1 hogs & household goods to Julia A. FURGASEN; Meredith & James FURGASON rent her place & farm produce. Signed Isaac M. McBEE, Executor, 6 Sep 1848. Recorded 19 Oct 1848 E. TATE, clerk.

p. 83   Inventory - Jonathan WILLIAMS, decd. Mentions: one judgement on note Wm ROACH signed by Samuel P. ROACH. Signed 2 Oct 1848 Isaac F. McCARTY, Adm. Recorded 19 Oct 1848 E. TATE, clerk.

Account of Sale - Jonathan WILLIAMS, decd. Mentions: Tamar WILLIAMS,

J. C. WILLIAMS, Susan WILLIAMS, Eli SPOON, A. L. WILLIAMS, John C. WILLIAMS, Wm
M. GRAY, E. L. TATE, Wm G. McDANIEL, Jesse HODGES, E. T. TATE, G. W. McDANIEL,
Isaac DONEL, Rufus A. WILLIAMS, James MAYES, E. D. SUNDERLAND, F. B. S. COCKE.
Signed 2 Oct 1848 Isaac F. McCARTY, Adm. Recorded 20 Oct 1848 E. TATE, clerk.

p. 84   Report of the Proratio Division of the Estate of David HORNER, decd.
Mentions: Robert CARDWELL, Jr., Adm; Clisbe AUSTON for shrouding & burying
clothes; MAYES & SULLENBARGER for 3 coffins; John L. MOSES for printing notice;
James MAYES for cyring sale & Isaac DANIEL, clerk for same; amount set apart for
support of 2 children of decd under age of 14 yrs; creditors - Isaac DANIEL, Wm
T. TATE & Co., Clisbe AUSTIN, Hiram COX, F. & H. BOYD, Sam'l N. TATE, David
N. TATE, James JAMES, Robert CARDWELL, Sr., RICE & McFARLAND, M. B. MILLAR, E.
L. TATE, Jacob KINDAR, Sr., Robert CARDWELL, Jr., Wm DANIEL, John ROACH. 21 Oct
1848 by E. TATE, clerk. Recorded 14 Nov 1848.

p. 85   Additional Account of Sale - Lea McDANIEL, decd, at the residence of
John McDANIEL, decd. Mentions: Green ROACH, Samuel _____, Robert M. WEST, Lena
Ann McDANIEL. Signed 22 Sep 1848 John CALLISON, Adm. Recorded 21 Nov 1848.

p. 86   Inventory - 22 Sep 1848. Estate of Susan McDANIEL, decd. One cow, one
bedstead, one blanket & coverlet, 3 dollars. Signed John CALLISON, Adm, 6 Nov
1848. Recorded 21 Nov 1848 E. TATE.

         Account of Sale - 22 Sep 1848, Susan McDANIEL, decd, at her residence.
Mentions: Robert M. WEST, Elizabeth McDANIEL, Frances YOUNG, James MORGAN.
Signed 6 Nov 1848 John CALLISON, Adm. Recorded 21 Nov 1848 E. TATE, clerk.

         Inventory - Mary DEVAULT, decd. 14 Aug 1848. Mentions: note on Ira
DARTER. Signed George LAY & G. P. MYNATT, Adm of the Estate of John DEVAULT,
decd. Recorded 23 Nov 1848 E. TATE, clerk.

p. 88   Account of Sale - John DEVAULT, decd. 24 Aug 1848. Mentions: J. L.
DEVAULT, Saml SHARP, Wm BOOKER, Ira DARTER, Wm DEVAULT, Elizabeth ZACHARY, C. M.
GOODLIN, Pryor HARLSON, John ROBINSON, John BAKER, Gordon MYNATT, hire of Slave
JULIA & CHILD, AMANDA, HANNAH, JONAS & JERRAMICAH, Wm WALLIS, Jacob HARRIS,
Wm DONAHOO, John HUBBS, Saml WALLIS, G. B. CARDEN, M. WYRICK, Wm T. CARDEN,
Joel FIELDS, J. C. H. SAWYERS, Silas MYNAT, Joseph HILL, Andrew GRAHAM, John
SAWYERS, L. DAMEWOOD, Houston RUTHERFORD, J. P. SHARP, Nathan KELLY, Andrew
FURGASON, ___ LAWSON, Henry KITTS, Wm PETERS, Wm CRISPIN, Amos SHARP, Valentine
WYRICK. Signed George LAY, G. P. MYNATT, Adm. Recorded 23 Nov 1848 E. TATE.

p. 91   Account of Sale - John McDANIEL, decd. 2 Sep 1848. Mentions: Isaac
DANIEL, Levi SATTERFIELD, Thos DAVIS, Jas FURGASON, John CALLISON, Allen D.
MORGAN, Wm MORGAN, Richd FURGASON, John MOODY, David MANLY, Jacob SMITH, John
HOLLY, Edward TATE, George KINDAR, Daniel NOE, Nancy MORGAN, David LIVINGSTON,
Bennett CUNNINGHAM, Wm SMITH, Eli McDANIEL, Jr., Mary MORGAN, Francis YOUNG,
Edward MORGAN, Elisha OWENS, Chesley MORGAN, Lina Ann McDANIEL, Nancy McDANIEL,
Drury ROACH, Edward HODGES, George W. TATE, Reuben L. CATE, Jas FURGASON, Wm
HAMMER, Samuel JONES, Green ROACH, Robt CORUM. "The executor is chargable with
the follow'g amt (to wit) Cash come to hand Since the Marriage of the Widow of
said Decd. Note on self." Signed Robert LOYD, Executor. Recorded 23 Nov 1848.

p. 93   Will - William JAMES, decd. My son Elijah JAMES, my dau Barbara

WILLSON, my dau Elizabeth YOUNG, my dau Nancy MORGAN, my son Wm JAMES, my dau Martha McCOY, my son Isaac JAMES, my son James JAMES land in District 5, Robert LOYD, Executor. Signed 17 Jul 1844 William JAMES. Att: Isaac DANIEL, John DANIEL. Recorded 6 Dec 1848.

Report of Commissioners - Set apart 1 year support for Cynthia HARREL, widow, & family of Wm M. HARREL, decd. Signed 22 Oct 1848 Reuben WOLFENBARGER, John DODSON, Franklin SAUNDERS, Commissioners. Recorded 7 Dec 1848 E. TATE.

p. 94   Inventory - Wm M. HARREL, decd. Signed Cynthia x HARREL, Admx. Recorded 7 Dec 1848.

Guardian Report - Andrew BOWER, Guardian of the minor heirs of John HILL, decd. 29 Nov 1848. Mentions: cash on hand on 1 Sep 1847; hiring wards SLAVES for 1848; renting wards lands for 1848; Olliver P. FIELDS for tuition & board for Wm R. HILL, a ward; Lewis A. GARRET, Clerk & Master; T. W. TURLEY, Atto. for taking depositions in a suit against John HUBBS & Stephen FROST; Octavus YOE, Revenue Collector, taxes 1848; pd Peter WOLFENBARGER for Booker DYER on behalf of wards; Wm T. TATE & Co. for goods for Wm R. HILL, a ward; Robert CARDWELL for goods for same; Guardian boarding & clothing Penina Palestine HILL, a ward; James DYER for damages; O. P. FIELDS. Signed Andrew x BOWER, Guardian 29 Nov 1848. Recorded 7 Dec 1848 E. TATE, clerk.

p. 95   Settlement - John A. McKINNY & Eli SKAGGS, Executors of the Estate of Edward HANKINS, decd. 29 Nov 1848. Mentions: notes on John A. McKINNY, James BOYD & C. M. GOODLIN; Edward HANKINS notes to G. B. MITCHEL, Katherine HAMILTON, James HANKINS, Thos HANKINS, C. M. GOODLIN, Thos STRINGFIELD; THORNTON & McMILLAN; Wm C. & J. S. MOFFET; CASWELL & HOPPER; Jas SALLING, Dpt Shff, taxes 1844. Recorded 8 Dec 1848 E. TATE, clerk.

p. 96   Commissioners Report - 1 year support for Mary DODSON & family, widow of Samuel DODSON, decd. Signed 9 Nov 1848 James GREENLEE, Reuben GROVE, Eli GREENLEE, Commissioners. Recorded 8 Dec 1848.

p. 97   Inventory - S. E. DODSON, decd. Signed W. H. D. McANALLY, Admt.

Account of Sale - S. E. DODSON, decd. 28 Nov 1848. Signed W. H. D. McANALLY, Admt. Recorded 8 Dec 1848 E. TATE, clerk.

p. 98   Account of Sale - Ellis RIGGS, decd. Sold 4 Sep 1848. Mentions: James GRAY, John F. NOE, Adeline RIGGS, Eliza J. RIGGS, Simpson RYAN, Felps RIGGS, Saml RIGGS, W. J. REED, John B. NEWEL, Jehu MORRIS, John BULL, Jas O. SENTER, Wm CHANEY, Ellis RIGGS, Jas L. RYAN, Jonathan MORELOCK, Wesley MILLAR, William BAKER, James CUNNINGHAM, Elisha BULL, Wm P. LONG, Thos SHIPLEY, Drury MORRIS, S. INMAN, Russel RIGGS, Murphy BOATMAN, F. W. TAYLOR, S. S. HUFFMASTER, Thos BIRDWELL, Ambrose CARTWRIGHT, Chesley BURNETT, Alexd CARTWRIGHT, Edward ALLEN, D. McANALLY, Wm MOSKAL, M. ARNOT, Joseph THRASHER, Edward RIGGS, Wm PASKAL, Joseph SHANNON, C. W. MILLAR, Chislee RIGGS, Winsfiford GARRESTON. Signed Chislee RIGGS, Shadarick INMAN, Adms. Recorded 9 Dec 1848 E. TATE.

p. 100   Will - John WILLIAMS, decd. My wife, Elizabeth, my plantation & at her d. divided equally between my 2 sons David WILLIAMS & John Alfred WILLIAMS;

William WILLIAMS; my son James WILLIAMS; my dau Lucenda WOLFENBARGER; my dau
Elizabeth WOLFENBARGER; John Alfred WILLIAMS is to pay to Mary WILLIS if she
lives with me until she is 18; Executors my sons David & John Alfred WILLIAMS.
Signed 1847 John WILLIAMS. Wit: Joseph CLARK, Joseph WILLIAMS. Recorded 3
Jan 1849 E. TATE, clerk.

p. 101   Will - Stephen JOHNSON, decd. My son James JOHNSON 3 Negroes, SYLVIA
& CHILDREN & a boy named DAVE; my son Hardy JOHNSON; my dau Polly STUBBLEFIELD
& her children 4 Negroes, JOHN, CLARA, the younger, MARIAH & ALLEN; disposition
of Slaves CLARA, the elder & the Negro man ARTHUR; George STUBBLEFIELD, hus of
my dau Polly; Executor, my son Hardy JOHNSON, my nephew Larkin JOHNSON & Elisha
DODSON, Esq. Signed 24 Oct 1845 Stephen JOHNSON. Wit: John McANALLY, Joseph F.
SEAVER. Recorded 5 Jan 1849 E. TATE, clerk.

p. 103   Commissioners Report - 1 year support to Nancy SENTER & family, widow of
William T. SENTER, decd. Signed 13 Oct 1848 Samuel LIVINGSTON, John IVY, Jesse
HOWEL. Recorded 19 Jan 1849 E. TATE, clerk.

        Inventory - Wm T. SENTER, decd. Sold at the sale 25 Nov 1848. Signed
Nancy SENTER, Admx. Recorded 19 Jan 1849.

p. 104   Account of Sale - Wm T. SENTER, decd. Mentions: Warham EASLEY, J.
KELLY, O. R. WATKINS, A. AUSTIN, David NOE, B. H. BAGWELL, J. L. GIVENS, Hiram
COX, A. D. HOSS, James O. SENTER, Massy HILL, Allen KELLY, Robert POTTER, R.
CARSON, Sterling C. PERRIMAN, John IVY, H. PECK, George LACY, James C. MILES,
B. SMITH, Thos WALKER, James P. CONWAY. Signed Nancy SENTER, Admx. Recorded
22 Jan 1849 E. TATE, clerk.

p. 106   Commissioners Report - 1 year support for Jane MAYES & family, widow
of John MAYES, Sr., decd. Signed E. THOMASON, Parrott GODWIN, James x LACY,
Commissioners. Recorded 20 Jan 1849.

        Inventory - Edward M. WHIT, decd. Mentions: cash in hands of E.
THOMASON. Signed T. W. TURLEY, Adm. 15 Jan 1849. Recorded 20 Jan 1849.

        Account of Sale - Wm H. HARREL, decd. Sold by Cynthia HARREL, Admx
19 Dec 1848. Mentions: tools, hogs, horse, cow & saddle bought by Thos ACUFF
for the widow. Signed Cynthia HARREL, Admx. Recorded 20 Jan 1849 E. TATE.

p. 107   Guardian Report - Benjamin SMITH, Guardian of Mary SMITH, Frances
SMITH, Alexander SMITH, Juba SMITH & Rachel SMITH. Mentions: last report 23
Aug 1847; taxes 1848; by amt of Frances SMITH, a ward, who is now of full age,
dates 10 Sep 1848. Signed Benjamin SMITH, Guardian, 2 Oct 1848. Recorded
20 Jan 1849 E. TATE, clerk.

        Settlement - Joseph CLARK one of Beanstation Road Commissioners for
1848. Mentions: Willie SANDERS, Marvel NASH, overseer, Henry WILLIAMS, Ed.
TATE, Joseph LANHAM, Charles McANALLY, John W. BUNCH, Jacob CLOUD, other
Comms. Signed J. GODWIN, Daniel McKINNY, Wm T. TATE, Comms. Recorded 20 Jul
1849 E. TATE, clerk.

p. 108   Account of Sale - Sold 20 Nov 1844 at residence of Lucy EATON, decd.

Mentions: William BASSETT, O. JOHNSON, Elizabeth HENDERSON, Sarah JOHNSON, David HARRIS, Albert SULLENBERGER, Larkin GRAY, John WALKER, William GRAY, Adam HOPPER, Emeline HENDERSON, Henry LONG, Frederick SHELTON, Mrs. O. JOHNSON, John SHELTON, Thomas DODSON, Peter SAMPSEL, David HARRIS, Edmund COLLINS, Aquilla JONES, William JOHNSON, James O. SENTER, Reuben LONG, Pleasant M. SENTER, A. G. SULLENBARGER, James DODSON, A. M. WINKLE, Joe RENFRO, Sanford JOHNSON, B. F. HENDERSON, David SHELTON, Nelson A. SENTER, Eli JONES, Jacob GODWIN, E. D. WINKLE, P. M. SENTER. Signed Larkin JOHNSON, Adm. Recorded 24 Jan 1849.

p. 112   Inventory - S. E. DODSON, decd. Signed W. H. D. McANALLY, Adm.. Nov 1848. Recorded 7 Feb 1849 E. TATE, clerk.

Account of Sale - S. E. DODSON, decd. 18 Nov 1848. Signed W. H. D. McANALLY, Adm. Recorded 7 Feb 1849.

Inventory - Epaphroditus HIGHTOWER, decd. 28 Aug 1848. Mentions: Negroes JANE & CHILD, man DICK c53, MANDA c 7, boy TOM 4, 1 man GEORGE 63. Signed William P. JONES, Adm. Recorded 7 Feb 1849.

p. 113   Account of Sale - Epaphroditus HIGHTOWER, decd. 3 Oct 1848. Mentions: sale of slaves JANE & CHILD to Thomas WEST, AMANDA to Robert MASSENGILL, TOM to Thomas WEST, boy DICK to E. HIGHTOWER & boy GEORGE to Calow LYONS; Thomas LYONS; Chester JARNAGIN; William HIGHTOWER, Jr; Harcute (?) LEA; Susan CURLE. Signed William P. JONES, Adm, with the will annexed. Recorded 7 Feb 1849.

Settlement - Robert LOYD, Adm of the Estate of Amos STALSWORTH, decd. 16 Sep 1848. Mentions: notes on George SPARKMAN & Wm J. LOWE, executed by Aquilla MITCHEL former Adm; note given by Catherine STALSWORTH, Wm TOWNSLEY & B. E. GAINS to former Adm; note given by James DAVIS & James TALBOT to former Adm; note given by Joel COFFEE to former Adm; note given by Amos STALSWORTH, decd, in his lifetime to Robert STONE; Wm STONE; BLACKBURN & BURNETT; note to Hiram M. NEMO; note to James SWINGLER; Thomas SMITH; B. E. GAINS, Dpt Shff, recpt for judgement S. & T. SMITH vs Amos STALSWORTH; W. L. LATHIM; note to J. JARNIGAN; Daniel McKINNY award against Estate; note to Samuel SMITH; Jeremiah JARNIGAN; Wm H. & J. S. MOFFITT; Warham EASLEY, Jr; Thos W. TURLEY; Robt H. HINDS, Atto; G. B. MITCHEL, Adm of the Estate of Aquilla MITCHEL, decd; James T. WEST; James G. WALKER; James S. TALBOTT, Probate of the presentation of George HANKINS provd account & M. THORNBURG recpt for the same. Recorded 7 Feb 1849 E. TATE, clerk.

p. 114   Inventory - Nancy SMITH, decd. Signed John A. SMITH, Adm. Recorded 10 Feb 1849 E. TATE, clerk.

Inventory - Of the property that was sold at the Sale of Nancy & Josiah SMITH, decd, that was there at the death of Josiah SMITH, that came into my hands as Adm. Mentions: notes that were there at Nancy SMITH's death - 1 note on Allen HURST, 1 on Joshiah SMITH, 1 on John A. SMITH. Signed James A. SMITH, Adm. Recorded 10 Feb 1849 E. TATE, clerk.

p. 116   Account of Sale - 18 Dec 1848. Nancy SMITH, decd. Mentions: David PARKEY, Jas B. SMITH, Allen HURST, Ezra BUCKNER, Jno F. HUDDLESTONE, Leety McCRAY, Calvin HUDDLESTONE, Isaac CONDRY, Owen DYER, Josiah SMITH, Presley

BUCKNER, J. A. J. BROCK, Amos EVANS, Lawson DAMEWOOD, Bowyer BEELAR, Wm CALVIN,
Thos BLACKBURN, Henry LAMBDEN, Allen McCOY, Charles S. BERRY, John COX, Jr.,
John BULLARD, John BALLARD, Richd WADE, Granville COX, A. J. DYER, Loid COX,
Jno SWAFFORD, Wm DYER, Robt McBEE, Calvin HICKLE, Bale BURNETT, Ezra BUCKNER,
Thos ROBERTS, Isaac CONDRAY, Thos WILLSON, Alex SHARP, Frances PHILIPS, Wm T.
CARDEN, Jas SNODGRASS, Wm COLVIN, Jerry SELVAGE, Robt McBEE, Roddy SAVAGE, Amos
EVANS, Jordan HANDLEY, John WALTERS, Jesse WAGNER, Peter BEELAR, Jas JOHNSON.
Signed John A. SMITH, Adm. Recorded 10 Feb 1849 E. TATE, clerk.

p. 118   Account of Sale - Josiah SMITH, decd. 18 Dec 1848. Mentions: Allen
HURST, Ezra BUCKNER, A. J. BROCK, Josiah SMITH, David PARKEY, J. F. HUDDLESTONE,
Lawson DAMEWOOD, Thomas WAGNER, Jesse WAGNER, Presley BUCKNER, Richd WADE, Isaac
CONDRAY, John BEELAR, James JOHNSON, John BULLARD, Peter BEELAR, Jno SWAFFORD,
J. B. SMITH, Owen DYER, J. C. BAKER, Calvin HUDDLESTONE, John BOWMAN, John
WALTERS. Signed John A. SMITH, Adm. Recorded 10 Feb 1849 E. TATE, clerk.

p. 119   Inventory - William T. SENTER, decd. Mentions: notes on account - Wm
PIPER (1838), Preston LAWSON (2-1840), Alexander POWELL (1841), _____ McGEE
(1839), John JEFFERS (1840), Tandy KILE (1831), John SELLINGS & COCKS (1831),
John SELLINGS (1830), Lebum SENTER (2-1835, 1- 1834), John GRIGSBE (1840),
John McGEE (1840), James KIRKHAM (1845), Aaron DOOLY (1841), David VETTIESON
from Clinton ARMSTRONG to Wm T. SENTER (1842), John COCKRUM note on S. D. MOORE
(1841), Jesse CREECH (1842) from Clinton ARMSTRONG to W. T. SENTER, David
VETTIESON (1840), George BROWN (1841), A. COOLY (1840), James ALLEN (1841),
Samuel GOODMAN (1849). Signed Nancy SENTER, Adm. Recorded 10 Mar 1849.

p. 120   Inventory - John MAYES, decd. Mentions: note on John T. ROBERTS;
acc against John B. CREWS, Wm VAUGHN, John MAYES, Jr., M. S. DANIEL & George
BURDEN. Signed 1 Mar 1849 John MAYES, Jr. & M. S. DANIEL, Adm. Recorded 10
Mar 1849 E. TATE, clerk.

p. 121   Inventory - Wm JAMES, decd. Mentions: note on James JAMES. Signed
5 Mar 1849 Robert LOYD, Executor. Recorded 10 Mar 1849 E. TATE, clerk.

          Will - James M. LEACH, decd. My beloved wife, Mary LEACH; land claim
for voluntary service in the war with Mexico; my 2 bros Abraham & John; wife
Executor. Signed 16 Sep 1848 James M. LEACH. Wit: Jas SALLING, Calvin
HUDDLESTONE, John C. BAKER. Recorded 10 Mar 1849.

p. 122   Guardian Report - Edward TATE, Guardian of the minor heirs of Thomas
CHURCHMAN, decd. Mentions: last report 1 Aug 1842; rents of wards land 1843
to 1848; 2/3 conveyed by Margaret CHURCHMAN, the mother of said minor heirs & 1
of them having arrived at full age & conveyed his share of said land on 11 Feb
1842, to wit, Lowry P. CHURCHMAN; taxes 1843 to 1848; postage to IN 1843 to
1848; Philip SNIDAR became purchaser of Lowry P. & Margaret CHURCHMAN's lands
1843 & 1844. Signed E. TATE, Guardian. Recorded 12 Mar 1849.

p. 123   Guardian Report - George WILLIAMS & Margaret WILLIAMS, Guardians of the
minor heirs of John M. WILLIAMS, decd. Mentions: last report 24 Apr 1848;
Parrott GODWIN, Adm of the Estate of John M. WILLIAMS, decd; rent of wards lands
1848; John NETHERLAND, Atto, for attending to petition for division of land;
Henry MILLS fencing wards farm; Octavus YOE, Rev. Coll, taxes 1848. Signed

George WILLIAMS & Margaret WILLIAMS, Guardians. Recorded 12 Mar 1849 E. TATE.

p. 124   Settlement - Peter WOLFENBARGER, Adm of the Estate of Tandy WOLFENBARGER,
decd.   6 Feb 1849. Mentions: a/c & notes on G. W. VITTITOE, James WELSH,
Nicholas SATTERFIELD, Joseph WILLIAMS, G. W. DYER, Peter WOLFENBARGER, B.
BRANSEN, John CHANDLER, Isaac BEELAR, Jackson BULLIN, Wm WILLIAMS, L. M. ELLIS,
Martin CLEVELAND, Pleasant STARNES, Ruben WOLFENBARGER; Rebecca WOLFENBARGER,
widow, 1 yr allowance; Elijah SMITH; Robert FRY; Frederick LONG; John CHANDLER;
John B. GRIGSBY; Wm CLEVELAND; Robert W. WOLFENBARGER, Guardian of the minor
heirs of Tandy WOLFENBARGER. Recorded 12 Mar 1849.

p. 125   Settlement - Parrott GODWIN, Adm of the Estate of John M. WILLIAMS,
decd. 20 Feb 1849. Mentions: notes & a/c on James H. COFFEE, Wm F. DANIEL,
Lewis CARTER, John B. GRIGSBY, James McCRARY, Samuel LANE, Robertson McKINNY,
Robert P. MOORE, George POWELL & others, Wm RICE, Presley RICE, John B. STAPLES,
George K. LARIMORE, Russel RIGGS, R. L. HOWELL, Jesse RIGGS, Thomas RUSSEL,
Joseph N. SHANNON, Tolliver ROBINSON, A. G. WATKINS, Stokely D. WILLIAMS, George
W. WARHAM, Wm F. DANIEL; Constable Wm RICE; Dpt Shff John I. NOE; notes on
Philomen HODGES, John WALKER, Wm MURRY, H. D. HYNSON, Ann K. WILLIAMS, Mrs.
McCONNEL; George WILLIAMS, Adm of the Estate of Hugh G. MOORE, decd, a balance
due John M. WILLIAMS, decd, part of his share of the said is of H. G. MOORE,
decd; cash from G. R. POWELL; Henry HARRISON; George & Margaret WILLIAMS,
Guardians of the minor heirs; Margaret WILLIAMS, widow & relect of John WILLIAMS,
decd; Levi CAMPBELL; Wm KELLY; Hiram L. SHAVER; note to George WILLIAMS; Wilson
OLLIVER; David NAFF, Registar; James FULLAR, Clerk; Joshua D. CURLE, Dpt Shff
taxes 1847; John NETHERLAND, Atto; Dr. Wm MURRY; W. L. LATHIM, Clerk of Circuit
Court; Robert P. MOORE; Robt P. & John M. MOORE; A. R. SULLENBARGER; note to
P. G. YOE; Massy HILL;. S. L. HALE, Rev. Coll, taxes on town lot 1844; John P.
CONWAY; Wm F. DANIEL; Samuel GILL, discount of note. Recorded 13 Mar 1849.

p. 128   Will - Noah JARNAGIN, decd. My dau Jemima HINES; my son Asa JARNAGIN;
my dau Anna CURLE; my youngest son Paschel L. JARNAGIN; land in Poor Valley
adjoining land conveyed to me by Caswell JARNIGAN; my wife Mary JARNIGAN;
Paschel JARNIGAN, Executor. Signed 1 Jan 1836 N. JARNAGIN. Att: Chesley
JARNAGIN, William WILLIAMS, Harmon G. LEA.
          Codicil - My son George R. JARNAGIN, the $50 bequeathed to my dau
Jemima HINES, she being now decd; $75 to son Paschal L. JARNAGIN I bequested to
my dau Anna CURLE. Signed 28 Feb 1849 N. JARNAGIN. Att: Harmon G. LEA, A. P.
GREEN. Recorded 19 May 1849.

p. 130   Will - Magness MOORE, Planter. My wife, Sally, entire estate; my
beloved dau Sally entire estate at d. of mo; I have done what was wright for my
other children. Esteemed neighbors & friends Samuel B. TATE, David McANALLY,
& John RICE, Executors. Signed 28 Oct 1849 Magnes x MOORE. Wit: N. A. SENTER,
David McANALLY, Saml B. TATE, John RICE, Sr. Recorded 19 May 1849 E. TATE.

          Will - Charles McANALLY. My three sons, David, Thomas & Charles W. F.
McANALLY; my two daus Matilda DODSON & Saraphina HAYES; my grdau Elizabeth
WILLIAMS; all the children of my dau Patsy NASH, decd; my sister Sally to be
taken care of by daus husbands, Wm DODSON & James HAYES; my 2 grsons, Charles
& David, sons of David R. McANALLY; my 2 grsons Lefaett & Joseph, sons of Thomas
P. McANALLY; my 4 grsons Charles, Samuel, Clabourn & David DODSON, sons of my

dau Matilda & wife of Wm DODSEN; 2 grsons Thomas & Charles NASH, sons of my dau
Patsy NASH, decd; dau Elizabeth WILLIAMS, no issue; to the 2 children of Telitha
HUTCHESON, now Teletha HARVEY, who are said to be the children of my son James M.
McANALLY, decd, towit, Alhale & James Madison; land owned in common with the
heirs of Stephen W. SENTER in Poor Vally adjoining land of David HOLD (?) & on
the Bryier Fork of German Creek & a tract lying the So. side of the Knoles So
of Ceekville (?) joining lands with Thomas WHITESIDE & Estate of James MAYES,
decd.   Executors, my son David R. McANALLY & David M. McANALLY, son of my bro
John McANALLY.   Signed 6 Dec 1848 Charles McANALLY.   Wit: Wm B. CUNNINGHAM,
Wm T. TATE, Warham EASLEY, Jr.   Recorded 19 May 1849 E. TATE, clerk.

p. 132   Account of Sale - 25 Jan 1849, Estate of John & Mary DEVAULT, decd.
Mentions: William DEVAULT, John ROBERTSON, Isaac DEVAULT, Lawson DAMEWOOD,
Amos SHARP, Elizabeth ZACHARY, Jacob SHARP, Ira DARTING.   Signed George LAY &
G. P. MYNATT, Adm of the Estate of John DEVAULT, decd.   Recorded 21 May 1849.

p. 133   Account of Sale - Henry MOODY, decd.   22 Feb 1849.   Mentions: Nancy
N. MOODY, John MOODY, Sr., Nelson A. BOWEN, Parrott GODWIN, Wm M. MOODY, Reuben
G. MOODY, George M. LACY, James GREENLEA, Edward L. TATE, William AUSTIN,
Archibald AUSTIN, John MOODY, Jr., George MOODY, Jno B. CREWS, F. B. COCKE.
Signed Levi CAMPBELL, Adm.   Recorded 21 May 1849.

p. 134   Guardian Report - Elizabeth RIGGS, Guardian of the minor heirs of
Nenian RIGGS, decd.   8 May 1849.   Mentions: last report 8 Mar 1844; James
JONES, Adm of the Estate of Henry BOATMAN, decd; O. YOE, Rev. Coll, taxes for
1848; D. McANALLY, Dpt Shff, Taxes 1844 to 1848; Wm CROW who intermarried with
one of the wards.   Signed Elizabeth x WARD, Guardian.   Recorded 21 May 1849.

         Settlement - Godwin MAYES, Adm of the Estate of Elizabeth MAYES, decd.
8 May 1849.   Mentions: sale of personal property recd 16 May 1847; 1 judgements pd by Dr. C. S. HARRIS; M. L. DANIEL, Constable for a judgement against
Adm in favor of James CHARMICHAEL & Wortham JOICE; John COCKE, Att; John
CHURNEY; note to Jesse LIVINGSTON; John A. MILES; John NOE, Dpt Shff taxes
1846; Joseph RICHE; Clisbe AUSTIN; W. L. LATHIM, Clk of the Circuit Court.
Recorded 21 May 1849, E. TATE, clerk.

p. 136   Guardian Report - Lewis ATKINS, Guardian of the minor heirs of Nathan
ATKINS, decd.   1 Jun 1849.   Mentions: last report 6 Jun 1848.   Signed Lewis 𝍤
his mark ATKINS, Guardian.   Recorded 12 Jun 1849 E. TATE, clerk.

p. 137   Second Settlement - Jacob BEELAR, Executor of the Estate of Joseph
BEELAR, decd.   19 Apr 1849.   Mentions: last report 30 Mar 1848; John LONG who
intermarried with Katharine BEELAR, a legatee; Henry MOYERS who intermarried
with Mary BEELAR, a legatee; Isaac BEELAR a legatee; Daniel BEELAR a legatee;
John BEELAR a legatee; Henry MOYERS & John BEELAR, affidavit for $1 proved to
be paid by said Executor which was a Counterfeit & received by the Executor as
part of said Estate; Smith STRANGE; W. L. LATHIM, Clk of Circ Ct, cost of
suit vs Estate; Jacob BEELAR, a legatee.   Recorded 13 Jun 1849 E. TATE, clerk.

p. 138   Inventory - Robert D. DUFF Estate.   Mentions: a/c & notes on Edward
CLARK, James KENNON, Samuel H. BUNCH, P. L. JARNAGIN, Alexander WEST, L. M.
ELLIS, C. G. LEA; Asa JARNAGIN, Wm P. JONES, James H. STARNES, Joseph LONG, G. R.

JARNAGIN, Hugh DUFF, A. P. GREEN, J. B. GRIGSBEE, Pleasant STARNES, Pleasant
JENNINGS. Signed 4 Jun 1849 I. G. WALKER, Adm. Recorded 12 Jun 1849 E. TATE.

p. 139 Account of Sale - Robt R. DUFF, decd. Mentions: B. E. GAINS, Barney
SIMPSON, John STEPHENS, Anderson YATES, A. P. GREEN, L. M. ELLIS, Thoe MALONE,
J. B. GRIGSBY, John LONG, Thos WALKER, Jas H. STARNES, Jas LONG, B. PECK, Jr.,
Wm O. CLARK, Wm MAPLES, Kennon LOWE, Jno B. GRIGSBY, Jas GOINS, Joel COFFEE, Wm
WEST, Henry SPARKMAN, Daniel GREEN, Matthias CROWE (?), Paschal JARNIGAN,
Patrick SHULEY, Thos PASCHAL, Jas PATTERSON, Lunah LOWE, Polk SHIRLEY, Wm SMITH,
Henry ALSUP, Wm G. EATON, James DUFF, Louisa DUFF, Wm B. CUNNINGHAM, James
LONG, Patrick SHIRLEY, Samuel WHITE, Thomas MAPLES, John VANDAGRIFF, Buck
CLARK, W. G. EATON, A. AUSTIN, Wm MAPLES, B. G. SIMPSON, Robert TILMAN, Jas
PECK, Preston BECKHAM, Benjamin PECK, Reuben CATE, John DUFF, Jacob LONG, James
GAINS, Samuel SMITH, Wm R. JARNAGIN, Archy AUSTIN, W. S. DYER, James MORRIS.
Signed 11 May 1849 J. G. WALKER, Adm. Recorded 15 Jun 1849 E. TATE, clerk.

p. 141 Settlement - Samuel GILL, Executor of Thomas GILL, decd. 25 Jan 1849.
Mentions: dau of Thomas GILL, decd, Elizabeth KNIGHT, wife of Trestrain Day
KNIGHT, Mary SHIELDS, widow of John SHIELDS, decd, & Martha JARNAGIN, wife of
Chesley JARNAGIN; son Samuel GILL. Recorded 26 Jun 1849 E. TATE, clerk.

Inventory - John BETHEL, decd. 14 May 1849. Signed David K. LIVING-
STON, Adm. Mentions property in dispute claimed by Rhoda BETHEL. Recorded
27 Jun 1849 E. TATE, clerk.

p. 142 Will - Mary Susan HENDERSON. My mother, Mary HENDERSON, widow of my
father Thomas HENDERSON; money in the hands of William GODWIN who was appointed
to settle the Estate of my father in place of James MOOR, who was the Executor
of my fathers last will & testament; my mother Mary HENDERSON, Executor.
Signed 4 May 1849 Mary Susan HENDERSON. Wit: Saml B. TATE, Wm S. JONES, Eli
A. JONES, James CONN. Recorded 27 Jun 1849.

p. 143 Will - William Y. HENDERSON. My mother, Mary HENDERSON; land So of the
State Road; NEGROES to be sold; tombstones to be placed at the graves of my
father & sisters & to the grave of Thomas GODWIN & my own; at d. of mother any
money to be paid to Trustees of MOORS Chapel; Larkin JOHNSON, Executor. Signed
28 May 1844 William Y. HENDERSON. Wit: A. G. SULLENERGER, Thomas SHELTON.
Recorded 7 Jul 1849 E. TATE, clerk.

p. 144 Inventory - Magness MOOR, decd. Mentions: a/c & notes on Joseph
PROFFITT, Peter SHAVER, 1 judmt on John _____. Signed John RICE, Saml B. TATE,
Executors. Recorded 16 Jul 1849 E. TATE, clerk.

Will - William WAGGONER, Sr. Wife, Sarah WAGGONER; my 3 sons William
WAGGONER, Jr., Jesse WAGGONER & Gabriel WAGGONER; Gabriel being an idiot I appt
his bros guardians; to the heirs of my dau Nancy CAPPS $1.00; my son Samuel
WAGGONER $1.00; Thomas WAGGONER, my son, Sally DAVIS, my dau, & Benjamin CAPPS,
grson; two sons William & Jesse WAGGONER, my Executors. Signed 21 Apr 1849
William x WAGGONER. Wit: James SALLING, John COX, Sr. Recorded 9 Aug 1849.

p. 145 Will - Lavinia LEA, Relict of Major LEA, decd. My son, Albert Millar
LEA 1/2 land known as Dower Tract & land on Bushy Ridge & all my SLAVES; 1/2

land in trust for Mary, wife of my son Luke LEA and their son now an infant &
named Albert Major LEA; to my son, Harmon Graves LEA, my servant WILLIAM, son
of MARIA, & Slave, for life; to my son Albert Millar LEA, $550, the price of
my former Slave CHARLES, my servant HENRY, a Slave for life, the eldest son of
MARIA, wishing him to always be a body servant on account of the lameness of my
said son; son, Harmon Graves LEA, Executor. Signed 6 May 1848 Lavinia LEA.
Wit: Saml SHIELDS, John H. SHIELDS, Williston T. LEA, Rachel T. LEA. Recorded
9 Aug 1849 E. TATE, clerk.

p. 147   Inventory - Lavinia LEA, decd. Mentions: Negro man SAM, 51 1/3,
Negro boy WILLIAM, 17, Negro woman MARIAH, 37, Negro man HENRY 21, Negro boy
HORACE, 3. Signed Harmon G. LEA, Executor. Recorded 13 Aug 1849.

          Inventory - Charles McANALLY, decd. Signed 30 May 1849 D. R. McANALLY,
D. McANALLY, Executors. Recorded 13 Aug 1849 E. TATE, clerk.

p. 148   Commissioners Report - 1 year support to minor heirs (under 15 yrs) of
Robert R. DUFF & wife, decd (towit), Robert Hugh, Thomas Rufus, Temple Albert &
Caroline E. Signed 10 May 1849 Robt D. EATON, Paschal L. JARNAGIN, A. P. GREEN.
Recorded 10 Sep 1849 E. TATE, clerk.

          Inventory - Delpha DOLTON, decd. Signed Coleby DOLTON, Executor.
Recorded 10 Sep 1849 E. TATE, clerk.

          Inventory - 25 Aug 1849. William WAGNER, decd. Mentions: 1 judge-
ment on Stephen MASSA. Signed Jesse M. WAGNER & Wm WAGGONER, Executors.
Recorded 10 Sep 1849 E. TATE, clerk.

p. 149   Guardian Report - Benjamin SMITH, Guardian of Mary SMITH, Juba SMITH
& Rachel SMITH. Mentions: last report 2 Oct 1848; James C. CLARK, Tax Coll,
taxes wards money 1849. Signed 17 Aug 1849 Benjamin SMITH, Guardian. Recorded
10 Sep 1849 E. TATE, clerk.

p. 150   Guardian Report - Robert CALDWELL, Guardian of Jeremiah CHAMBERLAIN &
Mary Jane CHAMBERLAIN, minor heirs of Andrew CHAMBERLAIN, decd. Mentions:
last report 24 Apr 1848; rent of wards lands 1847; Octavus YOE, Rev. Col., taxes
1848; Wm J. BOWMAN, tuition for Jane CHAMBERLAIN, a ward; Dr. Samuel N. TATE
for ward Jane. Signed 7 Aug 1849 Robt CARDWELL, Guardian. Recorded 22 Sep
1849 E. TATE, clerk.

          Guardian Report - John LAFFERTY, Guardian of the minor heirs of James
MAYES, decd (to wit) Thomas MAYES & Elizabeth MAYES. 1 Sep 1849. Mentions:
1 Nov 1847 last report; rents 1848; Reuben GROVE for board & clothing Thomas
MAYES, a ward; George G. TAYLOR for tuition of Thomas MAYES; Wm DAVIS for
tuition of Thos MAYES; Reuben GROVES for boarding & clothing Eliza MAYES, a
ward; Wm DAVIS tuition for Eliza; George G. TAYLOR for tuition for Eliza.
Signed 1 Sep 1849, John LAFFERTY, Guardian. Recorded 11 Sep 1849 E. TATE.

p. 152   Guardian Report - Thomas McBROOM, Guardian of the minor heirs of John
DENNIS, decd. 30 Aug 1849. Mentions: last report 3 Apr 1847. Signed Thos Mc
BROOM, Guardian. Recorded 11 Sep 1849 E. TATE, clerk.

Inventory - Martin CLEVELAND, decd. Mentions: notes on William TEAGUE (1849), Royal JENNINGS (1849), Samuel DODSON (1846), Jackson FRY (1842), Aaron HAMILTON (1841), Hugh WHITE (1848), Benjamin NEALEY (1840), John SHIRLEY (1824), Wm P. McBEE (1841), Joshua BIBAS (1836), G. B. CARDEN (1840), Stephen FROST (1839), Joseph LARGE (1831), Arnold CABBAGE (1828), Adam THOMPSON (1827), Henry CAMPBELL (1833), Martin HAMMOCK (1828), James JOHNSON (1842), Eli WYRICK (1836), William ROACH (1840), Hiram BAKER (1839), John MYNATT (1842), Martin THORNBURY (1838), Samuel SHOCKLEY (1842), Mat HUNTER (1842), Henry GRIGSBY (1844), Robert MASSINGILL (1819), Wm STARNES (1831), John DENNIS (1833 - 1829), Joseph WYRICK (1829), Christopher HITCH (1842), Lea H. MONROW (1842), Jacob VANDARIFF (1843), Alfred MOORE (1842); L. M. ELLIS, officers recpt on notes on Joseph SMITH (1840), Jesse HILL (1839), John HILL (1840), Israel WALTERS (1839), John KITTS (1840), James SMITH (1840) George COFFMAN (1840), Solomon WYRICK (1842); S. B. BEELAR, officers recpt on notes on John CAPPS (1845), James BRANSEN (1847); book accts on Robert FRY (1838 to 1844), Abner DODSON (1840 to 1844), Jesse F. BEELAR (1840 to 1843), L. M. ELLIS (1842 to 1846), John GAMBLE (1838 to 1839), David DODSON (1838), Ralph SHELTON (1839 to 1841), Wm ARWINE (1843), Saml MOORE (1846), John CHANDLER (1839 to 1848), John CLARK (1839 to 1846), Pleasant STARNES (1847 to 1848), Thomas VITTITOE (1839 to 1848), Wm HUBBS (1843), Sterling HAYNES (1846), David H. BRYAN (1848), John BRANSON (1849), James PHIPPS (1847), John BEELAR, Jr. (1847), Benjamin ACUFF (1843 to 1847), Jacob BEELAR (1845 to 1849), Smith STRANGE (1848), Thomas BLACKBURN (1848), John GRAY (1845 to 1848), James STRANGE (1847 to 1848), Wm JONES (1848), Wm VITTITOE, Sr. (1839 to 1849), Dedman NASH (1845), James STARNES (1842 to 1849), Anderson ACUFF (1848-1849), Stephen ATKINS (1848-1849), Eliza ATKINS (1839), John DYER (1839), John BAKER (1839), George DYER (no date), Joseph WOLFINBARGER (1840), Abel HILL (1848), James SELLARS (1843-1846), James JOHNSON (no date), Benjamin BRANSON (no date), George HACKER (1840-1841), Claibourn ACUFF (1847), Andrew J. SMITH (no date), Pleasant JENNINGS (1840-46), Joseph GREASE (?) (1845), Wm ACUFF (1839-40), Reuben WOLFINBARGER (1842), John BOILES (1840-49), Royal JENNINGS (1843-44), John DUNN 1843), John PERRIN (1841), Joel DODSON (1840-42), John BRECK (1840), Mr. JONES (1845), _____ McQURSTON (1845), Samuel PLEMING (1844), Hugh GRAHAM (1839), Henry WISER (1839), Allen HURST (1843-48), Reece WILLIAMS (1843-46), Chesley ARWINE (1841-42), John McBEE (1841), Jackson BULLEN (1848), John COFFMAN (1840), Elijah SMITH (1847), Wm VITTITOE, Jr. (1846-48), Joseph WILLIAMS (1839-46), James NICELY (1840-41), Jacob VANDAGRIFF (no date), John CHANDLER (1843-45), Alfred MOORE (1844), Lewis LAY (no date), John GOANS (1842-43), Nathaniel BRANSON (1839), Fredarick COFFMAN (1839-40), George SEMORE (1843-44), Goldman CARDEN (1841), David WATSON (1839-42), Isaac VITTITOE (1840), Alfred BUNCH (1839-41), Alfred CLEVELAND (1845-47), Boyer BULLARD (1842), Asa EVANS (1839-41), Doctor A. NOEL (1844), Christopher BULLARD (1842), Doctor John STARNES (1841), Jacob YADEN (1841), John GREST (1841-43), John LONG (1841), John McANALLY (1840), Doctor WESTERFIELD (1840), John MERRETT (1842-46), Drury GIPSON (1840), John BARNARD (1840), John BOWERS (1840-42), William McFETRIDGE (1840), Pleasant D. AKIN (1843), John B. GRIGSBY (1846-47), Mat HUNTER (no date), Jesse F. DIAL (1843), Wm ROBINSON (1840), James HOWEL (1839), James DAMEWOOD (1840), Jacob SHARP (1840-45), Solomon SHIPLEY (1840), John CARTER (1840), Jonathan POWEL (1842), Pryor JENNINGS (1841), Nicholas GIBBS (1842), Alexander HAMILTON (1841), Joab JANUARY (1842-43), Perry HARRELL (1842), John TANNER (1843-44), Kinata HILL (no date), Isaac HAYNES (1842), Robert SANDERS (1842), John WHITINGTON (1842), Joseph VANCE (1846), John DODSON (1842), Albartis ARNWINE (1839), Daniel ARNWINE (1839), Hiram ARNWINE (1839), James DYER, Jr. (1839-43), James DYER, Sr.

(1843), Mr. GOLDMAN (1841), Wm HOLLEN (1840), Rhodeman HARREL (1840-42), Wm
HAMILTON (1840), David JANUARY (1842-44), Jonas NICELY (1847), John OLLIVER
(1838), Elizabeth VITTITOE (1840), Washington VITTITOE (1839-43), Isaac SHEWMAKE
(1847), B. W. SCOTT; 1 note on Wm H. NORTON; James A. KLINE, tanner; $2 from
Daniel ARNWINE for rent of ferryboat; 12 NEGRO slaves. Signed 1 Oct 1849 Jacob
BEELAR, Wm M. CLEVELAND, Adms. Recorded 18 Oct 1849 E. TATE, clerk.

p. 158   Commissioners Report - 1 yr support to Anna CLEVELAND & family, widow
of Martin CLEVELAND, decd. Signed 4 Sep 1849 Joseph CLARK, Robt P. MOORE, Reuben
WOLFENBARGER, Comms. Recorded 19 Oct 1849.

p. 159   Account of Sale - Martin CLEVELAND, decd. 5 Sep 1849. Mentions: Anna
MARTIN, Franklin SAUNDERS, L. M. ELLIS, Henry WALKER, John A. CLEVELAND, James
DOLTON, Matelda CLEVELAND, Pleasant JENNINGS, Kenady HILL, James HILL, Henry
HIPSHEAR, John LONG, Jr., John BAKER, John LAY, William WYRICK, Thomas BLACK-
BURN, James GRAY, James VITTITOE, Fredarick SMITH, Stephen ADKINS, John LONG, Sr.,
James PHIPPS, Joshua D. CURLE, Benjamin PECK, Thomas WAGGONER, Samuel WALLACE,
Henry WILLIAMS, James MOUNTAIN, Thomas MAJORS, James H. STARNES, George W. DYER,
Alfred M. CLEVELAND, John CLARK, Peter WOLFINBARGER, Jr., James WAGGONER, Shad-
arick WILLIAMS, Joseph WOLFINBARGER, John GODWIN, Harrison BROWN, Calvin KIRK,
Joseph WILLIAMS, David BRANSON, Stephen ROUTH, Robt P. MOORE, Olliver P. FIELDS,
William DENNIS, G. W. VITTITOE, Joel DODSON, Rhodeman HARREL, James L. ACUFF,
Daniel ARNWINE, James BROCK, Jr., Robert WOLFINBARGER, Pleasant STARNES, David
SANDERS, Daniel GREEN, Allen HURST, William CRUTCHFIELD, Jackson BULLEN, John
DODSON, James M. VITTITOE, John HOLLEY, Jacob KLINE, George McMAHAN, Henry
JENNINGS, Joseph WOLFINBARGER, Abel HILL, David NICELY, William OWEN. Signed
8 Sep 1849 J. W. BRANSON, John CLARK, Clerks. Jacob BEELAR & Wm M. CLEVELAND,
Adm. Recorded 20 Oct 1849 E. TATE, clerk.

p. 163   Commissioners Report - 1 yr support of widow and family of John BETHEL,
decd. Signed 30 Jun 1849 Joseph NOE, Jacob KINDAR, Thos WEST, Sr. Recorded
20 Oct 1849 E. TATE, clerk.

p. 164   Inventory - John COLVIN, decd. Mentions: notes on Joseph SMITH, Jas
LEMORE & J. HILL (1831). Signed 1 Oct 1849 Wm COLVIN, Admt. Recorded 23 Oct
1849.

p. 165   Account of Sale - John COLVIN, decd. Mentions: Elijah COLVIN, James
SALLING, John MONROW, Sr., James COLVIN, J. F. HUDDLESTONE, Mark MONROW, Mark
KITTS, Pryor MUNROW, Wm P. OWEN, John W. WARWICK, Wm HICKLE, Enoch BRANSON,
Richard WADE, Calvin MONROW, John A. BLACKBURN, Allen HURST, D. F. HUDDLESTONE,
George W. VITTITOE, Samuel SHOCKLEY, Margaret COLVIN, Wm P. OWEN, Andrew J.
TROUT, Owen DYER, G. B. CARDEN, Robert KITTS, Thos BLACKBURN, Wm WYRICK, David
PARKEY, Thos L. BRANSON, Isaac DAVIS, John ROBERTSON, J. F. HUDDLESTONE, Calvin
MONROW, James MERRITT, Elias WARWICK, John HILL, A. M. COLVIN, Isaac CONDREY,
John SHARP, Mark KITTS, Thomas BLACKBURN. Signed 12 Oct 1849 Wm COLVIN, Adm.
Recorded 23 Oct 1849 E. TATE, clerk.

p. 167   Account of Sale - John BETHEL, decd. Sold 30 Jun 1849. Mentions:
Margaret BETHEL, Willson MANLEY, Rhoda BETHEL, Michael McGUIRE, Sterling COTNER,
George H. PRATT, Albert DAVIS, R. M. WEST, Wm B. WEST, James RAY. Signed David
K. LIVINGSTON, Adm. Recorded 24 Oct 1849 E. TATE, clerk.

p. 169   Account of Sale - Delpha DOLTON, decd. Mentions: A. J. DOLTON, Azra
DOLTON, James McGINNIS, Thomas DOLTON, Reuben DOLTON, John DOLTON, George DOLTON,
Thos HARVEY, Jno DOLTON, C. RUCKER, Colbert HIPSHEAR, Samuel RUCKER, T. W.
SCARCE (?), Timothy DOLTON, Wm HIPSHEAR, Claburn RUCKER, Malden LADY, C. J.
DOLTON, Murpithy HOWEL, John HAYES, Coleby HAYES. Signed Coleby DOLTON, Executor.
Recorded 24 Oct 1849 E. TATE, clerk.

p. 170   Inventory - Samuel BUNCH, decd. Mentions: the sorrel mare is claimed
by T. H. BUNCH as a gift of his father the late Cl. Sml BUNCH, the Sorrel
horse c4 yrs is claimed by Saml H. BUNCH as a gift from his father the late Col.
Saml BUNCH; a field of corn adjoining E. THOMASON; a field of corn adjoining T.
W. TURLEY; Negros MAJOR c50 yrs, ANAKA, a woman c40, JOHN c24 or 25, MARIAH c20,
FRANCES c3, WESLEY c1 both children of MARIAH, LUCAS c10 & LAZ c8; accounts and
notes on Hopkins ANDERSON to Joel EMBREE (1831), Janus M. LINDAMOOD (1848), Jas
PHIPPS (1845), Thomas BRADY to Jno F. PATE (1838), W. C. DUNLAP TO C___ JOHNSON
(1837), G. R. JARNIGAN (1840), Dennis PARISH (1839), Samuel SMITH (1838), Wm
CHASE (1840), Robt MITCHEL (1839), John LOWRY (1819), Joshua HICKY (1833), F. A.
CASH (1816), Henry COUNTZ (1832), Samuel CLARK to Jacob PECK (1809), John SHIRLEY
to Silas HALL (1807), Nancy HENDERSON & James CONN to James H. PECK (1815), Eli
CLARK (1833), James DEES to Jacob PECK (1817), Benjamin LEWIS (1831), Ch. CONDRY
& Dennis CONDRY (1806), J. C. BUNCH (1824 & 1828), J. G. MURDOCK (1819), Th C.
CLARK (1816), E. WITT (1825), Samuel MOORE (1830), Henry GAMBLE (1832), Edward
WHITT (1825), Saml ALLEN (1819), Isaac DANIEL (1836) on his return from Washing-
ton for a note on Benj. BITTLE (1830), Josiah MIDKIFF (1836), John IVY (1834),
John O. OATS (1837), John ROGERS to John LOWRY (1828), Hamilton MALLICOAT to Wm
T. TATE & Co. (1841), John H. ANDERSON (1840), Martin CLEVELAND (1826); suit
McKINNY vs GAMBLE (1827); an apple mill at farm of Mr. Jos BRYAN. Signed W. L.
LATHIM, Adm. Recorded 25 Oct 1849 E. TATE, clerk.

p. 175   Additional Inventory - Samuel BUNCH, decd. Mentions: a portrait Mrs.
BUNCH, Col BUNCH, Joseph ANDERSON, decd; sale 25 Oct 1849; note on John H.
ANDERSON (1845) came into hands of Adm through Benjamin SHERWOOD of Hawkins Co.
& among the papers of ANDERSON; note by Pryor H. DYER (1845). Signed W. L.
LATHIM, Adm. 5 Nov 1849. Recorded 10 Nov 1849 E. TATE, clerk.

          Commissioners Report - 1 yr support to Amanda BUNCH, the widow, &
family of Samuel BUNCH, decd. Signed 25 Oct 1849 Parrott GODWIN, T. W. TURLEY,
James x HELTON, Comm. Recorded 10 Nov 1849.

p. 176   Account of Sale - 25 & 26 Oct 1849. Samuel BUNCH, decd. Mentions:
Daniel TURLEY, B. G. SIMPSON, R. P. MOOR, A. AUSTIN, Jr., W. H. NORTON, Joel
THOMASON, James McGEE, T. W. TURLEY, Benj SHERWOOD, Samuel I. BUNCH, Edmund
PEMBERTON, E. THOMASON, M. L. DANIEL, John GREENLEE, Jr., W. McCONNEL, Emonauel
RAY, James JAMES, Parrott GODWIN, William WILLIAMS, Dennis ROBERTS, James
ROBERTS, D. W. PRENTICE, S. D. WILLIAMS, Octavus YOE, Wm M. COCKE, John COCKE,
Jr., Saml I. BUNCH, John MALLICOAT, Richard EPPS, James McDANIEL, Presley
BECHAM, Samuel GILL, John LAFFERTY, Larkin WHITT, Reece BOWEN, Saml H. BUNCH,
Wm B. CUNNINGHAM, John CALLISON, John LONG. See pages 180, 181 & 182.

p. 178   Inventory - Charles CATES, an insane person. Mentions: rent corn from
Andrew COLLINS & Alfred KEY; crop owned partly by R. LOYD, accounts against
Jas R. MITCHEL, Reuben CATES. Signed 5 Nov 1849 John CALLISON, Guardian.

Recorded 13 Nov 1849 E. TATE, clerk.

Account of Sale - 18 Aug 1849. John DEVAULT, decd. Mentions: Wm
DEVAULT, Saml SHARP, John ROBERTSON hired JERRY, John VANDAGRIFF hired JONAS,
Elizy ZACHEARY hired JULIAN, Isaac DEVAULT hired AMANDA, Saml SHARP hired
HANNAH, Martin HUBBS hired LEWIS. Signed George LAY & G. P. MYNATT, Adms.
Recorded 13 Nov 1849 E. TATE, clerk.

p. 179   Third Settlement - Jacob BEELAR, Executor of Joseph BEELAR, decd.
11 Sep 1849. Mentions: from A. P. GREEN part of debt due by Richard BRAGG;
last settlement 19 Apr 1849; John LONG who intermarried with Katherine BEELAR,
a legatee; Isaac BEELAR, a legatee; Danl BEELAR, a legatee; Jno BEELAR; recpt of
the heirs of Henry MOYERS, decd, who intermarried with Mary BEELAR, a legatee;
Jacob BEELAR, Executor, a legatee. Recorded 13 Nov 1849 E. TATE, clerk.

p. 180   Account of Sale - continued from p. 177 - Samuel BUNCH, decd. Mentions:
George R. CHILTON, C. C. SMITH, Jas K. McANALLY, Wm McCONNEL, John BOWEN,
Fredarick MAY, O. YOE, O. McCONNEL, Thos McBROOM, E. THOMASON, Samuel I. BUNCH,
Warham EASLEY, R. P. MOORE, L. M. ELLIS, Dennis ROBERTS, James A. KLINE, S. A.
LATHIM, Mrs. Amanda BUNCH, W. H. DANIEL, W. B. CUNNINGHAM. Signed W. L. LATHIM,
Adm. Recorded 13 Nov 1849.

p. 182   Account of Sale - S. E. DODSON, decd, & sold by Wm H. D. McANALLY, Adm.
Recorded 13 Nov 1849 E. TATE, clerk.

p. 183   Guardian Report - Andrew BOWER, Guardian of the minor heirs of John
HILL, decd. 13 Oct 1849. Mentions: last report 29 Nov 1848; hiring SLAVES;
rents of wards lands; Wm T. TATE & Co. for saddle for ward Wm R. HILL; taxes
1849; Peter WOLFINBARGER; boarding & clothing Penina Palestine HILL, a ward.
Signed 13 Oct 1849 Andrew x BOWER, Guardian. Recorded 13 Nov 1849 E. TATE.

p. 184   Guardian Report - James G. WALKER, Guardian of the minor heirs of James
WHITLOCK, decd. Mentions: last report 21 Sep 1848; rents recd for Mary
WITLOCK, a ward & Eliza E. WHITLOCK, a ward; John DUGLAS, Dpt Shff, Taxes 1844
& 45; Jas C. CLARK, Rev Coll., taxes 1849; Dr. John B. GRIGSBY for attendance &
medicine for Mary WHITLOCK, a ward. Signed James G. WALKER, Guardian, 3 Nov
1849. Recorded 14 Nov 1849 E. TATE, clerk.

Guardian Report - Henry ALSUP, Guardian of the minor heirs of David &
William COFFMAN, decd. 11 Oct 1849. Mentions: last report 1 Oct Oct 1848;
amt pd Enos HAMMER who has been appt Guardian to Susan COFFMAN, one of said
minors. Signed Henry ALSUP. Recorded 14 Nov 1849 E. TATE, clerk.

p. 185   Second Settlement - James SUNDERLAND, Adm for the Estate of George
BURKET, decd. 9 Oct 1849. Mentions: last settlement 24 Jan 1845; Wilson
CAMRON; Mary BURKET, a legatee; Warham EASLEY, Jr., Registering deed. Recorded
14 Nov 1849 E.TATE, clerk.

p. 186   Will - John HICKMAN. My wife Mary HICKMAN; my 3 daus Elizabeth HICK-
MAN, Catherine GRAY, formerly HICKMAN & Hannah HICKMAN; land up & down the creek
beginning on John HICKMAN, decd, line & running to Moses B. ATKINS line; my
daus Margaret HICKMAN alias Margaret MARTIN, Elizabeth HICKMAN & Hannah

HICKMAN; my 3 sons Daniel HICKMAN, Elijah HICKMAN & Francis HICKMAN; my dau
Pricilla LASLEY formerly HICKMAN; my 3 grddaus Mary HICKMAN, Lucenda HICKMAN &
Amy HICKMAN, Heirs at Law of John HICKMAN, decd; wife Mary HICKMAN, Executor.
Signed 19 Aug 1846 John x HICKMAN. Wit: Wm SHARP, James x PHEPPS. Recorded
7 Dec 1849 E. TATE, clerk.

Guardian Report - Francis YOUNG, Guardian of Preston YOUNG & Adaline
YOUNG, formerly Adaline McDANIEL. Mentions: cash recd from Robert LOYD, Executor of the last will & testament of John McDANIEL, decd, belonging to his
wards; Dr. John B. GRIGSBY for medicine & attendance to his wards. Signed
Francis YOUNG, Guardian 30 Nov 1849. Recorded 8 Dec 1849 E. TATE, clerk.

p. 187   Guardian Report - Thomas DYER, Guardian of the minor heirs of Nelson
ORE, decd. 24 Nov 1849. Mentions: last report 10 Jul 1846; rents for 1846, 47
& 48 & divided between wards, Viz, Mary E. ORE, Calvin ORE, Amanda ORE & Sarah
Jane ORE; rents 1846, 47 & 48 belonging to 3 of his younger wards, Viz, Calvin
ORE, Amanda ORE & Sarah Jane ORE: schooling & clothing Calvin ORE, Amanda ORE
& Sarah Jane ORE; Theo I. BRADFORD, Clerk of Jefferson Co., recpt for lawsuit on
wards behalf; John H. PECK, lawyer; Shff THOMASON, taxes 1845 & 46; Dpt Shff B.
E. GAINS, taxes 1847; O. YOE, Rev. Coll., taxes 1848; R. FIELDING, Rev. Coll,
for Jefferson Co., taxes 1847 & 48; Joel DYER who intermarried with Mary Elizabeth ORE, a ward. Signed Thomas DYER, Guardian, 24 Nov 1849. Recorded 8 Dec
1849 E. TATE, clerk.

p. 188   Second Settlement - Wm T. TATE, Adm of the Estate of James MALLICOAT,
decd. 1 Dec 1849. Mentions: last settlement 3 Dec 1847; Mrs. E. MALLICOAT;
wit. certificates recd of W. L. LATHIM & Dr. Wm E. COCKE; rents 1848; land sold
5 Aug 1848; Thos W. TURLEY, Atto. Recorded 8 Dec 1849 E. TATE, clerk.

p. 190   Settlement - Robert LOYD, Executor of Enos HAMMERS, decd. 31 Mar 1849.
Mentions: notes on John CALLISON, Wm HAMMER, Jas L. CHURCHMAN & Francis YOUNG &
assigned to Thos HANKINS, Jno GRAY, Pierce CODY & R. LOYD, Elisha THOMASON,
James GALLIAN & Isaac FLORA, Edward & Wm B. HODGES, Jacob KLINE & Sons; Cla-
bourn & Martha ACUFF, legatees; Elizabeth HAMMER, a legatee; Henry GROVE; Wm T.
TATE & Co.; Dr. Wm E. COCKE; John GRAY; Abraham HAMMER, probate; E. THOMASON,
Shff, taxes 1846; Clabourn ACUFF who intermarried with Martha HAMMER, a legatee.
Recorded 8 Dec 1849 E. TATE, clerk.

p. 191   Settlement - George COLLINS, Executor of Elish CARBACK, decd. 8 Dec
1849. Mentions: will states all property to belong to his wife, Sarah CAR-
BACK, at her d. to be the property of his son-in-law George COLLINS; Joseph
ORE; John M. BURNETT; Thos SMITH; Jacob COPPACK; Sarah x CARBACK, widow, recd
full amt of estate from Executor 11 Sep 1844, attested by John CARBACK & D. K.
LIVINGSTON; Jas TROTT; Joseph B. M. REECE; Levi SATTERFIELD; note to Wm
BRAZELTON; John CARBACK, a legatee, recd part of estate 19 Dec 1846, attested
by Daniel McKINNEY. Recorded 18 Jan 1850 E. TATE, clerk.

p. 192   Will - Pierce CODY. Lands & personal property to be sold in such a
way as to support my wife & family; land sold to James L. CHURCHMAN; my
worthy friend Robert LOYD, my sole Executor. Signed 18 Jun 1848 Pierce x
CODY. Wit: Francis YOUNG, James CAMRON. Recorded 10 Jan 1850 E. TATE, clerk.

Will - Nuncupative - Jane O. HOWEL. Made 21 & 23 Nov 1849 in her home in her last sickness; my dau Prudence CARMICHAEL; my dau Jane GROVE; ROSE, my old Black Woman; PRUDY's children. Made by us 7 Dec 1849 Elias WESTER, Pleasant WESTERN. Proved in court Jan Term 1850. Recorded 10 Jan 1850.

p. 193   Will - Jane SHIELDS of Shields Station, Grainger Co., TN. Being age 82; to be buried next to my decd hus, James SHIELDS, on the plantation I removed from when I came to this place to live in the Co. of Green, grave was back on the top of a high hill in an old field front of his old dwelling house in said Green Co. on Lock Creek; a mulatto girl JANE, who was by my decd hus will to be freed when reaching age 21, that date being 19 Jul 1856, said will on file in Green Co., should I d. before this date, my dau Joanna LEA, is to care for her, if dau d. then my son Melton SHIELDS is to care for her, if JANE has issue, they are to be liberated also, if JANE should d. & have no issue, all bequests are to go to Sophia SHIELDS, mother of JANE; my grdau Mary Jane SHIELDS dau of my son Samuel SHIELDS; my grdau Jane BOYD, dau of Michael & Esther WOODS; Sophia SHIELDS, a woman of color, that my decd husband set free & a cow & calf he bequeathed her; my dau Esther WOODS; my son William SHIELDS who lives in the State of MO; my son Henry W. SHIELDS; my son James SHIELDS; my son Milton SHIELDS, sole Executor. Signed 25 Mar 1842 Jane SHIELDS. Recorded 11 Jan 1850.

p. 196   Settlement - Alsa COOK, Adm of the Estate of James T. COOK, decd, with a will annexed. 7 Dec 1849. Mentions: accounts on Allen HURST, John ROBINSON, Jacob SHARP's Estate, Thomas HARDEN, James ROBINSON, Martin COOK; John COX, Constable; James SALLING, Dpt Shff, taxes 1844 & 45; B. E. GAINS, Dpt Shff, taxes 1846; J. F. HUDDLESTONE, Dpt Shff, taxes 1847; O. YOE, Rev. Col., taxes 1848; James C. CLARK, Rev. Col., taxes 1849. Recorded 18 Jan 1850 E. Tate.

p. 197   Third Settlement - Preston MITCHEL, Executor of the Estate of Edward CHURCHMAN, decd. 24 Dec 1849. Mentions: a bond on James MILLS payable to Edward CHURCHMAN due at d. of Elizabeth CHURCHMAN, stepmother of said Edward; notes on Nathan STANLEY, Alexander REEDER, Banister WILLS, Jesse DELOZER, Robert BLAIN; John MITCHEL & wf, Delilah MITCHEL, formerly Delilah CHURCHMAN; Joab PERRIN & Rabecca PERRIN, his wf, formerly Rabecca CHURCHMAN; Wm MITCHEL & wf, Margaret, formerly Margaret CHURCHMAN; John MILLS & wf, Nancy, formerly Nancy CHURCHMAN; Jefferson NANCE & wf, Jane, formerly Jane CHURCHMAN; Lewis COLLECT & wf, Cynthia, formerly Cynthia CHURCHMAN; Jiles J. BLEDSOE & wf, Mary, formerly Mary CHURCHMAN; John BRADLEY & wf, Hannah, formerly Hannah CHURCHMAN; James MILLS & wf, Naoma, formerly Naoma CHURCHMAN; John BRADLEY, Executor of the Estate of Matilda CHURCHMAN, a legatee; James MILLS, Guardian of John P. PERRIN, an heir; Executor Preston MITCHEL by his m. with Rachel CHURCHMAN, a legatee, retains in his hands a part of the Estate due his wife. Recorded 18 Jan 1850 E. TATE, clerk.

p. 198   Final Settlement - John SUGGS, Executor of R. M. SUGGS, decd. 7 Jan 1850. Mentions: received from Wm P. JONES, surviving partner of the R. M. SUGGS & Co. for sale of NEGROS & property; Wm P. JONES for himself & wife; Wm P. JONES, Guardian of the minor heirs of R. M. SUGGS, decd. Recorded 18 Jan 1850.

p. 199   Inventory - John COLVIN, decd. Signed Wm COLVIN, Adm. 4 Jan 1850. Recorded 19 Jan 1850 E. TATE, clerk.

        Account of Sale - John COLVIN, decd. Mentions: John SEXTON, Elijah
COLVIN, Thomas BLACKBURN, Calvin MONROW, Eli OUSLEY, Wm P. OWEN, J. A. BLACK-
BURN, Thos H. ROBERTS. Signed 4 Jan 1845 Wm COLVIN, Adm. Recorded 19 Jan 1850.

p. 200   Guardian Report - James MILLS, Guardian of John P. PERRIN. 24 Dec 1849.
Mentions: last report 24 Apr 1848; BRANNER & INMAN for overcoat for ward;
money recd from Preston MITCHEL, Executor of the Estate of Edward CHURCHMAN,
decd. Signed James MILLS, Guardian. Recorded 19 Jan 1850 E. TATE, clerk.

        Commissioners Report - 1 yr allowance to Nancy BOWERS, widow of Andrew
BOWERS, and family. Signed Joseph CLARK, John CLARK, Reuben WOLFINBARGER.
Recorded 19 Jan 1850.

p. 201   Account of Sale - Martin CLEVELAND, decd. Commencing 11 Dec 1849.
Mentions: John LONG, Wm HERREN, James BROCK, Jr., John ROBERTSON, James
WAGGONER, Alfred CLEVELAND, Joel FIELDS, Carter T. DOLTON, David A. BRYANT,
J. B. ODEL, William CRUTCHFIELD, J. D. JONES Negroes MILLA, GEORGE & JULIA,
William P. CRISPIN Negro PHILLIP, Matilda CLEVELAND Negros CELIA, BETTY & JIM,
David WATSON Negro PATRICK, James H. DYER Negros MARY, JACK & TOM, Edward TATE
Negro HANNAH, G. W. DYER, William HARREL, Reuben WOLFINBARGER, Hezekiah ROUTH,
Pleasant STARNES, William L. WAGGONER, Archibald MULLINS, Jesse NANCE, James
DOLTON, John DODSON, L. M. ELLIS, Benjamin C. ACUFF, Ann CLEVELAND, John
CLEVELAND, B. E. GAINS, John CHANDLER. Signed J. W. BRANSON, John CLARK, clks.
Additional sales - Charles M. ACUFF & Stephen ROUTH corn at Wm VITTETOES, James
H. STARNES, John BRANSON, John MERRET, Pleasant JENNINGS, Matilda CLEVELAND &
Eliza CLEVELAND, Berry KERBY a judgement against B. W. SCOTT, Wm CLEVELAND
renter of a machine 1849. Signed Jacob BEELAR, Wm M. CLEVELAND, Adms. Recorded
19 Jan 1850, E. TATE, clerk.

p. 203   Guardian Report - G. B. MITCHEL, Guardian of Russel SMALLWOOD's heirs.
1 Jan 1850. Mentions: last report 16 Sep 1848; taxes 1849; none of wards of
full age. Signed G. B. MITCHEL, Guardian. Recorded 21 Jan 1850.

p. 204   Guardian Report - G. B. MITCHEL, Guardian of the minor heirs of Aquilla
MITCHEL, Jr., decd. 1 Jan 1850. Mentions: rents 1848-49; Alfred WILHITE
tuition of Robert F. MITCHEL, a ward; Jas R. MITCHEL for tuition of Robt F.
MITCHEL, a ward; James C. CLARK, Rev. Col., taxes 1849; last report 21 Aug 1847.
Signed 21 Jan 1850.

        Commissioners Report - 1 yr support to Mrs. Elizabeth McCOY, widow of
Clabourn McCOY, decd, & family. Signed 28 Nov 1849 Samuel GILL, Tandy W. x
DOLTON, W. L. LATHIM. Recorded 21 Jan 1850 E. TATE, clerk.

p. 205   Guardian Report - Robert L. TURLEY, Guardian of James MAYES. Mentions:
from time of appt to time his ward reached full age; Wm M. MOODY, former
Guardian, cash recd 6 Dec 1847; cash recd from James LAFFERTY 1 Jan 1847; recpt
of ward arrived at full age, dates 1 Jan 1850. Signed Robert TURLEY, Guardian
1 Jan 1850. Recorded 21 Jan 1850 E. TATE, clerk.

        Account of Sale - Clabourn McCOY, decd. Sold 28 & 29 Dec 1849.
Mentions: John HIPSHEAR, Osburn COFFEE, Thomas DOLTON, John RUCKER, George
WOLFE, Jr., Nick'l ANDRAKIN, Anderson DOLTON, Arch McCOY, William McCOY,

Ans. E. McCOY, Peter OGAN, James JORDAN, George BREAF, George WOLFE, Jephta
McCOY, Peter WOLFE, Green B. WOLF, Elijah COFFEE, J. K. McANALLY, Eli JONES, Wm
T. ASBURY, John HARPS, Adam WOLF, Jr., Mrs. E. McCOY, Meredith HARVEL, M. B.
DOLTON, Wm COFFEE, John RUCKER, Wm E. McCOY, Azariah DOLTON, Anderson DOLTON,
An. ANDRIKIN, Charles WOLFE, Arch McCOY, Adam WOLF, Sr. Signed David McCOY,
Adm. Recorded 22 Jan 1850 E. TATE, clerk.

p. 208   Inventory - Cash in hands of Elizabeth McCOY, widow of Clabourn McCOY,
decd. Mentions: notes on A. COFFEE, George WOLF, Edley DOLTON, Andrew McGINNIS
& Adam WOLF. Signed David McCOY, Adm. Recorded 22 Jan 1850 E. TATE, clerk.

p. 209   Account of Sale - Charles McANALLY, decd. Mentions: Charles W. F.
McANALLY, James M. HAYES, A. G. HELTON, James K. McANALLY, Deadman MALLICOAT,
James ASBERRY, James GODWIN, Marvell NASH, Anderson MALLICOAT, William IMES,
Green ALLEN, John FORRESTER, Henry HIPSHEAR, Wm HARREL, Andrew McGINNIS, Insley
COLLINS, I. J. HARVEY, Wm F. TONEY, E. RALEY, Thomas DOLTON, Green BURDEN, J. J.
HARRELLE, Henry WILLIAMS, Sarah McANALLY, Wm DODSON, Edward SLAVENS, Ralph
SHELTON, Pleasant HOLT, A. J. McANALLY, J. J. BAKER, William PAYNE, Isaac HARVEY,
George COFFEE, Elijah COFFEE, W. LANCOCK, Madison HARVEY, Sarah BURNS, John
GODWIN, Colby DOLTON, Thomas P. McANALLY, James BULLEN. List of sales on 24 Aug
1849 mentions: Thomas P. McANALLY, John GODWIN, C. W. F. McANALLY, John
FORRESTER, Alexander HELTON, James M. HAYES, Edward SLAVENS, Wm IMES, C. W.
LATHIM, Sarah BURNS, James ASBERRY. Sales on 2 Nov 1849 mention: C. W. F.
McANALLY, James M. HAYES, John GODWIN, corn at J. HUTCHISON, R. MURPHY, D.
THACKER, John RUCKER, William MALLICOAT. Signed D. McANALLY an Executor.
Recorded 8 Feb 1850 E. TATE, clerk.

p. 214   List of notes of the Estate of Charles McANALLY, decd. Mentions:
Hezekiah MILLS (1848, 49 & 50), James M. HAYES (1848), Marvel NASH (1843), James
M. & Anderson HAYES (1846), Thos P. McANALLY (2 1837), Pendleton TAYLOR (1845),
Wm H. ODEL (1846), John ALLEN (1847), Pleasant JENNINGS (1843), Henry GAMBLE
(1833), Wm ROGERS (1842), James ASBERRY (1832,34), Thomas ADAMS (1833), Dand-
ridge THACKER (1847), Robert MURPHY (1848), David & John P. McANALLY (1844),
Coleby COFFEE (1831), John SHIRLEY (1819), A. & A. HELTON (1841), E. McKEY said
to be paid 2 yrs ago, John DODSON (1849). Signed D. M. Mc ANALLY, an Executor.
Recorded 9 Feb 1850 E. TATE, clerk.

p. 215   Inventory - Andrew BOWERS, decd. Mentions: NEGRO boy 13 yrs. Signed
George SELLARS, Adm. Recorded 9 Feb 1850 E. TATE, clerk.

p. 216   Account of Sale - Andrew BOWERS, decd. 25 Jan 1850. Mentions: Wm
DENNIS, James SELLARS, Nancy DAULTON, John DYER, Arthur MALLICOAT, Joel TAYLOR,
Wm HOPSON, Willie B. DYER, Nancy BOWERS, Benjamin BRANSON, Harlen LEFFEW, James
BROCK, Wesley SIMMONS, John CAMPBELL, Jacob BEELAR, Jesse F. BEELAR, John
MALICOAT, Daniel HURST, John CLARK, Nicholas SATTERFIELD, James DAULTON, Wm
LEFFEW, John WHITE (hiring BLACK boy), H. HURST, Nancy WILLIAMS, Elijah JONES,
Pleasant JENNINGS, Albartis ARNWINE, Samuel DODSON, Valentine WYRICK, Thomas
MAJORS, G. B. CARDEN, Jeremiah WYRICK, William HILL, L. B. BEELAR, John DYER,
Daniel HURST. Signed George SELLARS, Adm. Recorded 9 Feb 1850 E. TATE, clerk.

p. 218   Commissioners Report - 1 yr support to Deborah CODY, widow of Pierce
CODY, decd, & her family. Signed 28 Jan 1850 Daniel McKINNEY, Jacob KINDAR, Sr.,

Francis YOUNG, Comms. Recorded 9 Feb 1850 E. TATE, clerk.

p. 219   Guardian Report - William DENNIS, Guardian of the minor heirs of John
HILL, decd. Mentions: Guardian appt began 21 Jan 1850; cash notes recd from
Adm of the Estate of Andrew BOWER, decd, former Guardian of said heirs, 19 Dec
1849. Signed 21 Jan 1850 William DENNIS, Guardian. Recorded 9 Feb 1850.

        Inventory - John LONG, decd. Mentions: d. intestate with no personal
property other than such as widow by love is entitled; a sum of money due from
Col. Thomas WHITESIDE. Signed John COCKE, Adm. Recorded 8 Mar 1850 E. TATE.

p. 220   Inventory - Corban JACKSON, decd., taken 19 Jan 1850. Mentions: notes
on A. DOLIN, Joseph HOLLY, Wm WADKINS, Francis LYONS, F. JAME (?), H. MASSEN-
GILL & M. H. STONE, Thomas HUMES, Wm BOWEN, Wm CHASE, Jonathan JACKSON. Signed
John A. McKINNY, B. E. GAINS, Admts. Recorded 8 Mar 1850 E. TATE, clerk.

        Account of Sale - 19 Jan 1850. Corban JACKSON, decd. Mentions: T. A.
McKINNY, Norman JACKSON, Andrew JACKSON, Calliway KELLY, Andrew GRAHAM, Isaac
SHARP, Preston MYNATT, Nelson MYNATT, Aaron HARBISON, Alxd CAMPBELL, Robert
W. BLAIN, And FURGASON, James DYER, John NANCE, Eliza DAVIS, Saml SHARP, John
COATES, James CAMPBELL, Matthew CAMPBELL, H. G. LEA, Major MINCY, John YORK,
Richard MYNATT, Frank LYONS, Willis PRATT, William MARTIN, John A. RENTFRO,
Robert MARTIN, Henry ETTER, Preston MITCHEL, Saml JOHNS, Theophilus MALONE, T.
A. McKINNY, Anson DOLIN, Dotson P. MYNATT, Joseph SLAGLE, John CHASE, Wm P.
HARBINSON, Andrew FURGASON, Stephen CAMPBELL, O. YOE, G. B. MITCHEL, Calvin
MAGGOT, John SAWYERS, G. P. MYNATT, Lewis FOREST, John PERIN. Signed John A.
McKINNY, B. E. GAINS, Admts. Recorded 8 Mar 1850 E, TATE, clerk.

p. 222   Inventory - Pierce CODY, decd. Signed Robert LOYD, Executor 4 Mar 1850.
Recorded 8 Mar 1850 E. TATE, clerk.

        Additional Account of Sale - John DEVAULT, decd. Sold 5 Jan 1850.
Mentions: Samuel SHARP, Robert ROBINSON, Susanna DAMEWOOD, N. PETERS. Signed
Green C. MYNATT, George LAY, Admts. Recorded 8 Mar 1850 E. TATE, clerk.

p. 223   Inventory - Jane O. HOWEL, decd. Feb 1850. Mentions: notes & accts
on David NOE & Jehu MORRIS, Joseph NOE, G. B. MAYES, Johua KIDWELL, D. C.
CARMICHAEL. Signed D. C. CARMICHAEL, Adm. Recorded 8 Mar 1850 E. TATE, clerk.

        Guardian Report - Final Settlement made with Thomas McBROOM, former
Guardian of the minor heirs of John DENNIS, decd. 5 Mar 1850. Mentions: last
report 30 Aug 3849; the present Guardian, L. M. ELLIS. Recorded 8 Mar 1850.

p. 224   Guardian Report - Lewis M. ELLIS, Guardian of the minor heirs of John
DENNIS, decd. 5 Mar 1850. Mentions: Thomas McBROOM, former Guardian. Signed
L. M. ELLIS, Guardian. Recorded 8 Mar 1850 E. TATE, clerk.

        Guardian Report - Isaac LEBOW, Guardian of Pheba BASSETT. 20 Feb 1850.
Mentions: last report 30 Aug 1847; Wm GRAY, Executor of the Estate of John
LEBOW, decd; Executor of the Estate of Katherine LEBOW, decd, said Pheba BASSETT
being an heir; price of a NEGRO girl slave part of the Estate of Katherine
LEBOW, decd. Signed Isaac LEBOW, Guardian. Recorded 8 Mar 1850 E. TATE.

p. 225   Guardian Report - Godwin MAYES, Guardian of Nancy, Susanna, Martha, Elizabeth & Rachel MAYES. 16 Feb 1850. Mentions: cash recd from G. B. MITCHEL, Executor of the Estate of Aquilla MITCHEL, Sr., decd, from 17 May 1836 to 6 Mar 1837 & sale of property; James & Nancy JOICE (1838); Vardeman & Susanna BURNETT (1837), Wm & Elizabeth BOWERS (1841); Martha MAYES (1846); Rachel MAYES (1850); Elizabeth MAYES for store goods; pd Godwin MAYES for services 5 Feb 1838 to present. Recorded 8 Mar 1850 E. TATE, clerk.

Guardian Report - Amos STROUD, Guardian of Anna STROUD, Christopher STROUD, Joseph STROUD & Rachel STROUD. Mentions: amt of cash recd from David SEVIER, Clerk of the Chancery Court at Greenville, TN in Sep 1849. Signed Amos STROUD 5 Feb 1850. Recorded 8 Mar 1850 E. TATE, clerk.

p. 226   Will - Job GARRISTON. My wife Winniford GARRISTON; my esteemed friends Jacob PECK & Jehu MORRIS, Executors. Signed 21 Apr 1850 Job GARISTON. Wit: Meton SHIELDS, John H. L. PECK, William THOMPSON, M. HILL. Recorded 26 May 1850.

Inventory - Isaac PERKAPILE, decd. Signed 1 Feb 1850 John WALKER, Adm. Recorded 26 May 1850 E. TATE, clerk.

Commissioners Report - 1 yr support of the widow of Thomas P. McANALLY, decd. Mentions: one small judgement on Isaac HARVEY. Signed 21 Feb 1850 Hamilton EVANS, John P. JENNINGS, Claibourn BULLS. Recorded 26 Apr 1850.

p. 227   Account of Sale - Pierce CODY, decd. Mentions: Jacob KINDAR, Wm DONAHOO, Benjamin MITCHEL, James CAMRON, James MAYES, Deborah CODY, Massy COCKRUM, Preston YOUNG, Alfred ROACH, Robert TURLEY, Willson MANLEY, Isaac DANIEL, Reuben MOODY, Jesse MOODY, John OWENS, Dennis McKENNY, Benjamin PECK, David LIVINGSTON, Wm B. CUNNINGHAM, James L. GREENLEA, George W. TATE, James E. MORGAN, John GRAY, David N. TATE, Francis YOUNG, John SANDERS, James McDANIEL, Eli McDANIEL, James JAMES, Isaac DANIEL, Samuel JONES, Wm SMITH, John ROACH, Jr., James CLARK, Wm WATSON, Samuel SMITH, Jas S. CHURCHMAN, Edward L. TATE, Wm HAMMER, James R. MITCHEL, Albert YOUNG, Absolom MANLY, Preston YOUNG, a note on Jeremiah BOWMAN (1841). Signed Robert LOYD, Executor. Recorded 16 May 1850.

p. 228   Account of Sale - Isaac PERKAPILE, decd. 16 Feb 1850. Mentions: G. M. LONG, John PERKAPILE, John ESTES, Stephen ESTES, Isaac NOE, Nathan SHIPLEY, Alexander CARTRIGHT. Signed Russel RIGGS, Clerk. John WALKER, Adm. Recorded 26 May 1850.

p. 229   Inventory - Charles CATES, decd. Signed 2 Apr 1850 James KINDAR, Reuben L. CATES, Adms. Recorded 26 May 1850.

p. 230   Commissioners Report - 1 yr support for Anna MITCHEL & her family, widow of Benjamin MITCHEL, decd. Signed 24 Apr 1850 Jacob x KINDAR, John COLLISON, James JAMES. Recorded 26 May 1850 E. TATE, clerk.

Commissioners Report - 1 yr support for Elizabeth CATES & family, widow of Charles CATES, decd. Signed 24 Apr 1850 Daniel McKINNY, Thos WEST, George COLLINS. Recorded 26 May 1850 E. TATE, clerk.

Fourth Settlement - Hughs W. & Elka A. TAYLOR, Executors of the

Estate of Hughs O. TAYLOR, decd. 29 Apr 1850. Mentions: last report 8 Dec
1847; C. H. BOATRIGHT & Louisa BOATRIGHT, she a legatee; Amelia WITT, a legatee;
George G. TAYLOR, a legatee; Amanda A. PATTON, a legatee; Thos D. TAYLOR, a
legatee; Elbert E. TAYLOR, a legatee; C. W. WITT & Rachel WITT, legatees; Jabin
L. TAYLOR, a legatee; D. C. JACKSON, Adm of the Estate of Edna E. JACKSON, decd.
Recorded 26 May 1850 E. TATE, clerk.

p. 231   Settlement - Mary Louisa BEWLEY, Adm of the Will of Calvin F. BEWLEY,
decd. 4 May 1850. Mentions: note to G. W. ALEXANDER; Allen BAKER; Adam A.
ROGAN; note to John G. BEWLEY; note to Wm A. CAMPBELL; George W. DRAKE.
Recorded 26 May 1850 E. TATE, clerk.

p. 232   Guardian Report - George WILLIAMS, Guardian of the minor heirs of John
M. WILLIAMS, decd. Mentions: last report 23 Feb 1849; rent recd from Francis
BOYD for Panther Spring property; Jas C. CLARK, Rev. Coll., taxes 1849; Jas
HUFFMASTER, Rev. Coll. for Hawkins Co., taxes 1849; Abraham McCONNEL fee selling
wards rents. Signed 23 Apr 1850 George WILLIAMS, Guardian. Confirmed May Term
of Court.

p. 233   Guardian Report - Jacob BEELAR, Adm of the Estate of Martin CLEVELAND,
decd. 19 Mar 1850. Mentions: cash remaining in the hands of Martin CLEVELAND,
decd, at the time of his d. as Guardian of the minor heirs of Wm HAYES, decd,
repted to be in his hands 18 May 1847; Joseph & Catherine POWEL, she being a
ward (1847); Daniel HAYNES, present Guardian. Signed Jacob BEELAR, Admt.
Recorded 17 May 1850 E. TATE, clerk.

        Guardian Report - Greenberry MITCHEL, Guardian of Russel SMALLWOOD's
heirs. 24 Apr 1850. Mentions: last report 1 Jan 1850; Russel SMALLWOOD
Attorney in Fact for said heirs. Recorded 17 May 1850 E. TATE, clerk.

p. 234   Settlement - John CALLISON, Adm of the Estate of Lea McDANIEL, decd.
22 Feb 1850. Mentions: first sale 19 Jan 1848; second sale 22 Sep 1848; Wm
A. ROGERS; Edward WEST; James ZACHARY; Eli McDANIEL; Daniel McKINNY; Wm G.
EATON; Nancy McDANIEL; James JAMES; Lena McDANIEL, widow; John CLARK, Guardian
of Lenna McDANIEL, an heir; Chesley MORGAN; Thos WILLIAMS. Recorded 27 May 1850.

p. 235   Guardian Report - John CLARK, Guardian of Lenna McDANIEL. 19 Mar 1850.
Mentions: cash recd from John CALLISON, Adm of the Estate of Lea McDANIEL,
decd & James E. MORGAN; pd Elizabeth McDANIEL in pursuance of contracts made
by John McDANIEL in his lifetime for years 1848 & 49; pd Lina Ann McDANIEL for
care of ward; James C. CLARK, Rev. coll., taxes, wards lands 1849; cash recd
from Jesse HODGES. Signed John CLARK, Guardian. Recorded 17 May 1850.

        Settlement - Hughs W. TAYLOR, surviving Executor of the Estate of
Eli HODGES, decd. Done 28 Dec 1848. Mentions: Wm P. MASSENGILL; Job
GARRESTON; Jehu MORRIS & REGGIS; John J. NOE, Dpt Shff, taxes 1846; note to
John M. PATTON; the Executor, Ellis RIGGS; Benj. COX; John M. HODGES, an heir,
receipt 26 Jan 1849; I. B. HODGES, agent for John HURST who intermarried with
Lucinda HODGES, a legatee; Nicholas McBRIDE who intermarried with Mary HODGES,
a legatee; Jacob E. HODGES, a legatee; Isaac B. HODGES, a legatee; Thos C.
HODGES, a legatee. Recorded 17 May 1850 E. TATE, clerk.

p. 236   Settlement - James THOMPSON surviving Executor of the Estate of George
G. REED, decd. 23 Apr 1850. Mentions: James THOMPSON, Executor, & Shaderick
INMAN & Clesbe RIGGS, Admts of the Estate of Ellis RIGGS, decd; 15 Oct 1837 amt
left in George G. REED's pocket Book at his d. of $500 of which proved to be
counterfeit; 19 Apr 1838 amt recd of Isaiah REECE; 15 May 1838 amt recd of Wm
MITCHEL; 10 Jun 1838 amt recd of David SHEPHERD of Wm POINDEXTER & of John
MILLER; 13 Jan 1838 amt recd of Leroy PULLEN; 15 Sep 1838 amt recd of Bartley
McGEE & of Saml WITT; 20 Oct 1838 amt recd of Isaiah REECE; 20 Dec 1838 amt of
Wm A. REED & of William DONALSON; 1 Feb 1839 amt recd of Jesse RIGGS; 1 May 1839
amt recd of Clisbe RIGGS for clock; 13 May 1839 amt recd of David W. REECE; 15
May 1839 amt recd of John WALKER; 18 May 1841 amt rect of Leroy PULLEN; 30 Nov
1844 amt recd of David McANALLY & amt purchased at sale; 22 Feb 1847 amt recd
from Black JOHN for hire; 20 Oct 1847 amt recd of Eli KERN note; 1 Feb 1848 amt
recd on Adam SHIPLEY note; 13 Feb 1845 amt recd Adam SHIPLEY note; 5 Dec 1838
amt recd of Wm ORR; 29 Jan 1840 amt recd of Wm ORR; pd Isaac BARTON (1838);
Job GARRESTON; pd Noah JARNAGIN for boarding Thos & Noah REED c3 mos, 20 Feb
1838; pd Dr. Wm MURRY & James WHITE 7 Dec 1838; pd Ezekiel INMAN, Wm R. CASWELL
& John HIDE 26 Mar 1838; pd Mrs. SHEPHERD for keeping Adalaid 15 Jan 1838; pd
John HURST 30 Apr 1838; pd C. F. P. JARNAGIN 19 May 1838; pd George ROBERTSON 20
Jun 1838; pd Obadiah BOOZE 30 Jun 1838; taxes 1844; pd Wm S. MANSON 30 Jun 1838;
pd John MEEK & Henry HARRISON 1 Dec 1838; pd Clisbe AUSTIN, Thos S. WALKER &
Joseph WILLIAMS 1 Aug 1838; pd R. M. LANDRUM 10 May 1839; pd C. S. HARRIS, 1 Aug
1840; pd taxes 1838, 39 & 40; pd for Mary's saddle to NEILL 1 May 1841; pd
Joseph SHANNON & Job GARRESTON 20 May 1841; pd Jehu MORRIS 15 Apr 1842; pd
H. W. TAYLOR for smith work on farm 10 Jun 1842; taxes 1841, 42, 43; pd Thos
REED for saddle 1 Aug 1843; pd to TAYLOR for schooling 8 Oct 1846; taxes 1845,
46, 47; the Wm ORR debt recd by Mary THOMPSON 29 Jan 1840; pd Dr. C. S. HARRIS
1 Aug 1841; John F. NOE, being an heir by m. with Mary REED, the dau of Thos.
REED, 7 Aug 1838. Confirmed in May Term 1850. Recorded 27 May 1850 E. TATE.

p. 240   Guardian Report - Robert W. WOLFINBARGER, Guardian of the minor heirs
of Tandy WOLFINBARGER, decd. 1 Jun 1850. Mentions: Peter WOLFINBARGER, Adm
of Tandy WOLFINBARGER, decd; last report 6 Feb 1849. Signed Robert W. WOLFIN-
BARGER. Recorded 10 Jun 1850 E. TATE, clerk.

p. 241   Guardian Report - Lewis ATKINS, Guardian of the minor heirs of Nathan
ATKINS, decd. 31 May 1850. Mentions: last report 1 Jun 1849; Ira & Talbott
ATKINS, two wards. Signed Lewis his A mark ATKINS, Guardian. Recorded 10 Jun
1850 E. TATE, clerk.

          Guardian Report - Elias WESTER, Guardian of the minor heirs of Nanian
RIGGS, decd. 3 Jun 1850. Mentions: cash recd from Elizabeth RIGGS, former
Guardian, dated 3 Jun 1849; rents of wards lands 1850. Signed Elias WESTER,
Guardian. Recorded 10 Jun 1850 E. TATE, clerk.

p. 242   Guardian Report - John CALLISON, Guardian of Charles CATES who was an
idiot & not capable of transacting his own business & who has since d. in the
Lunatic Hospital at Nashville. 22 May 1850. Mentions: cash recd from Robert
LOYD, Reed MITCHEL & Boyd McNARY, Superintendant & Physician of the hospital;
Dr. Samuel N. TATE for services; John DUNAVANT; John HOLLEY for carrying Charles
CATES to Nashville; Wm M. COCKE & John NETHERLAND, Atto fees. Signed John
CALLISON, Guardian 22 May 1850. Recorded 10 Jun 1850 E. TATE, clerk.

p. 243   Inventory - Benjamin MITCHEL, decd. 25 Apr 1850. Mentions: account on John CLARK. Signed Robert LOYD, Adm. Recorded 10 Jun 1850 E. TATE, clerk.

Account of Sale - Charles CATES, decd. 25 Apr 1850. Mentions: G. W. TATE, Albert DAVIS, George KINDAR, James JAMES, E. CATES, D. McKINNY, R. LOYD, John SANDERS, J. B. GRIGSBY, Alexd MANLY, E. MORGAN, John KINDAR, Urijah KEY, Joel COFFEE, Absalom ROACH, Abner K. LOWE, Willson MANLEY, George COLLINS, S. D. WILLIAMS, Gooldsby SANDERS, Danl McKINNY, Eli McDANIEL, Sr., Thos DAVIS, Thos WEST, James GAINS, J. L. CHURCHMAN, J. R. MITCHEL, Anderson YATES, R. LAY. Signed James M. KINDAR, Reuben CATES, Adms. Recorded 10 Jun 1850.

p. 245   On the day of the sale 25 Apr 1850 the widow took property out of the hands of Adm. Signed James M. KINDAR & Reuben L. CATES, Adm. Recorded 10 Jun 1850 E. TATE, clerk.

Guardian Report - Wm T. TATE, Guardian of Evalina CARMICHAEL, formerly Evalina LATHIM & Martha LATHIM, minor heirs of John LATHIM, decd. 17 May 1850. Mentions: rents of wards lands & slaves 1849 & 50; last report 6 Aug 1848; taxes 1849; C. W. LATHIM, Wm M. COCKE, Atto, in case of Guardian vs James LATHIM & others (1845); S. M. EPPERSON for work done; James T. CARMICHAEL, hus. of Elvira, one of his wards. Signed Wm T. TATE.
     Also added: James T. CARMICHAEL who intermarried with Sarah E. LATHIM, a ward; James T. CARMICHAEL who pd Wortham JOICE for 2 coffins to bury 2 NEGROS belonging to both wards; Dr. James L. EASLEY for medical attendance on 3 SLAVES; James T. LATHIM, cash pd to Martha LATHIM; hiring of Negro man, ALFRED. Recorded 15 Jul 1850 E. TATE, clerk.

p. 247   Settlement - Levi CAMPBELL, Adm of the Estate of Henry M. MOODY, decd. 29 Jun 1850. Mentions: Reece BOWEN; Jas C. CLARK, Rev. col, taxes 1849; note to John MOODY; O. YOE, rev. col, taxes 1848; note to Thomas LATHIM; note to John CALLISON, Adm of the Estate of Lea McDANIEL; note to Wm T. TATE & Co.; J. P. LEGG; James G. WALKER, trustee of Gr Co.; MAYES & SULLENBARGER; W. L. LATHIM, Clerk of Circuit Ct; Dr. Wm E. COCKE; John HOLLY; Nancy N. MOODY, widow & relict; fee on deed for the benefit of H. M. MOODY Estate; Wm T. TATE; RICE & McFARLAND; insolvent note against Benjamin BRAY. Recorded Jul 1850.

p. 248   Inventory - Job GARRESTON, decd. Signed Jehu MORRIS, Executor. Recorded 16 Jul 1850 E. TATE, clerk.

p. 249   Account of Sale - 22 May 1850, Job GARRESTON, decd. H. W. TAYLOR, Crier of Sale. Mentions: W. P. GARRESTON, Saml RIGGS, Jas ESTES, G. M. LONG (cherry tree on Harry RIGGS land), John F. NOE, Hughs W. TAYLOR, John H. FLORA, John RICE, Wm A. HARRIS, Jacob LIVINGSTON, Jr., Drury MORRIS, M. M. ROGERS, Jas MONTGOMERY, Wm MURIK, Caswell GREGORY, Wm B. CUNNINGHAM, C. B. STAPLES, Russel RIGGS, Jno H. FLOWERS, Clisbe RIGGS, G. W. MOYERS, G. W. MYERS, Jacob PECK, S. L. HUFFMASTER, John BIGGS, H. H. PECK, Alxd CARTWRIGHT, Thomas MILLAR, J. H. MILLAR, W. J. REECE, John GARRESTON, S. D. MILES, J. MORELACK, Rowland ESTES, Wm MERRIK, J. S. RYAN, Harmon COX, W. STUBBLEFIELD, Hughs O. TAYLOR, Alxd WILLIAMS, Jno WALKER, John ESTERLY, S. PERRYMAN, Jas O. SENTER, S. INMAN, G. W. HOUSLEY. Signed Clisbe RIGGS, clerk, Jehu MORRIS, Executor. Recorded 16 Jul 1850 E. TATE, clerk.

p. 252   Settlement - Cynthia HARRELL, Admx of the Estate of Wm M. HARREL, decd.
23 Oct 1849. Mentions: sale of Military Land Warrant; Jacob SHOULTZ, M.
CARRIGAR; Hugh GRAHAM; George W. ROSE; there being but 2 heirs, Cynthia HARREL
is entitled to ½ Estate. Recorded 16 Jul 1850 E. TATE, clerk.

        Commissioners Report - 1 yr support to Barbara KITTS & family, widow
of John KITTS, decd. Signed 20 Jul 1850 J. F. HUDDLESTON, Calvin HUDDLESTON,
Alexander HAMILTON, Commissioners. Recorded 13 Aug 1850 E. TATE, clerk.

p. 253   Second Settlement - Robert LOYD & Eli McDANIEL, Exeuctors of the
Estate of John McDANIEL, decd. 25 Jul 1850. Mentions: last report 11 Mar
1848; sale 22 Sep 1848 & 22 Sep 1849; share of the hire of Boy ALFRED; cash
recd from Widow; John CALLISON, Guardian of Martha & Rachel Minerva McDANIEL;
John CALLISON, Adm of the Estate of Susan McDANIEL, decd; John CALLISON Adm of
the Estate of Susan & Wm McDANIEL, decd; Francis YOUNG, Guardian of Adaline
YOUNG; Wm T. TATE & Co. for medicine & burying clothes for Susan McDANIEL, an
heir & legatee; Robert H. HINES, Atto; Wm SMITH for tuition fee; Isaac DANIEL;
B. E. GAINS, Dpt Shff, taxes 1847; O. YOE, rev col, taxes 1848; J. C. CLARK, rev
col, taxes 1849; Jacob GODWIN; Nicholas NOE note; Preston YOUNG, Guardian of
Adaline YOUNG. Recorded 13 Aug 1850 E. TATE, clerk.

p. 255   Settlement - L. M. ELLIS, Executor of the Estate of David JANUARY, decd.
22 Jul 1850. Mentions: 5 notes on George SPARKMAN, 1846 to 1850 for a tract
of land; Thos PATTERSON; James G. WALKER; note to Wm T. TATE & Co; Chesley
TROGDON; note to Wm H. DAVIS; Wm LOWE; Eli MANLEY; Thos SMITH; Samuel WEST;
W. P. WHITLOCK; Anderson ATKINS; James T. WEST; Thos & Wm READER; Wm G. EATON;
Wm HARRIS; J. D. CURLE, Constable; Reuben YATES; Alfred M. KEY; B. E. GAINS,
Dpt Shff, taxes 1846; Hiram YATES; G. B. SIMPSON; acct on Absalom ROACH for acc
against the Widow PARROTT & a note against R. D. EZELL. Recorded 15 Aug 1850.

p. 256   Guardian Report - Isaac HARRIS, Guardian of the minor heirs of Samuel
RAY, decd. 20 Jul 1850. Mentions: last report 21 Sep 1848. Signed Isaac
HARRIS, Guardian. Recorded 14 Aug 1850 E. TATE, clerk.

p. 157   Second Settlement - Joseph HILL, Adm with a will annexed of the Estate
of Isaac DYER, decd. 4 Jun 1850. Mentions: last settlement 9 Oct 1838; interest recd from 10 Mar 1837 to 9 Oct 1838; Isaac DYER recpt 1839, an heir;
George DYER, an heir, recpt dated 1839; Robert DYER, an heir, recpt dated 1838;
Peter CARDWELL & Susan CARDWELL, an heir, recpt dated 1844; Martin WYRICK &
Nancy WYRICK, an heir, recpt 1844; Ira DENNIS & Elizabeth DENNIS, an heir, recpt
dated 1840 & 41; Pleasant DYER, an heir, recpt dated 1839; Elizabeth SATTER-
FIELD recpt dated 1838; taxes 1839, 40, 41; N. PETERS, Dpt Shff, taxes 1842;
taxes 1843; James SALLING, Dpt Shff, taxes 1844 & 45; B. E. GAINS, Dpt Shff,
taxes 1847 & 48; notes on Thomas ROOKARD & John McKINNY; acct on Wm DYER who is
insolvent; note on Robert DYER who is insolvent & taken by Fanny DYER in her
lifetime; Judgement on Joel FIELDS & Abel HILL on a note on Estate taken by
Fanny DYER in her life time & being insolvent; Jeremiah JARNAGIN. Recorded
14 Aug 1850 E. TATE, clerk.

p. 258   Settlement - Beanstation Turnpike Commission. Report for 1849.
Mentions: balance in hands of former treasurer Joseph CLARK for yr ending
1849; Joseph LANHAM, overseer; Marvel NASH, overseer; Charles McANALLY;

Daniel G. MILLAR, overseer; Henry WILLIAMS, overseer; C. W. LATHIM, Comm; John
HARRIS, Comm; Hugh JONES, Comm. Signed J. A. KLINE, Wm H. NORTON & Wm B.
CUNNINGHAM, Comms. Recorded 13 Aug 1850 E. TATE, clerk.

p. 259   Inventory - Wm WAGGONER, decd. Mentions: notes on Asa TOLLIVER,
Allen HURST security; note on Wm HAMMOCK, Marcarias COOK & Pleasant COOK,
security; note on Wm L. WAGGONER & James A. WAGGONER, security; note on Charles
S. BERRY, Allen HURST security; cash pd by James DAVIS. Signed 7 Jan 1850
Jesse M. WAGGONER & Wm WAGGONER, Executors. Recorded 24 Sep 1850 E. TATE.

Additional Account of Sale - 6 Aug 1850. John DEVAULT, decd.
Mentions: William BOOKER, Lawson DAMEWOOD, Wm DEVAULT, Isaac DEVAULT, John
ROBERTSON, Samuel SHARP; hire of Negros - boy JERRY to John ROBERTSON, man
JONAS, WOMAN & CHILD, 2 GIRLS & 1 BOY to Isaac DEVAULT. Signed George LAY &
G. P. MYNATT, Adms. Recorded 24 Sep 1850 E. TATE, clerk.

p. 261   Settlement - David McANALLY one of the Executors of the Last Will &
Testament of Charles McANALLY, decd, who was the Adm of the Estate of James M.
McANALLY, decd, which remained in his hands at the time of his d. Mentions:
Chas McANALLY made last settlement 27 Aug 1845; Thomas WHITESIDE; John P.
McANALLY; James M. McANALLY note to Thos WHITESIDE; Wm T. TATE & Co.; James M.
McANALLY note to Jacob SHOULTZ; George BARNARD; Gray GARRETT; Aquilla PAYNE;
James BULLEN acct of Thos P. McANALLY; Zorababel HARVEY; Estate of Chas McANALLY,
decd, is chargable with interest on the sum of $231.28 from 28 Oct 1843 to this
date. Recorded 24 Sep 1850.

Settlement - Isaac McBEE, Executor, of Elizabeth CHURCHMAN, decd. 28
Aug 1850. Mentions: notes on Daniel VINEYARD, Thomas SHARP (insolvent), John
WILLIS (insolvent); bequeaths to James FURGASON, Meredith FURGASON, Nancy COLLET
by Lewis COLLET, Nancy Jane FURGASON, dau of William FURGASON, Julia Ann FURGA-
SON, dau of William FURGASON, Joseph HODGES. Recorded 26 Sep 1850 E. TATE.

p. 263   Settlement - Clesbe RIGGS & Shadareck INMAN, Adms of the Estate of
Ellis RIGGS, decd. 28 Aug 1850. Mentions: sale of SLAVES & lands payable
24 Nov 1849 & 24 Nov 1850; Warham EASLEY; Wm ESTES; Elisha BULL; Russel RIGGS;
L. M. ELLIS, Shff; O. YOE, rev coll, taxes 1848; F. W. TAYLOR; John H. NELSON;
Thos SHIPLEY; Felps READ; MORRIS, RIGGS & MILLIKAN; James L. JENNINGS; John
GARRISON; James THOMPSON, Executor of G. G. READ, decd; note to Wright STUBB-
LEFIELD; Felps RIGGS; B. F. SPIKER; note to Russ (?) I. DAVIS; note to W. L.
DIXON & Mary MOORE; note to Jehu MORRIS & Co.; note to C. T. P. JARNAGIN;
Jonathan MORELOCK; note to Wm H. RIGGS; W. W. NEIL, S. L. HUFFMASTER; note
to Daniel NOE; note to G. G. READ, Jehu MORRIS & W. C. NEWEL; note to J. W.
PATTERSON, Executor of R. L. RIGHT, decd; James THOMPSON. Recorded 27 Sep 1850.

p. 264   Settlement - Wm T. TATE, Adm of the Estate of James MALLICOAT, decd.
4 Oct 1850. Mentions: sale of land 5 Mar 1850; T. W. TURLEY; W. L. LATHIM;
other settlement 1 Dec 1849; sell of lands. Signed W. B. CUNNINGHAM, J. GODWIN,
Comms. Recorded 12 Oct 1850 E. TATE, clerk.

p. 265   First Settlement - George LAY & G. P. MYNATT, Executors of John DEVAULT,
decd. 3 Dec 1850. Mentions: note on Ira DARTER due 1848; 5 sales; S. & M.
SHIELDS; Dr. SHIELDS; Wm A. ROGERS; Dr. C. M. GOODLIN; Fanny PETRES; Isaac

DEVAULT; O. YOE, rev coll, taxes 1848; J. C. CLARK, rev col, tax 1849; W. L.
LATHIM, Clk of Cir Ct; Wm T. CARDEN; Wm P. CRISPIN; Nathaniel POPEJOY; Isaac
DEVAULT, an heir; Elizabeth DOLTON & hus, Carter T. DOLTON; Jacob MILLAR,
Guardian of Mary Ann DAMEWOOD, formerly Mary Ann DEVAULT, an heir; Samuel
SHARP, who intermarried with Meneesa DEVAULT, an heir; Elizabeth ZACHARY, an
heir; Wm C. DEVAULT, an heir; George LAY, Adm, he being an heir by his m. with
Susan DEVAULT, one of the Destributes; Green P. MYNATT, an Adm, he being
an heir by his m. with Sarah DEVAULT, one of the Destributes. Recorded 12
Oct 1850 E. TATE, clerk.

p. 266   Settlement - Joseph WILLIAMS, Adm of the Estate of Hannah WILLIAMS,
decd. Mentions: last settlement 5 Oct 1843; Saml DODSON who intermarried with
Mary WILLIAMS, an heir, recpt dated 2 Nov 1843; Sarah SHELTON, formerly Sarah
WILLIAMS, recpt dated 16 Dec 1846; Saml WILLIAMS, an heir, recpt dated 27 Jul
1845. Recorded 12 Oct 1850 E. TATE, clerk.

p. 267   Additional Account of Sale - Martin CLEVELAND, decd. 19 Jul 1850.
Mentions: Pleasant STARNES, Wm T. CARDIN, James A. WAGGONER, Leroy CLARK,
G. V. CARDIN, David BRANSON, Daniel BEELAR, John LONG, Thomas WAGGONER, note
on Albartes ARNWINE. Signed John CLARK, Alfred M. CLEVELAND.   28 Sep 1850:
John CHANDLER, Pleasant STARNES, James WAGGONER, R. WOLFINBARGER, Jno CAMPBELL,
Wm SHARP, Wm HERRON. Signed Wm SHARP, Saml CLARK. Mentions: W. L. LATHIM,
note on Stephen ATKINS & James STARNES; recd of G. W. DYER for Martin CLEVELAND
tending the Circuit Court as a witness, Jesse F. BEELAR vs George W. DYER.
Signed Jacob BEELAR, Adm. Recorded 14 Oct 1850 E. TATE, clerk.

p. 268   Inventory - Elizabeth CLARK, decd. Mentions: note on B. BRANSON &
Thomas MAJORS & Elijah JONES. Signed David BRANSON, Adm. Recorded 14 Oct 1850.

p. 269   Inventory - John KITTS, decd. Signed Wm COLVIN, Adm. Recorded 14 Oct
1850 E. TATE, clerk.

       Account of Sale - John KITTS, decd. Mentions: Isaac KITTS, G. B.
CARDIN, Barbara KITTS, John A. BLACKBURN, John KITTS, Mark KITTS, Solomon
KITTS, Dicy KITTS, Allen HURST, David SMITH, Davidson KITTS, John F. HUDDLESTON,
Barbary KITTS. Signed 7 Oct 1850 Wm COLVIN, Adm. Recorded 14 Oct 1850.

p. 270   Additional Account of Sale - D. DOLTON. Mentions: Margaret DOLTON,
George W. HAYES, Anderson DOLTON. Signed Coleby DOLTON, Executor. Recorded
14 Oct 1850 E. TATE, clerk.

       Will - Benjamin PECK. Being aged & feble; family burying ground near
Massy Creek in Jefferson Co.; my dau Nancy Jane LEGG land in the town of
Rutledge, east of W. B. CUNNINGHAM's brick offices & farm (gives description
includes line of R. P. MOORE); my son Benjamin PECK land (gives description);
my son James H. PECK; interest in the DYER place which was conveyed to me under
the will of my last wife Mary which said DYER place is to belong to F. M.
WILLIAMSON when he becomes 21 yrs; my dau Eliza CUNNINGHAM & her children; my
Negro girl MARGARET & her offspring; my grandson Kindreck CUNNINGHAM; my dau
Mary LEA; my dau Sarah Ann DICK; Dr. LEGG, my son-in-law; Negros- boy KINDRICK,
boy NELSON, Black girl LUCY & AMANDA & their offspring, boy YOUNG DICK, girl
ORLENA & her offspring, boy OLD DICK, JEFF, CRESA & offspring, boy JOHN, girl

MADGE & her offspring, boy RUFUS, ADALINE & her offspring, boys CHARLES & GEORGE, girl NERIE & her offspring; Executors John H. PECK & Henry J. DICK. Signed 24 Oct 1850 Benjamin PECK. Wit: Wm GRAVES, R. P. MOORE, Henry H. PECK. Recorded 5 Nov 1850 E. TATE, clerk.

p. 272   Will - Sarah DENNIS. "I give & bequeath unto my beloved William DENNIS", no relation given. Signed 26 Mar 1843 Sarah x DENNIS. Wit: William SHARP, Levi DENNIS, Wm DENNIS, Sr., John WHITE. Recorded 8 Nov 1850 E. TATE.

p. 273   Settlement - Thomas W. TURLEY, Adm of the Estate of Edward M. WHITT, decd. 25 Oct 1850. Mentions: Dr.'s Wm T. THURMAN & M. N. JEFFREY; P. HERRELL. Recorded 12 Nov 1850 E. TATE, clerk.

Guardian Report - Elizabeth HODGES, Guardian of the minor heirs of Eli HODGES, Sr., decd. 31 Oct 1850. Mentions: last report 25 Feb 1844; Isaac B. HODGES; taxes 1847, 48, 49; Jacob E. HODGES, a ward; Thomas C. HODGES, a ward; Elizabeth HODGES, a ward; Cornelice or Camelia HODGES, a ward. Signed Elizabeth x HODGES, Guardian. Recorded 12 Nov 1850 E. TATE, clerk.

p. 274   Guardian Report - Nicholas McBRIDE, Guardian of the minor heirs of Preston LOYD, decd. 24 Sep 1850. Mentions: last report 19 Sep 1846; rents on wards lands 1847, 48, 49; wards, 2 in number, clothing & schooling; taxes 1847, 48, 49 & 50; Elizabeth HODGES, the undivided interest of James D. HODGES to the real estate of Eli HODGES, Sr., decd, which interest now belongs to the heirs of Preston LOYD, decd. Recorded 12 Nov 1850 E. TATE, clerk.

p. 275   Commissioners Report - 1 yr support to Elizabeth J. CLARK being the only minor heir of Elizabeth CLARK, decd, under age 15 yrs. Signed John CHANDLER, Pleasant STARNES, Clabourn ACUFF, Comms. Recorded 12 Nov 1850.

Commissioners Report - 1 yr support to Caroline M. MORRIS, widow of Jehu MORRIS, decd, & family. Signed 25 Oct 1850 Melton SHIELDS, Wm A. HARRIS, Jas O. SENTER. Recorded 12 Nov 1850 E. TATE, clerk.

Inventory - Martha ACUFF, decd. Signed 4 Nov 1850 Clabourn ACUFF, Adm. Recorded 12 Nov 1850 E. TATE, clerk.

p. 276   Inventory - Jehu MORRIS, decd. Book Accounts. 6 Aug 1850. Mentions: Mrs. Louisa LADD (?), Amos CARR, Josiah SPARKS, Elisha LAWSON, Wm BROOKS, John H. NELSON, Major L. WALKER, James WOODS, Ambrose CARTWRIGHT, Edward ALLEN, John SPOON, Alexander CARTWRIGHT, Elijah STANBERRY, C. W. MILLAR, Peter POPE, Henry WILLIAMS, Garrett L. READ, INMAN BILL (Black), Layfaett BROOKS, Thomas RUSSEL, Jesse POE, Walter SHROPSHIRE, ELIAS READ (Black), Peter SPOON, Isaac B. BOATMAN, Miss Nancy JARNIGAN, John MANSFIELD, James JARNAGIN, John WALKER, Mrs. George PETTY, Newton McALLESTER, John T. TURNER, Daniel CARR, Allen W. SNODGRASS, Wm N. CLARKSTON, John B. NEWEL, Thomas C. MILLAR, James E. THOMPSON, Widow BULL, Saml D. WADKINS, Peter CLINE, Alfred H. TARR, John CROWE, John CHANEY, John M. HODGES, Adam TREECE, Charles STATHAM, James WALKER, Mrs. Henry BOATMAN, Thomas H. ELLEDGE, Willie J. READ, Morristown Acedamy, Isaac NOE, Mrs. Jonathan NOE, Elihu MILIKAN, Nicholas NOE, Abraham COOTER, Landon R. TUDOR, Miss Jane HOLSTEN, Elijah BULL, Reece Wm WALL, Wm BRIGHT, A. G. SMITH, A. E. STAPLES, Alexander BROOKS, Caleb HOWELL, HALE ISAAC (Black), Thomas SHIPLEY, Nicholas LONG,

Nathaniel COX, Richard THORNHILL, W. DARNELL, Andrew COX, Wm A. JETT, Daniel
D. NOLEN, John COX, Thomas C. MILLAR, Miss Sarah LONG, Mrs. Soloman COX, Isaac
GREGGARY, Wm DAVIS, James L. NEWEL, James L. JENNINGS, James WHITE, Thomas
LAWLACE, John NOE (my John), George FAY, David HOLT, Shadarick GORDEN, Wm
WHITE, Paschal JONES, Wm NOE, Solomon SUNDERLAND, Hickery McKINNY, Robert LONG,
Sophia TEMPLETON, John HARRIS, Esqr., James HELTON, John McKINNY, Samuel MOORE,
David PERKAPILE, Thomas BROOSE, Miss Tamanda STEERMAN, Alexander McDANIEL, Mrs.
Ellis RIGGS, Wm P. ROGERS, G. A. TREBUCK, John V. BREWSTER, Joseph NOE, Felps
READ, Miss Louisa HAZELWOOD, John BULL, Col. C. D. GREGORY, L. W. IVY, Robert
MILLAR, Thos SHEPHERD, John L. WHITE, Silas B. STEPHENS, David GRANT, A. J.
THOMAS, Nathan SHIPLEY, Miss Sarah RUSKY, Job GARRISTON, Henry WOODS, George G.
RHEA, Wm JOHNSTON, Abraham MILLAR, Wm SHERWOOD, John COX of Jerremiah, Alxd
McCLANAHAN, John A. CARR, Benjamin SMITH, John PYOTT, Susan HAYNES, David N.
PANGLE, Madison HALE, James WHITE, J. W. R. MOORE, Miss Elizabeth WILLFORD,
Owen ANGLE, Jacob ANGLE, Garland BROWN, John BROWN, Dr. Edward CARSON, James D.
KINNER, Isaac GRANT, Shadarick INMAN, Joseph CARSON, James WILLIFORD, Paschal
TURNER, Miss Sarah THORNHILL, Nancy MILLAR, B. F. SPIKER, George W. RUSSEL, Job
GARRESTON, James L. NEAL, James ANDREWS, Jacob PERKY, Sr., John H. MILLAR, C.
B. STAPLES, W. SAMPLES, Thos M. JONES, John ROBERTSON of McKey, James H. GRAY,
Dr. W. F. M. HELMS, John RIGHTSILLE, J. A. LEWIS, Robert WELSH, John M. PATTON,
J. C. WHITT, John ANGLE, Elisha BULL, Martin SUMMERS, J. H. H. FLOWERS, George
A. RUSSEL, D. D. KEER, W. CARTWRIGHT, Mrs. Winny GARRESTON, James KING, Alfred
McCLANAHAN, Daniel NOE, Nat. BROOSE, John LAWRENCE, Martin KILGORE, Thos
SHIPLEY, Marcus McBRIDE, Wm DAVIS, Abraham SPOON, John MAY, Harry MEFFORD,
Samuel D. PRINCE, Joshua HAZELWOOD, David COX, Sterling C. PERRYMAN, Wm ESTES,
John B. JACKSON, Joseph N. SHANNON, Jesse HOWEL, Esqr., Redden S. TAYLOR, Joab
BLAKE, Col. Wm P. LONG, James B. BOYD, Alisce COBB, Thomas MORRIS, E. B. SNODDY,
Thos READ, Chesley ROGERS, John WILLIAMS of Ezekeil, Jesse LIVINGSTON, Russel
RIGGS, David REDWELL, Thos HODGES, George McFARLAND, David HETON of Goler, Mrs.
Elizabeth HODGES, Dr. W. C. SMITH, John DRENNON, Samuel SITZLER, Rachel MORRIS,
Willie B. READ, Miss Polly CLARK, James BARTON, Marvin ARNETT, Joseph HUDGGEON,
Hardy JOHNSON, Wm THOMPSON, Sr., John BROCK, Blana ? HAZELWOOD, Wm BAKER of
Knobles, Adam SIMMERMAN, Robert POTTER, Jr., James CARMICHAEL, Jr., Miss Nancy
READ, George WILLIAMS, Jacob LIVINGSTON, Wm SETZLER, Nelson B. SHELTON, Jacob
HODGES, Wm C. HEATON, Wm M. THOMPSON, James THOMPSON, Sr., Richard M. HUFFMASTER,
John F. NOE, Maj. Joseph NOE, Dr. C. S. HARRIS, James M. BUTLER, J. T. CAR-
MICHAEL, Jr., Wm A. HOWELL, Wm BAKER (D.R), Jacob LIVINGSTON, Wm A. HARRIS,
Clisbe RIGGS, David NOE, Y. I. MORRIS, Alxd TALLY, Dr. Josiah RHOTON, James O.
SENTER, Miss W. P. JONES, Henry COUNTZ, James ESTES, H. ANDREWS, George WILL-
IAMS, James WOODS, D. MORRIS, Mrs. Jeremiah HALE, John RICE, Wm H. POE, S. L.
HUFFMASTER, Lewis RIGGS, E. MOORE, E. ROGERS, A. B. EDGAR, Wyatt STUBBLEFIELD,
N. McBRIDE, P. M. MILLIKAN, S. D. MILES, TAYLOR & ECHLE, Mary CLARK; notes due:
Harry RIGGS, Harry MEFFORD, John MORRIS, Jas THOMPSON, Chesley BURNETT, Joseph
WESLEY, Clisbe RIGGS, L. D. MILES, Jno F. & Jos NOE, David COX, Willie L. REECE,
Felps RIGGS, S. L. HUFFMASTER, Thos MORRIS, John MORRIS, Thos ELLEDGE, Dr. J.
RHOTON, Rachel MORRIS, J. W. BUNDY (?), Jas C. DAVIS & Massy HILL, Y. I. MORRIS,
James O. SENTER, P. M. MILLIKAN, Gideon MORRIS, Joseph NOE, Jr., Wm D. NELSON,
James B. BOYD, Wyatt STUBBLEFIELD, Joseph NOE, Harry RIGGS, Francis WILLIAMS,
Wm SUNDERLAND, T. W. JONES, Abraham & Joseph COOTEN, L. R. TUDOR, S. RYAN,
Nicholas LONG, Wm H. DANIEL, Thos BROOKS, J. J. NOE, Wm M. PATTON, Jas HUTCHE-
SON, Alex HELTON, Wm F. DANIEL, Wm RAMSEY, Alxd McCLANAHAN, Cyrus JENNINGS,
James S. JENNINGS, Abraham SPOON, Malon SPOON, Isam WALKER, James WILLIAMS,

L. J. RHOTON, J. J. TREECE, George G. READ, W. S. RYAN, J. W. PATTON, Jos.
MORGAN, Hugh K. DUNCAN, J. H. MILLAR & E. BULL, James W. RUSSEL, James H. JONES
& Co., G. W. FRY & Isaac GREGORY, James KNIGHT, Nicholas McBRIDE, Robert DENNIS-
TON, Eliza BOWLIN, Thos W. READ in MO, J. H. MILLAR, Wm S. CREECE, Walter
SHROPSHIRE, R. G. ESTES, Russel CROWE, John BULL, C. B. STAPLES, R. SUMMERS, John
SHAW, Peter SMITH, Wm ORR, Daniel NOE, Wm WILLIAMS, James D. TURNER, Abraham
TOWREY, Elbert HORNER, John L. WHITE, Ezekiel GOAN, Thos GLASCO, Henry HARRISON,
John S. WOODARD, John GARRESTON, M. W. BLACK, Thos REECE, Katherine KIDWELL, Wm
COCKRUM, _____ McALESTER, David NEWEL, Thos M. ANDERSON, Henry WILLIAMS, Garrett
CLARKSON, Wm CLARK, Elisha BOGAN, James HUTCHENS, A. ROWE, Marion MEFFORD,
Edward ALLEN, Peter POPE, James JARNEGIN, Ambrose CARTWRIGHT, David HELTON, Wm
SHROPSHIRE, I. G. L. NEWEL, Jas L. NEAL, W. R. READ, T. D. L. POPE, W. R. KING,
Vincent McKINNY, Robert SHIPLEY, Clisbe RIGGS, John COX, J. H. HILL, T. D. PRICE,
Gideon MORRIS, C. B. STAPLES, John B. CAMRON, Michael LONG, Paschal TURNER,
Horry MEFFORD, Alex McCLANAHAN, Wm A. JETT, John BROWN, Nicholas McBRIDE, Daniel
NOE, Andrew MILES, John M. PATTON, Marvin MEFFORD, Stanford COLLINS, George
EDGAR, D. K. LIVINGSTON. W. V. CLARKSON, D. R. NOE, Robertson WELCH, S. L.
HUFFMASTER, firm of MORRIS, RIGGS & MILLIKAN. Signed T. R. READ & D. MORRIS,
Adms. Recorded 12 Nov 1850 E. TATE, clerk.

p. 282   Inventory - Personal Property of Jehu MORRIS, decd, unsold 1 Nov 1850.
Mentions: an account of Bacon in SC, amt of salt in KY. Signed Thos R. READ,
D. MORRIS, Adms. Recorded 13 Nov 1850 E. TATE, clerk.

p. 284   Account of Sale - Jehu MORRIS, decd. Mentions: C. M. MORRIS, Nich
McBRIDE, M. M. ROGERS, John COOTER, Jeff JONES, A. CARTWRIGHT, Wm Am HARRIS, J.
CLARK, P. J. JONES, J. C. HODGES, M. ARNOT, J. B. JACKSON, P. GODWIN, Jno MORRIS,
Wm CREED, J. B. MOORE, Saml RIGGS, Felps RIGGS, John MORRIS, O. R. WATKINS,
Parott GODWIN, Abraham COOTER, W. STUBBLEFIELD, Geo MOORE, E. WESTER, Harvey
RIGGS, Samuel L. HUFFMASTER, John COX, James SMITH, Thos HODGES, John COOTER, S.
D. WILLIAMS, James O. SENTER, P. A. WITT, Daniel JONES, M. M. ROGERS, W. C.
SCRUGGS, J. B. JACKSON, Wm A. HARRIS, A. MARCHBANKS, Wm B. HEATON, James SMITH,
James KNIGHT, Wm BAKER, George M. LONG, Gordon SATTERFIELD, Wm L. RYAN, John
HUNT, Clisbe RIGGS, Jno W. HEROLD, Daniel TURLEY, P. HORNER, James THOMPSON,
John BALLARD, Lewis RIGGS, Ellis RIGGS, James W. READ, Dr. DOAK, Stokely
WILLIAMS, H. W. TAYLOR, B. SHERWOOD, A. G. GULLY, Benj SMITH, Henry HALE, Jas
KNITE, Benj CLUCK, Harvey STEFFORD, Simp RYAN, Wm TURLEY, James WOOD, Wm C.
SCRUGGS, N. A. READ, Elkany HOSS, Gideon MORRIS, George MOORE, Hu CAIN, Josh
HAZELWOOD, Neal McBRIDE, J. H. GREY, Lewis CARTER, Jos. HAZELWOOD, A. J. GULLY,
Wm BROOKS, Thos JONES, W. STUBBLEFIELD, W. O. SNIDAR, Y. J. MORRIS, W. F. READ,
Edward RIGGS, Jesse HUNT, Jas GRAY, S. D. MILES, E. JACKSON, Thomas JONES,
John H. MILLAR, Geo W. RIGHTSEL, R. E. RICE, David McALESTER, Barnett SMITH,
Thos L. HANES, S. C. ODEL, John HARRIS, Wm P. LONG, James S. NEAL, Pleasant
HORNER, Samuel ODEL, G. CROSBY, Isaac HOGES, Samuel LANE, James LEWIS, George
HAUN, Danl CARMICHAEL, James SMITH, Elijah HAYES, W. S. CREED, Jno LANE, Dr.
RHOTON, John CLARK, Thos BROOKS, James M. RANKIN, Wm WHITE, Emeline MILLIKAN,
J. NEWMAN, P. S. HOSKINS, James GRAY, Jno F. NOE, N. BROOSE, Leburn SENTER,
Dr. HOGAN, David McALESTER, Thomas LAWLESS, N. SHANNON, Wm M. GOAN, George HILL,
Isaac ESTES, Thos GREEN, Ben SHERWOOD, Wm GOAN, John HOLT, David HOLT, T. J.
LEA, Dct HARRIS, James NEAL, Jr., J. F. MIDDLECOFF, M. WALL, W. WALL, P. BOGER,
T. T. MIDDLECOFF, Geo SQUIBB, Jos KIDWELL, Ed JACKSON Amb CARTWRIGHT, Gid
MORRIS, Wyatt STUBBLEFIELD, Wm PROFFIT, R. STUBBLEFIELD, Daniel TAYLOR, Wm

HUMBLE, C. B. STAPLES, Ed RIGGS, Wm S. CREED, Wm HUMMEL, H. HEALE, George RAY, Robt STUBBLEFIELD, Jno MYERS, Jno MILLAR, Henry SMITH, Wm MITCHEL, Martin SUMMERS, Jno INMAN, R. BULL, J. M. PATTON, James NEIL, Richd HUFFMASTER, Wm McFARLAND, Jerry BIVINS, John MILLAR, Jno LAFFERTY, O. BOAZ, Shade INMAN, Jno IVY, Wm MITCHEL, W. WILHELMS, Wm DAVIS, Wm THOMPSON, H. FARBUSH, Frank WILLIAMS, H. B. FAWBUSH, A. ANDREWS. O. BOOZE, Thos K. DODSON, Josh KIDWELL, Andrew MILLS, Wm MILLIKAN, Wm HELMS, Isaac ROGERS, Ches ROGERS, P. J. JARNAGIN, Jno M. DOLTON, Jesse BALLARD, J. FRANKLIN, Peter CLINE, J. J. KING, John HARRIS, Saml LANE. Sales held Sep 3, 4, 5, 6 & Oct 1, 2, 1850. Recorded 14 to 20 Nov 1850.

p. 303   Will - Rebecca CLAY. Having become old & infirmed; possessions left to me by my husband William CLAY in his last will & testament; my beloved son Clement C. CLAY, my Negro boy EPHRAIM; Samuel SHIELDS, Executor. Signed 5 Jan 1846 Rebacka x CLAY. Wit: John A. McKINNY, Harmon G. LEA. Recorded 9 Dec 1850.

p. 304   Commissioners Report - Estate of Isaac DANIEL, 1 yr support to widow & family. Signed 20 Nov 1850 F. B. S. COCKE, Warham EASLEY, Abner x JOLLY. Recorded 10 Dec 1850 E. TATE, clerk.

Commissioners Report - 1 yr support to Nancy WYRICK & family, widow of Martin WYRICK, decd. Signed 6 Nov 1850 Wm SHARP, John H. FORT, William HUBBS, Comms. Recorded 10 Dec 1850 E. TATE, clerk.

Additional Account of Sale - S. E. DODSON, decd. Signed W. H. D. McANALLY, Adm. Recorded 10 Dec 1850 E. TATE, clerk.

p. 305   Guardian Report - Jeremiah JARNAGEN, Guardian of the minor heirs of Joseph H. DAVIS, decd. 27 Nov 1850. Mentions: last report 13 Oct 1847; hire SLAVES to F. TAYLOR 1848, 49; B. CLARK, rent of wards lands 1848; W. ROGERS & CLARK, rent 1848, 49; E. TATE for hire of slave GILBERT 1849, 50; SCRUGGS hire of SLAVES 1850; J. JARNAGIN hire of SLAVES 1850; clothing & schooling wards. Signed Jeremiah JARNAGIN, Guardian, 27 Nov 1850. Recorded 10 Dec 1850.

p. 306   Additional Account of Sale - Andrew BOWEN, decd. Mentions: Willie B. DYER, Nancy BOWEN, James SELLARS, William HOPSON, Peter WOLFINBARGER, David HOPSON, John MALLICOAT, John McNEW, Jackson DYER, Adam IDOL. Signed George SELLARS, Adm. Recorded 10 Dec 1850 E. TATE, clerk.

Will - John LATHIM. My wife, Rachel; my children Thomas, William, John H., Matilda who intermarried with George H. EVANS, Mary who intermarried with Henry WILLIAMS, Martha who intermarried with Michael FARMER, Eveline who intermarried with Aquilla FARMER & the children of Susan, decd, who intermarried with Joseph CLARK; land in Hawkins Co., TN on the Poor Valley Creek; Wm LATHIM, my son, Executor. Signed 7 Arp 1849 John LATHIM. Att: S. S. SHIPLEY, Thos McBROOM, Wm MURRY. Recorded 22 Feb 1851 E. TATE, clerk.

p. 307   Guardian Report - Robert CARDWELL, Sr., Guardian of Jeremiah CHAMBER-LAIN & Elizabeth Jane CHAMBERLAIN minor heirs of Andrew CHAMBERLAIN, decd. 20 Dec 1850. Mentions: last report 7 Aug 1847; rent of wards lands 1849; Samuel N. TATE present Guardian of Elizabeth Jane TATE, formerly Elizabeth Jane CHAMBERLAIN; Harmon G. LEA for surveying; Lea DYER, Commissioner in dividing lands; J. H. DYER, rev col, taxes 1850; J. C. CLARK, rev col, taxes 1849;

also Massy COCKRUM, John CALLISON, John CLARK, Comms. in dividing lands. Signed 20 Dec 1850 Robert CARDWELL, Sr., Guardian. Recorded 23 Jan 1851 E. TATE.

p. 308   Fourth Settlement - Preston MITCHEL, Executor of the Last Will & Testament of Edward CHURCHMAN, decd. 31 Dec 1850. Mentions: last settlement 24 Dec 1849. Recorded 23 Jan 1850 E. TATE, clerk.

p. 309   Guardian Report - John LONG, former Guardian of the minor heirs of David BEELAR, decd. 1 Jan 1851. Mentions: last report 2 Nov 1847; taxes 1847; Jesse F. BEELAR present Guardian. Recorded 23 Jan 1851 E. TATE, clerk.

        Guardian Report - G. B. MITCHEL & Wm MITCHEL, Guardians of the minor heirs of Aquilla MITCHEL, Jr., decd. 30 Dec 1850. Mentions: last report 1 Jan 1850; rents 1849; John STATSWORTH for digging well; Robt Franklin MITCHEL, a ward; J. H. DYER, rev col, taxes 1850. Signed G. B. MITCHEL, Wm MITCHEL, Guardians. Recorded 23 Feb 1851 E. TATE, clerk.

p. 310   First Guardian Report - T. W. TURLEY, Guardian of Margaretta SENTER, appointed Guardian Sep Term County Ct 1849. 1 Jan 1851. Mentions: S. P. SENTER, decd, former Guardian; notes on S. W. SENTER & others (1848), S. W. & P. M. SENTER (1849), S. B. TATE & Wm HAWKINS (1849), James LONG & others (1849), Walter SHROPSHIRE & others (1849), James DAVIS & John LONG (1848); hiring Girl MARY; L. A. GARRETT; hired MARY & child to R. M. BARTON; M. HILL renting lot at Springs; Wm T. TATE for sale of LENA; note on Dr. MURRY (1850); dividing HOGAN SLAVES; rent of HOGAN lands; note on Harry LONG; recd of John OAKLEY BY Const. JONES; recd of J. PERKAPILE by Jonathan NOE; money recd in AL; H. G. LEA for surveying; B. K. CUNNINGHAM for renting P. S. place; John LONG for carrying chain; taxes in Jefferson Co., 11th Dist; R. M. BARTON, Atto fee; Mrs. E. SENTER for board & clothing wards; W. L. LATHIM, clerk. Signed T. W. TURLEY, Guardian 1 Jan 1851. Also 2 Slaves sold - MARY to Samuel GILL & MARIAH to R. M. BARTON. Recorded 23 Jan 1851 E. TATE, clerk.

p. 312   Guardian Report - Lewis M. ELLIS, Guardian of the minor heirs of Thos P. McANALLY, decd. 17 Dec 1850. Mentions: rents of wards land 1850. Signed L. M. ELLIS, Guardian. Recorded 23 Jan 1851 E. TATE, clerk.

        Guardian Report - Benjamin SMITH, Guardian of Juba SMITH & Rachel SMITH. 25 Dec 1850. Mentions: last report 27 Aug 1850; taxes 1850; boarding & clothing Rachel SMITH, the youngest ward, 1850. Signed Benjamin SMITH, Guardian. Recorded 23 Jan 1851 E. TATE, clerk.

p. 313   Guardian Report - Albartes ARWINE who was appointed Guardian of the widow and minor heirs of John SATTERFIELD, decd. 30 Dec 1850. Mentions: selling a Military Land Warrant. Recorded 23 Jan 1851 E. TATE, clerk.

        Inventory - Benjamin PECK, decd. Signed John H. PECK, H. J. DICK, Executors. Recorded 23 Jan 1851 E. TATE, clerk.

p. 314   Inventory - Benjamin PECK, decd. Money & notes on hand. Mentions: notes on Wm COCKE (1849), Thos WALKER & Benjamin WALKER (1848), Jas FURGASON (1849), Joseph NOE (1850), Wm B. CUNNINGHAM (1841), John H. PECK (1846), Wm CLARK (1848), Wm CLEVELAND (1850), Isaac PHILLIPS (1850), John GODWIN (1841).

Signed John H. PECK & H. J. DICK, Executors. Recorded 23 Jan 1851 E. TATE.

        Account of Sale - Benjamin PECK, decd. 21 Nov 1850. Mentions: James
H. PECK, Wm B. CUNNINGHAM, J. P. LEGG, P. J. LEA, Benjamin PECK, Hugh McELHANY,
Jacob GODWIN, Saml LAIN, James GAINS, Wm H. NORTON, James WEST, John DOUGLAS,
Thos WEST, N. L. PECK, Pleasant STARNES, John MALLICOAT, Robt P. MOORE, Michael
GOLDMAN, Wm C. GRAVES, John T. CURLE, Samuel GOINS, John H. PECK, John CAMPBELL,
H. J. DICK. Signed John H. PECK, H. J. DICK, Executors. Recorded 27 Jan 1851.

p. 317   Inventory - Martin WYRICK, decd. Mentions: notes and accts on Wm
BLANSETT, Cardwell LEAMORE, Isaac DAMEWOOD, Moses B. ATKINS, Gilbert VANDAGRIFF,
Sterling CHESNEY, Wm DYER, John BURNETT. Signed 6 Jan 1851 Wm WYRICK, Adm.
Recorded 28 Jan 1851 E. TATE, clerk.

        Account of Sale - Martin WYRICK, decd. Mentions: Pleasant DYER, James
HUNTER, Valentine WYRICK, Thomas McMILLIN, Solomon WYRICK. Signed 20 Nov 1850
Wm WYRICK. Recorded 28 Jan 1851 E. TATE, clerk.

        Inventory - Isaac DANIEL, decd. 23 Nov 1850. Mentions: notes & accts
on Wm DANIEL (1836, 1848), James MAGEE (1849), John DANIEL (1833), Willie B.
McGEE (1836), Alphius OWENS (1843), Wm B. HODGES (1849), Joseph DANIEL (1848),
Absalom CAMRON (1848), J. E. C. HODGES 1850 pd, John DANIEL (1838) payable to
Jerrell D. MAYES; Nicholas NOE (1839) payable to Robert CARDWELL, Henry MAYES
(1841), James ROACH (1841), Loyd COCKRUM (1850), David KITTS (1846, 47), Jarrel
D. MAYES (1847), Thomas MAYES (1833), James BOX payable to Isaac HALL (1836),
Daniel SUNDERLAND payable to Levi SATTERFIELD (1845), Sterling LAY (1837), Thos
WILLIAMS (1841), Charles BROWN & assigned by John IVY (1845), Adam HOPPER (1850),
N. M. JEFFREYS (1848), Mary MORGAN (1843), R. L. TURLEY (no date), Henry TURNER
(1850), Fountain NORTON (1848) to be pad at Centervillforge in Campbell Co. to
William CAIN, Nicholas COUNTZ (1838), Nicholas & Joel KOUNTZ. Signed 6 Jan 1851
B. F. McFARLAND, Adm. Recorded 28 Nov 1851 E. TATE, clerk.

p. 319   List of Accts on 2 School Articles in the hands of Isaac DANIEL at the
time of his Death & came into my hands as Administrator of said Isaac DANIEL,
decd. 23 Nov 1850. Mentions: accounts against R. CARDWELL, Jr., John YOUNG,
John KINDAR, Loyd COCRUM, Anderson CATES, Pierce COODY, Francis YOUNG, William
MANLEY, Stephen FAVER, Sarah FREEMAN, Elizabeth MANLEY, Wm DONEHOO, Jas L.
CHURCHMAN, R. CARDWELL, Sr., F. B. S. COCKE, John POTTER, James MAYES, John
POGUE (Worthless 3.37[2]), Thos WILLIFORD, John BROOKS, Daniel WIDDERS, Wm M.
MOODY, John GRAY for schooling, Isaac PRATT, Jno C. WILLIAMS, Zack GLOSSEP,
James LACY, R. A. WILLIAMS, Saml MARTIN, Wm LACY. Recorded 25 Jan 1850.

p. 320   Account of Sale - Isaac DANIEL, decd. 23 Nov 1850. Mentions: Josiah
KIDWELL, James MAYES, James SUNDERLAND, Alpheus OWENS, Wm PHILIP, J. E. C.
HODGES, Wm M. MOODY, Warham EASLEY, Sr., John DANIEL, Jr., Robert CARDWELL, Jr.,
James LONG, James HOOKER, John MOODY, Sr., Wm DANIEL, Jesse MOODY, Robert
TILLMAN, John A. COCKE, Wm SMITH. Signed B. F. McFARLAND, Adm. Recorded 28
Jan 1851 E. TATE, clerk.

p. 321   Account of Sale - 2 Dec 1850. Estate of John DEVAULT, decd. Mentions:
Samuel WALLACE, Nathaniel PETERS, Samuel SHARP, Lawson DAMEWOOD, John ROBERTSON.
Signed George LAY & G. P. MYNATT, Adms. Recorded 5 Feb 1851 E. TATE, clerk.

Additional Account of Sale - Charles CATES, decd. 25 Apr 1850. H. ALSUP, Esq., D. McKINNY, Esq., Elizabeth CATES. Signed James M. KINDAR, Reuben L. CATES, Adms. Recorded 5 Feb 1851 E. TATE, clerk.

Additional Account of Sale - 16 Jan 1851. Clabourn McCOY, decd. Mentions: Henry HIPSHEAR, Jr. Signed David McCOY, Adm. Recorded 5 Feb 1851.

p. 322   Account of Sale - John MAYES, decd. Mentions: John B. CREWS, Jane MAYES, Faderick MAYES, John OLLIVER, Jennings PEMBERTON, Jesse LIVINGSTON, Elisha THOMASON, Philip HODGES, Edmund PEMBERTON, Edward HODGES, Nimrod CREWS, Pleasant WESTERN, Hugh DUFF, Seth WHITT, John McDANIEL, David RICH, Parrott GODWIN, Jacob GODWIN, Wm HAMMERS, James K. McANALLY, Larkin WHITT, Wm BOATMAN, Alexander JOICE, Thomas SOLOMON, James GREENLEA, William HODGES, John HOLLY, Anderson HOPPER, W. H. DANIEL, James T. CARMICHAEL, John PHILIPS, James HELTON, George GREENLEA, Richard EPPS, Dennis ROBERTS, Emanuel RAY, Richard RAY, John GREENLEA, Reece BOWEN, James LAY, Robert L. TURLEY, James MAYES, Thomas POLLARD, Mary MAY, E. P. WRIGHT, Berry MAYES, accounts against M. L. DANIEL, John MAYES, Wm VAUGHN, John B. CRUSE, Alexd JOICE & John T. ROBERTS. Signed M. L. DANIEL, John MAYES, Adms. Recorded 5 Feb 1851 E. TATE, clerk.

p. 324   Additional Account of Sale - John MAYES, decd. Mentions: Richard RAY, John LACY, Frederick MAY, Larkin WHITT, Edmond PEMBERTON, Philip HODGES, William MAY, John HOLLY, James K. McANALLY, Jane MAYES. Signed M. L. DANIEL, John MAYES, Adms. Recorded 5 Feb 1851 E. TATE, clerk.

p. 325   Inventory - John LATHIM, decd. Signed Wm LATHIM, Executor. Recorded 6 Feb 1851 E. TATE, clerk.

Relinquishment of Claim on Personal Property - Rachel LATHIM, wife of John LATHIM, decd, gives to her sons Thomas & William LATHIM, all the property left to her in deceased husband's Last Will & Testament, with the understanding they sell the property to pay all debts against his estate. Signed Rachel x LATHIM. Wit: C. W. LATHIM, John E. WALKER. Recorded 6 Feb 1851.

Guardian Report - John McNEW, Guardian of the minor heirs of William BOWER, decd. 7 Jan 1851. Mentions: recd of James H. DYER the share of his wards in a NEGRO Boy belonging to the Estate of Andrew BOWERS, decd; last report 16 Aug 1850. Signed John McNEW, Guardian. Recorded 6 Feb 1851 E. TATE.

p. 326   Settlement - Thomas RUSSEL, Adm of the Estate of George C. SPECK, decd. 7 Jan 1851. Mentions: E. TATE, clerk, recpt dated 1 Nov 1847; Mary D. SPECK, widow. Recorded 5 Feb 1851 E. TATE, clerk.

p. 327   Settlement - David WILLIAMS, Executor of John WILLIAMS, decd. 9 Jan 1851. Mentions: Wm WILLIAMS, a son & legatee; James WILLIAMS, a son & legatee; Marie Elizabeth WOLFINBARGER, a dau, & Robert WOLFINBARGER, legatees; notes to Peter WOLFINBARGER, Wm T. TATE & Co., Joseph WILLIAMS, George W. DYER & Hugh FARMER; accounts against this estate: M. CAREGER, Robert FRY, R. CARDWELL, Wm NORTON, M. GOLDMAN, Jacob BEELAR, Wm HILL & Danl W. HURST & others. Recorded 5 Feb 1851 E. TATE, clerk.

p. 328   Guardian Report - Jesse F. BEELAR, Guardian of Cynthia Jane, Mary

Orlena, Matilda Caroline, Martha Elizabeth & Melissa Ann BEELAR, minor heirs.
28 Feb 1851. Mentions: sale of Negro girl CLARESSA; money decreed by Chancery
Ct at Tazwell to them of the Estate of Wm DYER bequeathed to their mother by
said DYER & interest on same for a term of 5 yrs; boarding & clothing wards.
Signed 28 Feb 1851 Jesse F. BEELAR, Guardian. Recorded 10 May 1851 E. TATE.

Guardian Report - Jesse F. BEELAR, Guardian of the minor heirs of David
BEELAR, decd. 28 Feb 1851. Mentions: cash recd from John LONG, former
Guardian, dates 1 Jan 1851; rents for 1846, 47, 48, 49 & 50; 4/9 of a legacy
willed by Wm DYER, decd, to Mary BEELAR, decd & interest from 1 Mar 1846; George
W. BEELAR, a ward & heir of George DYER, decd, said ward hired himself to Jacob
BEELAR; John BULLEN for board at school; Charles RAGAN for tuition; BUCKHANNON
for school books; Robert FRY for clothing; GILL & CLARK for clothing, books,
etc; Katherine & Sarah Margaret, 2 of his wards. Signed Jesse F. BEELAR,
Guardian. Recorded 10 Mar 1851 E. TATE, clerk.

p. 330   Guardian Report - Edward TATE, Guardian of Amanda Ann CHURCHMAN, one of
the heirs of Thomas CHURCHMAN, decd. 26 Feb 1851. Mentions: last report 12
Feb 1849; taxes 1849, 50; sale of wards lands in the landed Estate of Thomas
CHURCHMAN, decd, father of his ward, sold on 21 Dec 1850 by order of Co. Ct;
postage for letters from IN; Margaret CHURCHMAN, the widow & Leavy CHURCHMAN,
a ward, who became of lawful age, sent to them by mail; cash sent by letter to
Amanda Ann CHURCHMAN, a ward. Signed E. TATE, Guardian. Recorded 10 Mar 1851.

p. 331   Settlement - Ausburn COFFEE, Adm of the Estate of N. P. WHITSETT, decd.
28 Feb 1851. Mentions: Elizabeth WHITSETT, widow; Enoch MOBLEY; Dr. Josiah
RHOTON; John HIPSHEAR; Wm COFFEE; John LAFFERTY; Moses McGINNIS; note to Wm
DAY: Colbert HIPSHEAR; Levenia HOPSON; note to George COFFEE; Pendleton TAYLOR;
Hiram TUCKER; note to John RUCKER; Marvel NASH; Joel MILLS; Wm HIPSHEAR; James
BULLEN; Jacob WOLF; Margaret TURNMIRE; Harmon HAYES; W. W. WALKER; Thos COFFEE;
note to Henry WILLIAMS; note to George COFFEE; Solomon MILLIKAN; note to J. &
J. LAFFERTY; note to Enoch JORDAN, George HAYES; Delpha DOLTON; Wm RUCKER;
Sarah M. PARKESSON; Dowel COLLINS; Reuben DOLTON; John WOLF; S. M. EPPERSON;
Henry HIPSHEAR; note to George TUCKER. Recorded 10 Mar 1851 E. TATE, clerk.

p. 333   Second Settlement - Smith STRANGE, Adm of the Estate of Nicholas
NICELY, decd. 17 Feb 1851. Mentions: last settlement 29 Apr 1844; notes on
Benjamin BRANSON (1841 & 42); note on Jeremiah BOWMAN (1840); Isaac PHILLIPS,
Constable, on judgement against decd (1842); Isaac M. LOWE (1844) judgement;
A. P. GREEN, Shff, taxes 1844; Robert CARDWELL; note to Wm M. MOODY; note to
John NANCE; E. THOMASON, taxes 1841; L. M. ELLIS, Dpt Shff, taxes; Wm ARNWINE,
Const, judgement for Willie DYER; John CAMPBELL; John ACUFF, Sr.; note to A.
P. GREEN; note to Campbell GAINS; note to Wm T. TATE & Co.; note to H. JONES.
Recorded 11 Mar 1851 E. TATE, clerk.

p. 334   Settlement - John A. SMITH, Adm of the Estate of Nancy SMITH, decd, &
balance of the Estate of Josiah SMITH, decd. 6 Feb 1851. Mentions: personal
property sales on both decd; John BULLARD; D. F. HUDDLESTON; John COX; Wm T.
CARDEN; Wm COLVIN; Allen HURST; C. M. GOODLIN; Josiah SMITH, an heir; Wm P.
BUCKNER who intermarried with Nancy SMITH, an heir; James B. SMITH, an heir;
Calvin HUDDLESTONE who intermarried with Dorca SMITH, an heir; J. F. HUDDLESTONE
who intermarried with Mary SMITH, an heir; John A. SMITH, Adm & heir; John A.

SMITH, Adm, an heir; R. T. CABBAGE, Constable. Recorded 11 Mar 1851 E. TATE.

p. 335   Guardian Report - John CLARK, Guardian of Leanner McDANIEL, a minor orphan & heir of Lea McDANIEL, decd. 4 Apr 1851. Mentions: last report 29 Mar 1850; rent of wards land 1850; John CALLISON, Adm of the Estate of Lea McDANIEL; Lena Ann McDANIEL for keeping ward; W. L. LATHIM, clerk of Cir Ct, cost for partitioning lands of John McDANIEL, decd; Eli McDANIEL repair fence; Thomas W. TURLEY, Att; Chesley MORGAN. Signed 4 Apr 1851. Recorded 14 Apr 1851.

p. 336   Account of Sale - Sale of lands belonging to the Estate of Charles McANALLY, decd, sold on 6 Apr 1850. Mentions: 100 acres in Poor Vally known as FENDLEY Tract to Thomas WHITESIDE; 1/2 of 160 acres lying in Poor Vally known as the PARTEN Tract to Samuel B. TATE; 1/2 of 135 acres lying in the 3rd Civil Dist to Reuben GROVE. Signed D. R. McANALLY & D. McANALLY, Executors. Recorded 15 Apr 1851 E. TATE, clerk.

Inventory - 5 Mar 1851. John CAPPS, decd. Signed Wm DAVIS, Adm. Recorded 15 Apr 1851 E. TATE, clerk.

p. 337   Account of Sale - John CAPPS, decd. Mentions: Charles RAGAN, Wm GRIMES, Wm WALTERS, John HAUL, J. C. CAPPS, Thomas WALTERS, John CABBAGE, Wm NICELY, Wm WAGGONER, Abraham HAYNES, Melton McPHETTRIDGE, Jesse RAGAN, Henry NEEDHAM. Signed 28 Mar 1851 Charles RAGAN, Joab C. CAPPS, Clerks. Wm DAVIS, Adm. Recorded 15 Apr 1851 E. TATE, clerk.

p. 338   Account of Sale - 22 Mar 1851. Abner LOWE, decd, sale. Mentions: A. K. LOWE, Barton LOWE, E. LOWE, Edward LOWE, Samuel WEST, Sr., Wm M. MOODY, Mrs. MAPLES, Wm SMITH, W. P. WHITLOCK, Looney LOWE, Wm MAPLES, Isaac M. LOWE, James PECK, James FURGASON, James MAPLES, Saml WEST, Jr., James PATTERSON, James PECK, Thos H. PASCHAL, Wm SMITH, Lunah LOWE. Signed William J. LOWE, Adm. Recorded 15 Apr 1851 E. TATE, clerk.

p. 339   Inventory - Mrs. Rabecca CLAY, decd. Mentions: Negro man EPHRAIM; accounts against the Estate of Samuel BUNCH, decd; Wm P. JONES, decd, for money retained while he was acting as Pension agent for Rebecca CLAY & proved by Rabecca C. LEA, 1847; Negro child ADALINE, a bill of sale from E. HIGHTOWER, 1846, who was never in hands of decd; witness W. L. A. HIGHTOWER & S. S. MASSENGIL; accts on S. H. BUNCH, John BOYLES & Charles M. LEA. Signed Saml SHIELDS, Executor. Recorded 15 Apr 1851 E. TATE, clerk.

Account of Sale - William CLAY, decd. Mentions: a Will Annexed, & property sold as per Last Will & Testament; sell held 20 Jan 1851 & 21 Mar 1851; Preston MITCHEL, Robert G. GAINS, John A. McKINNY, Wm E. NANCE, G. C. McBEE, J. T. MITCHEL, H. G. LEA, B. E. GAINS, Henry ETTER, C. B. NANCE, Wylie FIELDING, and GRAHAM, C. C. CLAY, Sr. - bought Negroes HARRIETT, ELIZABETH, EMALY & ADALINE, Wm P. KENDRICK, who brought Negros - woman MILLA, man JACK, BRADOCK, EMALY, JUDA & MARY, C. C. GREEN who bought Negros MARY, RICHMOND, BALTIMORE, CORDELIA, MARGARET & EMALY, L. DAMEWOOD, James MAPLES, A. DOLIN, Jas DANWIDDY, Thos NUGEN, Daniel GOWANS, Nelson MYNATT, Henry ALSUP, H. DUFF, H. N. DALE, James SHEROD, Val WYRICK, Wm DONAHOO, Alvis McMILLAN, Wm HIGHTOWER, James DYER, Sr., J. JARNAGAN, Benjamin PECK, Nancy HIGHTOWER, E. TATE, Joshua D. CURLE, Wm POPEJOY, Wm E. NANCE, J. H. SHIELDS, P. SHIRLEY, Thos WALKER, Wm DENNIS, Isaac

MITCHEL, Mrs. C. GREEN, J. B. GRIGSBY, M. FURGASON, Bill by Jono RENFROW (1839).
Signed Saml SHIELDS, Adm. Recorded 15 Apr 1851 E. TATE, clerk.

p. 343   Inventory - Elizabeth CLARK, decd. 1 May 1851. Mentions: David BRAN-
SON, Adm of the Estate of Elizabeth CLARK, decd, has hired 2 NEGRO's belonging
to the heirs of Wm CLARK & Elizabeth CLARK, decd, to Daniel BEELAR; Leroy CLARK
to pay taxes on hiring the Servants CYNTHIA & FREDERICK; notes on Thomas MAJORS,
Elijah JONES, Benjamin BRANSON & Nicholas SATTERFIELD. Signed David BRANSON,
Adm. Recorded 14 May 1851 E. TATE, clerk.

    Account of Sale - 27 Sep 1851, Elizabeth CLARK, decd. Mentions: Leroy
CLARK, Joseph CLARK, Harrison BROWN, John CLARK, Daniel SMITH, Joseph BEELAR,
Calvin KIRK, L. M. ELLIS, John JOHNSON, Pleasant O. JENNINGS, Benjamin BRANSON,
George W. JENNINGS, Pleasant STARNES, Harber LEFFEW, Lewis BRANSON, William
BARKER, James DOLTON, David HIPSHEAR, Barney G. SIMPSON. Signed John CLARK,
James CLARK, David N. SANDERS, Benjamin BRANSON, Clerks. David BRANSON, Adm.
Recorded 14 May 1851 E. TATE, clerk.

p. 344   Inventory - State of TN, Gr Co., I certify that I have made a deligent
inquiry & cannot find any of the goods, chattles, rights & credits of Andrew
BOWER, decd, the former Adm having taken into his possession & sold all the
Goods and Chattles, Rights & Credits of said Decd & refuses to hand over the
proceeds of said sale. Signed 6 May 1851 L. M. ELLIS, Adm. Sworn to in Open
Court May Term 1851. E. TATE, clerk.

p. 345   Guardian Report - George WILLIAMS, Guardian of the minor heirs of John
M. WILLIAMS, decd. 20 Apr 1851. Mentions: last report 23 Feb 1850; sale of
lands; rents & taxes on Panther Creek 1847-1851. Signed 23 Feb 1851 George
WILLIAMS, Guardian. Recorded 16 May 1851 E. TATE, clerk.

p. 346   Settlement - Colby DOLTON, Executor of the Estate of Meredith DOLTON,
decd. 27 Jan 1851. Mentions: Wm RUCKER; Delpha DOLTON notes to C. M. & D. L.
COFFIN; Richard COOPER; Saml GILL; Forababel HARVEY; James MOUNTAIN; Azariah
DOLTON; Thomas DOLTON, a legatee; Claburn RUCKER, a legatee; James McGINNIS, a
legatee; John W. DOLTON, a legatee; A. B. DOLTON, a legatee; John W. DOLTON,
Guardian of Carter & Margaret DOLTON, 2 minor heirs; George W. HAYES, a
legatee; And DOLTON & John W. DOLTON, Guardian of Carter & Margaret DOLTON; Jon
W. DOLTON, a legatee; James McGINNIS, a legatee. Recorded 16 May 1851 E. TATE.

    Additional Inventory - Abner LOWE, decd. Mentions: notes on Thomas
MAPLES; acct on Wm J. LOWE; judgement on Thomas WALKER & Benjamin WALKER in the
name of Samuel RIGHT for the use of Isaac M. LOWE rendered before Samuel WEST,
Esq. in Chancery Ct at Rutledge 1850; note on Abraham LOWE. Signed William J.
LOWE, Adm. Recorded 16 May 1851 E. TATE, clerk.

p. 348   Settlement - Paschal L. JARNAGIN, Executor of the Estate of Noah
JARNAGIN, decd. 15 Apr 1851. Mentions: bequest to son George R. JARNAGIN in
the Last Will & Testament; note to Wm P. JONES. Recorded 16 May 1851.

    Commissioners Report - 1 yr support to Catherine WOLF, widow of Moses
WOLF, decd. Signed A. DOLTON, Maldin LADDY, William McCOY, Comm. Recorded
9 Jun 1851 E. TATE, clerk.

p. 349   Inventory - Stephen JONSON, decd. Mentions: notes on S. YATES & James
SHIELDS (1847), James SHIELDS & John HARRIS, Esq. (1847), James HODGES (1843),
George PILANT (1848), Joseph HICKS (1843), Hardy JOHNSON (1844 & 1845); SLAVES -
1 man 50 to 53 yrs, woman 50 to 60 yrs. Signed 25 Jan 1849 Hardy JOHNSON &
Larkin JOHNSON, Executors. Recorded 9 Jun 1851 E. TATE, clerk.

p. 350   Commissioners Report - 1 yr support to Rhoda MORGAN, widow of Allen D.
MORGAN, decd, & family. Signed 24 May 1851 William SMITH, James FURGASON,
Richard FURGASON, Comm. Recorded 9 Jun 1851.

        Inventory - Allen D. MORGAN, decd. 5 May 1851. Mentions: notes on
Levi SATTERFIELD. Signed 31 May 1851 Massy COCKRUM, Adm. Recorded 9 Jun 1851.

p. 351   Account of Sale - A. D. MORGAN, decd. 24 May 1851. Mentions: Robert
N. CORUM, Edward P. MORGAN, Wm A. MORGAN, John KINDAR, John CALLISON, Eli McDAN-
IEL, Jr., Rhoda MORGAN, Albert DAVIS, Allen D. MORGAN, James FURGASON, Samuel
CALLISON, James JAMES, Philip SNIDER. 31 May 1851 Massy COCKRUM, Adm. Recorded
9 Jun 1851 E. TATE, clerk.

p. 352   Settlement - W. H. D. McANALLY, Adm of the Estate of S. E. DODSON, decd.
30 May 1851. Mentions: Note on James H. LANDMAN; sale 15 Oct 1849, 18 Nov 1849
& 18 Oct 1850; Wm A. BROWN; E. L. TATE; Henry GROVE; Wm T. TATE; James DODSON;
RICE & McFARLAND; George BASSETT; notes to J. SUNDERLAND, Landon CARTER, Wm T.
TATE & Co. & W. H. D. McANALLY. Recorded 9 Jun 1851 E. TATE, clerk.

p. 353   5th and Final Settlement - John HUBBS & Stephen FROST, Executors of John
HILL, decd. 17 May 1851. Mentions: Wm HILL; Joseph HILL, Const; last settlement 3 Oct 1845; Wm DENNIS, Guardian of the minor heirs of John HILL, decd;
judgement against Wm HILL & Jas VITTETOE; suit Able HILL vs Executor. Recorded
9 Jun 1851 E. TATE, clerk.

p. 354   Settlement - David McANALLY & David R. McANALLY, Executors of Charles
McANALLY. 6 May 1851. Mentions: note to Samuel GILL; Thos P. & James M.
McANALLY; note to James BARNETT & pd by Executors, it being due by Charles
McANALLY as Adm of James M. McANALLY, decd; notes to Jacob SHOULTZ & Wm
WILLIAMS; James K. McANALLY; C. W. F. McANALLY; John GODWIN; Evan B. SPENCER;
Wm A. BROWN; Hamilton EVANS; James ASBURY; BROWN & COX; J. P. EVANS; Wm PAYNE;
Anderson CARDEN; M. CARRIGER; James M. HAYES; Wm C. MALLICOAT; Pleasant HOLT;
Lewis HARMON; Calvin HARRELL; James CLARK, rev coll, taxes 1849; J. H. DYER,
rev coll, taxes 1850; W. EASLEY, Jr.; L. M. ELLIS, Shff; Sally RUSSELL; Saraphina
HAYES & James M. HAYES, legatees; Henry WILLIAMS, Guardian of Elizabeth PROCTOR
formerly Elizabeth WILLIAMS, a legatee; note to James & Wm WILLIAMS; judgement
vs Thos S. COCKE & Charles McANALLY; note to Wm T. TATE & Co.; note to Ethelred
WILLIAMS; Jacob GODWIN; Wm DODSON, a legatee; notes on Pendleton TAYLOR, Wm H.
ODEL, Pleasant JENNINGS, Henry GAMBLE, Wm ROGERS, Thomas CRAWSBY, Dandridge
TACKER, Colby COFFEE, John SHIRLEY, A. & A. HELTON, Thomas ADAMS & Robert
MURPHY. Recorded 10 Jun 1851 E. TATE, clerk.

p. 356   Guardian Report - Pleasant DYER, Guardian of the minor heirs of Isaac
DYER, decd. 6 Jun 1851. Mentions: Joseph HILL, Adm; Hampton DYER, a ward;
taxes. Signed Pleasant x DYER, Guardian. Recorded 17 Jul 1851 E. TATE, clerk.

p. 357   Second Settlement - Clesbe RIGGS & Shadarick INMAN, Adm of the Estate
of Ellis RIGGS, decd.   17 Jun 1851.   Mentions: last settlement 28 Aug 1850;
Edward RIGGS surviving trustee of the Slave FILL, formerly belonging to the
Estate of Clesbe RIGGS, Sr., decd; note to Wm H. RIGGS; John F. NOE, Dpt Shff;
judgement against Wm H. RIGGS, Clisbe RIGGS & others in the Circuit Ct of
Hawkins Co.; Adaline RIGGS, widow & relict of Ellis RIGGS, decd, 1 yr support
dated 18 Aug 1850; Elisha BULL.   Recorded 17 Jul 1851 E. TATE, clerk.

p. 358   Additional Account of Sale - Jehu MORRIS, decd, sold at public auction
15 May 1851.   Mentions: Wm S. CREED, Wm HARRIS, Saml HUFFMASTER, E. D. HOSS,
R. STUBBLEFIELD, Thos LAWLES, J. B. JACKSON, S. RIGGS, John F. NOE, S. D.
WILLIAMS, John HOLT, Wm MOORE, Wm LYMAN, Jos SHANNON, M. M. ROGERS, John MILLAR,
James MOORE, R. RIGGS, G. MOORIS, Ambrose CARTWRIGHT, Henry MEFFORD, N. F. READ,
Newton SHANNON, Will HELMS, Wm DAVIS, Jas THOMPSON, Jr., Wyatt STUBBLEFIELD,
Daniel NOE, John INMAN, Jas WITT, Horry MEFFORD, Shields DYER, H. W. TAYLOR, F.
W. TAYLOR, S. D. WILLIAMS, Gideon MORRIS, James MOORE, John B. JACKSON, Stodely
WILLIAMS, James KING, Jas NEAL, Sr., Col. GREGORY, Simpson RYAN, Ben SHERWOOD,
E. RIGGS, James Moore TAYLOR, John FLOWERS, Wm RYAN, Robert BUMBAS, H. H.
HUBBARD, John CLARK, Russel RIGGS, Jno ANDERSON, Jno MILLAR, J. B. MOORE, T. W.
TAYLOR, James BROWN, James KENNER, B. EDGAR, Ed RIGGS, Wm D. SHURMAN, Jacob
HODGES, Thos DOTSON, James O. SENTER, Saml LANE, W. B. LYMAN, Lea WITT, James
ESTES, Andrew MILES, B. ELLEDGE, R. LONG.   Signed T. R. READ & Drury MORRIS,
Adms.   19 Jul 1851 E. TATE, clerk.

p. 362   Settlement - Parrott GODWIN & B. F. McFARLAND, remaining Comm. appt to
superintend building new Courthouse. Mentions: report made by Thomas WHITESIDE,
Robert LOYD & Martin CLEVELAND in Apr 1849; J. C. CLARK, former Rev. Coll; John
DAMRON, Contractor; J. H. DYER, Rev. Col.; note held by E. TATE to the Trustees
of Madison Acadamy; notes to John DAMERON; Wm T. TATE & Co. for money loaned for
use of said House; entire contract cost 2,125.23.   Recorded 22 Jul 1850 E. TATE.

p. 363   Will - John NEEDHAM. My wife Nancy NEEDHAM; at her d. divided property
among her 7 children as she wishes; my dau Lousany & Margaret, Rebecca, Louisa,
Mariam & Martha; land on Creek running to George SEAMORE; my son Zachariah; my
2 sons Ira & John; Katherine WOLFINBARGER, my dau to receive $15 from Ira;
Elizabeth VITTITOE (no relation given) to receive $15 from John; my wife Nancy
NEEDHAM & Deadman NASH, sole Executors.   Signed 17 Mar 1851 John NEEDHAM.   Att:
Steven ATKINS, Andrew J. NASH.   Recorded 9 Aug 1851 E. TATE, clerk.

        Guardian Report - Lewis ATKINS, Guardian of the minor heirs of Nathan
ATKINS, decd.   11 Jan 1851.   Mentions: last report 31 May 1850; pd Joel DYER
for spelling book & clothing for Lewretta ATKINS, Ira ATKINS & Talbot ATKINS,
wards; EASLEY & Co. for goods.   Recorded 9 Aug 1851 E. TATE, clerk.

p. 364   Will - Thomas WHITESIDES. Being feeble; my trusty friends John NETHER-
LAND & Thomas Whitesides TURLEY, Executors; lands contained in the English Grant
known as the Beanstation tract in 2 entrys made by Joseph COBB & conveyed by
COBB to Jenkins WHITESIDE; land purchased by me of John PROFFIT & another of
Joseph PROFFET; land entered by Wm WHITESIDE; land bought of the Estate of
McANALLY & SENTER in Poor Valley adjoining David HOLT; mentions tavern, grist
mill leased to James LINDAMOOD, contract with Lawson LONG & his son John, lands
in Middle TN & sell all SLAVES except DANIEL & JENNY who are to be supported

for the rest of their lives & goes into detail how and what is to be sold; my
sister, Issabelle McGOLDRICK; my nephew Thomas C. WHITESIDE; John NETHERLAND &
T. W. TURLEY, Guardians of my children & grandchildren to age 21; my little son
who bears a name endeared to me, Jinkin, to engage in legal profession if he
desires; my dau Eliza Jane to go to the Odd Fellow Collegate Institution at
Rogersville; my son William also the law; my son, David WHITESIDE; my dau
Harriett; my son Thomas, the elder; my son Thomas the younger; my children:
David WHITESIDE, Thomas the elder, William, Eliza Jane, Thomas the younger,
Harriett, Richard, Issabella, Lucy, Jenkins & James & my grand son Thomas A.
DONALSON, my grand son Francis LINDAMOOD, son of my dau Mary. Signed 10 Jun
1851 Thos WHITESIDE. Wit: Saml B. TATE, Reuben GROVE, Jr., Jos B. HASKELL.
          Codicil - give & bequeath land rented to Mr. SHIPLEY to Wm M. COCKE,
James T. SHIELDS, Levi CAMPBELL, Wm MURRY & T. W. TURLEY as Trustees, Presby-
terian Church to be erected. Signed 21 Jul 1851 Thos WHITESIDE. Wit: S. S.
SHIPLEY, J. R. McCURRY. Recorded 11 & 12 Aug 1851 E. TATE, clerk.

p. 373   Settlement - Jacob BEELAR, Adm of the Estate of Martin CLEVELAND,
decd. 14 Jul 1851. Mentions: personal property sales 5 Sep 1849 & 11 & 12 Dec
1851; rents of ferry boats; steed horse book; sale 19 Jul & 28 Sep 1850; John
BRANSON; note to Tandy WOLFINBARGER, Guardian; J. W. BRANSON & John CLARK,
clerks at sales; John CHANDLER; John LONG; Benjamin C. ACUFF; Robert W. WATSON;
Anna CLEVELAND, widow, 1 yr support; Clabourn ACUFF; Wm T. TATE; state tax &
fee for stud license 1849; note to John P. JENNINGS; L. M. ELLIS, Shff, as
Security of B. W. SCOTT for fine; James C. CLARK, Rev Coll, 1849; Alexander
HAMILTON; Deadman NASH; Wm HUBBS; Stephen ATKINS; George SEEMORE; Barry KERB;
bill due to John LONG; Wm SHARPS & Saml CLARK; Jacob GODWIN; note to Andrew
BEELAR, Guardian; T. W. TURLEY, Atto; note to Robt FRY; Robt P. MOORE & Joseph
CLARK for laying off widow support; James C. STRANGE; Wm M. CLEVELAND; Daniel
WIDDER; John D. HOLLY; James DOLTON, Constable; Pheba SHARP; Dr. J. P. LIGG;
note to A. P. GREEN; John C. CLARK & A. M. CLEVELAND; James A. WAGONER; John
BOILES; M. CLEVELAND, Guardian of the minor heirs of Wm HAYES, decd; Dr. John
B. GRIGSBE: David A. BRYAN; John NEEDHAM; Smith STRANGE; James GRAY; Joseph
WILLIAMS; James H. STARNES; R. WOLFINBARGER; Jonas NICELY; John CHANDLER; Mary
MYERS; Robert CARDWELL; note to John NANCE; note to James DAVIS; note to Wm P.
JONES surviving partner of R. M. SCUGGS & Co.; note to Jno A. McKINNY; joint
note with P. STARNES to Jacob BEELAR, Executor of the Estate of Henry MEYERS,
decd; note to Ethelred WILLIAMS; Daniel HAYNES, Guardian of the minor heirs of
Wm HAYNES, decd, M. CLEVELAND, decd, former Guardian; John H. CARDWELL, Const.;
Thos J. JOHNSON, Clk of the Co Ct of Clabourn Co. & John EASLEY, Esqr; note to
James & Wm WILLIAMS; note to J. & J. B. CLEVELAND; James W. LINDAMOOD; RICE &
McFARLAND; note to Wm T. TATE & Co.; Jno Millar McKEE; note to Madison County;
George MYERS; L. M. ELLIS, taxes, 1842 & 43; Allen HURST; Wm COLVIN, Esqr.; Wm
TEDFORD; Eli CLEVELAND; John BOILES; J. J. HERRELL; Wm HERRON; W. L. LATHIM,
clerk; Wm M. CLEVELAND one of the Adm to 1 Monday of Sep 1850, the time he
resigned; note to John BEELAR; G. W. LEWIS; Kenada HILL; John COX; note to Thos
McBROOM, Guardian of the minor heirs of John DENNIS, decd; note to Jacob BEELAR:
Wm T. TATE, Guardian of Martin A., Eli M., Green F., Martha E. & Robert H.
CLEVELAND, minor heirs; Kenada HILL & Mary HILL, formerly Mary CLEVELAND, an
heir; Matilda CLEVELAND, an heir; L. M. ELLIS, Atto in fact for Aly & Pleasant
JENNINGS, an heir; Green BUNDEN, Guardian of Eliza BUNDEN, formerly Eliza
CLEVELAND & Atto in fact for John A. CLEVELAND & Wm M. CLEVELAND for part of
their distrubterie shares; Jacob BEELAR & his wife, Nancy, formerly Nancy

CLEVELAND, an heir; note on Royal JENNINGS. Recorded 18 Aug 1851 E. TATE, clerk.

p. 377   Settlement - Beanstation Turnpike Commissioners. Year 1850. Mentions:
last settlement 1 Jan 1850; A. M. McGINNIS, Gatekeeper; D. McANALLY, as Executor
of Charles McANALLY, decd; overseers Danl G. MILLAR, Henry WILLIAMS; commers
John HARRIS, C. W. LATHIM, Hugh JONES, Wm B. CUNNINGHAM, Jacob GODWIN. Signed
12 Jul 1851 Wm B. CUNNINGHAM, W. L. LATHIM, J. GODWIN, Comms. Recorded 19 Aug
1851 E. TATE, clerk.

p. 378   Inventory - Estate of Col. Thomas WHITESIDE, decd. Mentions: notes
due on Green BURDEN (1846, 47), M. B. DOLTON (1847), Redman BIRD (1842), W. L.
EVANS, Wm HIGHTOWER, E. JONES & Jonathan HODGES (?) (1850), L. A. GARRETT (1845),
David NOE (1842), by Reuben GROVE to Levi LONG (1851), J. K. McANALLY (1843), T.
W. TURLEY by Hardy LONG (1842), Harmon LEA (1846), H. WILLIAMS (1847), W. L.
LATHIM (1851), Harmon G. LEA (1851), Andrew McGINNIS & Green BUNDEN (1848),
Joseph NOE, Jr. (1846), E. THOMASON (1851), S. S. SHIPLEY (1844), T. W. TURLEY
(1844), Jacob NOE & Wm T. TATE, security (1850), A. P. GREEN (1843), A. COFFEE
(1844), Hillard BIRD (1842), Reuben DOLTON (1848), Marine DUVAL (1842), Hardy
LONG (1840), James LACY (1842), by Green BUNDEN to Huffare (?) WHITE (1844),
Nancy HENDERSON (1842), John A. McKINNY (1841), Charles McGINNIS (1844), John
L. PERRY (1848), Josiah RHOTON (1842), D. HARRIS & Peter MEEKS (1848), H.
HARRIS (1850), T. L. HARRIS (1849), H. WILLIAMS & Wm DODSON (1844), Hamilton
EVANS (1842), T. P. McANALLY & P. HOLT (1844), G. W. JENNINGS (1850), John B.
CREWS (1842), C. W. LATHIM (1838), Isaac BULLEN (1842), F. H. BRACKER (1841),
John CREACH & Henry HIPSHEAR (1842), John MATHEWS (1842), Henry HIPSHEAR (1844),
John COFFEE (1841), Harvy MILLS (1849), Peter HOPPER (1842), James K. McANALLY
(1834), Wm JONES (1844), James McGINNIS (1842), Joseph McGINNIS (1841), R.
SULLENBARGER & John MAYES (1848), James SHIELDS (1848), C. COFFY (1849) Aaron Mc
McGINNIS (1844), B. H. BAGWELL (1841), D. HARRIS & Peter MEEKS (1844), Henry
BOWEN (1840), James CHECK (1844), Saml BOWERS (1847), Ben COFFY (1844), Jeremiah
BOWMAN (1846), Nimrod CREWS (1846), Edward DAVIS (1840), M. BROMAN (1842),
Diannah CONN (1842), John HARVEL (1847), W. D. COIN (1842), Robt G. BAREKLEY
(1842), A. C. EATON (1842), Jno A. ANDERSON (1842), Rabecca DANIEL (1842), Thos
ELLEDGE (1842), W. G. McDANIEL (1842), Wm McCROWE (1844), CLOUD & GRAY (1849),
Martin GREENLEA (1841), Thos LAWLESS (1846), Henry JENNINGS (1842), Jno LONG
given by R. M. YANCY (1841), Parmelia LYNN (1842), Robt M. LUCKY (1840), James
JOICE (1842), John KIDWELL (1843), James KENNER (1840), Wm ELDER (1843), John
HICKSON (1841), John LONG (1837, 40), Jacob LONG (1840), Lawson A. LONG (1841),
M. HART & M. MORELY (1840), ABNER GRIPHIN (1842), Nicholas HAYNES (1842), James
C. HODGES (1841), Levi LONG (1843), N. B. HUDNELL (1841), L. K. GRAY (1841),
James C. JONES (1843), Bosh HARVEY (1843), Abel LAWLES (1840), David MILES
(1841), John MYNATT (1843), Thomas McGOLDRICK (1842), A. R. SULLENBARGER & W.
W. NIXON (1842), Wm McGOLDRICK (1840), Ab MILLAR & T. WATSON (1839), Jos NANCE
(1842), John NEWMAN (1841), Ab MILLAR (1842), Larkin McNEIL (1841), George W.
RICH (1839), George B. ROGERS (1841), Jas PENNINGTON (1844), Joseph PROFFIT
(1843), Saml M. POLLARD (1842), Ab SPOON (1842), H. YOUNG & Thos ROBERTSON
(1840), Walter SHROPSHIRE (1841), W. B. SNELSON (1841), Abijah WELLFORD (1838),
Richard SINGLETREE (1844), A. G. SULLENBARGER (1841), Wm SANDERS (1842), A. R.
SULLENBARGER (1842), Charles WILBOURN (1841), Wm WOLF (1844), L. WEBB & Jas
McDANIEL (1842), Thos WILLFORD & James CROWE (1841), James WATSON (1843), Jos
A. WALKER (1845) N. P. WHITSETT (1842), J. WILLSON (1841), Thomas NASH (1841),
Amos STROUD & Thos STROUD (1838), John HICKSON given to Jno KIDWELL (1840),

Elizabeth COX given to J. B. CREWS (1838), P. B. COBB given to David COUNTZ &
by him assigned to E. WILLIAMS (1833), Stephen DANIEL & C. W. LATHIM (1831),
Robert MARTIN (1841), T. M. ANDERSON (1842), Spenser BASSETT (1841 & 1842),
John HICKSON (1844 & 1841); accounts & claims due the Estate on C. M. RENAU for
keeping state horses & blacksmithing, S. S. SHIPLEY for oil & carriage (1849),
John NETHERLAND for hogs, Wm M. WILLIAMS, Wm E. COCKE former clerk, JAMES &
JONES for boarding self & family (1849), Hugh JONES, E. THOMASON, Wm PROFFITT,
J. M. BLAND to pay David WHITESIDE, Reuben GROVE, Green BURDEN to pay Jacob
GODWIN; receipts from collecting officers: Wm HAMMONS, Cons, notes of Peter
OGAN (1842), E. THOMASON, Shff, for 3 executions against Ausburn COFFEY (1847),
George R. WARD, Const., notes on James BARRETT (1842) & Farrer ROSE (1842),
Thomas LATHIM, Const, notes on Pleasant JENNINGS (1842 & 1841), A. McCONNEL
note on John COX (1842), Charles BROOKS (1841), Rowland McGILL (1840), John
McGILL (1841), John HELTON, Jr. (1840 & 41), Thos HILL (1841), A. P. GREEN, Dpt
Sheff, notes on John DUNAVANT (1841), Wm HAYES, Const, note on Riley MILLS
(1842), Abr McCONNEL note on George HOPPER (1841) & Joseph LYNN, Thos LATHIM,
Const, note on Thomas HAYES (Creek) (1840, 1841), John T. CURLE, Const, notes
on F. B. S. COCKE (1842) & T. S. COCKE (1842), R. LOYD, Shff, note on George
MATLOCK (1842), Thos LATHIM, Const, note on And COLLINS (1839), Wm HAYES, Const,
notes on Thos EVANS (1841), Hezekiah MILLS (1842), Abr McCONNEL note on Henry
LONG (1840) with judgement for balance at Jos RICHES, M. L. DANIEL, Const, notes
on John OAKLEY (1841), Thomas JOICE (1841), Goodwin SOLOMON (1841), Richard
PEMBERTON (1842), Hudson PEMBERTON (1841), Edmund PEMBERTON (1840), Thomas STROUD
(1842), John MAYES (1842), Joel MILLS, Const, account on Semion R. FROST, R.
LOYD, Shff, note on Wm MAYES, Sr. (1842), Wm PHILLIPS (1841), Thos C. POLLARD
(1841), P. J. JEFFREYS (1842), Wm PHILLIPS (1843), Thos LATHIM, Const, note on
Thomas McANALLY (1842), D. McANALLY note on Thomas McGOLDRICK (1842), R. LOYD,
Shff, notes on Elizabeth & Wm P. JACK (1841), John HOWELL (1842), Thomas LATHIM,
Const, note on W. HARVELL (1842), E. THOMASON, Shff, notes on John CHANEY (1840),
Nimrod CREWS (1839 & 1840), A. P. GREEN, D. Shff, notes on Thos ACUFF (1842),
John MALLICOAT (1842), Enoch MOBLEY (1842), James NASH (1841), Wm NASH (1841),
Edmund MASON (1842), Nathl MALLICOAT (1843), Wm OWENS (1842), John MALLICOAT
(1843), M. MAYERS & Jno McGINNIS (1841), Winwright ATKINS (1843), Joshua COX
(1843), Clabourn BULL (1843), Harrison ATKINS (1842), Aaron COLLINS (1842), Thos
P. McANALLY (1843), James JONES (1840), John HIPSHEAR (1842), Henry HIPSHEAR,
Jr. (1843), Hiram HAYES (1838, 1840 & 1842), Cobert HIPSHEAR (1842), Jacob
HIPSHEAR (1842), Thomas LAYCOCKE (1842), _____ MOOR (1842), Tandy DOLTON (1842),
Thos DOLTON (1842 & 1841), Enoch DOLTON (1840), S. PARKISSON & H. HIPSHEAR
(1842), Wm TAYLOR (1841), Pendleton TAYLOR (1843), Colbert HAYES (1842), Wm
HIPSHEAR (1842), Geo W. HAYES (1842), Zerabell HARVEY (1841), A. P. GREEN, Dpt
SHFF, notes on W. G. McDANIEL (1841), Henry JOICE (1842), James WESTERN (1839 &
1842), Proyor BIBA (1841 & 1842), E. THOMASON, Shff, notes on Samuel POLLARD
(1841), John FLORA (1841), Daniel FLORA (1841), Wm MAYES (1840), Thos LATHIM,
Const, notes on Elisah WALKER (1841 & 1842), Elisha WALKER (1841), Lewis TILLY
(1841), Christopher COLLINS (1841), John CREACH (1841), Duncan COLLINS (1847),
Wm WOLF (1841), Thos LATHIM, Const, notes on Aquilla PAYNE (1842), Simeon
ACUFF (1842), T. D. ACUFF (1842), Abendigo FARMER (1841), Edley DOLTON (1842),
George R. WARD, Constable, notes on Robert BENNETT (1841), Hiram BUNDEN executed
to John GODWIN (1840 & 1842), J. GODWIN note on Daniel NOE (1845), Wm DONALSON,
D. Shff, who has been decd several years, note on H. ATKINSON (1841), H. ARNETT
(1840). Articles of agreement - copartnership in Mercantile Business at Thorn-
hill between Thos. WHITESIDE, Andrew McGINNIS & C. W. LATHIM (1839), Thomas

WHITESIDE & John WALKER, WALKER to rent Beanstation Tavern (1843), LAFFERTY,
WHITESIDE & S. S. SHIPLEY renting a house at the old store (1843) & SHIPLEY
renting Beanstation Tavern for 5 yrs from 1 Mar 1851, also renting tan yard,
WHITESIDE & WYATT renting store for 5 yrs from 1 Aug 1850, Green BUNDEN purch-
ase of Hogs for self & WHITESIDE. List of personal property & Slaves NIMROD,
ISAAC, PAT, WASH, BUCK, JOHN, HARRY, CALVIN, MANDY, MARTHA, DORCAS & 5 children
(namely DEB, JOE, DAN, SOL & WILLIE), CLARY & 4 children (namely LAURA, JIM,
DAVID & MARIAH), MARY & 2 children (namely WILLIAM & MARY), SAM & family (to wit
POLLY, his wife, & 4 children named LAURA, SYNTHY, LEA & PRESTON). Old Slaves
DANIEL & JENNY are to be supported by estate. Lands: Beanstation tract 2
entrys made by Joseph COBB & conveyed by COBB TO Jinkins WHITESIDE, one made by
John PROFFIT & an entry made by Joseph PROFFIT; tract in Poor Valley bought of
heirs of SENTER & McANALLY; tract on big Ridge entered by Wm WHITESIDE & tract
called the COULTER entry lying back of LAFFERTIES; farm called the PROFFIT
Place including mill of a parole (?) lease to James LINDAMOOD; an old still
house; place on German Creek in 3rd Civil Dist; the Jack KENNON place where Col.
COCKE lives & also John CREWS; COOKWOOD place to go to old slaves DANIEL &
JENNY; BOWMAN place given to Mrs. McGOLDRICK; lands in Middle TN including lots
in Nashville; the JENNINGS place N. Clinch Mts; small tracts on the big ridge
& in the neighborhood of NOES mill; the HENDERSON place & interest in the Widows
Dower, and entry made by H. G. LEA. Signed T. W. TURLEY, Executor. Recorded
15 Sep 1851 E. TATE, clerk.

p. 388   Inventory - Jacob NOE, decd. 1 Sep 1851. Mentions: the Widow; accts
& notes on Wm Henry HANESON, Robt W. TURLEY, Reuben GROVE, Jr., John LONG, Marine
DUVAUL, S. S. SHIPLEY, D. R. McANALLY, S. W. CENTER, Wm T. THURMAN, Wm SPOON,
Thos WHITESIDE, James KENNER, George BUTTS, John WALKER, Frederick T. WINKLE.
Signed Wm T. TATE, Adm. Recorded 24 Sep 1851 E. TATE, clerk.

p. 389   Commissioners Report - 1 yr support for widow & family of Jacob NOE,
decd. Signed D. C. CARMICHAEL, James CARMICHAEL, Jno MAYES. Recorded 24 Sep
1851 E. TATE, clerk.

p. 390   Guardian Report - Henry ALSUP, Guardian of the minor heirs of David &
Wm COFFMAN, decd. 24 Aug 1851. Mentions: last report 11 Oct 1849; Thomas
McBROOM, Atto in fact for David COFFMAN, Jr. one of the minor heirs has arrived
at full age, recpt dated 1 Apr 1850; Wm M. COCKE, Atto fee in case Henry ALSUP,
Guardian vs Joseph & David NOE. Signed Henry ALSUP, Guardian. Recorded 24 Sep
1851 E. TATE, clerk.

     Third Settlement - Calvin HUDDLESTONE, Adm of the Estate of B. C.
McCRARY, decd. 29 Aug 1851. Mentions: last settlement 4 Aug 1845; Wm M. COCKE
Atto fee in case G. W. ROSE vs Guardian; Zachariah HODGES for costs in case G.
W. ROSE vs Guardian; W. L. LATHIM, Clk of Cir Ct costs in case G. W. ROSE vs
Guardian; John BULLARD, ditto; Letty McCRARY, widow & relect; J. F. HUDDLESTONE,
Executor of the Estate of Robert HUDDLESTON, decd. Recorded 24 Sep 1851.

p. 392   Settlement - T. R. READ & Drury P. MORRIS, Adms of the Estate of Jehu
MORRIS, decd. 6 Aug 1851. Mentions: private sale of goods bought in Baltimore;
David WHITESIDE judgement against John MANSFIELD; James CUNNINGHAM; Wm THOMPSON
as a witness; Wm CARTWRIGHT; HOPKINS & HULLS for goods bought in Baltimore by
decd; D. C. CARMICHAEL; note to C. & M. H. WILLIAMS; N. F. READ; Russel CROW's

attendance as a witness in Jehu MORRIS vs Wm T. MANSON; Wm EVANS; Wm T. GRAY
witness in case Jehu MORRIS vs Wm T. MANSON; Clisbe RIGGS ditto; E. B. SNODDY
ditto; Thomas RICHARD & Son for goods purchased by decd in Augusta, GA; Josiah
RHOTEN; S. S. HUFFMASTER; Drury MORRIS, ditto case; David McANALLY;   Russel
RIGGS ditto case; Joseph SHANNON; Elisha BULL for amt pd D. L. KERR; Jonathan
MERELOCK; Alexander WILLIAMS; note to Wm C. HEATON; Martin MOORE; note to Henry
HALL; J. H. MILLAR; F. W. TAYLOR; J. E. JACKSON; Wm L. CREED; Daniel J. READ;
Nathl BROOKS; Hughs W. TAYLOR; Ben SHERWOOD; note to Wyatt STUBBLEFIELD; J. H.
DYER, Rev Col, taxes 1850; note to Hyatt McBURNEY & Co.; note to James T.
CARMICHAEL; note to Mary MOORE & Wm S. DICKSON; note to CHAMBERLAIN, BANCROFT &
Co.; Wm PERKINS for Post Office dues; Joel DENISON; Ephrium MOORE; John COX;
James A. LEWIS & N. F. REED probate; J. F. MILLAR; Wm ROGERS; note to Amelia
WITT; James MOORE probate of Counterfiet Bank bills recd of N. F. READ acting
for Jehu MORRIS; E. B. SNODDY & S. L. HUFFMASTER; Gideon MORRIS; Rachel MORRIS;
John F. NOE; James L. JENNINGS; Eli SHIPLEY; Dr. David JONES; R. STUBBLEFIELD;
Mary G. CLARK; John ESTERLY; Samuel GILL. Recorded 29 Sep 1851 E. TATE, clerk.

p. 395   Account of Sale - Celie E. COFFEE, decd. Mentions: Jackson COFFEE.
Signed C. COFFEE, Adm. Recorded 14 Oct 1851 E. TATE, clerk.

        Inventory - Thomas CAIN, decd. 1 Oct 1851. Signed Hugh CAIN, Adm.
Recorded 14 Oct 1851 E. TATE, clerk.

        Inventory - John NEEDHAM, decd. Mentions: one Bounty Land Warrant
for 80 acres. Signed Dedman NASH, Executor. Recorded 14 Oct 1851 E. TATE.

p. 396   Additional Inventory - W. L. LATHIM, Adm of Col. Saml BUNCH Estate.
Mentions: notes by M. J. BUNCH of MS, 1841 & 1849, made by Thomas M. ANDERSON.
Recorded 14 Oct 1851 E. TATE, clerk.

        Inventory - Doc Luther BROWN, decd. Mentions: notes on James H.
BIDDLE, Isaac LANE, Tydon RODDY, Armstead TALLY, Merince BEWLEY, Samuel H. WITT,
Wm ROGERS, Christopher, STROUD, George G. GENTLE, Wm HAUN (removed), Henry
HANSEL, Robert B. MARTIN, Robt JONES, John RIGHT, Kutchen CARY, Jacob MEFFORD,
G. L. BOGAL, John A. BUDON, Abram ROE, Genl BAKER, James BURCHELL, John RAIDER,
George COURTNEY; cash received Joseph WILLIAMS, Bartley MAGEE, Wm GRIGSBY, Wm
COURTNEY, Elizabeth HOLLAWAY, Adam HAUN, William BROWN, John SHANNON, Joseph
LONG, John WHINNERY, Wm B. BAKER, Mrs. E. M. GILLISPIE, E. B. SNODDY; accounts
on James KNIGHT, Thos RUSSEL (runaway), Mrs. Jesse YOUNG now Mrs. COLE, H. W.
ATKINSON, decd, Wm MORRIS, John SNIDER (removed), Elijah HAYES, David JACKSON,
James COURTNEY, Sr., James COURTNEY, James CUNNINGHAM, William LEA, William
GRIGSBY, Thomas M. ANDERSON, George MOORE, Mr. Wallace WELDEZGER (gone), Varner
SHIPLEY, John GRIFFIN, decd, Thomas PERRIN, Jack MORGAN, Wm M. RAYL, Sally
BARNES, Capt James LONG, Hugh L. McCLUNG, _____ YATES, Isaac M. REECE of
Kingston, Miss PHIPPS, Sam HENDERSON, _____ CONNER, Estate of Thos BIGGS, Albert
BAKER, Right CHRISTIAN (now no more), John HODGE, Andrew STROUD (moved off), Wm
R. RODDY, decd. Signed 27 Sep 1851 Obadiah BOAZ, Adm. Recorded 15 Oct 1851.

p. 399   Commissioners Report - 1 yr support of widow & family of James COFFEE,
decd. Signed 10 Sep 1851 Henry ALSUP, John DAVIS, Williford P. WHITLOCK.
Recorded 16 Oct 1851 E. TATE, clerk.

Commissioners Report - set apart 1 yr support to heirs of Joel COFFEE, decd, who are under age of 15 being 4 in number, to wit, Susan, Jacob, Elvira & Sarah. Signed Henry ALSUP, William MITCHEL, David VINEYARD. Recorded 16 Oct 1851 E. TATE, clerk.

p. 400   Guardian Report - Wm M. WILLIAMS, Surviving Guardian of the minor heirs of Wm F. WILLIAMS, decd. 8 Sep 1851. Mentions: rents of lands & SLAVES since 1 Mar 1850; Cornelia C. WILLIAMS, a ward; A. L. WILLIAMS, a ward; Thos H. WILLIAMS, a ward; Saml C. WILLIAMS, a ward; Lucy J. WILLIAMS, a ward. Signed Wm M. WILLIAMS, Surviving Guardian. Recorded 18 Oct 1851 E. TATE, clerk.

Guardian Report - Mary SHIELDS, Guardian of James T. SHIELDS & E. J. SHIELDS, minor heirs of John SHIELDS, decd. 8 Sep 1851. Mentions: last report 5 Oct 1842; James T. SHIELDS & E. J. SHIELDS who have both arrived to the age of 21. Mary SHIELDS by James T. SHIELDS. Recorded 18 Oct 1851 E. TATE, clerk.

p. 401   Guardian Report - Samuel GILL, Guardian of Thomas MAYES. 8 Sep 1851. Mentions: Daniel C. CARMICHAEL, Adm of the Estate of James MAYES, decd; John LAFFERTY former Guardian; Thos B. JARNAGIN for tuition; boarding Thos MAYES at school; R. C. GLENN tuition; T. D. KNIGHT board; R. C. CRAFFORD for silver watch; S. S SHIPLEY for saddle; GILL & CLARK for goods. Signed Saml GILL, Guardian. Recorded 18 Oct 1851 E. TATE, clerk.

p. 402   Guardian Report - Cynthia CHANDLER, Guardian of Nancy HARREL minor heir of Wm M. HARREL, decd. 26 Sep 1851. Mentions: cash recd from Pension Agent at Knoxville; Thos ACUFF for going to Knoxville regarding pension. Signed Cynthia HARREL, Guardian. Recorded 18 Oct 1851 E. TATE, clerk.

Guardian Report - John DOLTON, Guardian of Margaret DOLTON & Carter DOLTON. 5 Sep 1851. Mentions: Coleby DOLTON Executor of Meredith DOLTON, decd; rent of wards lands 1850; Saml GILL for clothing for Carter DOLTON, a ward. Signed John W. DOLTON, Guardian. Recorded 18 Oct 1851 E. TATE, clerk.

p. 403   Account of Sale - Stephen JOHNSON, decd. 15 Feb 1849. Mentions: James JOHNSON, Thomas DODSON, Pleasant A. WITT, Richard STUBBLEFIELD, James LONG, John MASON, Willson S. CREED, Rawleigh DODSON, William LEA, Isaac ROGERS, Thos R. DODSON, John HOLDMAN, John MASON, James GRANTHAM, William STUBBLEFIELD, David McANALLY, William R. WITT, John McANALLY, Elisha DODSON, Russell WYATT, George G. TAYLOR, Thomas JOHNSON, John B. PROFFITT, Thomas DODSON, Jr., William HOUSLEY, William OLLIVER, John WRIGHT, Abraham BURCHELL, Robert DODSON, James POINDEXTER, Hardy JOHNSON, Eli COX, Joshua JONES, W. M. CLARKSON, Adam HOPPER, R. L. STUBBLEFIELD, George PILANT, John HARRIS, Almariah JOHNSON. Signed Larkin JOHNSON, Hardy JOHNSON, Executors. Recorded 5 Nov 1851 E. TATE, clerk.

p. 407   Inventory - James COFFEE, Jr., decd. 8 Sep 1851. Signed John T. MITCHEL, Adm, 3 Nov 1851. Recorded 5 Nov 1851 E. TATE, clerk.

p. 408   Account of Sale - James COFFEE, Jr., decd. 3 Nov 1851. Mentions: Jno STALSWORTH, Jno B. GRIGSBY, Pleasant VINEYARD, Eliza DAVIS, Willie FIELDING, Jubal MITCHEL, Elijah MITCHEL, John CLAWSON, John HINSHAW, Hugh DUFF, John BIRLES, Thos HANKINS, M. H. STONE, Pleasant WHITLOCK, John CARBACK. Signed John T. MITCHEL, Adm. Recorded 5 Nov 1851 E. TATE, clerk.

Inventory - Joel COFFEE, decd. Signed Wilford P. WHITLOCK, John HENSHAW, Adm., 3 Nov 1851. Sworn in Open Court Nov Term 1851.

p. 410   Inventory - Notes on hand & due dates of the Estate of Joel COFFEE, decd. Mentions: John INMAN (1850), Archibald MULLINS (1850), John HOWSLEY (1850), William BRADLEY (1843), Charles CAMPBELL (1835), Zachariah HINES (1850). Recorded 6 Nov 1851 E. TATE, clerk.

Account of Sale - Joel COFFEE, decd. Sold 10 & 11 Oct 1851. Mentions: Daniel VINEYARD, Thos MORGAN, Andrew VINEYARD, Willie FIELDING, Wm LOWE, James COFFEE, Wm HAYWORTH, Pryor NANCE, J. H. DINWIDDY, Henry ALSUP, Levi SATTERFIELD, Saml SHIELDS, Wm S. DYER, Richard HAYWORTH, Thornton COWAN, James L. COLLINS, Theophilus MALONE, Pleasant VINEYARD, G. W. VITTITOE, Danl GOWANS, Jno NORTHERN, Jacob HINSHAW, James RYAN, John DAVIS, James YATES, Thos BROGDON, Jas G. WALKER, Alfred PARSON, John EASLEY, Elijah MITCHEL, Jackson COTNER, Aquilla MITCHEL, Thos MORGAN, Robt M. CORUM, Hugh DUFF, Orvil VINEYARD, Anderson TALLY, John T. MITCHEL, Joseph PARROTT, Ramsey HAWKINS, John CLAWSON, Malin McDOWELL, Willeston PATE, Elza DAVIS, Seth BEALS, Robert GAINS, James GAINS, Thomas DAVIS, Alfred PARSON, Ramsey HACKNEY, Goldin HENSHAW. Signed W. P. WHITLOCK, John HENSHAW, Adm. Recorded 6 Nov 1851 E. TATE, clerk.

p. 412   Commissioners Report - 1 yr support for widow & family of Sterling HAYNES. Signed 13 Sep 1851 Joseph CLARK, Joseph YADON, Wm DAVIS. Recorded 6 Nov 1851 E. TATE, clerk.

p. 413   Inventory - Sterling HAYNES, decd. Mentions: Jerson HAYNES, John BULLARD, Wm GRIMES, W. B. BUTCHER, J. M. WAGGONER, James WALKER, Henry JONES, Susan HAYNES, Britton McBEE, Polen McBEE, Thomas HAYNES, Jacob HAYNES. Sold by A. HAYNES, Adm., J. C. BULLARD, Clerk. Recorded 8 Nov 1851 E. TATE, clerk.

p. 414   Account of Sale - Hannah BLAKEMAN, decd. Mentions: Willie B. EPPERSON, T. J. EPPERSON, Clabourn BULL, John L. EPPERSON, Peter OGAN, James BULL, Elijah BARBEY, one note on R. P. PROCKTOR, one account on Wm PAYNE. Signed Clabourn BULL, Adm. Recorded 8 Nov 1851 E. TATE, clerk.

Guardian Report - James M. MITCHEL, Guardian of the minor heirs of Benjamin MITCHEL, decd. 13 Oct 1851. Mentions: rents of wards lands. Signed James M. MITCHEL, Guardian. Recorded 8 Nov 1851 E. TATE, clerk.

p. 415   Guardian Report - Elias WESTER, Guardian of the minor heirs of Nenian RIGGS, decd. 31 Oct 1851. Mentions: last report 3 Jun 1850; rents due two of wards yet under age; Joshua N. RIGGS agent for Loinia (?) McCALLUM (?) a minor; Joshua N. RIGGS, an heir, who is now of full age, receipt dated 23 Aug 1851; J. H. DYER, Rev. Coll., taxes 1850-51. Signed Elias WESTER, Guardian. Recorded 8 Nov 1851.

Additional Account of Sale - S. E. DODSON, decd. Mentions: sold by W. H. D. McANALLY, Adm, 29 Oct 1851. Recorded 10 Dec 1851 E. TATE, clerk.

p. 416   Account of Sale - Thomas CAIN, dec. 22 Oct 1851. Mentions: Thos R. READ, O. BOAZE, Jesse BULLARD, J. MASTERSON, John TAYLOR, G. W. MOORE. Signed Hugh CAIN, Adm. Recorded 10 Dec 1851 E. TATE, clerk.

        Inventory - Samuel WRIGHT, decd.   8 Nov 1851.   Signed Henry ALSUP,
Adm.   Recorded 10 Dec 1851 E. TATE, clerk.

p. 417   Account of Sale - Samuel WRIGHT, decd.   Sold 25 Nov 1851.   Mentions:
D. P. MORRIS, Charity WRIGHT, William LOWE, J. B. GRIGSBY, Wm B. WEST, Thos
DAVIS, Jr., Thos WALKER, Hiram YATES, Thos DAVIS, Sr., Wm H. DAVIS, Charles
WRIGHT, B. E. GAINS, Jubal MITCHEL, Leroy FINDLEY, Thos WEST, Jno WILKINS,
Samuel WEST, Wm WRIGHT, J. T. CHESHIN, Wylie GALIAN note given by Thomas D.
MAPLES to S. WRIGHT, note on Alexander WEST, note on John RAY, due bill on Wm
WILLIAMSON, note on William & Margaret GRIFFIN, note on George K. WARD, note
on Wm G. ARNETT, note on Henry JANUARY & John SPARKMAN, note on Thomas GREEN,
note on James BROWN by J. BOILES, account against Meredith YATES, account on
James RAY.   Signed Henry ALSUP, Adm.   Recorded 10 Dec 1851 E. TATE, clerk.

p. 419   Account of Sale - Benjamin MITCHEL, decd.   Mentions: Wesley YOUNG,
Anderson YATES, Jas L. CHURCHMAN, George BRIGHT, Edward L. TATE, George COLLINS,
Wm KELLY, S. S. MASSENGILL, Nicholas NOE, Geo W. PRATT, Sterling DAVIS, Goldsby
COLE, James McDANIEL, Anderson CATES, Anna MITCHEL, Chesley MORGAN, Wm HAMMER,
Eli McDANIEL, Jr., Robert OWENS, M. McGUYRE, Wm M. MOODY, Alfred ROACH, Albert
DAVIS, Jno COLLISON, Stephen ATKINS, James JAMES, Reuben MOODY, Henry ALSUP,
James McDANIEL, John MALLICOAT, J. B. GRIGSBY, Mabel CULLEFER, James M. MITCHEL,
James GRIGSBY, Jr., H. MALLICOAT, Alexd MANLY, John OWENS, Abner K. LOWE, Mary
BURKET, H. G. LEA.   Signed Robert LOYD, Adm.   Recorded 10 Dec 1851 E. TATE.

p. 420   Guardian Report - Robert W. WOLFINBARGER, Guardian of the minor heirs
of Tandy WOLFINBARGER, decd.   27 Nov 1851.   Mentions: last report 1 Jan 1850;
Rebecca WOLFINBARGER, widow.   Signed Robt W. WOLFINBARGER, Guardian.   Recorded
10 Dec 1851 E. TATE, clerk.

        Guardian report - Wm T. TATE, Guardian of the minor heirs of John
LATHIM, decd, towit, Sarah E. CARMICHAEL formerly Sarah E. LATHIM & Martha
PATTERSON formerly Martha LATHIM.   18 Nov 1851.   Mentions: last report 18 May
1850; rent of lands 1851; J. H. DYER, Rev Coll, taxes 1850 & 51; James T.
CARMICHAEL medicine & attendance to sick NEGROES; James T. CARMICHAEL who intermarried with Sarah E. LATHIM, a ward; James T. SHIELDS for Boarding & tuition of
Martha LATHIM, a ward, at school; W. T. TATE & Co. for cash & merchandise;
Samuel GILL for goods; EASLEY & Co. for goods; GILL & CLARK for goods; Wm NORTON
saddle, etc for Martha; RICE & McFARLAND for goods; Thos PATTERSON who intermarried with Martha LATHIM, a ward; James T. CARMICHAEL for boarding, washing &
lodging Martha LATHIM 127 weeks; SLAVES sold 22 Jan 1851.   Recorded 10 Dec 1851.

p. 423   Will - Abigail BURGES.   Everything to my present husband William BURGES.
William BURGESS & A. P. GREEN, Executors.   Signed 1 Aug 1851 Abigail x BURGES.
Wit: William DENNIS, Clabourn JOHNSON.   Recorded 7 Feb 1852 E. TATE, clerk.

        Inventory - Ann K. WILLIAMS, decd.   Mentions: a note on Joseph NOE.
Signed Wm M. WILLIAMS, Adm.   Recorded 12 Mar 1852 E. TATE, clerk.

p. 424   Account of Sale - Ann K. WILLIAMS, decd.   Mentions: James JONES,
Octavus NOE, John RHEA, Saml GILL, James T. SHIELDS, Marine DUVAUL, Levi
CAMPBELL.   Signed Wm M. WILLIAMS, Adm.   Recorded 12 Mar 1852 E. TATE, clerk.

p. 425 Inventory and Account of Sale - James COFFEE, decd. Mentions: account on Joel COFFEE, decd & James DYER, Elza DAVIS, Pleasant VINEYARD, Saml STALS-WORTH. Signed Jno T. MITCHEL, Adm. Recorded 12 Mar 1852.

p. 426 Guardian Report - John PERKAPILE, Guardian of the minor heirs of Isaac PERKAPILE, decd. 31 Dec 1851. Mentions: has not recd a cent from the Adm for the two years he has been Guardian; he has spent the sum of $5.25. Signed John x PERKAPILE, Guardian. Recorded 12 Mar 1852 E. TATE, clerk.

Guardian REPORT -· Benjamin SMITH, Guardian of Juba SMITH & Rachel SMITH. Mentions: last report 24 Dec 1850; state & county taxes 1851. Signed Benjamin SMITH, Guardian. Recorded 12 Mar 1852 E. TATE, clerk.

p. 427 Second Settlement - Parrott GODWIN, Adm for the Estate of John M. WILLIAMS, decd. 17 Jan 1851. Mentions last settlement 20 Feb 1849; amt reserved to make the Widow equal the two minor heirs; Octavus YOE for 1/2 amt of sales of the old store held jointly by John M. WILLIAMS & said YOE; James LACY, Esq. money collected from Warham EASLEY. Recorded 12 Mar 1852 E. TATE, clerk.

p. 428 Settlement - Wm COLVIN, Esqr, Adm of the Estate of John COLVIN, decd. 3 Dec 1851. Mentions: note on Joseph SMITH, note on James SEAMORE; 2 sales; James SALLING for clerking sale; Isaac CONDRA for clerking sale; John BULLARD for crying the sale; note to James COLVIN; McCOLLUM; D. F. HUDDLESTONE; Wm A. ROGERS; Owen DYER; James SALLING, Dpt Shff, taxes 1845; Wm P. OWENS; James COLLIER; J. C. CLARK, R. Col, taxes 1849; J. H. DYER, R. Col, taxes 1850 & 51; Isaac MILLAR; Alxd HAMILTON; James COLVIN an heir; John A. BLACKBURN who inter-married with Anna COLVIN, an heir; Mark COLVIN, an heir; Rosanna MONROW form-erly Rosanna COLVIN, an heir; Alxd COLVIN, an heir; Margaret COLVIN, an heir; Elijah COLVIN, an heir; Wm COLVIN, Adm & also an heir. Recorded 12 Mar 1852.

p. 429 Guardian Report - Wm WILLIAMS, surviving Guardian of the minor heirs of Wm F. WILLIAMS, decd. 8 Sep 1851. Mentions: Ann K. WILLIAMS & Wm WILLIAMS, Guardians; hire of SLAVES from 1845 to 1850; sale of 2 SLAVES; board, clothing & tuition for Caroline C. WILLIAMS, a ward, for 9 yrs, 2 mos; board, clothing, tuition for Mary L. WILLIAMS, a ward, for 9 yrs, 2 mos; board, clothing, tuition of Thomas H. WILLIAMS, a ward, for 9 yrs, 2 mos; board clothing, tuition for Lucy Jane WILLIAMS, a ward, for 9 yrs, 2 mos; board, clothing & tuition for Samuel C. WILLIAMS, a ward, 9 yrs 2 mos; ditto James E. WILLIAMS, a ward for 3 yrs; ditto Wm M. WILLIAMS, a ward for 4 yrs; Thomas WHITESIDE for cost & taxes on PARTIN tract, sold for taxes; taxes for 1845 to 1849. Signed Wm WILLIAMS, Guardian. Recorded 12 Mar 1852.

p. 430 Settlement - John WALKER, Adm of the Estate of Isaac PERKAPILE, decd. 2 Feb 1852. Mentions: Wm H. HARRIS, John L. EASTERLY. Recorded 12 Mar 1852.

p. 431 Guardian Report - Thomas W. TURLEY, Guardian of Margaretta SENTER. Mentions: last report 1 Jan 1851; A. DOLTON, sale of NEGRO; amt recd from AL rents; from L. A. GARRETT in note on Seburn W. SENTER & others; note on P. M. SENTER & others; recd of J. E. HOGAN wards part of compromise with heirs; note on Mrs. SENTER; note on Wm MURRY; recd at Nashville from A. G. SHEWSBERRY; note on S. GILL for girl MARY; note on R. M. BARTON for girl MARIAH; note on B. K. CUNNINGHAM; J. H. DYER, Rev Col, taxes 1851; R. FIELDING, Rev Col, for

Jefferson Co., taxes. Signed T. W. TURLEY, Guardian. Recorded 12 Mar 1852.

p. 432   Additional Account of Sale - C. McCOY, decd. Mentions: notes on Henry HIPSHEAR; note on Arch McCOY. Signed David McCOY, Adm. Recorded 12 Mar 1852.

Commissioners Report - 1 yr support for widow of Samuel RIGHT, decd.   8 Nov 1851. Signed Wilford P. WHITLOCK, Jubal MITCHEL, Meredith YATES, Comms. Sworn in Open Court Feb Term 1852. Recorded 12 Mar 1852 E. TATE, clerk.

p. 433   Additional Account of Sale - 22 Dec 1851. John DEVAULT, decd. Mentions: Isaac L. DEVAULT, Lawson DAMEWOOD, Calloway KELARY, Wm C. DEVAULT, John BRADLEY, J. E. COLLINS, J. L. COLLINS. Signed George LAY & G. P. MYNATT, Adms of John DEVAULT with a Will annexed. Recorded 12 Mar 1852 E. TATE, clerk.

Commissioners Report - 1 yr support of widow & family of Jacob GODWIN, decd. Signed 9 Feb 1852 Joseph BRYAN, Jas P. LEGG & Ben PECK, Comms. Recorded 12 Mar 1852 E. TATE, clerk.

p. 434   Settlement - David McCOY, Adm of the Estate of Clabourn McCOY, decd. 21 Feb 1852. Mentions: sale 28 & 29 Dec 1849; notes on A. COFFEE, George WOLF, Easley DOLTON, Andrew McGINNIS & Andrew WOLF; amt of additional sale 16 Jan 1851 from Jacob HIPSHEAR, Jr.; S. S. SHIPLEY; Wm MURRY; Zora HARVEY; Samuel GILL; Nicholas ANTRIKIN; Michael GOLDMAN; John LAFFERTY; Warham EASLEY; David WHITESIDE; Ausburn COFFEE; John A. SIMPSON; Ben SHERWOOD; J. H. DYER, Rev Col, taxes 1850; Elizabeth McCOY, widow & Guardian of the minor heirs; note on Edley DOLTON. Recorded 13 Mar 1852 E. TATE, clerk.

p. 435   Guardian Report - Elizabeth McCOY, Guardian of the minor heirs of Clabourn McCOY, decd. 20 Feb 1852. Mentions: David McCOY, Adm; rent & taxes of wards lands 1851; boarding, clothing & taking care of her two wards. Signed Elizabeth McCOY, Guardian. Recorded 13 Mar 1852 E. TATE, clerk.

p. 436   Settlement - Edward TATE, Clerk of Co. Ct for Gr. Co., Submit report of the Proratio Division of the Estate of Isaac DANIEL, decd., amongst the Creditors of said decd, by an act of the General Assembly. Mentions: B. F. McFARLAND, Adm; to be paid E. TATE, Jacob GODWIN, BROWNLOW & OBRIAN, Pheba DANIEL, widow 1 yr support, John DOUGLAS, F. B. S. COCKE for Shrouding, James MAYES for Coffin; creditors: notes to Bank, Wm M. COCKE, M. L. DANIEL, P. L. DANIEL, James CAMERON, A. P. GREEN, Joseph HOOKER, Building Committee, Ab. McCONNEL, John MAYES, A. AUSTIN, Zack HAMMER, A. CALDWELL, James MAYES, J. R. HAGGARD, Wm SMITH, RICE & McFARLAND, Churety VENOY, Wm T. TATE & Co., F. B. L. COCKE, Wm GREY, John BROOKS, Josiah KIDWELL, Wm B. HODGES, R. LOYD, D. McKINNY, D. C. CARMICHAEL, J. B. GRIGSBY, Loyd COCKRUM. Wm A. LAY, Robert CARDWELL, J. H. & J. S. MOSES, Dr. James EASLEY. Recorded 15 Mar 1852 E. TATE, clerk.

www.ingramcontent.com/pod-product-compliance
Lightning Source LLC
Chambersburg PA
CBHW021905020426
42334CB00013B/496